The three-volume *Encyclopedia of Rock* is simply the best, most comprehensive Rock reference work ever written. Compiled by an international team of specialists working under expert editorial control, it combines hard accurate facts with lively critical comment. Clearly arranged in alphabetical order the *Encyclopedia* is the essential and definitive book for anyone – from the serious student to the casual fan – who wants to know more about what lies behind the music.

The first volume (also available in Panther Books) deals with the earliest origins of rock'n'roll through to the coming of the Beatles. This volume covers the music of the Sixties – Merseybeat, R&B and the British invasion of the US rock scene; flower power music, the emergence of underground and heavy rock; soul and blues rock; the West Coast sounds and much more. The extraordinary performers who came to fame in this era – the Stones, Dylan, Ray Charles, the Hollies, Janis Joplin, Hendrix, and Cream, to name just a few – are given full coverage. But the unknowns and little-knowns who contributed to the music of this astonishing decade are also treated fully, making this the most in-depth, thorough reference book on rock ever published.

Also available in Panther Books

The Encyclopedia of Rock Volume I

The Encyclopedia of Rock
Edited by Phil Hardy and Dave Laing

Consultant Editors:
Charlie Gillett
Greil Marcus
Bill Millar
Greg Shaw

The Encyclopedia of Rock

Volume II
*From Liverpool
to San Francisco*

Edited by Phil Hardy and Dave Laing

Panther

Granada Publishing Limited
Published in 1976 by Panther Books Ltd
Frogmore, St Albans, Herts AL2 2NF

Reprinted 1977

Copyright © Aquarius Books, Phil Hardy and
Dave Laing 1976
This volume first published in
Great Britain by Hanover Books in
cooperation with Panther Books Ltd 1976
Made and printed in Great Britain by
Hazell Watson & Viney Ltd
Aylesbury, Bucks
Set in Linotype Times

This book is dedicated to Lillian Roxon

Contributors to this volume:

STEPHEN BARNARD
RON BROWN
JOHN COLLIS
ROBIN DENSELOW
DAVID DOWNING
ROB FINNIS
MIKE FLOOD PAGE
PETE FOWLER
SIMON FRITH
MICHAEL GRAY
PHIL HARDY
MARTIN HAWKINS
IAN HOARE
MICK HOUGHTON
DAVE LAING
DAVID McGILLIVRAY
BILL MILLAR
JONATHAN MORRISH
JOHN MORTHLAND
JOHN PIDGEON
CLIVE RICHARDSON
GREG SHAW
ROBERT SHELTON
PETER SIMONS
GRAHAM TAYLOR
JOHN TOBLER
DAVID WALTERS
CLIFF WHITE
RICHARD WILLIAMS

ACKNOWLEDGEMENTS

The editors and contributors freely acknowledge the considerable debt they owe to the following:
Bigtown Review, Billboard, Bim Bam Boom, Blues & Soul, Blues Research, Blues Unlimited, Blues World, Boppin' News, Cashbox, Barrett Hansen, *Jazz & Blues, Let It Rock, Living Blues, Melody Maker, New Musical Express, Penniman News, Record Mirror, Rock File, R&B Monthly, R&B Magazine, Rollin' Rock, Rolling Stone, Shout, Soul Bag,* Joel Whitburn and *Who Put the Bomp.*

INTRODUCTION

This is Volume II of a three-volume Encyclopedia of Rock. It covers the periods from the English Invasion to San Francisco. The criteria for inclusion are two-fold. The first is success: rock artists whose records were very successful in the hit parades of America and/or Britain will almost invariably be included. The second basis for inclusion involves our assessment of historical influence and artistic significance. Here we have drawn heavily on our Consultant Editors and contributors, all of whom are acknowledged experts in the field. The length of each entry has been dictated by our estimate of the importance of its subject to rock music as a whole. The people behind the scenes have been as influential as the performers, so here, in many cases for the first time, is recognition of the contribution made by the record company bosses, record producers, session musicians and songwriters. The Encyclopedia gives due weight to the work of these often neglected figures, and also to musicians from areas of music which border on rock, and which have exerted considerable influence on it. Thus, in addition to an entry on gospel music, there are individual entries on six major gospel artists.

Because the aim of the Encyclopedia is to provide information and informed comment for the general reader, no discographies are included as such, though in many cases reference is made to an artist's significant recordings in the body of the entry. In any case, a definitive discography of all the artists in this volume would fill a book at least as big as this. Leadbitter and Slaven's *Blues Records* provides such information for blues artists, and a comparable work in the field of rock is urgently needed, as interest in the past of the music grows apace. The only equivalents in rock at present are Joel Whitburn's collection of the Billboard charts in America and Pete and Annie Fowler's collation of the British charts in *Rock File*.* Except where noted, all chart positions noted in the Encyclopedia refer to these charts.

After a hiatus in the early Sixties, excitement returned to pop with the emergence of a whole range of innovative performers and styles. The period covered in this volume opens with the vast expansion in the scope of pop by the Beatles and the English Invasion, by Bob Dylan and folk-rock, and by the birth of soul music out of R&B and gospel music. The book takes the story up to the growth of the underground and progressive sounds of the late Sixties, which spread outwards from San Francisco to be reflected in different ways in different places.

Although we are covering a specific period in rock history, many of those mentioned have careers stretching before or beyond the Sixties. In these instances, the entry appears here rather than in Volume I or III, because the individual's greatest significance for mainstream pop was during this period. Thus, city-blues musicians like Muddy Waters and Little Walter are included despite the fact that their greatest commercial success with black audiences occurred in the Fifties. More important for the development of rock was their seminal influence on white R&B groups like the Rolling Stones and the Paul Butterfield Blues Band. Similarly, the Pink Floyd, whose largest-selling albums were made in the Seventies, belong here because their approach to music remains rooted in the particular avant-garde stance of the late Sixties. In the case of major music centres and record companies, a separate entry appears in each volume.

Finally, the editors welcome any corrections or suggested additions to the information contained in this book, so that they may be included in future editions.

*Volumes II and III are available in Panther Books.

Acappella, derived from the Italian *cappella* (chapel) and originally applied to 16th century church music, is the term currently used to describe almost any unaccompanied singing, though it most often refers specifically to vocal groups.

The absence of instrumentation was normal in the pre-war gospel field, but some early secular black groups, the Four Vagabonds and the Virginia Four for example, also sang without backing. Acappella enjoyed a brief boom between 1964 and 1966 on the East Coast, partly in reaction to the Beatles (who were anathema to most doo-wop fans) and partly through the discovery of ten-year-old acappella practice tapes by the Nutmegs. The tapes, which included 'Let Me Tell You' and 'Down In Mexico', were issued on the Times Square label by Slim Rose. They sold a mere 2,000 copies but inspired all the kids who had been singing the old songs down in the subway (because of the echo) to try their hand at recording. Rose, Eddie Gries (Relic) and Stan Krause (Catamount) were besieged by street corner quartets.

Mediaeval, Old Timer, Siamese and Harlequin were among the dozens of acappella labels. Some recorded up to thirty groups, most of whom were white, i.e. Spanish, Italian and Puerto Rican (young blacks had moved on to soul). They were often absurdly polished with high, pure, strong voices which avoided the graceless vibrato so common in imitative R&B.

Acappella discography is riddled with oldies: songs originally cut by the Skyliners, Harptones, Orioles and Moonglows were revived with an honesty and affection unparalleled in rock. The form is now carried on almost single-handedly by the Persuasions, but the Zircons, Dennis Ostrum and the Citadels and the Velvet Angels – just three of the best groups from the golden years – deserve to be remembered.

David Ackles, born at Little Rock, Illinois, in 1937 into a showbusiness family, started in vaudeville at the age of four, and became the child-star of a series of successful B-films featuring a dog called Rusty. He studied literature at college while writing ballet and choral music; later he gained experience in musical comedy, theatre and film.

Elektra signed him as a songwriter after hearing 'Blue Ribbons' (which resurfaced on his first album); eventually they were persuaded to allow him to record. In the course of three Elektra albums he achieved huge critical acclaim but little commercial success. His brooding, elegant and eclectic style – seen at its best on *American Gothic* – is an acquired taste; superficially it can seem simply depressing. Ackles is a writer and performer of remarkable power, perhaps doomed to remain under-rated. Elektra dropped him in 1972; one Columbia album followed, but he is currently without a contract.

Barbara Acklin, born in Chicago on Feb. 28, 1943, first sang in a gospel choir. In 1964, her mellow voice was heard on background sessions for the St Lawrence label where she also recorded as Barbara Allen. On moving to Brunswick, she recorded 'Love Makes A Woman' (a Top Twenty hit in 1968), and 'Just Ain't No Love' and 'Am I The Same Girl' – the original vocal version of Young-Holt Unlimited's million-selling 'Soulful Strut' – in 1969. She also recorded duets with Gene Chandler, the best known of which is 'From The Teacher To The Preacher', a Top Sixty disc in 1968. Her songwriting career – she wrote Jackie Wilson's enormous hit, 'Whispers' – developed in partnership with Eugene Record of the Chi-Lites. Together they wrote 'Love Makes A Woman' and many others, while Record produced her discs for Brunswick. Acklin currently records for Capitol.

Lou Adler is one of the key figures in the development of California pop. He was active as early as 1959 when he managed Jan and Dean and worked with Herb Alpert on his first records (mostly teen novelties). Together they collaborated on early Sam Cooke hits including 'Only Sixteen', under the pseudonym of Barbara Campbell. He next became involved with Screen Gems and their Colpix and Dimension labels. At Colpix he met Shelly Fabares, whom he later married, while at Dimension he worked with Carole King and the rest of Don Kirshner's Brill Building stable, and also discovered a number of young artists including Steve Barri, P. F. Sloan, and Carol Connors.

In 1964 he started Dunhill Productions and Trousdale Music, employing the talents of Steve Barri and P. F. Sloan, who wrote, produced and recorded hundreds of songs in styles ranging from surf music to protest rock, a style which found its home on the Dunhill label, launched in 1965. After two years of hits by the Mamas and Papas, P. F. Sloan, the Grass Roots, Barry McGuire, the Brass Ring and Richard Harris, and hit productions for non-Dunhill artists including Johnny Rivers and Jan and Dean, Adler became one of the organizers of the Monterey Pop Festival, which brought the whole California music explosion into focus in June, 1967.

After he sold Dunhill Records to ABC in 1966, Adler formed Ode Records, whose first hit was 'San Francisco (Be Sure To Wear Some Flowers In Your Hair)' by Scott McKenzie in 1967. Other early Ode acts included Spirit ('I Got A Line On You', 1969) and the City, featuring Carole King. King, who'd been in a commercial slump since 1963, made one of the most successful comebacks in the history of rock on Ode in 1971 where, under Adler's direction, she led the singer-songwriter trend. Other recent successes on Ode include Cheech and Chong, and the symphonic version of *Tommy*.

In recent years, Adler has become involved in films (*Phantom of the Paradise*), theatre (he produced the L.A. production of *Rocky Horror Show*) and club management, in addition to producing Carole King's records and running Ode Records.

Laurel Aitken was originally from Cuba. His 'Little Sheila' was the first Jamaican record ever issued in Britain (on the Melodisc label in 1953). He settled in Britain in the early

11

Sixties and helped pioneer ska with 'Bugaboo', 'The Lion Of Judah' and 'You Was Up', having earlier achieved success amongst West Indians in Britain with 'blues' numbers like 'Bartender' and straightforward gospel on 'Daniel Saw The Stone'. He remained popular throughout the Sixties and recorded in a variety of styles which included plaintive love songs ('You Left Me Standing'), rude reggae ('Pussy Price') and political commentary ('Landlords And Tenants').

Steve Alaimo, born in Rochester, New York, on Dec. 12, 1940, formed his group, the Redcoats, at the University of Miami where he studied medicine. Exposure on Dick Clark's *American Bandstand* led to the Top Fifty hit, 'Everyday I Have To Cry' on Checker in 1963. The song became a soul standard. After a series of minor hits on Imperial and ABC, he pursued his interest in black music by becoming a producer for the group of Miami labels owned by his manager, Henry Stone, including TK and Alston.

Arthur Alexander, born in Sheffield, Alabama, in 1942, was the first hit artist to emerge from Rick Hall's Muscle Shoals studio with a beautifully understated interpretation of the self-penned 'You Better Move On' (1962) – a seminal performance, reflected by many later southern soul hits.

Recorded before Hall had formed his own Fame label, it was released by Dot who proceeded to market Alexander as a pop singer. Despite less sensitive productions, he was equally impressive on the Mann/Weil song 'Where Have You Been' and his own 'Anna' (1962) and 'Go Home Girl' (1963), and although he was indifferently received at home, all four records were much admired and covered by British acts (including the Rolling Stones and the Beatles). Subsequent records for Dot, Sound Stage 7 (1965–9), Monument (1968), and most recently a fine album on Warner Bros., nearly all excellent examples of southern country soul, were ignored until he returned to the Hot Hundred with his own 'Everyday I Have To Cry A Little' in 1975.

J. W. Alexander, born in Tulsa, Oklahoma, in 1917, was one of the key back-room men in the Los Angeles black music scene. Alexander's first involvement was with gospel music, singing with, managing and recording various groups including the Pilgrim Travellers and Sam Cooke's Soul Stirrers.

In 1961 he set up the Sar and Derby labels with Cooke, helping to launch the careers of Johnnie Taylor, Mel Carter, the Valentinos and Billy Preston. On Sam Cooke's death in 1964, Alexander concentrated on Lou Rawls, signing him to a Capitol Records contract which led to his international success. More recently, he has recorded some fine blues sides for his own label, Truth.

Mose Allison, jazz singer/pianist/trumpeter, was born in Tippo, Mississippi on Nov. 11, 1927. His early influences included the blues of John Lee Hooker, Sonny Boy Williamson and Charles Brown and the jazz of Duke Ellington and Charlie Parker. The result was a richly individual style first heard on record in 1957 with the critically acclaimed *Back Country Suite* (Prestige) and other accomplished compositions.

Allison's greatest impact on rock has been through the dry, idiosyncratic singing on 'Parchman Farm', 'Seventh Son' and 'I Love The Life I Live' which has exerted a lasting influence on British singers, notably Georgie Fame. Allison's later recordings were for Columbia and Atlantic.

Herb Alpert, born March 31, 1937, took up the trumpet at eight and was turned on to jazz while in the US Army. His early career was as a songwriter, in partnership with Lou Adler, writing for Keen Records, notably the Sam Cooke/Herman's Hermits hit 'Wonderful World'. They became producers for Dore Records, handling the early hits by Jan and Dean and together with Lou Rawls set up Shardee, but after friction over Alpert's own recording and acting ambitions they separated. Acting took him no further than being an extra for *The Ten Commandments*, and initially recording was equally fruitless.

He found a new partner, Jerry Moss, a promoter and co-producer of the sole Dore Alpert single for RCA, and they set up Carnival Records, later A&M. Their third venture was the Mexican sounding 'The Lonely Bull' by the Tijuana Brass, on A&M. It launched simultaneously Herb Alpert recording star and middle-of-the-road label executive. He became a household name with a run of gold albums, sell-out concerts and television specials. In 1969, facing declining popularity, he took a five-year sabbatical, concentrating on the production side of A&M and discovering the Carpenters.

The Amboy Dukes – Ted Nugent, guitar; Steve Farmer, rhythm guitar; Dave Palmer, drums; Bill White, bass (replaced by Greg Arama); Rick Lober, piano, organ (replaced by Andy Solomon) and John Drake, vocals (replaced by Rusty Day, ex-Detroit Wheels) – hailed from Detroit. They broke nationally with the Top Twenty hit 'Journey To The Centre Of The Mind' in 1968 on Mainstream. Personnel changes didn't deter their rank bad taste: Steve Farmer really knew how to write a pretentious lyric and brash, abrasive Ted Nugent, the first to put himself in a class with Hendrix or Beck, was a dab hand at adapting to other influences. He pulled out all the stops in their wild stage shows, and still does with the new Amboy Dukes which resurfaced in 1974 with *Call Of The Wild* (DiscReet). The man who learnt his licks from Keith Richard and Jim McCarthy of the Godz can still turn in the grossest ever version of 'Maybelline'. The closest they came to a good album was *Migration*, their last in 1969.

Amen Corner, a leading Cardiff group by 1966, strong on image – Andy Fairweather Low, vocals; Neil Jones, guitar; Blue Weaver, organ; Clive Taylor, bass; Dennis Bryn, drums; Allen Jones, baritone sax; Mike Smith, tenor – had their first British Top Twenty record in 1967 at the end of the mod wave with the powerful 'Gin House' (Deram). Their material became progressively more commercial, never fulfilling early promise. After providing Immediate with a No. 1 with 'Half As Nice', they were caught up in the label's collapse. As Fairweather they dropped the brass section and had a Top Five hit, 'Natural Sinner', in 1970, but were disillusioned, and disbanded. Blue Weaver went to the Strawbs, Dennis Bryn to the Bee Gees, and Andy Fairweather Low rested his thin voice through several years' isolation in Wales before re-emerging with *Spider Jiving* (A&M) in 1974.

The American Breed formed in Chicago in 1966 – Gary Loizzo, vocals and guitar (born Aug. 16, 1945); Chuck Colbert, bass (Aug. 29, 1944); Al Ciner, guitar (May 14, 1947) and Lee Graziano, drums (Nov. 9, 1943) – and had five chart records in the years 1967–8, all produced by Bill Traut of Dunwich Productions. Originally called Gary and the Nite Lights, the group had a soul-influenced sound, best presented in their biggest hit 'Bend Me, Shape Me' (Acta) which reached No. 5 in America in 1967. Other hits included their first, 'Step Out Of Your Mind' (No. 24) and 'Green Light' (a No. 39 in 1968). After several personnel changes, the group evolved into Rufus.

American Radio in the early Sixties hadn't changed significantly in a decade. Stations were dominated by larger-than-life disc jockeys full of rapid-fire chatter, jingles, promotions, and above all, free to play whatever records they wanted. As in the Fifties, deejays accepted composer credits or other 'honorariums' in return for helping to expose a new record or artist. Because of the competition to 'break' and claim credit for new hits, it was relatively easy for America's thousands of local groups to get their records aired, if only locally. Out of this grew an incredible proliferation of groups, records, labels, and musical trends. The years 1964–7, in particular, probably saw more records released than any other three-year period in history.

Then in 1965, a new programming theory took hold in American radio. A programme director named Bill Drake (at KHJ, Los Angeles) discovered that he could get higher ratings playing 20 records in constant rotation (as opposed to the 40 or even 60 aired previously), and within a year AM radio was plunged into a cut-throat competition to see who could play the fewest records – at one point, WLS in Chicago (the nation's most powerful station) was playing less than 15. While great for the ratings, it effectively eliminated all avenues for new acts to gain radio exposure. However, this coincided with the birth of 'progressive' FM radio and the dance/concert phenomenon developing in the big cities. So there grew up, for the first time in rock, a duality: certain groups (mostly studio concoctions) holding forth on AM and selling singles, while the 'underground' rock groups confined themselves to concerts, FM radio and album sales. Progressive FM was begun in early 1967 by KMPX in San Francisco, WABX in Detroit, WBCN in Boston, and a few other pioneers. At first, these stations and those who followed tried to offer a clear alternative to the restrictions of AM, playing whatever the jocks wanted (be it classical, folk, avant-garde jazz, electronic music, or obscure album cuts), but as ratings increased and commercial pressures grew, FM in turn became competitive, with most stations establishing limited playlists of 'most popular album cuts' from popular current albums, with only a small percentage of airtime allowed for oldies or other programming. This in turn has spawned 'progressive AM' in the Seventies, leading to a great confusion of definitions and formats that has yet to be resolved. But as far as the Sixties are concerned, it's doubtful if we'll ever again see the kind of free-form programming or the disc-jockey cultism that flourished in that decade, for better or for worse.

American Television and its attitude to rock in the early Sixties was dominated by Saturday afternoon dance shows patterned on *American Bandstand*. There were also nighttime appearances by exceptionally big stars (such as Presley) on Ed Sullivan's and other variety shows. Rock'n' roll was not taken seriously as an audience attraction until the Beatles' guest spots on Ed Sullivan's Sunday night show in 1964 drew unprecedented ratings. The ABC network, in conjunction with British entrepreneur Jack Good, launched *Shindig* in 1965 – a prime-time, weekly half-hour devoted to

16

nothing but rock, presented in a go-go setting. The series was extremely successful, and within a year it had expanded to an hour, then twice a week, with competition from NBC with *Hullabaloo*. During this time, every major city developed local shows which presented a combination of nationally known stars and local groups, hosted by popular disc jockeys. Some of these were modelled on *Bandstand*, while others had a more theatrical cast, presenting live groups on stage. There were literally hundreds of these shows, many of them syndicated nationally.

They began dying off around 1967, however, after *Shindig* and *Hullabaloo* had been cancelled and the British Invasion had tapered off and, with it, the teen mania that had made the TV boom possible. The hardy *American Bandstand* survived, in addition to which Dick Clark launched other series, chiefly *Where the Action Is*, which lasted a few years and introduced a number of important groups, notably Paul Revere and the Raiders. Despite abortive attempts (such as ABC's *Music Scene*, in 1970) to present modern rock on TV, no successful format was evolved until 1973 when ABC's *In Concert*, NBC's *Midnight Special*, and Don Kirshner's syndicated *Rock Concert* found their niche in late-night time slots.

Anders and Poncia, a New York songwriting team responsible for many studio hits in the Sixties, Peter Anders (Andreoli) and Vinnie Poncia started as members of the Videls, whose 'Mr Lonely' was a minor hit in 1960. As contract writers for Hill and Range, they wrote a lot of songs and eventually met Phil Spector, for whom they wrote hits for the Ronettes, Crystals and Darlene Love as well as Cher's non-hit, 'I Love You, Ringo', released under the name of Bonnie Jo Mason. Leaving Spector in 1964, they formed their own production company, and wrote, produced and sang (as the Tradewinds) 'New York's A Lonely Town', which became a No. 32 hit on Red Bird. Later, they joined Kama Sutra where they recorded both as the Tradewinds ('Mind Excursion') and the Innocence ('There's Got To Be A Word!').

17

In 1969, they issued *The Anders and Poncia Album* (Warner Bros.) and then split. Peter Anders subsequently recorded a solo album (Family, 1972) while Vinnie Poncia went into production with Richard Perry. His most recent credits include Fanny and Melissa Manchester.

Eric Andersen was born in Pittsburgh on Feb. 14, 1943. He was 'discovered' by Tom Paxton who brought him to New York as 'the new Dylan'. Andersen impressed many with his poetic lyrics, his handsome, ethereal presence and his gift for haunting melodies. Among his strongest works were the romantic 'Violets Of Dawn', the passionate 'Come To My Bedside', the socially conscious 'Thirsty Boots' and the anti-Dylan 'The Hustler'.

After recording for Vanguard and Warner Bros., he moved to Columbia, developing strong background arrangements that never detracted from his supple, involved singing. Beatles manager Brian Epstein had planned a major management push for Andersen only months before his death. While strongly influenced by the romantic side of Dylan and Presley, Andersen soon had an identifiable style of gentle, wistful lyricism. He's been on the brink of stardom for years, yet has mostly a coterie following. In 1974 he was signed by Clive Davis to the Arista label.

Chris Andrews. During the rock'n'roll era Andrews – born in Romford, Essex in 1938 – first worked as a singer in Hamburg. In 1958 he became an *Oh Boy!* regular and later formed a moderately successful group, Chris Ravel and the Ravers. Throughout this period he was writing his own material and, after meeting Adam Faith, wrote a Top Five hit, 'The First Time', for him in 1963. He then went on to write most (and produce some) of Sandie Shaw's early singles, and their jerky, upbeat rhythm became one of the most familiar British sounds of the mid-Sixties.

In 1965 he recorded one of his own songs, 'Yesterday Man' for Decca, and despite his squeaky voice and tubby appearance, both this record and its follow-up, 'To Whom It

May Concern', did well. He continued recording throughout the Sixties with little chart success.

The Animals, perhaps the greatest stylists among the bands
that led the British R&B boom and certainly the most significant force to emerge outside London's suburbs, were
formed as the Alan Price Combo in Newcastle, where they
played all night on Saturdays at the shabby, crowded Down-
beat club. The combo – Alan Price, organ (born April 19,
1942); Hilton Valentine, guitar (May 2, 1943); Bryan 'Chas'
Chandler, bass (Dec. 18, 1938); John Steel, drums (Feb. 4,
1941) – gained a singer, Eric Burdon (May 19, 1941), moved
to the smarter Club A Go-Go and eventually, at the start of
1964, to London, changing its name en route to the Animals.
  The group at once attracted a following on the
London-based club circuit as ardent as they'd left in Newcastle, drawing crowds with their electric repertoire, a driving sound whose core was the counterpoint of Burdon's
'black' voice and Price's engine-room organ, and an aggression which prompted one American bluesman they backed
to admit, 'Man, them Geordies are really mean – I gotta
fight to keep the limelight when they're playing.' With
record companies looking for R&B groups in the wake of
the Rolling Stones' Top Ten success with 'I Wanna Be Your
Man', the Animals were signed by EMI's Columbia label
where they were produced by Mickie Most. For their first
single, however, Most ignored the R&B classics which went
down so well on stage, opting instead for an unfamiliar
blues standard which had recently appeared on Bob Dylan's
first album as 'Baby Let Me Take You Home', and in doing
so anticipated public taste as he would so often again. Released in March 1964, it made the British Top Twenty six
weeks later. The follow-up, 'House Of The Rising Sun',
came from the same source, but Price's compellingly powerful arrangement transformed it into a rock classic. Besides
topping the transatlantic charts, selling several million
copies throughout the world, and lifting the group to stardom, it reputedly inspired Dylan to start working with a
rock band himself. The group emerged as part of the R&B

19

boom in Britain but in America was seen as part of the folk-rock movement.

After recording their own 'I'm Crying', which hinted at their later inability to make the transition from interpretations to originals, they returned in 1965 to American material with Nina Simone's 'Don't Let Me Be Misunderstood', Sam Cooke's 'Bring It On Home To Me' and interestingly, with 'We've Gotta Get Out Of This Place' by Brill Building writers Mann and Weil. After two albums, *The Animals* (1964) and *Animal Tracks* (1965), Alan Price left in May, 1965. He was replaced by Dave Rowberry (born July 4, 1940) from the Mike Cotton Sound, who imitated his style completely, and in February, 1966, the Nashville Teens' Barry Jenkins took over from John Steel.

The reshaped Animals moved to Decca for 'Inside Looking Out', 'Don't Bring Me Down' and *Animalisms*, but, in September, Burdon unexpectedly broke up the group. He re-emerged at the end of the year as the leader of Eric Burdon and the Animals – John Weider (guitar, violin), Vic Briggs (guitar), Danny McCulloch (bass), Barry Jenkins (drums) – which had a further string of psychedelically inspired hits in America where the group was based. These included Burdon's twin hymns to hippydom, 'San Franciscan Nights' and 'Monterey' (1967) and 'Sky Pilot' the following year. In 1969 Burdon finally laid the Animals to rest to follow an erratic solo career.

P. P. Arnold, born in 1946 in Los Angeles, arrived in Britain as a member of the Ikettes – the backing group for Ike and Tina Turner – in 1966. She decided to stay and after working as a session singer signed with Andrew Oldham's Immediate label. Her impassioned version of Cat Stevens' 'The First Cut Is The Deepest' was a Top Twenty hit in Britain in 1967 but further chart success eluded her – though not her backing group, the Nice – despite an album, *Kafunta*, produced by Mick Jagger and Steve Marriott. She appeared in *Catch My Soul* in 1969 and *Jesus Christ Superstar* in 1970 before returning to session singing.

The Association were a vocal harmony group who straddled the worlds of conventional pop and the new California consciousness of the late Sixties. The group included Russ Giguere (vocals, guitar), Ted Bluechel (drums), Brian Cole (bass, vocals), Terry Kirkman (reeds), Larry Ramos (replaced by Gary Alexander) (lead guitar, vocals) and Jim Yester (guitar, vocals). 'Along Comes Mary' and 'Cherish' – their first two records – were both Top Ten hits on Valiant in 1966, despite accusations that 'Mary' was a 'drug song'. The Association followed with another ambiguous ditty, 'Pandora's Golden Heebie Jeebies', but after they joined Warner Bros. in 1967, their material became straightforwardly romantic. 'Windy' and 'Never My Love' got to No. 1 and No. 2 respectively, while 'Everything That Touches You' and 'Time For Livin'' were smaller hits. By 1972, when they recorded for Columbia, their popularity had waned.

Brian Auger, born in London on July 18, 1939, abandoned a promising career as a jazz pianist – he won the 'New Star' section in the *Melody Maker* readers' jazz poll – to play R&B and a Hammond organ in 1964. He folded his first group, which included John McLaughlin (guitar) and Rick Laird (bass), to form the Brian Auger Trinity with Rick Brown (bass) and Mickey Waller (drums). By mid-1965 Long John Baldry had joined with Rod Stewart, followed by guitarist Vic Briggs and Julie Driscoll to complete Steampacket.

The band lasted only a year, but Auger stayed with Driscoll, recording their only hit, 'This Wheel's On Fire' (Marmalade), in 1968. He survived Driscoll's departure, record flops and contractual problems until July 1970, and subsequently reappeared leading Oblivion Express, a heavy jazz-rock band which enjoyed success on the American college circuit.

Autosalvage – Thomas Donaher, vocals, rhythm guitar; Darius LaNoue Davenport, vocals, piano, oboe, trombone, krummhorn, guitar, bass, drums; Rick Turner, guitar, banjo; Skip Boone, bass, guitar, piano – both group and album (RCA, 1968), are quite unique. Thomas Donaher and Darius LaNoue Davenport, son of a noted musician, formed the group in 1966, Rick Turner came via Ian and Sylvia and Skip Boone is brother of Lovin' Spoonful's Steve Boone. The Mothers reputedly discovered them during their New York sojourn and Zappa is rumoured to have played some role on their only album, one of the earliest attempts to marry rock lyrics to avant-garde music.

Burt Bacharach, now rarely credited for his innovation in the fields of pop composition and arrangement, was one of the most interesting and quietly influential figures of the early Sixties. Born in Kansas City, Missouri, on May 12, 1929, he studied music at McGill University in Montreal and, upon graduating, chose the classic route of becoming a piano accompanist to balladeers like Vic Damone and Steve Lawrence. By 1958, he had become a songwriter in partnership with Hal David. They were immediately successful with neat songs like 'The Story Of My Life' (Marty Robbins, 1957) and 'Magic Moments' (Perry Como, 1958). Bacharach worked briefly with Bob Hilliard, with whom he composed two memorable songs for the Drifters, 'Mexican Divorce' and 'Please Stay' (1961).

It was, however, with David that Bacharach formed his most famous and productive partnership: Hal David, a lyricist who had toiled long in the Broadway vineyards, and whose sharp, witty, literate images provided the perfect foil for Bacharach's increasingly sophisticated melodies. Both men were steeped in a tradition which went back way beyond pop music to the classic show songs of Cole Porter, Irving Berlin, and George Gershwin, yet both had enough appreciation of the finer points of pop consciousness to be able to roll off dozens of hit songs in the early Sixties. Dionne Warwick – discovered by Bacharach singing backgrounds on a Drifters session – was their *protégée*, their mouthpiece, and success came immediately through her with songs like her first hit 'Don't Make Me Over' (No. 21

22

in 1962), 'Anyone Who Had A Heart', 'Walk On By' (both Top Ten in 1963), 'You'll Never Get To Heaven', 'Reach Out For Me,' 'Here I Am', and many others on Scepter. Instantly apparent was the iconoclasm of Bacharach's melodic sense: few other singers could have coped with the daringly wide intervals, odd phrase-lengths, and uneven rhythms with which he confronted Miss Warwick. Given his head as producer and arranger, he emphasized the more eccentric aspects of the songs, employing unusual instrumental groupings and almost melodramatic orchestral punctuation. By the standards of contemporary pop he kept to no rules, and his exemplary knowledge and taste allowed him to get away with it. During this period Bacharach and David also composed for other performers, and among their greatest artistic successes were Gene Pitney's smash '24 Hours From Tulsa' (with its famous two-trumpet phrase) and Jimmy Radcliffe's lesser known but equally attractive 'Long After Tonight Is All Over'.

Inevitably, as the rest of the world plagiarized their methods, the couple's success ratio declined, but as recently as 1970 one of their earliest songs, 'One Less Bell To Answer', was renovated and became a No. 2 hit for the Fifth Dimension, thanks to its typical combination of sumptuous melody and imaginative lyric idea. Towards the end of the Sixties they wrote a Broadway musical called *Promises, Promises* – but it was not as successful as their previous efforts and ultimately the partnership was dissolved. Since 1963 Bacharach had been recording (for MCA and A&M) in his own right, largely due to the popularity of TV specials and series built around him, and his own albums contain interestingly developed versions of songs like 'Walk On By', 'Close To You', 'The Look Of Love', 'Any Day Now', 'I Say A Little Prayer', and 'This Guy's In Love With You'. Since his last major hit with 'Raindrops Keep Falling On My Head' a No. 1 for B. J. Thomas in 1969 (from the soundtrack of the hit movie *Butch Cassidy And The Sundance Kid*), Bacharach's creative energy appears to have dwindled, and it's now doubtful if he will again achieve the heights of earlier years. But he and Hal David gave pop many of its most intelligent and attractive songs as well as providing a different perspective which altered, in subtle but vital ways, its sound and style.

The Bachelors were originally a harmonica trio, the Harmonichords. Formed in Dublin in 1953, by the Sixties the Bachelors had become a singing trio. The two brothers Con (born Nov. 18, 1941) and Declan Clusky (Dec. 12, 1942) played acoustic guitars and Sean James Stokes (born August 13, 1940) played bass. With their first hit, 'Charmaine' (Decca), they established the winning formula of dressing up old standards in a familiar style. Con usually sang lead, laying the Irish accent on as thick as the head on a glass of Guinness.

Apart from a high nostalgia quotient, they had an image that couldn't fail: clean-cut, cardigan-clad and always smiling. Moreover, the Bachelors appeared in the charts simultaneously with the Beatles' 'Please, Please Me' (1963) and up to 1965 they had hit after hit – 'Diane' (their only No. 1), 'I Believe', 'Ramona', etc. – a constant reminder of the British pop tradition the Beatles and their like were undermining.

Showbiz-oriented and without a substantial hit since their opportunistic version of 'Sounds Of Silence' in March, 1966, they remain firm favourites of the cabaret and variety show circuit. They mix comedy with their singalong-down-memory-lane approach, a twin appeal unlikely ever to find them on the breadline.

Joan Baez. Whatever her theme, her voice always rings with strength and clarity. Whether singing folk or contemporary material in her purling soprano, or enunciating her views on pacifism and brotherhood (and sisterhood), Joan Baez projects an identifiable, persuasive and compelling sound. Her fusion of music and social conscience was an Old Left folk-movement convention, which she carried along into the New Left of the Sixties.

She made a striking debut at the first Newport Folk Festival, in 1959, and has been a star ever since. But a star obdurately indifferent to showbizzy image or style. She was born in New York City on Jan. 9, 1941, daughter of an English-Scots mother, a drama teacher, and a Mexican-American physicist. Both her grandfathers had been ministers. Her Latin descent gave her a command of Spanish as well as early experience with discrimination in California. To keep up with her father's shifting assignments, the family moved to Boston after high school. Joan fell in with the Harvard Square folk scene in her first tentative attempts to sing and play guitar. She attended Boston University for only one month, then pursued a career in music, folklore and humanist politics that was entirely self-taught. Baez's first few albums featured traditional material. Then she fell under the sway of Bob Dylan and the topical song movement. By the end of the decade, she was writing her own songs.

The Baez voice is generally regarded as a marvel of untrained purity, always controlled, often rolling with reined passion, light in texture, quite unforgettable once heard. Her singing has a stunning projection, clear-as-glass intonation, a focus that many a highly schooled conservatory singer would envy. Her acoustic guitar-playing is consistently secure, supple and refined. Whatever her stylistic excursions, even into country music, she is a master of idiom. Among her best early recordings were 'Silver Dagger,' 'All My Trials', 'Donna Donna', 'Engine 143', 'What Have They Done to the Rain?', 'Mary Hamilton', 'There But For Fortune', and 'Bachianas Brasilieras No. 5'. *The First Ten Years* double album recapitulates her first decade with Vanguard Records. After 17 albums on that label, she switched to A&M. Among her most unusual work have been an unreleased experiment into folk-rock, co-produced by the late Richard Fariña, her brother-in-law; *Any Day Now*, a double album of Dylan material in which she began recording in Nashville; *Where Are You Now, My Son?*, including tapes from North Vietnam, and *Gracias a La Vida*, a Spanish collection.

Joan's influence has been in political activism, music and in her lifestyle, as well. Her diffidence towards stardom and towards false shibboleths was widely imitated. Her career was never just in music, but on the battlefronts of social reform. In 1962, her three Southern concert tours maintained a strict non-discrimination policy. She began, in 1964, a running battle with American tax authorities by withholding that proportion earmarked for arms and war. In 1965, as an outgrowth of her interest in pacifism, she founded the Institute for the Study of Nonviolence near her home in Carmel, California. In 1967, after participating in a draft-resistance action, she, her mother and sister Mimi, spent 10 days in jail. Later that year, Joan was jailed again briefly for a similar violation. Her autobiographical book, *Daybreak*, appeared in 1968, the year she was married to David Harris, a peace activist who served a long prison term. Their son, Gabriel Earl Harris, was born in December, 1969. The couple were divorced later. In the Seventies, Baez became active with Amnesty International, ultimately joining the American chapter's board. Late in 1972, on a visit to Hanoi, she survived the 11-day American bombing of the North Vietnamese capital. The experience underscored her long opposition to war. 1975 saw her returning to the rock mainstream with *Diamonds And The Rust*. Recorded in Los Angeles rather than Nashville, it was her most commercially successful record for some time.

Peter 'Ginger' Baker, teenage racing cyclist and trumpeter from Lewisham, South London, where he was born on Aug. 19, 1939, gained early experience as a drummer with the increasingly popular traditional jazz bands of the late Fifties, including Acker Bilk's and Terry Lightfoot's. Following a residency at Ronnie Scott's Jazz Club in London, he joined Blues Incorporated in 1962, replacing Charlie Watts. In February, 1963, he broke away with Graham Bond and Jack Bruce and stayed with the Graham Bond Organization until 1966, when he formed Cream with Bruce and Eric Clapton. He and Clapton stuck together after

Cream broke up late in 1968 and teamed up with Stevie Winwood and Rick Grech in the short-lived Blind Faith.

Widely acclaimed as the world's best rock drummer, Baker developed an interest in African music, which provided the impetus for his ten-piece Airforce in 1970 and prompted his move to Akeja, Nigeria, where he built a recording studio and made a TV documentary about Nigerian music. He visited Europe with Fela Ransome Kuti and Salt, and returned to England in 1974 where he formed the Baker-Gurvitz Army with Adrian Gurvitz, ex-leader of Gun.

'Long' John Baldry. A folk and jazz singer in the Fifties, Baldry – born on Jan. 12, 1941 in London – left Blues Incorporated a few months after its formation in 1962 to tour Germany with a jazz band, joining Cyril Davies' breakaway R&B All-Stars on his return. On Davies' death in January 1964 he renamed the band the Hoochie Coochie Men and led it for more than a year with Rod Stewart as second singer, then took Stewart to join Steampacket.

After a subsequent stint with Bluesology, he was tempted into pop in 1967 and for the only hits of his career – the British chart topper 'Let The Heartaches Begin' (Pye) and 'Mexico' (1968). In the Seventies he attempted a return to blues, but despite label changes and the assistance of former colleagues, Rod Stewart and Elton John (Bluesology's Reg Dwight), he met with little success.

The Band consists of Levon Helm, drums (born in 1935); Jaime Robbie Robertson, guitar (July 5, 1943); Garth Hudson, organ (Aug. 2, 1937); Richard Manuel, piano (April 3, 1943); and Rick Danko, bass (Dec. 29, 1942). The group is versatile and all members play other instruments in addition to their principal one. They came together in the late Fifties as the Hawks, the backing group of the Toronto-based rock'n'roller, Ronnie Hawkins. All are Canadian, except for Helm who is originally from Arkansas. With Hawkins, they toured Canada and recorded R&B standards like 'Who Do

You Love?' and Muddy Waters' '19 Years Old', which featured Robertson's tough but understated guitar playing and Helm's vocals.

Leaving Hawkins, they played small venues across Canada and the United States, billed as the Canadian Squires or Levon and the Hawks, cutting a few singles including Robertson's 'The Stones I Throw'. In New York, they played with white blues singer John Hammond Jr., and through him met Bob Dylan, who saw them as the ideal group to accompany his intended move into electric music. The first recording that Dylan and The Band made together was the single 'Can You Please Crawl Out Your Window' (1965) and some members played on selected *Blonde On Blonde* tracks. But certainly the most powerful music made by Dylan and The Band at this time were the rock concerts of Dylan's 1965–6 tour. Their sound has been preserved on 'Just Like Tom Thumb's Blues' (issued on the flip side of 'I Want You') and on a widely circulated bootleg recording of Dylan's Albert Hall, London concert which demonstrates that The Band had made Dylan's sound more anarchic and turbulent than his studio recordings. On this tour Mickey Jones played drums instead of Helm, and the rhythm section propelled Dylan's voice along like a battering ram while Robertson played searing guitar lines on top, leading Dylan to praise him as 'a mathematical guitar genius'. After Dylan's motorbike crash in July 1966, The Band settled in Woodstock, to make music with him while he recuperated. These sessions resulted in a collection of songs, originally widely circulated in bootleg recordings, known as *The Basement Tapes* and finally officially released by Columbia in 1975. These songs possessed a more subdued, mellow funky feeling, and were indicative of the effect Dylan and The Band were having on each other.

The Band, particularly Robertson as a songwriter, assimilated some of Dylan's gift for metaphor and imagery, while Dylan developed a less violent, more rural musical vocabulary. The results of this interaction were first heard on Dylan's *John Wesley Harding* album, and subsequently on the first recording released under the name of The Band,

Music From Big Pink (Capitol, 1968). The album was remarkable for the 'white soul' sound of the singing, primitive but powerfully honest, the 'natural' sound of the instruments, undistorted by electronic tampering, the ease with which lead vocals were tossed around the group on 'We Can Talk', and the subtlety with which the shifting rhythms wove 'The Weight' together. *Big Pink* was a powerful stylistic achievement, synthesizing influences from country, soul, fairground music, Baptist hymns, Bob Dylan, and rock'n'roll, and succeeding through a gift for understatement and subtlety which came as a distinct contrast to the aggressive virtuosity of the 'progressive' rock scene. However, on their second album, *The Band*, Robertson created a set of songs which, verbally, displayed the same range as The Band's musical resources, e.g. 'The Night They Drove Old Dixie Down', 'King Harvest' and 'Up On Cripple Creek'. Despite its timeless feel, the album evoked a strong response in the America of late 1969. A sense of disillusion surrounded youth and rock culture and *The Band* was welcomed as the work of adults, displaying a broader grasp of American experiences than the transient obsessions of one age group or one moment in history – an achievement which wasn't compromised by any ponderous, self-conscious artistry, or loss of rock'n'roll vitality.

Having emerged from Dylan's shadow they undertook some lengthy tours which led to the title song of their third album, *Stage Fright*, which dealt with the perils of performing. Equally powerful was the album's closing song, 'The Rumor', in which The Band brought their history of the American identity up to date to embrace the paranoid and vindictive quality of life in the Seventies under Nixon and Agnew. As a whole, though, *Stage Fright* lacked the stylistic coherence of *The Band*, a result of emerging from their protective bubble of historical perspectives to look at the present. This process continued on *Cahoots* (1971) where they seemed to be expressing despair at the values of contemporary society and began to sound ponderous in their role of custodians of traditional values as their rock energy began to be neutralized by their 'maturity'.

They've produced no new material in the years since *Cahoots*, suggesting that their misgivings about life in the Seventies have, to some extent, stifled their creativity. They have produced a good live album, *Rock Of Ages*, and also a 'golden oldies' album, *Moondog Matinee*, their liveliest recordings since *The Band*. The album displayed the strength of their affection for the roots of rock, and renewed conviction as musicians and singers. They have also worked twice more as Bob Dylan's back-up band: on his *Planet Waves* album, a pleasant piece of work but scarcely a triumph for Dylan or The Band, and also on Dylan's 1974 tour, recorded and released as *Before The Flood*. Noticeably backing Dylan, The Band displayed more musical daring and attack (particularly Hudson's organ and Robertson's guitar) than when playing their own songs, which sounded like rather wooden versions of acknowledged masterpieces.

Steve Barri is a writer, producer, singer, record executive and trendsetter who, in partnership with P. F. Sloan and Lou Adler, virtually launched folk-rock/protest music on the West Coast. Barri's career started in 1959, with solo singles on Rona, and songs written for the Nortones and Carol Connors. With the latter, he formed the Storytellers (Dimension) as a result of which he met Lou Adler, who teamed him with Phil Sloan to form the key songwriting team for his Dunhill/Trousdale publishing/production company.

Not only as writers, but as singers, arrangers, musicians, producers, and later as artists under their own and other names, Sloan and Barri were responsible for hundreds of songs. They did surf music as the Fantastic Baggys, backed Jan and Dean, wrote and sang all the early Grass Roots hits, wrote 'Secret Agent Man' for Johnny Rivers, and many other hits. In 1968, after many hits of his own, P. F. Sloan moved to New York, while Barri became an executive producer at Dunhill Records where he was acclaimed for his work with Bobby Bland.

Jeff Barry entered the music business in 1959 as a singer, recording about a dozen singles before 1962, at which time he met and married a young songwriter named Ellie Greenwich. He'd also written a few hits for others, notably 'Tell Laura I Love Her' (Ray Peterson, RCA) and 'Chip, Chip' (Gene McDaniels, Liberty), and with Greenwich he developed one of the hottest writing teams in New York, turning out hits for Lesley Gore, Ray Peterson, the Exciters, the Shirelles, the Chiffons and others.

In early 1963, he and Ellie began recording for Jubilee as the Raindrops, scoring two big hits with 'What A Guy' and 'Kind Of Boy You Can't Forget'. At the same time, they were involved heavily with Phil Spector, knocking out hits including 'Da Doo Ron Ron', 'Then He Kissed Me' (Crystals), 'Be My Baby', 'Baby I Love You', 'Chapel Of Love' (Ronettes), 'Wait Till My Bobby Gets Home' (Darlene Love), 'Not Too Young To Get Married' (Bob B. Soxx), and 'River Deep, Mountain High' (Ike and Tina Turner), as well as lesser hits for all these artists. In 1964, they were also working for Leiber and Stoller's newly formed Red Bird label, where they wrote, arranged and/or produced most of the label's output by the Jelly Beans, Dixie Cups and the Shangri-Las. It was there they discovered Neil Diamond, and took him to Bang Records in 1966, where they produced five albums and twelve singles with him, also writing most of his hits.

Barry's marriage to Greenwich ended in late 1965, and though they continued writing together, they were headed in. different directions. She got involved in production, while he cut singles for UA and Red Bird, and produced Andy Kim on Steed ('How'd We Ever Get This Way' and other Top Fifty hits). At the same time, he and Kim were writing, producing and playing on 'Sugar, Sugar' and other hits by the Archies, which kept them busy through 1970. Since then, Barry has worked primarily as a producer for A&M, and has also issued a single (1973) on that label.

Len Barry was the king of blue-eyed soul for six months during 1966. Born in Philadelphia on June 12, 1942 he is

31

thought to have sung on the Bosstones' wild rocker 'Mope-Itty Mope' on Boss in 1958. He moved on to chart success with the Dovells in 1961–3, performing on their series of hit dance records, initiated by 'Bristol Stomp'.

As a solo artist, he had his greatest moments with '1-2-3' and 'Like A Baby' (Decca), which have since become discotheque classics. Barry's high tenor singing kept him in business into the Seventies, with records on American Decca and RCA, but when the hits stopped coming he was forced to tone down his James Brown-inspired stage act and adapt his style for the cabaret circuit.

Fontella Bass, born on July 3, 1940, in St Louis, Missouri, first played organ and piano in Oliver Sain's band, with whom she made her first records on Ike Turner's Prann label and on Bobbin in 1963. Before Turner moved to the West Coast, she also recorded for another of his labels, Sonja, but her first hit came with 'Don't Mess Up A Good Thing', a duet with Bobby McClure on Checker which reached the Top Five in the R&B charts in 1965.

Bass followed up with 'Rescue Me', featuring a Motown-esque production by Billy Davis. It topped the R&B charts and reached No. 4 in the pop listings. Smaller hits from this period included 'Recovery' and 'I Surrender'. In 1969, in Paris, Fontella Bass recorded with her husband, jazz trumpeter Lester Bowie, for the Art Ensemble of Chicago. On her return to America in 1971 she returned to the R&B charts with records for Jewel/Paula produced by Oliver Sain.

Harold Battiste took his first step to becoming a respected recording producer when he was put in charge of Specialty's New Orleans branch office in 1957. At first his efforts to get the operation off the ground took second place to the label's success with Little Richard and Larry Williams, and so his discoveries like Irma Thomas, Ernie K-Doe and Chris Kenner had to wait a little longer for their Gold Discs, although Jerry Byrne had a local hit with 'Lights Out', a rock'n'roll classic. In 1960 Battiste joined the staff of Ric Records and arranged Joe Jones' Top Ten hit, 'You Talk Too Much'.

Alarmed at the way New Orleans musicians were being exploited Battiste masterminded the AFO ('All For One') label as a black co-operative and had an enormous hit with Barbara George's 'I Know'. But his ambitious plan of making AFO a black Atlantic ended in discord and he headed for the West Coast, where he arranged for Sam Cooke and others, notably for Sonny and Cher's 'I Got You Babe'. He evolved the Dr John character with Mac Rebennack in 1967, but Rebennack grabbed all the accolades for putting the Voodoo Rock and good old-fashioned New Orleans funk sound into the grooves, leaving Harold Battiste (who also recorded for Uptown) on the outside looking in – a man of good ideas reduced to a comfortable but obscure career in TV jingles.

The Beach Boys, formed in 1961, still extant in 1975 with no prospect of dissolution, were America's only real challenge to the Beatles and certainly the most prominent white American group of the pre-psychedelic era. The group's formation took place in a middle-class Los Angeles suburb of Hawthorne, and was centred around the teenage Wilson Brothers – Brian (born June 20, 1942); Dennis (Dec. 4, 1944); and Carl (Dec. 21, 1946) – their cousin Mike Love (March 15, 1941); and friend Alan Jardine (Sept. 3, 1942). Harmony singing had always been an important part of their family life, and when the Wilson parents took a holiday in Mexico in September 1961 it was a perfect opportunity for the kids to rent instruments and start a group in their living room.

It was Dennis's addiction to the Californian sport of surfing that gave the group their initial identity, one which survives indelibly in the minds of today's audiences. He suggested that the group sing about the pastime, and a song (written by Brian and Mike) called 'Surfin'' was the immediate result. Their father, Murray Wilson, himself a songwriter, took the boys along to his music publisher and the song was recorded in somewhat improvised conditions with

Carl on guitar, Alan on acoustic bass, and Brian providing percussive support on a garbage can. The publisher procured a release for the record on the local X label and then the slightly larger Candix label, and against all the odds it stuck around the lower limits of the American Hot Hundred for six weeks – based mainly on sales to Californian surfer boys and girls, no doubt. They also began to appear in public, initially as the Pendletones (after a make of heavy plaid shirt which surfers wore and which became their early uniform), briefly as Carl and the Passions, and ultimately as the Beach Boys, the last name being a suggestion from Candix's promotion man. Their concert debut under this name was in the Ritchie Valens Memorial Concert in Long Beach Municipal Auditorium on Dec. 31, 1961.

Jardine left around this time to pursue his dentistry studies and was replaced by neighbour David Marks who played rhythm guitar, enabling Brian to switch to bass guitar. Dennis played drums, while Mike Love shared the lead vocals with Brian.

When Candix, a small label, folded early in 1962, Murray Wilson took the boys along to Capitol Records and played producer Nik Venet acetates of 'Surfin' Safari' and '409' – the latter a hymn in praise of the singer's car. Venet grasped the possibilities, signed the group, and 'Surfin' Safari' became a national Top Twenty hit. 'Ten Little Indians', the follow-up, was a comparative flop, but the next one was big indeed: 'Surfin' USA' reached No. 3 in the early summer of 1963. In addition, it laid bare the influences behind the growing talent of Brian Wilson, who was coming to the forefront as the group's real creative force. For 'Surfin' USA' Brian had borrowed the tune and treatment from Chuck Berry's 'Sweet Little Sixteen', adding new words and a lead vocal surrounded by the beginnings of a cool, liquid harmony style strongly reminiscent of the Four Freshmen (and, by implication, the American glee-club tradition).

The next single, 'Surfer Girl', a wistful, yearning ballad emphasized the harmonies even more heavily as the voices began to twist and turn in creamy, close-packed, harmonically sophisticated chorales, topped off with a gimmick

34

adapted from East Coast vocal group records – Brian's cool, cruising falsetto, which became a major trademark. 'Surfin' USA' and 'Surfer Girl' marked the complementary modes which Brian and the group explored for the next three years. The up-tempo style led to 'Fun Fun Fun', 'I Get Around' (a No. 1), 'When I Grow Up (To Be A Man)', 'Dance Dance Dance', and 'Help Me Rhonda' (another No. 1) – all Top Ten hits in 1964 and 1965 – while the possibilities of the ballad form were explored with ever more trance-like effect in such classics as 'In My Room', 'The Lonely Sea', 'Girls On The Beach', 'Don't Worry Baby', 'The Warmth Of The Sun', 'She Knows Me Too Well', 'Kiss Me Baby', and 'Please Let Me Wonder' from the same period. By this time, too, Jardine had returned to the fold, displacing Marks.

On a wider front, the group's own influence had become widespread. Their early surfing records sparked off a complete genre, opening the way for performers like Jan and Dean ('Surf City'), Bruce (Johnston) and Terry (Melcher) with 'Summer Means Fun', Ronnie and the Daytonas ('Beach Boy'), Jack Nitszche ('The Lonely Surfer'), Dick Dale and the Del-Tones ('Surf Beat'), and hundreds of aspiring Californian garage bands. When surfing's vogue dropped off, the Beach Boys put out an album of car songs called *Little Deuce Coupe*, featuring '409' alongside other beauties like 'Our Car Club', 'Cherry Cherry Coupe', 'No-Go Showboat' and 'Custom Machine'. Sure enough, others responded: Jan and Dean with 'Dead Man's Curve' and 'Drag City', Bruce and Terry with 'Custom Machine' and 'Hot Rod USA', Ronnie and the Daytonas with 'GTO', the Rip-Chords with 'Hey Little Cobra' and 'Three Window Coupe'.

Through all this, Brian Wilson was as a journalist: absorbing and reflecting the emerging lifestyle of teenage California, a lifestyle which – luckily for him – kids from New York to London to Paris also decided they wanted to emulate. He wrote many of the early lyrics himself. In cold print they lack grace and wit, but sung by the group they are perfect expressions of teen *angst* in all its forms. Among

35

his external collaborators were Roger Christian, a local deejay who helped out with the car songs, and Garry Usher.

When the Beatles first blitzed America, at the beginning of 1964, the Beach Boys weren't much affected. In an apparently unassailable position, Brian strengthened the musical content of their records by adding elements of another influence: the production techniques of Phil Spector. From Spector, Brian borrowed the wall-of-sound technique, particularly the batteries of percussion instruments, which can be heard among the growing complexities of peak-era Beach Boys records like 'California Girls', 'The Little Girl I Once Knew', and 'Wendy', all perfect blends of teen consciousness and musical innovation. Brian reached his personal summit with *Pet Sounds* in 1966 and 'Good Vibrations', a No. 1 for the group later that year. Employing unusual instrumental grouping and apparently endless vocal overdubs with complete mastery and a tireless attention to detail, he was producing music which set the pop world on its ear.

A combination of circumstances, however, proved cumulatively tragic: *Pet Sounds* was badly upstaged by the Beatles' *Sergeant Pepper*, which followed it within a matter of months. Brian abandoned (amidst a mass of neuroses) his next project, an album called *Smile* which was to have dwarfed even *Pet Sounds*; and then the West Coast 'psychedelic revolution' occurred. Whereas the Beatles remained in the vanguard of the New Wave, wholeheartedly entering every new phase of discovery, the Beach Boys lagged fatally behind, the victims equally of Brian's personal uncertainties and of the innate conservatism of several other members of the group, who felt that they should never have left the simplicities of surf music. Within months they were old hat, and the tattered remnants of *Smile*, issued in skeletal form as *Smiley Smile*, did their reputation no good among the general public.

In the face of change, though, they stuck together. Bothered by partial deafness in one ear (which still renders him unable to hear stereo sound), Brian quit touring and was replaced in the road band first by Glen Campbell (briefly), and then by Bruce Johnston, who stayed to contribute a number of songs to their repertoire. But while other groups were exploring the possibilities of two- and three-hour sets, the Beach Boys continued to parade their 45-minute 'medley of hits' in front of concert audiences; they seemed sealed off from progress. Yet on record, and particularly in Europe, they maintained some semblance of hit status: 'Wild Honey', 'Darlin'', 'Do It Again', 'I Can Hear Music', and 'Break Away' were all fine – and successful – records, and albums like *Friends*, *20/20*, and *Sunflower* contained superb songs and matchless production, despite Brian's ever-diminishing participation.

They were also enmeshed in lawsuits with their former managers and with Capitol – the latter dispute boiling up after they'd formed their own label, Brother Records, in 1967, distributed first through Capitol and (from 1970) through Warner–Reprise Records. This, one of the early artist-run labels, was one of the many pioneering efforts for which they have received little credit – partly because they've always run into the difficulties which beset most pioneers.

In 1971, though, their affairs took a turn for the better when their management was taken over by a former journalist, Jack Rieley, who understood their position and their importance. As well as writing intelligent lyrics for songs by Brian and Carl, Rieley also unearthed the incomplete tapes of a song called 'Surf's Up', which was to have been the centrepiece on *Smile* back in 1967. He persuaded them to finish it off, made it the title-track of their new album, and went about refurbishing the group's image by abandoning stage uniforms and allowing them to play two-hour sets including both the hits and more obscure material. To a degree, Rieley's strategy worked – and the track 'Surf's Up', with controversial, typically elliptical words by Van Dyke Parks and fragile melodies by Brian, may well prove to be their masterpiece. Shortly after the release of this album, Bruce Johnston left to pursue a career with his own group.

In an attempt mainly to shake Brian out of his torpor, Rieley took the group in its entirety to Holland in 1972, built them a complete recording studio there, and came up

37

with an album called *Holland*. Critically well-received, it was not a major hit and when Rieley left them shortly afterwards the group resorted to releasing an accurate if unspectacular double album culled from live concerts. In person at this time they were highly impressive, thanks to a new rhythm section including two South Africans – Blondie Chaplin (guitar) and Ricky Fataar (drums) – but it seemed that they had lost the ability to make hit singles. Chaplin and Fataar left during 1974, James Guercio (of Blood Sweat And Tears and Chicago fame) took over their management, and the group reverted almost to its original 1961 configuration, with Guercio playing bass on stage in Brian's place. Though Dennis and Carl were by now composers of considerable strength, and despite having regained a place in the affections of the rock audience, business problems and their collective uncertainty as to the band's role kept their future insecure.

Nevertheless, no group in pop history has shown a more consistent creative development over a long period, and none has been more influential in the field of vocal harmonies. Moreover, the feeling persists that, if Brian Wilson ever regains his creative energy (for the ability and imagination are still there), they can again become a major force.

The Beatles. That the Beatles were the most important group in the history of rock does not need saying, but their very importance makes it impossible to provide a neat summary of their career and its significance. The Beatles became more than John Lennon, Paul McCartney, George Harrison, Ringo Starr, music makers; they became the worldwide representatives of the great explosion in British popular music in the Sixties, and the symbols of a new way of regarding the possibilities of pop. They were a *phenomenon* and if it was their music that gave the Beatles cultural force, their history is not just a musical one.

The Beatles were part of the generation, teenaged in the Fifties, of English working-class kids that grew up after the war, in conditions of comparative affluence and with, after the 1945 Education Act, at least a chance of secondary education and more. They were also among the kids who experienced the full impact of American rock'n'roll and its artistic and material possibilities. John Lennon (born Oct. 9, 1940) formed his rock'n'roll group, the Quarrymen, in 1955 while he was still at school; by 1958, when he was at art school, the group included Paul McCartney (June 18, 1942) and George Harrison (Feb. 25, 1943) who had previously had his own group, the Rebels. But the Quarrymen weren't just another English rock'n'roll group, they were a Liverpool rock'n'roll group, with the advantages of growing up in a cosmopolitan port. Musical advantages – American R&B records could be heard in Liverpool whatever the London pop industry's successes in cleaning up white rock'n'roll; material advantages – Liverpool had clubs where groups played gutsy, sexy music. It was possible to make a living from music and in 1959 the Silver Beatles were formed – John, Paul and George, Stuart Sutcliffe on guitar, Pete Best on drums. The living wasn't just in Liverpool – it meant frequent trips to the West German city of Hamburg, another port, another club scene, another centre of American music, – but it was a living.

It is impossible to overestimate the importance of these early *professional* years for the Beatles' subsequent music. The group learnt its basic technical and crowd-pleasing skills in very specific circumstances: the music had to be loud and hard, there was no space for subtlety; the clubs were small, the equipment poor, the resulting sound was dependent on the combined beat of drums, bass and rhythm guitar. Although the Beatles occasionally backed a lead singer, Tony Sheridan, as a group they didn't have a leader but rather built their vocals round harmonies and back-up voices, round techniques learnt from R&B and particularly from the gospel-based soul sound of early Motown records. By 1961 the Beatles were making a distinctive sort of music – the 'Liverpool sound' – and were making it better than anyone else. They had survived their apprenticeship and had, in John and Paul, two of the finest singers on the scene.

They had also become sufficiently popular – they were the winners of *Mersey Beat*'s first poll – to come to the attention of Brian Epstein, the manager of the record department (North End Music Stores) in his family's Liverpool furniture store. He became their manager and the Beatles became a national group. He groomed them (cleaning up their stage act, taking them out of leathers and into suits), he got them a record contract (with EMI's Parlophone label), he masterminded their successful assault on the charts, on the concert halls, on the nation's consciousness. But if Epstein's achievement was to make the Beatles the most successful act in the British music business, his significance was that he was not himself a part of that business. The key to the Beatles' career between 1961 and 1964 was that they became successful without having to tread the traditional pop path. Partly they were lucky – Epstein was an unusual manager, their EMI producer, George Martin, was not a pop person but had been making comedy records – but the crucial factor in their path-breaking success was John and Paul's songwriting ability – they wrote all their own hits – which was crucial for two reasons: it destroyed the aura of American rock records, and it completely broke the hold of the music publishing industry, with its hustling songwriting hacks, over British pop.

The group that Brian Epstein signed comprised George Harrison on guitar, Paul McCartney on bass, John Lennon on rhythm, Pete Best on drums (Stuart Sutcliffe had left the group in Hamburg and subsequently died of a brain tumour) – and shortly after Pete Best was replaced by Ringo Starr (born Richard Starkey on July 7, 1940) from Rory Storme and the Hurricanes. If it took Epstein months to get the EMI contract, success was then rapid. 'Love Me Do' made the Top Twenty in December, 1962, 'Please Please Me', 'From Me To You' and 'She Loves You' made No. 1 and established the Beatles in the summer of 1963 as teen idols. Record sales became accompanied by all the trappings of hysteria – sell-out, police-ringed concerts, obsessive press coverage, desperate record companies searching for 'new Beatles'.

But even then the group were more than just the latest flames, even then they were seen differently from previous pop stars. They didn't disappear into their own hype; they remained interesting, individual, articulate characters; as people, personalities, they were real in a way that Cliff Richard and the Shadows had never been. Their qualities were not those of showbiz – they came across as cynical, arrogant, restless. Beatle trappings – Beatle haircuts, Beatle jackets and Beatle boots – came to represent an attitude as well as the usual fan fervour. The Beatles brought pop appeal to a mass audience that had previously been uneasy in its relationship to pop. When Beatle music came out of the Cavern it was not just heard by other working-class kids, it also became the music of middle-class, sixth-form young people. This audience had had a similar generational experience to the Beatles themselves, and the Beatles were the first English pop group that didn't insult their intelligence. The contrast between the covers of the Beatles' first and second albums is symbolic: *Please, Please Me* had the boys grinning in their cheap suits, chirpy, very working-class; *With The Beatles* had four artistically posed heads, grainy, serious, black polo-necked, the Beatle cuts, soft and floppy – they looked like *students*.

If it was extraordinary that the Beatles' personalities could survive the success of their music, it was even more extraordinary that the music itself continued to carry weight. The group brought to the charts a fresh style of melody, of harmony, of rhythm, that was exhilarating and compulsive. The rough Hamburg edges were smoothed (the occasional album track was even schmaltzy) but the verve remained, the songs became more polished but retained their originality. By the end of 1963, in little over a year, the Beatles had achieved everything in Britain that a pop group could. The next and ultimate step was the conquest of America (Europe and the Commonwealth had already fallen) and this was achieved in stunning fashion in February, 1964. Thanks partly to careful planning by Brian Epstein (including a top billing on the *Ed Sullivan Show*), partly to £20,000 worth of hype from Capitol Records, but mostly to the then vacuum in American teenage pop, when the Beatles arrived in New York they took over the charts. Beatlemania flooded the States, bringing in its wake success for every group with an English accent, transforming attitudes to pop there as successfully as in Britain.

In retrospect, the real achievement of the Beatles in 1964 was not to arouse for the first time (and for ever) America's interest in British pop, but was to retain a musical creativity throughout the traumas and trappings of superstardom. From then on their career ran along separate, if parallel, lines – business success on the one hand, musical progress on the other. As a business, the Beatles made hit record after hit record, signed a new deal with EMI, formed a publishing company, Northern Songs; there were sell-out world tours (which finally stopped in 1966) complete with a growing entourage of hangers-on and ceaseless media attention. Everywhere the Beatles went so did the merchandisers, offering everything from Beatle wigs and Beatle knickers to Beatle tea-cloths. The quickest summary of the Beatles' career between 1964 and 1967 is that they made a lot of money – enough, in fact, to be honoured as an export industry when, as early as 1965, they were awarded MBEs.

Even in their attainment of riches the Beatles were original. Their films, *A Hard Day's Night* and *Help!* were not quick exploitations, but were inventively and artily directed by Dick Lester, and his tricks – plus the Beatles' own wit – won the films critical as well as box-office success. The key Beatle image occurred early in *A Hard Day's Night* – the boys enter their row of terraced houses to reveal, behind the façade, a huge communal, luxury pad. The Beatles, in their starry world, were cut off now from their roots. Their music was no longer, as in Hamburg days, a direct response to their performing situation, it was made *despite* the pressures. Their workplace was the studio, their musical history became a history of albums. And the significance of that history is that their music progressed – as they absorbed new influences, as they used their newly acquired wealth and resources, as their artistic ambitions grew. No one had expected the original rock'n'rollers to progress and few of them did, but the Beatles' music developed inexorably – despite the day-to-day pop pressures, despite the limitations of their musical origins. In transforming the attitudes of their audiences towards pop, the Beatles had transformed their own. By 1965, they were sustaining and being sustained by a new world of musicians – eclectic, ambitious, self-conscious. Pop was no longer a suitable word as the Beatles and Bob Dylan became mutual influences, as folk and rock'n'roll and blues and teenage ballads were swirled together in a new cultural frenzy; the Beatles were the first *rock* stars.

The staging posts of their progress were *Rubber Soul*, which came out in December, 1965, and *Revolver* (August, 1966). The albums still had their pretty tunes (if more elaborately orchestrated) but there were no more straight rockers, no more simple songs. Instead, the melodies became complex (as Paul McCartney moved from his instant standard, 'Yesterday', to the deliberate calculation of 'Eleanor Rigby'); the lyrics became 'interesting' (as Lennon absorbed Dylan and the group's philosophical pretensions showed); above all there was an outburst of new sounds – George's sitar, banks of strings, French horns, car horns, all George Martin's technical tricks. By 1967, it seemed that nothing was impossible for the Beatles as artists or for their audience as listeners, and in June they put out *Sergeant Pepper's Lonely Hearts Club Band* – elaborately packaged, elaborately conceived, an amazingly consistent pop package of all the elements of 1967 youth culture – drugs and electronics and mysticism and hope – and all with the familiar Beatle harmonies and tunes and charm.

The Beatles had become hippies. They grew their hair long, admitted to smoking dope, took up with the Maharishi; they believed in love, planned *The Magical Mystery Tour* for television, and put together Apple, the company that was going to use their profits creatively, joyously, for the people. Summer 1967 was the end of the beginning and the beginning of the end. Brian Epstein died, the *Magical Mystery Tour* flopped, Apple became a wheeling, dealing paradise. The Beatles began to be rent by the contradictions – between their role as the people's hippies and their lives as rich superstars; between their pop appeal and their increasing distance from 'ordinary' concerns; above all, between their individual musical and material ambitions. The break-up was slow and disguised, but between 1967 and 1969 the Beatles ceased to be the Beatles and became John Lennon and Paul McCartney and George Harrison and Ringo Starr. They continued to make records together. The double *White Album* (November, 1968) may be the finest showcase of the group's talent – as songwriters and singers and arrangers and performers and artists – but it is a showcase of *individual* talents. There are John songs and Paul songs and George songs, and they were now produced that way.

When the group finally split it hardly made a musical difference – the solo work had begun before then and the Beatles continued to be each other's sessionmen afterwards. But the split was symbolic – not just in its bitterness, in its business ramifications, but simply in the loss of a name. An era was over, an era in which the musical possibilities of rock'n'roll, of pop, had been first realized and explored, an era in which music had seemed to carry cultural, social, political, *revolutionary* force. The Beatles had symbolized optimism, their disintegration symbolized optimism fading. In the end the Beatles left us with not just a collection of fine songs (recorded by countless other artists as well as by themselves), but also with the reminder of a spoiled dream; they left us with the most nostalgic music in the history of rock.

The Beau Brummels were formed in San Francisco in 1964. Sal Valentino, Ron Elliott, Ron Meagher, John Peterson, and Declan Mulligan (who left the group early on, and later sued for damages after they became big), recorded for Tom Donahue's Autumn label. Both 'Laugh Laugh' and the follow-up 'Just A Little' (both produced by Sly Stone) were Top Twenty hits in early 1965, with a Searchers-like sound that caused the group to be dubbed 'America's answer to the British Invasion'. They used 12-string guitar, soft harmonies, plaintive harmonica and minor-key melodies to create a haunting sound that in turn spawned the Byrds and

44

folk-rock. Although a seminal group in this respect, their follow-ups over the next three years (on Autumn and Warner Bros.) were only minor hits. After their split in late 1968, Valentino made solo records and then formed Stoneground. Elliott had a group called Pan and also made a solo album. In 1974, the Beau Brummels re-formed, with a new album (4-75) on Warner Bros., only to disband in 1975.

The Bee Gees. The brothers Gibb began performing together publicly as children in Manchester and became a successful pop group in Australia (whence their family had emigrated) while still teenagers. In 1967, when Barry was 19 and Robin and Maurice 17, they returned to England, were signed up by Robert Stigwood and Polydor, and had their first English hit, 'New York Mining Disaster 1941'. Also in the group were Vince Melouney (guitar) and Colin Peterson (drums). This success was repeated in America and the Bee Gees quickly became established worldwide with such records as 'Massachusetts' and 'I've Gotta Get A Message To You'. In 1969, Robin Gibb left the group to go solo but he was comparatively unsuccessful and by 1972 the group was together again and getting American Top Twenty hits like 'My World' and 'Run To Me'. In 1975, after a period of little success, they returned to the top of the charts with two smash hits, 'Jive Talkin'' and 'Nights On Broadway', from the Arif Mardin-produced *Main Course* (RSO), an album that saw them producing their nasal harmonies in front of funkier rhythms than ever before.

The essence of Bee Gees music is the self-pitying ballad, lushly orchestrated around Robin's ingratiating tremulo and his brothers' distinctive nasal harmonies. In this style the Gibbs are facile songwriters (their songs are widely used by other cabaret artists) but doubts remain about their place in rock history. Their achievement was to take some aspects of the Sixties English group style – the harsh harmonies, the 'impure' lead voice, the risky melodies – and apply them to traditional pop; they were never a *rock* group. As the Beatles and other groups moved out of the world of pure

45

pop, the Bee Gees were left filling a significant gap, but they have failed to develop musically – *Bee Gees First* remains their most interesting album, 'New York Mining Disaster' their greatest song.

Harry Belafonte, born in Harlem, New York, in 1927, spent eight years in America, then five in Jamaica before returning to New York. He had an uneven career before establishing himself as the 'King of Calypso': it included a spell in the US Navy, attempting to become an actor, and succeeding in becoming a messenger. He then sang with a jazz group, quit to start a restaurant in Greenwich Village, and there became a convert to the folk scene. An engagement at the Village Vanguard, and a contract with Victor Records, followed. His album *Calypso* – which included his hit composition 'Banana Boat Song' – was released in 1956. Three years later it had sold a million copies. Belafonte's smooth singing style appealed to both folk and Easy Listening audiences, and by popularizing West Indian styles he was to lead the way for the folk and rock world's later fascination with the Caribbean.

William Bell, born in Memphis in 1939, was one of the Stax label's earliest recruits, first singing with the Del-Rios. Without achieving the same degree of success as their star turns, he remains a consistent if unspectacular reflection of the company's changing style, and a popular artist in the South. The best of his early records ('You Don't Miss Your Water', 'Any Other Way' – 1962; 'I'll Show You' – 1963) preceded national recognition of the Memphis Sound, but after Otis Redding and others had spread its popularity he scored his biggest hits from 1966 to 1968 with ballads – 'Everybody Loves A Winner', 'Tribute To A King' (i.e. Otis), 'I Forgot To Be Your Lover'; dance tunes – 'Never Like This Before', 'Eloise'; and a duet with Judy Clay – 'Private Number'. Further duets with Clay, Mavis Staples, and Carla Thomas; an attempt at soul-reggae; and some pretentious-sounding albums have done little for him since then. His songs have been widely recorded by other artists.

Cliff Bennett. From the Beatles onwards, everybody professed to respect Cliff Bennett in the British rock scene of the mid-Sixties, though people rarely bought his records. Bennett was born on June 4, 1940 and formed his group, the Rebel Rousers, in 1961. The group included Dave Wendells (lead guitar), Maurice Groves and Sid Phillips (saxes), Frank Allen (bass, replaced by Bobby Thompson) and Mike Burt (drums). His music was soul-based, and the band's repertoire included songs by Bobby Bland, the Drifters, Ray Charles and Bobby Parker. The eccentric-looking Allen would sing 'Mashed Potato' as well as the original. Later, Bennett added Roy Young to his band, a former Little Richard impersonator, who had now switched to Bobby Bland.

Bennett and the Rebel Rousers had two hits on Parlophone: the Drifters' 'One Way Love' (1964) and the Beatles' 'Got To Get You Into My Life' (1966), but their records never went beyond a highly efficient plagiarism. Bennett later formed an unsuccessful progressive rock band, Toe Fat.

Brook Benton is a warm-voiced balladeer who came into his own during the lull between rock'n'roll and the return of heavy rhythms in the mid-Sixties. Born on Sept. 19, 1931 in Camden, South Carolina, after singing with the Bill Landford and Golden Gate gospel quartets he recorded for Epic and Vik (scoring a minor hit, 'A Million Miles From Nowhere', in 1958), but survived by making demo recordings for writer/publisher Clyde Otis. Through Otis's successful association with Mercury records (he'd given them several winners, including 'The Diamonds' and 'The Stroll') Benton was signed to the company and together Belford Hendricks, Otis and Benton himself wrote his first three hits in 1959 – 'It's Just A Matter Of Time', 'Endlessly', and 'Thank You Pretty Baby'. For nearly four years he couldn't go wrong, recording a succession of smoky vocals flowing over banks of swirling strings and an ethereal chorus arranged and conducted by Hendricks – 'So Many Ways' (1959); 'Kiddio' and

'Fools Rush In' (1960); perhaps his finest sides, two million-selling duets with Dinah Washington, 'Baby (You've Got What It Takes)' and 'Rockin' Good Way' (1960); two folk songs, 'Boll Weevil Song' and 'Frankie And Johnny' (1961); and many more until 'I Got What I Wanted' and 'My True Confession' (produced by Shelby Singleton, arranged by Bill Justis) – his last big hits for Mercury in 1963. Sojourns with RCA (1965–7) and Reprise (1967–8) failed to revive his career, but he successfully adapted to the soul market on the Atlantic subsidiary Cotillion, scoring several hits including a particularly fine version of 'Rainy Night In Georgia' (1970). Subsequent releases on MGM, Brut, and Stax have not been so impressive.

Bert Berns was a new wave R&B producer and writer (also known as Bert Russell and Russell Byrd), a master at matching gospel voices with slow and climactic ballads of extraordinary passion.

Born in 1929, he worked first as a record salesman, music copyist and session pianist. In 1960 he began writing songs with Phil Medley. While Austin Taylor's 'Push Push' on Laurie was probably their first hit song, the most famous was 'Twist and Shout'. Originally written for the Topnotes on Atlantic, it became a Top Ten hit when revived by the Isley Brothers, on Wand, in 1962.

During the early Sixties, Berns compositions appeared on records from a number of small New York labels including Cameo (Don Covay), United Artists (the Electras, Marv Johnson, the Exciters, Garnet Mimms), Scepter (the Rocky Fellers), Diamond (Johnny Thunder), MGM (Conway Twitty) and his own label Keetch (Linda Laurie). At Atlantic/Atco, Berns took over from Leiber and Stoller in the dual role of songwriter-producer.

His publishing company, Webb IV, was formed to provide material for Barbara Lewis, Ben E. King, the Drifters, Tony Orlando, Tami Lynn, the Bluebelles and, most notably, Solomon Burke. 'Cry To Me', 'Down In The Valley', 'If You Need Me', 'Goodbye Baby' and 'Everybody Needs

Somebody To Love' were among Burke's best recordings and Berns helped to write and/or produce them all.

Berns also collaborated frequently with other top writers, producers and arrangers, producing a soul classic on almost every occasion. They included the Vibrations' 'My Girl Sloopy' (written with Wes Farrell), Betty Harris' 'Cry To Me' and 'His Kiss' on Jubilee (produced with Mike Stoller) and the Drifters' 'Under The Boardwalk' (arranged with Mike Leander). His compositions with Jerry Ragavoy established Garnet Mimms as Solomon Burke's only real rival. 'One Girl', 'Look Away', 'It Was Easier To Hurt Her' and 'I'll Take Good Care Of You' were among Mimms' deep soul masterpieces. In a more commercial vein, 'Little Lonely One' and 'A Little Bit Of Soap' (a Top Twenty hit in 1961) by the Jarmels were equally seminal Berns productions.

With assistance from Atlantic, Berns set up his Bang label in 1965. It was a sustained attempt to enter the white pop field and the Bang roster of artists included Neil Diamond, the Strangeloves and Van Morrison. Them had already recorded Berns' 'Here Comes The Night' and following the group's break-up, Berns brought Morrison to America. He also signed ethnic Spanish performers, and his interest in Latin music was reflected in the catchy 'La Bamba' rhythm which permeated some of his greatest hits: the McCoys' 'Hang On Sloopy', 'Twist And Shout' and Tami Lynn's 'I'm Gonna Run Away From You'. Bang's R&B subsidiary, Shout, featured a host of good soul performers including Roy C., George Freeman, Bobby Harris, Erma Franklin ('A Piece Of My Heart') and Freddy Scott ('Are You Lonely For Me, Baby', 'Cry To Me' and 'Am I Grooving You'). Berns also recognized the struggle for black identity when he wrote 'Up In The Streets Of Harlem' for the Drifters in 1966.

Apart from running Shout, he continued to write for Atlantic and other companies – Lorraine Ellison on Loma, Garnet Mimms on Veep – until the end. He died of a heart attack in a New York hotel on Dec. 31, 1967. Deprived of one of its major writers and producers, the golden era of deep soul died with him.

Dave Berry, an ardent admirer of Chuck Berry, was born David Grundy in Woodhouse, Sheffield, in 1941, changed his surname to that of his idol and formed the Cruisers, an R&B group, in 1961. Their first two records for Decca ('Memphis, Tennessee' in 1963 and 'My Baby Left Me' the following year) were pure British R&B.

Subsequently Berry was tempted into more commercial pop with Top Five songs like 'The Crying Game' (1964) and 'Mama' (1966) before moving into the Northern club circuit in the late Sixties. Berry always found it difficult to sing in tune, but compensated for this by evolving an enjoyably eccentric stage act revived by Alvin Stardust in the Seventies.

Big Brother and the Holding Company, formed in San Francisco in 1966, comprised Sam Andrew (born Aug. 12, 1941), guitar; James Gurly, guitar; Pete Albin, bass; Dave Getz, drums; and Janis Joplin, vocals. A supergroup in the Bay area, the one album that did them justice as a *group*, *Big Brother and The Holding Company* (Mainstream, 1967), was ironically a demo tape that the group fought against being released. But it showed a roughness behind the obvious excitement of Joplin's voice that Columbia, when they signed the group in 1968, was unwilling to risk on record again. By 1969, Big Brother and Janis were separate entities. *Be A Brother* (1970), on which the original members were augmented by Nick Gravenites, and David Schallok, saw the group developing a smoother, if less exciting, sound.

The Big Three, formerly members of Cass and the Casanovas – guitarist Brian Griffiths, bass guitarist Johnny Gustafson and drummer Johnny Hutchinson were among the top few Liverpool groups by the time the Beatles emerged in early 1963. They claimed to have a repertoire of 600 songs. Managed by Brian Epstein and signed to Decca, their studio recordings were disappointing. Only the EP *Live At The Cavern* did them justice, and that was released in 1964, six months after the break-up of the original group. Gustafson had gone first to the Merseybeats and much later to Quatermass, Hard Stuff and Roxy Music, while Griffiths just dropped out of sight. In 1973, Griffiths and Gustafson re-formed to make one album (*Resurrection* on Polydor). The drummer was Nigel Olsson from the Elton John Band.

Elvin Bishop, from Tulsa, Oklahoma, played guitar in the Paul Butterfield Blues Band until 1968 when he left to form his own group. Although Mike Bloomfield played lead guitar on the first three Butterfield records, Bishop had preceded him in the band, and took over for two later albums, including *In My Own Dream.* The Elvin Bishop Group was formed in San Francisco, and included Art Stavro (bass), Steve Miller (organ) and drummer John Chambers, formerly of Loading Zone. Three albums were cut for CBS/ Epic between 1968 and 1972, the band undergoing various personnel changes and moving through various blues, gospel and soul styles. In 1974, with a new band including Phil Aaberg (keyboards), Bishop signed with Capricorn Records to produce some pleasant albums very much in the Allman Brothers 'southern funk' mould, notably *Juke Joint Jump* (1975).

Cilla Black, born Priscilla White on May 27, 1943, used to check in the coats at Liverpool's Cavern and occasionally sang a song with one of the local groups. Brian Epstein saw her as perfect material for mainstream pop stardom and masterminded her rise to the top of middle-of-the-road show business in Britain. Her name was changed to Cilla Black, and after an unsuccessful debut with Lennon and McCartney's 'Love Of The Loved' (Parlophone, 1963), she resorted to the old tradition of covering American hits – Dionne Warwick's 'Anyone Who Had A Heart' and a fairly feeble version of 'You've Lost That Lovin' Feeling' among them – and a girl-next-door image was skilfully promoted. In Britain she had over a dozen Top Twenty hits which led by the Seventies to top cabaret appearances and a regular BBC television series.

51

Hal Blaine, a legendary West Coast session drummer of long standing, was born in 1932. He began playing at nine in his home town of Hartford, Connecticut, and then played in groups first in the Army and afterwards on the road with various acts. During the early Fifties he spent three years at the Roy Knapp School of Percussion in Chicago. Then, in 1957, he joined a Texan rockabilly group, the Raiders, and moved to Hollywood where they backed pop star Tommy Sands on stage and record until Sands was conscripted in 1960. Blaine then toured with Patti Page and in 1961 he met producer H. B. Barnum who persuaded him to stay in L.A. and work sessions.

Soon after, he played on the Crystals' 'He's A Rebel' session and became a regular member of Phil Spector's West Coast session crew. It was Spector who encouraged Blaine to unleash his full potential on hits like 'Be My Baby' and 'Da Doo Ron Ron'. From then on, everyone hired Blaine and since the early Sixties he has played drums on countless hits.

Blind Faith was a victim of the extraordinary demands made of the 'supergroups' of the late Sixties by businessmen and public alike and conclusive proof of the inability of Eric Clapton and Stevie Winwood to cope with such pressures. Blind Faith existed for a few months in 1969 when Clapton and Ginger Baker, on the rebound from Cream, teamed up with Winwood, temporarily separated from Traffic, and Family's bassist Rick Grech. They recorded one album, *Blind Faith* (Polydor, 1969), played a free concert in London in June that year and a series of American dates, then broke up.

Blood, Sweat and Tears was the brainchild of Al Kooper, following the demise of his Blues Project in 1968. One of the first rock bands with a full horn section, it was founded on the premise that rock is art, or at least arty eclecticism. On their debut album, *Child Is Father To The Man* (Columbia), the eclecticism worked more often than not. The original line-up was Kooper (keyboards, vocals), Steve Katz (guitar), Jim Fielder (bass), Bobby Colomby (drums), Randy Brecker, Jerry Weiss (trumpets), Dick Halligan (trombone) and Fred Lipsius (alto-sax). But Kooper left almost immediately, and leadership of the band fell to Katz (also ex-Blues Project) and new singer David Clayton-Thomas, a big-voiced Canadian. And where the first album had mixed rock, folk, blues, jazz and classical music into something resembling coherence, the second presented a taste of rock here, a smattering of jazz there, a classical interlude elsewhere. 'You Made Me So Happy' was a huge hit in 1969, and there was no turning back.

Commercial success grew by leaps and bounds, as did charges of pretentiousness. By 1970, most of the group's original audience was gone, replaced by the sort of man who picks his mood music by scanning the *Playboy* Jazz and Pop Poll. They duplicated their records almost note-for-note in concert. There followed Las Vegas engagements, State Department tours behind the Iron Curtain, and albums full of songs by Lennon–McCartney, Jagger–Richard, Satie, Little Walter, Prokofiev, and James Taylor – none of which bore any resemblance to the original in the BS&T versions, although they certainly sounded a lot like each other. Personnel changes increased until the group finally fell apart entirely in 1973. By then, for better or for worse, it had become one of the most influential groups ever, and the horn section in rock bands was here to stay.

Mike Bloomfield, the son of a wealthy Chicago restaurant supplies manufacturer, was born in 1943 and spent the early Sixties on that city's South Side, learning blues guitar from the black masters. It was also there that he met Bob Dylan.

When Dylan went electric in 1965, he brought along Bloomfield, already familiar with the studios by virtue of his sideman role on several blues albums. His fast, piercing guitar helped define the classic Dylan rock style. By then, he had also taken up with the Paul Butterfield Blues Band. Butterfield was another white veteran of the South Side, and his integrated band brought blues to the colleges and rock ballrooms, spawning a wave of white blues bands.

Bloomfield's technique was impeccable (he was often unjustly criticized for just that), and he was by now recognized as *the* guitarist. So much so that when Butterfield played New York, Bloomfield often stood with his back to the audience so all the guitarists in the front row couldn't watch his hands and steal his licks. The epochal *East–West*, which fused blues and Eastern modes, further enhanced his reputation.

In 1967, he moved to Northern California and formed the Electric Flag, with whom he played his last consistently good guitar. The complaint that he was all technique started looking more accurate as he freelanced – joining Al Kooper on the first *Super Session* (which, again, spawned many imitators); joining other white musicians and the Muddy Waters Band on a Chicago reunion, *Fathers And Sons*; dabbling in production; and releasing a solo album that was mostly uninspired country music. He hated to tour, and thus played only the Bay Area club circuit, with a makeshift band of other white blues veterans.

As the Seventies progressed he became less and less visible except for a 1973 'Supersession' with J. P. Hammond and Dr John (*Triumvirate*, Columbia), a 1974 Electric Flag reunion and a gig scoring porn movies for the Mitchell Brothers Film Group.

David Blue, a New York folkie, much influenced by Dylan, and his friend in the early Greenwich Village days, was born David Cohen in Rhode Island. He moved to New York at 18. Along with Eric Andersen, Tom Rush and Fred Neil, he gradually moved from folk to contemporary material, and described himself as 'a songwriter not a musician'. Recorded first for Warner Reprise, then for Elektra (as 'David S. Cohen'), and Asylum. 'Grand Hotel' from *David Blue* (1966) was one of the better known songs of yet another highly personal singer-songwriter who never made it huge.

Bluebeat. The Melodisc label, Bluebeat, existed from 1960 until 1967. Originally set up to provide West Indian immigrants living in London with home-grown boogie, 'blues' and gospel music from independent Jamaican producers Coxsone Dodd, Duke Reid, Smiths, Beverley, etc., it later found a market amongst white British youth who linked cult R&B with the raw JA sound, itself derivative of New Orleans 'second-line' jump. Discs featuring the offbeat piano rhythms and honking saxes of the new, uptempo 'ska' dance included Theo Beckford's 'Bringing In The Sheep' and Prince Buster's 'Tongue Will Tell'.

In the resulting confusion, the music became known as 'bluebeat' (after the label) by the British buyers while the West Indians themselves referred to it simply as 'the blues'. It was not, however, quite as simple as that. The very earliest recordings in the Bluebeat catalogue feature a very dissonant variety of styles, including Fifties teen doo-wop from the Jiving Juniors on 'My Heart's Desire'; ska-gospel from Laurel Aitken with 'Judgment Day'; mainstream low-church gospel from Basil Gabbidon's Mellow Larks on 'Time To Pray (Alleluia)'; and simple pop-flavoured love songs such as Derrick Morgan and the Ebonies' 'Don't Cry'. The legendary Folks Bros' 'Oh Carolina' was a pocomanic paean with Rastafarian overtones. Furthermore, many of the discs that were popular during the bluebeat craze of 1963–4 were not on the Bluebeat label: Millie's 'My Boy Lollipop' (Fontana); Derrick and Patsy's 'Gypsy Woman' (Island); Prince Buster's 'The Lion Roars' (Dice); Rezo Reco's 'King Of Kings' (Columbia).

The label continued to flourish long after 'bluebeat' had died its death. The older artists, Kentrick Patrick, Monty Morris, Cosmo, gave way to the Skatalites, the Charmers and the Maytals with 'Ska War'. The perennial Owen Gray, Prince Buster, Derrick Morgan and Laurel Aitken remained popular too. By 1967, however, Buster was the only one left. Apparently, Melodisc were unpopular in the record shops, and newer labels like Island, R&B, Doctor Bird and Pama were more forward-looking and popular with the record buyers. Bluebeat issued all the most important Prince Buster rock-steady sides including 'Judge Dread', 'Ghost Dance' and 'Judge Dread Dance The Pardon', before shutting shop to emerge with the Fab label, distributing all Prince Buster product, and later the Prince Buster label itself.

Blue Cheer. The early San Francisco bands progressed at a tangent to the influence of British power rock bands like Cream and the Jeff Beck Group, but many of their second and third generation outfits were completely overawed by the Britons. Accordingly, when Blue Cheer – Paul Whaley, drums (from Sacramento's Oxford Circle); Dick Peterson, bass, lead vocals; and Randy Holden, lead guitar – erupted on the scene with shatteringly loud performances and an excessively overburdened version of 'Summertime Blues' (Philips), a hit in summer 1968, there seemed little to distinguish them from British trios apart from extra volume. By their second album, *Outside Inside*, Holden had been replaced by Leigh Stevens. It is their most interesting album, noteworthy for Paul Whaley's excellent heavy rock drum technique. Like the Grateful Dead, they abounded in mystique and local legend but failed to project their aura of excitement on to any of their four albums. Too inward-looking, they nevertheless possessed a musical identity which in a later group, Grand Funk Railroad, proved to be a vehicle for enormous success.

The Blues Magoos, street kids from the Bronx, were regulars at the Café Wha on MacDougal Street and the Nite Owl Café in the Village before Mercury signed them. The Magoos – Ralph Scala, vocals, organ; Ron Gilbert, bass; Geoff Daking, drums; Mike Esposito, lead guitar; Peppy Thielhelm, rhythm guitar and vocals – notched up hit singles, notably '(We Ain't Got) Nothing Yet' – a No. 5 in 1966 – and 'There's A Chance We Can Make It', and had two good selling albums *Psychedelic Lollipop* (the first use of the word in an album title – complete with the 'play at high volume' tag) and *Electric Comic Book* (1967). They really knew how to hype. The second album contained a little comic book full of offers like the 'Psyche-de-lite' to turn you on while you played the album, itself 'a Blues Magoos Concert in your own home'. But unless seen on stage, the impact of the Vidal Sassoon hairstyles and Diana Dew-designed electric suits was missed. Their music, live or on record, was largely forgettable, rampant and discordant, reaching a new low point on *Basic Blues Magoos*, which featured a much changed group, and the electronic storm on *Gulf Coast Blues* (ABC, 1970), after which the group briefly mellowed their sound before disappearing.

The Blues Project were named after an Elektra blues collection involving various Village folk, when one of them, Danny Kalb, adopted the name for New York's first native electric blues band formed in 1965. The original line-up comprised: Tommy Flanders, vocals; Steve Katz, guitar, vocals; Danny Kalb, lead guitar; Al Kooper, organ, vocals; Andy Kulberg, bass, flute; and Ray Blumenfeld, drums. Katz had been in the Even Dozen Jug Band, Flanders in Boston's Trolls, Kulberg was studying music and Blumenfeld just hanging around. Al Kooper joined, to improve his nascent and highly praised organ-playing first heard on Dylan's *Blonde On Blonde*. The high-energy Project tore the New York scene apart, especially at Bleeker Street's Café A Go Go, venue for their first (live) album in 1966 on Verve. Genuinely exciting, it represents Flanders' only recorded work with the original band. Kooper and Katz filled the vocal roles on *Projections* (1966) and *Live At The Town Hall* (1967).

Friction with Kalb led Kooper to split, then Kalb fell ill and disappeared and finally Katz was enticed into Kooper's would-be Blood, Sweat and Tears. Kulberg and Blumenfeld added Richard Greene, violin, Don Kretmar, bass and sax, and John Gregory, guitar and vocals. They cut *Planned Obsolescence* as Blues Project though they were already metamorphosing into Sea Train. In 1971 Kalb, Blumenfeld and Kretmar came back with *Lazarus* and *Blues Project*, the latter plus Tommy Flanders and ex-Fish David Cohen. That version fell apart in April, 1972, and the final chapter so far is the reunion of the originals, minus Flanders, leading to *Reunion In Central Park*.

Bob And Earl. Despite their 20 years of activity in the R&B field, Bobby Relf and Earl Nelson are still best known for 'Harlem Shuffle', a shrill fat discotheque hit which reached the American Top Fifty on Marc in 1963 and the British Top Ten in 1969.

Originally, however, 'Bob' was Bobby Byrd (alias Bobby Day of 'Rockin' Robin' fame). He met Nelson when the latter joined Byrd's well-established group, the Hollywood Flames, in 1957. After recording as Bob and Earl for Class (1957–9), Byrd was replaced by Relf, and the duo continued to record prolifically for Chené, Tempe ('Don't Ever Leave Me', a small hit in 1962), Loma and Mirwood. Since 1954, Relf, who wrote Love Unlimited's 1974 hit, 'Walking In The Rain', has also recorded for Flair, Cash, Dot and (as Bobby Garrett) Mirwood. Nelson cut solo sides for Class Ebb, Mira (as Earl Cosby), Keyman, Mirwood (for example, 'The Duck', which he recorded under the name of Jackie Lee, reached the Top Twenty in 1965) and, as Jay Dee, for Warner Bros. in 1973. Nelson also sang lead on the Hollywood Flames' hit of 1957, 'Buzz Buzz Buzz'.

Graham Bond was voted one of British jazz's 'brightest hopes' in the early Sixties when he was still spending his days in a sales office, and his evenings playing Eric Dolphy-inspired alto sax with the Don Rendell jazz group. Bond left Rendell's group to join Blues Incorporated in place of Cyril Davies in November, 1962. Although hired as an alto saxophonist, he became increasingly interested in electric organ and quit in February, 1963, with Jack Bruce and Ginger Baker to form his own trio, expanded by the addition of guitarist John McLaughlin (replaced six months later by saxophonist Dick Heckstall-Smith). The Graham Bond Organization survived the departure of Bruce and Baker (replaced on drums by Jon Hiseman), but its jazzy, aggressive blues never found widespread success, and Bond moved to America after the group's final break-up.

On his return eighteen months later he became involved in a long series of abortive groups, including Ginger Baker's

Airforce, his own Magick and a band with poet-lyricist Pete Brown which ended with his death in 1974.

Bonner and Gordon. Gary Bonner and Alan Gordon were one of the hottest American Top Forty songwriting teams of 1965-7. They wrote hits for the Righteous Brothers, Petula Clark, Gary Lewis, Bobby Darin and many other artists, but were best known for the Turtles' No. 1, 'Happy Together', along with many subsequent Turtles' singles including 'You Know What I Mean', 'Me About You', 'She's My Girl' and 'She'd Rather Be With Me'. Originally half of the Magicians, a New York group that issued several fine singles on Columbia, Bonner and Gordon were affiliated with Koppelman and Rubin's songwriting/production stable. Bonner made a few solo singles until in 1974 the two reunited, and are currently writing songs again.

The Bonzo Dog (Doo Dah) Band's early (1966) publicity photographs implied that they were merely a reincarnation of the Temperance Seven, but interpretations of Twenties kitsch only formed part of their act. Formed by art students from several London colleges, the band began playing in pubs in 1965, and many of the members were still studying when the Bonzos moved on to clubs and cabaret in 1966.

The same year, the success of the New Vaudeville Band, another group of Twenties revivalists, encouraged the Bonzos to widen their musical range, and the result can be seen on their first, and most inventive, LP, *Gorilla* (Liberty, 1967), which includes characteristic Bonzo humour ('The Intro and the Outro'), Thirties novelty ('Mickey's Son And Daughter') and rock ('The Equestrian Statue'). The band personnel was now stabilized and the final line-up consisted of Vivian Stanshall (vocals, trumpet); Neil Innes (vocals, piano) who produced most of the band's comic and satirical song material; Roger Ruskin Spear, who generally supervised the props, dummies and robots; Rodney Slater (sax); 'Legs' Larry Smith (drums); Vernon Dudley Bohay-Nowell (guitar, banjo); and Sam Spoons (Martin Stafford) (percussion). Following their 1968 British Top Five single, 'I'm

The Urban Spaceman', the Bonzos became widely known through TV and concert appearances. Innes' influence made them increasingly psychedelic and rock-oriented, but Stanshall also retained his repertoire of pre-war curiosities, so that the Bonzos' act finally developed into a (literally) explosive display of school concert-like eclectisism.

The strain of having to devise new routines for their every appearance proved too great in 1970, and, after several albums, *The Doughnut In Granny's Greenhouse* (1968), *Tadpoles* (1969) and the legendary *Keynsham* (1969), the Bonzos went their separate ways. Stanshall formed several new groups but eventually went solo and is now a radio and TV personality; Innes is a prolific composer, working with Grimms and Fats; Spear now tours with his 'Kinetic Wardrobe', a one-man show; Slater left the business; and the others joined Bob Kerr's Whoopee Band, a cruder version of the Bonzos as they were in 1966.

Booker T and the MGs. Booker T Jones, born on Dec. 11, 1944, in Memphis, multi-instrumentalist, primarily keyboard, and the Memphis Group – Steve Cropper (born Oct. 21, 1941) guitar, originally Louis Steinberg on bass, later replaced by Donald 'Duck' Dunn (born Nov. 24, 1941), Al Jackson (born Nov. 17, 1945) drums – were for ten years the nucleus of the houseband for Stax records – the cornerstone of the company, its sound, and its success.

Originally the rhythm section of the Mar-Keys, the four men were recorded at an impromptu session minus horns, resulting in 'Green Onions', a bluesy organ riff slashed through by Cropper's razor-sharp tones, riding on a simple but persuasive bass and drum line. Issued on the new subsidiary Volt, it was transferred to the parent Stax label and distributed by Atlantic to a million sales in August, 1962. Much tighter than the average small R&B combo, their economic and expressive interplay of ideas was effective on moody, small-hours blues or hard-driving dance tunes, displayed in over a dozen albums and twenty more singles, including 'Bootleg' (1965), 'Hip Hug-Her', 'Groovin'' (1967), 'Soul Limbo' (1968), and 'Time Is Tight' (1969) from their soundtrack to the film 'Uptight'. Even more impressive was their contribution to virtually every hit created in the Stax studios in the Sixties. They backed not only the company's own stars, but also provided other Atlantic artists with the most consistently successful answer to the Motown Sound.

In 1971, tired of the pressures in a company which had long outgrown its intimate beginnings, Booker T escaped to a new career with his wife, Priscilla Coolidge, on the West Coast; Dunn stayed on in Memphis; Cropper has become a roving writer/producer and sessionman. Jackson remained a leading session drummer until his death in 1975.

The Box Tops – Alex Chilton, lead guitar; Billy Cunningham, bass; Gary Talley, guitar; Danny Smythe, drums; and John Evans, organ – were among the few white acts, along with the Gentrys, to achieve success from the soul-oriented studios of Memphis during the mid-Sixties. Formed in 1967, they recorded at American Recording Studios with Chips Moman, Dan Penn and Spooner Oldham, who wrote their third hit ('Cry Like A Baby', a No. 2 in 1968) and produced all their major hits, including their first, 'The Letter', a strong and intensely catchy record that went to No. 1 in the late summer of 1967, and has since been successfully covered by many others including Joe Cocker.

Although they had many subsequent Top Forty hits ('Neon Rainbow', 'Choo Choo Train', 'I Met Her In A Church', 'Sweet Cream Ladies, Forward March', and 'Soul Deep'), only 'Cry Like A Baby' approached the sales of 'The Letter' and the Box Tops never managed to sustain their popularity. After they disbanded in early 1970, lead singer Alex Chilton (whose winsome voice had made the Box Tops' records so appealing) joined up with Chris Bell and other pop-minded Mempheans at the newly formed Ardent Productions to form Big Star, a group which released two highly acclaimed albums during 1973–4.

British R&B. If, as has often been claimed, Alexis Korner was the father of British rhythm and blues, then Cyril Davies was the unlikely mother and Chris Barber the midwife. The partnership of Korner and Davies dates from 1955 when they transformed the Skiffle Centre at the Roundhouse pub in Wardour Street, in London's West End, into the London Blues and Barrelhouse Club. Their Thursday night sessions drew local enthusiasts and, later, visiting American bluesmen like Muddy Waters, Otis Spann, and Big Bill Broonzy.

Barber had been experimenting with blues within the framework of his traditional jazz band since 1953, when a blues trio featuring himself (bass), Beryl Bryden (washboard) and Tony 'Lonnie' Donegan (vocals, guitar) previewed the skiffle craze. Through the late Fifties, when his popularity was at a peak, he brought a series of blues artists to Britain to tour with his band – Bill Broonzy, Sister Rosetta Tharpe, Sonny Terry and Brownie McGhee, and, most significantly in 1958, Muddy Waters, whose use of amplification – which so offended the 'purists' – inspired Davies and Korner to wire up their own instruments.

After an American tour the following year, when he saw Waters play in Chicago, Barber invited Davies (harmonica) and Korner (guitar) to back his singer (and wife) Ottilie Patterson for brief rhythm and blues sets during his band's performances. So successful was this innovation that Davies and Korner left to form their own electric R&B band, Blues Incorporated. However, Barber stuck to jazz, seeing his music threatened by the debased 'trad' fad at the start of the Sixties, and didn't return to R&B until he replaced acoustic bass and banjo with bass and lead guitars in 1964 when, ironically, he was condemned as a bandwagoner.

Initially shunned by the clannish jazz club circuit, Davies and Korner opened their own club in a basement beneath the ABC teashop, near Ealing Broadway underground station, on March 17, 1962. Blues Incorporated was the houseband, but the club was a spawning ground for R&B groups like the Stones and Manfred Mann, whose future members would jam regularly. At the beginning of May, Blues Inc. were offered a residency for a Thursday 'Rhythm and Blues Night' at the Marquee Club, 165 Oxford Street, W1, where two months later the Rolling Stones made their first public appearance. During that summer another West End jazz club, the Flamingo in Wardour Street, was developing its own brand of rhythm and blues with the Blue Flames, whose leader, Georgie Fame, quickly absorbed the musical tastes of the predominantly black audience.

As the music's following grew, jazz clubs turned to R&B as a substitute for the increasingly lifeless trad, and new clubs opened around London's suburbs. By 1963 a distinct club circuit had evolved and a wave of bands had emerged to fill them.

Under the broad banner of R&B there were four basic forms: the long-hair-and-marracas rock style of the Stones and later groups like the Yardbirds, the Pretty Things and the Downliners Sect; the 'black' Flamingo sound, pioneered by Fame and adopted by Zoot Money's Big Roll Band, Chris Farlowe and the Thunderbirds, Ronnie Jones and the Nightimers, and other resident groups; and following Davies' split with Korner in November, 1962, the uncompromising revival of 1958 Muddy Waters by Davies' R&B All-Stars – which had parallels in John Mayall's self-styled blues crusade – and the subsequently jazzier, horn-driven riffing of Korner's Blues Inc. and Graham Bond's spin-off Organization.

So engrossed was the music industry with the Northern groups boom (and the feeble Home Counties competition from the Dave Clark Five and Brian Poole and the Tremeloes) that London's R&B movement flourished almost unnoticed by record companies and the pop press. Moreover, the music being played in the R&B clubs was generally considered too rough-hewn for conventional taste. What changed this notion was the Top Ten success of the Stones' second single, 'I Wanna Be Your Man', in the first week of January, 1964. Previously, only a handful of R&B records had been released – their status plainly indicated by the budget price tag on Blues Incorporated's *R&B From The Marquee*. But as 1964 progressed, the releases multiplied.

Hit singles, of course, forced groups out of the clubs into ballrooms across the country, and they were frequently obliged to dilute their style. The groups that replaced them in the clubs had invariably learned their repertoire from their predecessors, and this double effect of success brought about the grass roots breakdown of British R&B. The other factor was the source of the music itself. Faced in 1962 with an apparently inexhaustible reservoir of black music dating back over many years, few musicians had contemplated the possibility of it drying up and the need to provide their own material. Yet even before the boom started, influential figures like Chuck Berry, Bo Diddley, John Lee Hooker, Jimmy Reed and Muddy Waters had passed their creative peak, and by 1965 the music of black America had moved on to a level of sophistication that generally precluded recreation by British groups.

The Stones showed the way when, after several early derivative R&B-based attempts, Mick Jagger and Keith Richard developed a distinctive songwriting style of their own. Not every band had the inclination or the ability to adapt; some broke up, others hung on unchanged for a while. But for those who made the change, R&B had been an invaluable apprenticeship.

British Radio. Before 1964 there was little British pop radio. The only alternative to the evening broadcasts of the independent Radio Luxembourg, with its firm commitment to pop – and the heavy backing from the record companies which leased air time – was the BBC's Light Programme. An old-fashioned counterpart to the more 'serious' Third Programme (classical) and Home Service (non-musical), its content was epitomized by the perennial *Music While You Work*, which featured dance band arrangements of popular evergreens. Pop was virtually confined to two weekend shows, Saturday morning's *Saturday Club* – originally *Saturday Skiffle Club* – and Sunday morning's *Easy Beat*, hosted with patronizing benevolence by Brian Matthew. Both featured more studio sessions than records and a musical policy that was as broad as it was bland.

This situation was altered on Easter Saturday, 1964, when Radio Caroline, the brainchild of Ronan O'Rahilly, commenced broadcasting from international waters five miles off

Harwich. Within a week, the GPO had begun its campaign to ban offshore commercial radio, but on May 12, Radio Atlanta came on the air, merging with Caroline in July to create Caroline South and North (operating off the Isle of Man). Other stations followed, broadcasting from ships or disused wartime defence forts, and in December the powerful, businesslike Radio London opened. By this time the 'pirates' had an audience of millions.

Their popularity was easy to understand. Unrestricted needle time, flamboyant disc jockeys, and American-style format complete with call signs, jingles and commercials made a refreshing change from the Light Programme. Listening figures grew through 1965, but although increasing pressure was placed on the Government to outlaw the stations because of their interference with official wavelengths, there was no attempt at legislation until the introduction of the Marine Broadcasting (Offences) Bill in July, 1966, apparently hastened by the killing of Radio City owner, Reg Calvert, and the resultant exposure of genuine piracy behind the stations' breezy façades.

In December, 1966, the Government announced future plans for broadcasting, including the establishment of a pop wavelength and local BBC stations. The Marine Broadcasting (Offences) Bill became law on August 15, 1967 and only Caroline was prepared to risk prosecution, surviving until March, 1968.

BBC Radio One opened on Sept. 30, 1967, with the Move's 'Flowers In The Rain' and a format similar to that of the offshore stations, using ex-pirate disc jockeys – Tony Blackburn deejayed the opening programme – identical jingles, and a playlist centred on the Top Forty.

British Television. Many people who lived outside London during the beat boom now recall it largely in terms of the way it was reflected in the influential ITV programme, *Ready, Steady, Go!* (Aug. 9, 1963–Dec. 23, 1966). Swiftly developing into TV's most invaluable pop barometer, it faithfully recorded the changing fashions in music, clothes and dance, while everyone who was anyone dropped into the jam-

65

packed studio to chat or perform. Atmospherically it carried a charge unapproached since the days of *Oh Boy!* (1958–9), but technically it was way ahead of its time: no British pop show since has bettered its direction and camerawork. *RSG!* made a star out of its ideally ingenuous *commère*, Cathy McGowan, who (with Keith Fordyce and Michael Aldred) was a co-presenter before taking total control after miming was ditched in favour of live performances in 1965. Simultaneously, the programme was relocated in a larger studio, took some weeks to overcome the loss of intimacy, but triumphed. An arbiter of fashion to the last, it came off the air as British beat began to die.

Meanwhile, other programmes had sprouted. In 1963 both channels, acknowledging that 'the public for pops gets younger and younger', began supplying rock for children. The BBC offered Australian Rolf Harris in *A Swingin' Time*, while ITV revamped its two-year-old *Tuesday Rendezvous* as a junior version of *RSG!*, called *Five O'Clock Club*. New acts, trying to break into the charts, fought to appear even though it might mean sharing the bill with Sylvano's Sophisticated Chimps. On New Year's Day, 1964, BBC-1 offered a challenge to *RSG!* in the undernourished shape of *Top Of The Pops*, little more than an illustrated recital of the hit parade. At first clumsy and unimaginative, the programme has since become slick to the point of sterility. Also in 1964 BBC-2 presented its first pop show, *The Beat Room*, a sophisticated descendant of *Oh Boy!*

Most pop fans, however, remained tuned to ITV, whose coverage of contemporary music reached saturation point during the year. Apart from the programmes mentioned (plus the already established *Thank Your Lucky Stars*) the channel also staged the *RSG Mod Ball*, covered the *New Musical Express* Poll Winners' Concert and turned over peak-hour viewing to blues, gospel and folk as well as promoting *Ready, Steady – Win!*, a talent contest in which aspiring beat groups competed for £1,000 worth of musical equipment. The adverse criticism that such excesses aroused resulted in severe cutbacks the following year, and only the BBC premièred new shows. On BBC-2 *Gadzooks! It's All*

Happening (*The Beat Room* in all but name) begat *Gadzooks! It's the In Crowd* (an experimental mixture of pop, folk and comedy), which in turn begat plain *Gadzooks!*, which was without issue. BBC-1 made a brave but unsuccessful attempt to catalogue the Glaswegian pop scene in *Stramash!* and, in 1966, the year in which ITV axed practically all its pop shows, introduced *A Whole Scene Going*, the first programme to bring music into focus with the rest of pop culture (an idea expanded upon two years later when Tony Palmer presented his series *How It Is*). Between 1967 and 1968, TV relegated rock to the minority interests department, although two pop-based chat shows (Jonathan King's *Good Evening* and Simon Dee's legendarily awful *Dee Time*) won prime time. Typical of the new attitude, however, was BBC-2's late-night *Colour Me Pop* (1968), not only the first pop show in colour but the first to highlight heavier rock; it was a forerunner of *The Old Grey Whistle Test*.

Arthur Brown, born in Whitby on June 24, 1942, was a philosophy student at Reading University and had sung in small-time post-R&B boom bands before he teamed up with Vincent Crane in 1967. Working jointly – Crane supplied the music and Brown the lyrics – they developed their performance freely and bizarrely in the environment of the fledgeling underground clubs. Their act really built up from the UFO club appearances once they fell in with the Who's managers, Kit Lambert and Chris Stamp, who knew only too well the power of media outrage.

The Crazy World Of Arthur Brown were just right for the times. Clearly influenced by Screamin' Jay Hawkins, Brown came on stage grotesquely made up, wearing Sun God robes flowing freely as he gyrated around the stage singing, screaming and howling. The group, later adding drummer Carl Palmer, played frenzied and tight music as a perfect foil for Brown's antics which culminated in his blazing crown during 'Fire', their *tour de force*, which gave the group a transatlantic smash hit, led to a lawsuit with Ker and Finesilver who were later co-credited with its authorship, and also led to the break-up of the band. Earlier the group had cut a mostly exciting and timely album, *The Crazy World Of Arthur Brown*, but Brown's outrageousness soon became *passé* and, once Crane and Palmer left to form Atomic Rooster, his back-up musicians failed to come up to standard. In 1971 he re-emerged as the force behind an interesting rock theatre band, Kingdom Come. Following its demise he travelled widely, playing to Israeli troops with just a guitar and in 1975, after six months at a meditation school, returned with a new album and tour plans. He also secured a small part in Ken Russell's *Tommy*.

James Brown. The greatest or the most boring; overblown or underestimated; sincere or just plain shrewd? The only unanimous opinion about James Brown is that he's unique, and the only indisputable fact is that for nigh on fifteen years he's been the most consistently successful black entertainer bar none. Mixing gospel and blues roots with the energy of his own aggressive personality, he created some of the most fervent records of the late Fifties and a dynamic road show that, by 1962, had made him America's leading R&B star – 'Soul Brother No. 1'. Sidestepping the traditional fate of top black talent (limited rewards or compromise to mainstream, white-controlled showbiz) Brown then extended his music into an expression of defiant independence that was spiritually closer to the great jazz revolutionaries than to other 'soul' singers, but used compulsive dance rhythms to attract mass audiences, and ultimately brought about the polarization of jazz and soul in the form of Seventies 'street-funk'.

As one of the first entertainers to assume complete control of his own career, Brown paved the way for many other such independent ventures, and using his popularity as a platform for active participation in social reform he became a major figure in the fight for black equality. Now, disentangled from the main body of politics, he remains a champion of the underprivileged and is still a top selling name in an era when the changes he helped to pioneer have given birth to many equally committed performers. However, the startling paradoxes in his personality and music have so far robbed him of much of the critical acclaim usually heaped upon artists of similar stature. For never before had such an uncompromising talent made such a determined bid for commercial success, or indeed, been so successful.

Born near Augusta, Georgia, on May 3, 1928, Brown was first noticed in Macon leading the Famous Flames, the vocal group that he used as a foil on the gospel-style interaction of his early hits, and then disbanded in favour of complex rhythm accompaniment. Signed by Ralph Bass to Federal, a division of King records of Cincinnati, they recorded 'Please, Please, Please' in February, 1956. A strong regional hit, this raw wailing dirge was reworked in several less successful guises before a beautifully adapted gospel song, 'Try Me', put Brown in the national charts in November, 1958. On the strength of this success he was signed by Universal Attractions booking agency where he came to the attention of the owner Ben Bart, who chaperoned Brown's emergence as a major star and taught him how to take care of business. Given much wider exposure, and his first regular band, Brown expressed his restless imagination by redefining R&B in a succession of fiery hits that were even more persuasive on stage.

Using the fast numbers ('Good, Good Lovin'', 'I'll Go Crazy', 'Think', 'Night Train') as the basis of intricate dance routines; extending the slow songs ('Bewildered', 'I Don't Mind', 'Baby You're Right', 'Lost Someone') into hysterical sermons; and crowning the whole package with precision timing and a wardrobe that made his rivals look positively drab, Brown criss-crossed America, breaking box-office records in every major black venue with the wildest show ever assembled. In October, 1962, the show was captured on *Live At The Apollo*, resulting in a million-selling album – then unprecedented for an R&B album – that introduced an unsuspecting white market to 'The Hardest Working Man In Show Business'. Almost immediately he scored his first pop Top Twenty entry with an emotional interpretation of the schmaltz ballad, 'Prisoner Of Love', but before getting trapped in the middle of the same road as Ray Charles,

Brown and Bart risked a manoeuvre that enabled him to reach an even larger audience without diluting his music. Forming their own production company, Fair Deal, they sent new recordings to Smash, part of the nationwide Mercury Corporation. The third release, 'Out Of Sight' (1964), used a tighter band and a strong bass line to bind the co-ordination of his previous records into a solid dance rhythm that hit with an international *and* bi-racial audience. At the same time, he shrugged off conventional patterns of song construction. Returning to King, and aided by his band director, Nat Jones, he recorded progressively less formal hits ('Papa's Got A Brand New Bag', 'I Got You', 'Ain't That A Groove', 'Money Won't Change You', 'Bring It Up'), checked only by 'It's A Man's, Man's, Man's World', a wailing ballad with orchestra and chorus and a kids-stay-in-school special, 'Don't Be A Dropout'.

In 1967, Alfred Ellis succeeded Jones in shaping Brown's ideas. Their first collaboration, 'Cold Sweat', was completely divorced from any other form of popular music and introduced some of the most unique black records of the era, including 'There Was A Time' (a live extension of an earlier hit 'Let Yourself Go'), 'I Got The Feeling', 'Licking Stick', 'Give It Up Or Turnit A Loose', 'I Don't Want Nobody To Give Me Nothing', and the last three big hits with his famous Sixties band, 'Mother Popcorn', 'Let A Man Come In', 'It's A New Day'. During this period he was caught in the crossfire of racial conflict. Harangued for apparently supporting both factions with 'America Is My Home' and 'Say It Loud, I'm Black and I'm Proud' (actually two shades of the same emotion), he toned down his political involvement, but reaffirmed black roots in a series of superb Afro-rhythmic hits featuring younger musicians (including five who went on to join Funkadelic): 'Sex Machine', 'Get Up, Get Into It, And Get Involved', 'Superbad' (1970), 'Soul Power', 'Hot Pants' (1971); and two tracks that were issued after his switch to Polydor, 'Talking Loud And Saying Nothing', 'I'm A Greedy Man'.

Recording for Polydor since 1971 with yet another band, Fred Wesley and the JBs (including Maceo Parker, St Clair

Pinckney, and others who accompanied him in the Sixties), he has survived the changes stimulated by successors like Sly Stone and continues to produce exciting hits – 'Make It Funky' (1971), 'Get On The Good Foot' (1972), 'Doing It To Death' (1973), 'The Payback', 'Papa Don't Take No Mess' (1974). But with younger bands (Kool and the Gang, the Ohio Players) surpassing the JBs, and the increasing use of pre-recorded backing tracks destroying much of his spontaneous creativity, Brown has begun to seek new worlds to conquer. After scoring two successful movie soundtracks (*Black Caesar* and *Slaughter's Big Rip-Off*) in 1973, he has crossed the arc lights for a starring role in *Come To The Table*. Perhaps as an actor he will reach even wider audiences with the extraordinary personality that has dominated nearly one hundred hit records (including over forty accredited million-sellers) and a legendary rags-to-riches career.

Pete Brown, poet, songwriter and bandleader, was an important catalyst in the British rock scene of the Sixties, while more recently he has contributed lyrics to Jack Bruce's solo work. Born on Dec. 25, 1940, in London, Brown with Michael Horovitz initiated the jazz and poetry movement which involved several musicians who were to be active in the British R&B scene, notably Jack Bruce and Graham Bond. In the mid-Sixties, Brown founded a series of experimental rock groups – Battered Ornaments, Piblokto, etc. – whose members included Kokomo's Jim Mullen and guitarist Chris Spedding. He also wrote extensively with Bruce for Cream, composing such songs as 'Sunshine Of Your Love' ('It'll pay my rent for the rest of my life,' he once said) and 'Politician'. His records include three Piblokto albums on Harvest and *The Not Forgotten Association* (1973), a jazz-and-poetry album on Deram.

Bubblegum was the biggest commercial trend in American rock during 1968–9. What started as a rigidly defined formula (heavy, repetitive bass beat; simple, even moronic

71

lyrics; and affectedly nasal vocals) became the object of intense ridicule from the 'progressive' faction, and the term 'Bubblegum' came to symbolize just about anything that could be labelled 'commercial'. But, in fact, Bubblegum was a recognizable and valid genre, significant for its overwhelming success with the under-18 audience, and also, in retrospect, for many records of lasting worth.

Credit for its invention generally goes to Jerry Kasenetz and Jeff Katz, whose Super-K Productions began with seminal Bubblegum records by the Rare Breed and the Music Explosion on Attack Records, moved to Super-K (their own label), which found its spiritual home under the wing of Buddah Records, headed by Neil Bogart, formerly of Cameo Records – a label whose output was geared towards the same market that bought Bubblegum with such enthusiasm. The earliest Bubblegum classics – 'Try It' and 'Beg, Borrow and Steal' by the Ohio Express, 'Capt. Groovy and His Bubblegum Army' by Capt. Groovy, 'Shake' by the Shadows of Knight, and 'Go Away' by the 1910 Fruitgum Co., sounded more like punk or British rock than what most would call Bubblegum. But soon the formula emerged: the musical structure defined above, and a calculated distillation of sub-teen subject matter, expressing love in metaphors of candy, gumdrops, and children's games. And the kids ate it up.

At this point, late 1967, Katz and Kasenetz moved all their operations to Buddah, and were joined there by other young studio pioneers including Joey Levine, Artie Resnick, and Richie Cordell (from Kama Sutra Productions). At the same time, Andy Kim and Jeff Barry were leaving Red Bird Records to join Don Kirshner in creating the Archies, a faceless cartoon act designed to surpass even the Monkees in TV and record drawing power. The Archies' 'Sugar Sugar' subsequently became the biggest grossing record of 1969, thanks largely to the addition of Ron Dante from Ohio (Baskerville Hounds, Peppermint Rainbow) on vocals. Curiously, a large number of other bubblegum artists were also Ohio-based: the Ohio Express, of course, but also the Music Explosion, the Lemon Pipers, Dick Whittington, and the Royal Guardsmen. Although there were many interesting records by all these acts, and some very unusual recordings (ranging from Spector-imitations to hot-rod tunes) by other more ephemeral Bubblegum aggregations, the genre is best remembered for the hits of the Ohio Express ('Yummy Yummy Yummy', 'Chewy Chewy'), the 1910 Fruitgum Co. ('Simon Says', '1, 2, 3, Red Light', 'Indian Giver'), the Lemon Pipers ('Green Tambourine', 'Jelly Jungle'), Crazy Elephant ('Gimme Gimme Good Lovin'', another Super-K production) and the Archies ('Sugar Sugar', 'Jingle Jangle').

Like any artificial trend, Bubblegum lasted only a couple of years, but while it was around it provided a fertile breeding ground for some of today's leading producers, and for studio experiments and musical innovations whose effectiveness can't be denied.

Tim Buckley, born in Washington D.C. on April 12, 1947, was a leading figure on the fringes of mainstream rock after 1966. He started out in various Southern Californian country bands before moving on to the Los Angeles folk circuit. There he found a manager, Herb Cohen, and a record company, Jac Holzman's Elektra.

Holzman and Paul Rothchild produced Buckley's first album which, like the three that followed, was firmly folk-rooted but increasingly sophisticated musically. His most famous song of this period, 'Morning Glory' from the *Hello And Goodbye* album (1967, produced by Jerry Yester), was written with poet Larry Beckett, a partnership that continued sporadically. It was, however, the richness and variety of Buckley's singing which did most to establish his reputation. And the next phase of his career found him moving towards John Coltrane-style jazz on *Lorca* and *Starsailor* (1970), his first record for Straight, the label set up by Cohen and Frank Zappa. This free-form scat singing provoked mixed reactions, however, and *Greetings From L.A.* (1972) found Buckley returning to a more accessible urban R&B style, singing of sex rather than romance. *Selfronia* (1973, on another Cohen-Zappa label, DiscReet) was a synthesis of that hard-edged style with the earlier more lyrical singing. He died on June 19, 1975, in Los Angeles.

Buddah Records was formed in September, 1967, by Neil Bogart, formerly of Cameo–Parkway. Through arrangements with Kama Sutra Productions, Super-K Productions, Anders and Poncia, and other independent songwriting and production outfits, Buddah soon became one of the most prolific singles-oriented independents.

The label's initial success was with what became known as Bubblegum music. Early hits by the Lemon Pipers ('Green Tambourine'), the 1910 Fruitgum Co. ('Simon Says', '1, 2, 3, Red Light' and others) and the Ohio Express ('Yummy Yummy Yummy' and others) established Buddah as the home of Bubblegum, a sound – created almost entirely by a handful of producers – that was a huge commercial success during 1968–70 and disappeared almost completely thereafter.

But although few of Buddah's non-Bubblegum releases were hits in those years, they had built a solid roster of pop and R&B. The Brooklyn Bridge (featuring Johnny Maestro of the Crests) had numerous hits from 1968 on, starting with 'The Worst That Could Happen'. Lou Christie made the Top Ten in 1969 with 'I'm Gonna Make You Mine', and other established artists including Teddy Randazzo, Johnny Tillotson and Chubby Checker joined the label. In the early Seventies, having taken over Kama Sutra Records and affiliated with other labels including the Isley Brothers' T-Neck, Buddah's roster widened to include Melanie, Brewer and Shipley, the Five Stairsteps, the Edwin Hawkins Singers, Biff Rose, Freddy Cannon, Paul Anka, Len Barry, and a number of R&B acts – particularly Gladys Knight and the Pips, currently Buddah's most popular artist. Since Bogart's departure in 1974 to launch Casablanca Records, Buddah's mainstays have been Knight, Les Variations, Isis, Barbara Mason, and on Kama Sutra, Stories, Charlie Daniels and Sha Na Na.

Buffalo Springfield. Guitarists Steve Stills (born in Dallas on

Jan. 30, 1945) and Richie Furay (born in Dayton, Ohio, on May 9, 1944) were New York folksingers of meagre repute. Up in Toronto, Neil Young (born Nov. 12, 1945) was doing better with a similar act, but got restless for the big time anyhow. Drummer Dewey Martin (born in Chesterville, Ontario on Sept. 30, 1942) was with the Dillards, and bassist Bruce Palmer (born in Liverpool, Canada in 1947) was a friend of Neil's. They came together in Los Angeles in 1966, by chance more than anything else, and took their name from a steamroller. People who were there often insist that Buffalo Springfield was the best of the mid-Sixties L.A. groups.

They were certainly one of the most exciting live groups, thrilling Whisky audiences nightly with a show that featured two lead guitars (Stills and Young), three lead singers (Stills, Young and Furay), a rhythm section that had obviously been listening to the recent Stax singles, and an onstage kineticism that reintroduced showmanship to the Strip. That was live. On record, it was a different story. Their debut LP on Atlantic, *Buffalo Springfield* (1967), sounded sludgy, and it took them some time to learn their way around a studio. The exception was their first, and only, Top Ten single, the Stills-penned 'For What It's Worth' (1967), a most effective topical song about the recent Sunset Strip hippie riots that quickly became an anthem.

Hits or no hits, no one disputed their originality. They didn't play the folk-rock of their contemporaries, though folk was a major influence, and their country pop leanings were several years ahead of everyone else. Stills could move from hard rock ('Rock'n'Roll Woman') to Latin-influences ('Uno Mundo'). Young also had hard rock down ('Mr Soul'), but experimented with sound collages ('Broken Arrow'), showed a soft touch on ballads ('I Am A Child') and wrote lyrics that conveyed an intense, poetic sense of terror (as on 'Mr Soul'). Furay and Jim Messina (who replaced Palmer on bass) showed the strongest country predilections ('Kind Woman'). When all these talents merged cohesively, as often occurred live and as captured on *Buffalo Springfield Again* (1968), their second album, they added up to something many felt was the American answer to the Beatles.

But none of the Springfield's next four singles rose even to the top half of the charts. They suffered from poor management, and were never able to mount a single national tour. Stills and Young were often at each other's throats, to the extent that Young didn't even appear for their crucial Monterey Pop Festival engagement. *Last Time Around* (1969), their final album, was almost like the Beatles' *White Album*, with group dynamics being discarded and each member doing his own songs his own way. After that, each member went on to a Seventies supergroup, none of which showed half the range of the Springfield. Young and Stills also enjoyed success as solo acts.

Sandy Bull, multi-instrumentalist, extraordinary eclectic who mixed classical, Eastern and folk styles as early as 1963, is in some ways the American folk scene's equivalent of Davy Graham. Born in New York in 1941, he began playing folk banjo and guitar at the start of the folk boom, then incorporated jazz and Eastern influences. He signed with Vanguard records, and his first album *Fantasis* (1963) showed off all the varied styles. He went on to take in more influences, from Chuck Berry to learning to play the oud. Heroin addiction adversely affected his playing in the late Sixties, but he recovered and returned to successful performing – still mainly on the college circuit.

Eric Burdon retained the Animals' name following the break-up of the original group in 1966. Lead-singer Burdon formed a new group and pursued an increasingly erratic course across the counter-culture of the late Sixties. Under the influence of LSD, flower power and meditation, the hard-drinking white soul singer became the philosopher of a new lifestyle. With the first version of his new Animals, Burdon had hits on MGM with 'Good Times', 'San Franciscan Nights' and 'Monterey'. But a new line-up including Zoot Money, organ, and Andy Somers, guitar, was less successful and by 1968 Burdon quit. He returned two years later with black R&B group War, cutting two albums with them which included the remarkable song 'Spill The Wine', which suggested he was returning to his old form. But War split to make a series of hits on their own, while Burdon made an album with Jimmy Witherspoon (*Guilty!*, United Artists, 1971). The Seventies saw him ever on the verge of making a triumphant comeback with albums like *Stop* (Capitol, 1975).

Solomon Burke – King Heavy, The King of Rock'n'Soul – is the big man and big voice of black music. Born in Philadelphia in 1936, by the age of nine he was starring as the soloist in church, which led to local broadcasts on his own radio show *Solomon's Temple*, and stage appearances as 'The Wonder Boy Preacher'. His early recordings for the New York Apollo label (1955–8) were nearly all quasi-religious ballads or sentimental love songs, presumably aimed at the same audience that enjoyed Roy 'You'll Never Walk Alone' Hamilton, but after a few sides on Singular (1959, subsequently re-issued on Atlantic), including one untypical rocker, 'Be-Bop Grandma', he was signed by Atlantic where he became the first, and some say the greatest, of the company's formidable armoury of soul talent.

From his earliest sessions with the company (1960–62) he gave new meaning to a catholic selection of material, including country-weeper 'Just Out Of Reach (Of My Two Empty Arms)', the traditional 'Down In The Valley', and three Fifties R&B favourites, 'I Almost Lost My Mind', 'You Can Make It If You Try', and 'Send Me Some Lovin' '. But finest of all were two new songs, 'I'm Hanging Up My Heart For You' (a John Berry/Don Covay composition) and his most famous hit, 'Cry To Me', written and produced by Bert (Russell) Berns. Berns, the man behind many of New York's best contributions to soul, produced with Jerry Wexler all of Burke's greatest recordings, following the early hits with a smoother but equally convincing cover-version of Wilson Pickett's 'If You Need Me' (1963) – the first of several preaching scorchers, 'Can't Nobody Love You', 'You're Good For Me', 'Goodbye Baby (Baby Goodbye)', all arranged by Garry Sherman, climaxing with 'The Price' (1964), which even after so many other intense performances, was a stunning end to a fruitful relationship.

It may have been coincidence, but with Berns no longer in the studio Burke was never again so impressive on record, although he immediately scored his biggest hit with the catchy 'Got To Get You Off My Mind' (1965), arranged by Gene Page. The same year, 'Tonight's The Night' – coupled with an uncomfortable version of Dylan's 'Maggie's Farm' – were his last best-sellers. For three more years he continued to turn out performances that compared favourably with contemporary soul records but seemed lifeless against his earlier work. After minor hits with 'Take Me (Just As I Am)', recorded in Memphis in 1967, and 'I Wish I Knew' (1968), he left Atlantic.

Subsequent years have not been all bad. Recording in the South again, he cut some fine sides for Bell (including 'Proud Mary' and 'That Lucky Old Sun' – 1969) and then spent an erratic three years with MGM where several good issues (particularly 'Love's Street And Fool's Road' – 1972) were sandwiched between some of the worst recordings of his career. In 1974, after a partially successful tribute album to Dr Martin Luther King, *I Have A Dream*, he changed tack completely, jumping straight into the Seventies by re-uniting with Gene Page on two singles heavily influenced by hitmaker Barry White – 'Midnight And You' (Dunhill), 'You And Your Baby Blues' (Chess). A long way from 'Cry To Me', but at least he's getting hits again. In 1975 he released *Music To Make Love To* (Chess).

Paul Butterfield, born in Chicago on Dec. 17, 1942, is America's leading white blues harmonica virtuoso. He acquired his technique while playing the black clubs on Chicago's South Side. Influenced by the harp styles of Little Walter, Junior Wells and James Cotton, he formed his first blues outfit in 1963, bringing in two ex-members of Howlin' Wolf's band – Jerome Arnold (bass) and Sam Lay (drums), plus guitarist Smokey Smothers. Elvin Bishop later replaced Smothers, and in 1965 was joined by a session guitarist from Columbia records – Mike Bloomfield. Their first recordings were released that same year on the Elektra sampler *What's Shakin'*. Widely acclaimed as the most vital of the new American

R&B groups, a debut album quickly followed.

Butterfield was always at his best when accompanied by Bloomfield. They provided superb back-up on Chuck Berry's vintage 'It Wasn't Me' (1965) and they peaked on *East–West* (1966), which was highlighted by the 13-minute title track – a futuristic instrumental built on an Indian raga scale. Triumphant, the band came to Britain, but proved too way-out for London's blue-eyed soul scene. However, Butterfield did manage to cut an EP with John Mayall's Bluesbreakers, featuring Peter Green's guitar.

In 1967, Bloomfield quit the band to work with Bob Dylan and subsequently the Electric Flag. Butterfield released *The Resurrection Of Pigboy Crabshaw* (1967), adding a horn section for the first time. *In My Own Dream* followed, in pretty much the same style, but his 1969 recording, *Keep On Moving*, produced by Jerry Ragavoy, introduced a completely new line-up, and veered musically towards the soul/jazz market. Even so, he returned to his roots briefly that year to cut a double album for Chess called *Fathers And Sons.* It reunited Butterfield with Bloomfield, but was really a showcase for the legendary Muddy Waters. In 1971 Butterfield met with Todd Rundgren, who produced *The Paul Butterfield Band – Live* double album at the Troubador in Los Angeles. A few months later Butterfield cut his final album for Elektra – *Sometimes I Just Feel Like Smilin'*, this time featuring guitarist Ralph Wash, who was later to join Van Morrison's band.

The Paul Butterfield Blues Band finally disbanded in the autumn of 1972, after completing eight best-selling albums (plus the anthology, *Golden Butter*). Butterfield moved to Woodstock, where he met Ronnie Barron, Bobby Charles, Geoff Muldaur and Amos Garrett, recruiting them into a new band called Better Days. The debut album, released on Bearsville in 1973, was distinguished only by fairly sophisticated interpretations of folk-blues standards plus a couple of contemporary songs. A second album, *It All Comes Back*, was a little more out-going, but still failed to capture the excitement of the early albums. Butterfield is today content just to hang-out in Woodstock, making the occasional guest

79

appearance on albums by such artists as Maria Muldaur and Bonnie Raitt.

The Byrds, hailed as the American Beatles and the originators of folk-rock, dominated the American music scene for a brief period in 1965. They were never again to be as celebrated, yet with virtually each record between 'Mr Tambourine Man' (1965) and the *Sweetheart Of The Rodeo* (1968) album, moving from folk-rock through acid-rock and space-rock to country-rock, they outlined vast areas that other bands would later begin to explore. Moreover, the Byrds weren't merely musical pioneers. Their work also saw the creation of one of rock's most assured styles through which seemingly disparate musical elements were transformed into a unique Byrds sound.

In the early Sixties, while rock'n'roll was dying, across America in the coffee houses and colleges the folk boom in which most of the Byrds began their musical careers was getting underway. Jim (later Roger) McGuinn – born July 14, 1942, in Chicago – the only Byrd with a musical education, started backing the Limeliters, joined the Chad Mitchell Trio and in 1962 started session work and supporting Bobby Darin who had introduced a folk spot into his nightclub act. Similarly, Gene Clark – born Nov. 17, 1941, in Tipton, Missouri – had done a stint with the New Christy Minstrels and Dave Crosby – August 14, 1941 – had been a Les Baxter Balladeer for a while. Chris Hillman – Dec. 4, 1942 – began playing folk music in coffee bars, like McGuinn, before temporarily leaving it for bluegrass, first with the Scottsville Squirrel Breakers and then with his own group, the Hillmen, a joint folk and bluegrass outfit.

By 1964, the Byrds as individuals were old troupers of a folk scene that was rapidly changing. Peter, Paul and Mary had opened the door to the charts with their prettied-up versions of Dylan, and folk was quickly leaving the coffee bars for the concert halls: like rock'n'roll before it, folk was being swallowed up by the record industry. But if folk was happening, the event of 1964 for America was the Beatles, who opened up the floodgates of the British invasion and brought excitement back to rock. Suddenly the charts seemed important again, it seemed possible to play rock without having to be perpetually compromised, and McGuinn and a lot of other ex-folkies began starting rock groups. In the summer of 1964, McGuinn, Clark and Crosby began rehearsing as the Jet Set in Los Angeles. They quickly turned to Jim Dickson, who was trying to sell an album he'd produced for the Hillmen. When it became apparent the Jet Set wouldn't make it as a trio Dickson persuaded Hillman to join and trade in his mandolin for a Japanese bass guitar. With the addition of Michael Clarke – born June 3, 1944, in New York – a conga-playing acquaintance of Crosby's, on drums, the group was complete. Dickson had the run of World Pacific studios so they decided to rehearse there and make a tape of their songs. Later McGuinn would describe their early music as a synthesis of Dylan and the Beatles, but when those tapes were released eventually as *Preflyte* (Together Records) – which includes a trial version of 'Mr Tambourine Man' – it was the Beatles' influence that stood out. On the basis of that tape, Dickson secured the group a one-record-and-option deal with Elektra, for whom, as the Beefeaters, they put out the very Beatlish 'Please Let Me Love You' in the autumn of 1964. The record failed and the band, now officially the Byrds, switched to Columbia and began looking once again for a song to record.

Earlier that year the Animals recorded 'Baby Let Me Follow You Down' and 'House Of The Rising Sun' (an American No. 1), both rocked-up pieces of Dylan material if not Dylan compositions. So Dickson suggested they remake 'Mr Tambourine Man'. They did – with the aid of sessionmen Hal Blaine, Leon Russell and Larry Knetchel; of the group, only McGuinn played on the single. After six months it soared to the top of the American and British charts where it was seen as signalling the arrival of folk-rock and as stemming the tide of the British Invasion.

But the Byrds' chart success was short-lived: their second record, 'All I Really Want To Do', was beaten to the top by a Sonny and Cher cover version and though their third,

'Turn! Turn! Turn!', was a No. 1 in the autumn of 1965, from then on their singles struggled in the charts. Their last American Top Twenty single was 'Eight Miles High' which made No. 14 in September, 1966 before it was discovered to be a 'drug song' and promptly received no more airplay.

In the two years between 'Mr Tambourine Man' and 'Eight Miles High', the Byrds changed a lot. Columbia allowed the group to play on *Mr Tambourine Man* (1965), which was the expected mixture of Dylan, traditional folk songs and their own compositions. But if the material was straight folk-rock, the Byrds' treatment of it showed them to be more interested in three-part harmony, sound textures and circular rhythmic patterns as, song by song, the group stylized their material. By the next album, *Turn! Turn! Turn!* (1966), the group had folk-rock down pat and from material like Gene Clark's 'Set You Free This Time' and Dylan's 'Lay Down Your Weary Tune' they created diamonds of formal perfection that lacked only a sense of excitement: the Byrds seemed weary before their time. *Fifth Dimension* (1966), the third album, saw the Byrds tire of folk-rock and begin experimenting with electronics. Gene Clark, the group's major songwriter, had quit to pursue a solo career after *Turn! Turn! Turn!*

On the group's singles McGuinn was the Byrds; it was his voice and distinctive twelve-string guitar that were the trademarks, but on albums he was merely one of the group. This was amply demonstrated on *Younger Than Yesterday* (1967), which brought the electronic experimentation of *Fifth Dimension* to absolute perfection. McGuinn provided probably his strangest piece of 'space-rock', 'CTA 102', but the album belonged to Crosby ('Everybody's Been Burned' and 'Renaissance Fair') and Hillman ('Have You Seen Her Face' and 'Thoughts And Words'). Also featured was McGuinn and Hillman's world-weary 'So You Want To Be A Rock'n'Roll Star'. But if the group had never sounded tighter on record, outside the studio the incessant touring – the price of chart failure – led to bad feeling, with Crosby in particular for ever threatening to leave. The crisis came to a head during the recording of *Notorious Byrd Brothers*

82

(1968). Crosby refused to sing Goffin and King 'pop' songs – 'Goin' Back' and 'Wasn't Born To Follow' – demanded more political songs and then finally quit for a cash payment leaving the group with a half-completed album. The Byrds finished it as a trio and, once again, it was superb; even more importantly, it was well reviewed and sold well. Classified as a singles group, the Byrds were neglected by the new audience that sprang into being after 1967 and *Younger Than Yesterday*, the album that might have rescued them, was completely overshadowed by *Sergeant Pepper*. The good reception of *Notorious* in 1968 confirmed that the Byrds had a definite (and developing) cult following, and while the larger 1967 audience still eluded them, another *Notorious* might have given the group the San Franciscan seal of approval.

Instead, the Byrds added the honky 'Georgia Peach', Gram Parsons, from the International Submarine Band, replaced Mike Clarke with Kevin Kelley and headed for Nashville where they played the Grand Ole Opry and recorded *Sweetheart Of The Rodeo*, virtually creating country-rock and alienating their putative audiences at the same time. Later, *Sweetheart* would be seen as an enormously influential album, but in 1968 no one in either Nashville or Los Angeles was willing to accept a rock group singing songs by the Louvin brothers *and* William Bell *and* Dylan *and* Merle Haggard. *Sweetheart* not only lost the Byrds the 'progressive' audience, it also more or less destroyed the group. The next time they came to record, McGuinn would be the only Byrd left.

First Parsons quit rather than do a tour of South Africa and then on the group's return, when McGuinn wanted out of the country trip, Hillman, whose idea it had been, left to form the Flying Burritto Brothers with Parsons. The new Byrds' debut album, *Dr Byrds And Mr Hyde*, with Gene Parsons – born April 9, 1944 – on drums, Clarence White – born June 6, 1944, in Maine – on guitar and John York on bass, was uncharacteristically muddy. Moreover, to McGuinn's chagrin, he seemed unable to get away from country-influenced musicians and henceforth there would always be a country flavour to the Byrds' music. At this low point, luck entered the picture in the form of the phenomenally successful *Easy Rider* film which used some of their songs on its soundtrack. Almost respectable, and with a better album, *The Ballad Of Easy Rider* (1970), the Byrds seemed to be on the way up again.

In 1970 Skip Battin – born Feb. 2, 1934 – half of the Skip and Flip, an early Sixties imitation Everly Brothers, replaced John York and after some hard touring the group finally won themselves a reputation as a live band. Indeed they were so sure of themselves, that half of the double album, *Untitled* (1971), consisted of live recordings. And as if that wasn't enough, the other half saw McGuinn back on form as a writer. He'd been commissioned to write a rock musical version of Ibsen's *Peer Gynt* with Jacques Levy, *Gene Tryp*, and though that fell through, out of it came a batch of songs some of which, like 'Chestnut Mare' and 'Just A Season', fitted perfectly into the classic Byrds' mould of weary resignation. None the less, *Untitled* was just marking time and finally, in 1972, after two more desultory albums, *Byrdmaniax* and *Farther Along*, McGuinn folded the band to, of all things, re-form the original Byrds and see if, in an atmosphere of revived oldies, the group could take off again. The resulting album, *Byrds* (Asylum, 1973) was an artistic disaster, demonstrating that the individual Byrds had developed away from each other and completely lost any sense of balance. Where before they had played as a group, *Byrds* saw them acting as each other's sessionmen, which they were to continue to do in their various individual projects in the Seventies.

Roy C, born Roy Charles Hammond in New York City in 1943, changed his name to avoid confusion with Roy Hamilton and Ray Charles and sang lead with the Genies (Claude Johnson, Buddy Fason, Bill Gaines, Fred Jones) on Shad, Hollywood, Warwick and Forum. When the group split up, Roy went solo, scoring an R&B hit with 'Shotgun Wedding' which went to No. 14 in 1965 and reached the British Top Ten the following year.

Other discs on Black Hawk and Shout (produced by Bert Berns) made little impact and in 1969 he formed his own record company, Alaga. He issued a long series of consistently good soul singles, dealing blatantly with sexual problems and pleasures. 'Divorce Court', 'I Found A Man In My Bed', 'Gotta Get Enough Of Your Sweet Love Stuff' and others were later repackaged in album form as *Sex And Soul* by Mercury to whom he signed in 1973. Roy C also wrote and produced the Mark IV's million-selling 'Honey I Still Love You', for Mercury in 1972. He remains one of the least acclaimed masters of contemporary soul music.

Glen Campbell, born in Oklahoma on April 10, 1938, played guitar on recording sessions in Nashville and Los Angeles before producer Nik Venet recorded him as a singer in 1961. 'Turn Around Look At Me' was a minor hit on Crest, but soon after Campbell returned to session work, playing behind the Monkees, Mamas and Papas and others, as well as accompanying the Beach Boys for a short time. He resumed his own recording career with Capitol in the mid-Sixties, covering Buffy Sainte-Marie's 'Universal Soldier', then having a worldwide hit with 'Gentle On My Mind', composed by 'New Nashville' songwriter John Hartford. Since then, Campbell has had many hits in his pop/country crooning style, often with above-average ballads. In particular, he brought the work of Jim Webb to the fore with 'Wichita Lineman', 'Galveston' and others. In the Seventies, Campbell remained one of the better middle-of-the-road artists, introducing the songs of Kenny O'Dell, Kinky Friedman and Merle Haggard to audiences beyond the country and rock fraternity, although the frequent blandness of his singing – as on, say, his 1975 worldwide smash hit, 'Rhinestone Cowboy' – often contrasted with the original power of his chosen material.

Canned Heat achieved international prominence when their atmospheric version of the Memphis Jug Band's 'On The Road Again' reached No. 8 in Britain and No. 16 in America in 1968. The group was formed in 1965 by blues collector

Bob ('The Bear') Hite (vocals, born on Feb. 26, 1943), Henry Vestine (guitar, born on Dec. 25, 1944) and Al ('Blind Owl') Wilson (slide guitar, harmonica, vocals, born on Aug. 4, 1943). All were students of country blues and their first Liberty album – *Canned Heat* (1967) – was an expert reworking of rural songs in an electric blues style, with Larry Taylor (bass, born June 26, 1942) and Frank Cook (drums), replaced in 1968 by Fito De La Parra (born Feb. 8, 1946).

Both 'On The Road Again' and 'Going Up The Country' (another Top Twenty hit, in 1969) featured Wilson's high-pitched singing and established the band in the forefront of white blues exponents. Numerous Liberty albums followed including one with veteran bluesman John Lee Hooker (*Hooker 'n' Heat*, 1971). Their biggest European hit was a reworking of Wilbert Harrison's 'Let's Work Together' (a No. 2 in Britain) in 1970. Wilson's death on Sept. 3, 1970 precipitated several personnel changes with Taylor leaving to join John Mayall, a route later followed by Harvey Mandel who had replaced Wilson. By the mid-Seventies, only the 260 lb. Hite and Vestine remained of the original line-up, having been joined by Hite's brother Richard (guitar, bass, vocals, born in 1950), James Shane (guitar, bass, vocals) and Ed Beyer (keyboards).

Captain Beefheart and his Magic Band. Don Van Vliet, the Captain (born in Glendale, California on Jan. 15, 1941), was a little too bizarre for even the most steadfast crazies in the music biz. He first appeared with his band in 1966 with two singles – 'Diddy Wah Diddy' and 'Frying Pan' – of bone-crunching blues-rock. His cult started growing with the release of *Safe As Milk* (Kama Sutra) which featured Ry Cooder, Jimmy Semens, John Drumbo French and Herb Besman.

The Captain had an amazingly deep, gruff voice with an unprecedented range, and most felt he could have been the greatest white blues singer ever. But his own inclinations took him further and further from the mainstream. With his third album (*Trout Mask Replica*, Straight, 1969), he achieved his finest, and most avant garde, work. The album

86

featured a new Magic Band – Semens, guitar; Zoot Horn Rollo, guitar; The Mascara Snake, bass clarinet; and Rockette Morton, bass. It was rooted in Delta blues, but sounded nothing like the blues. There was a blues feeling to it, but the horn players were blowing lines more reminiscent of the New Wave jazz of Ornette Coleman and John Coltrane. Tempos jumped about crazily, melodies disappeared faster than they could be absorbed. The Captain's lyrics were an outrageously wacky series of word plays, puns and surrealist images which carried very serious thoughts. Beefheart considered his music great art, but saw no reason why he shouldn't reap the rewards of a pop musician. This attitude contributed greatly to a series of running battles with managers and record company executives who, he left, were trying to compromise his work. Most of his records came out on different labels, and live performances were irregular.

After *Trout Mask Replica*, he started moving slowly back towards the pop mainstream on his own initiative. By 1974, he had come up with *Unconditionally Guaranteed* (Mercury in America, Virgin in Britain), a baroque and bluesy album that was quite accessible. However, success still eluded him. Worse, perhaps the best incarnation of the Magic Band (including guitarists Zoot Horn Rollo and Rockette Morton) left him to form a group, Mallard. He had taught most of them to play from scratch and their looks and musicianship were integral to his music. In 1975 the Captain rejoined his oldest musical comrade, Frank Zappa, as vocalist with the Mothers Of Invention.

James Carr, a Southern soul wailer born in Memphis on June 13, 1942 started off sounding like Otis Redding, developed a similarity to Percy Sledge, and was considered by many to be better than either of them. After signing with the Soul Stirrers gospel group, he signed to Goldwax Records of Memphis and recorded a succession of intense performances ('You Got My Mind Messed Up', 'Love Attack', 'Pouring Water On A Drowning Man' in 1966; 'Dark End Of The Street', 'A Man Needs A Woman' in 1967) and a few uptempo sides (including 'That's What I Want To Know',

1966, and 'Freedom Train', 1968) that have since become disco favourites. He was last heard on Atlantic in 1971.

Clarence Carter, blind since childhood, first recorded with Calvin Scott (or Thomas) as Calvin and Clarence and the C and C Boys, for Fairlane, Duke and Atco. When Scott was injured in a car crash, Carter went solo for Rick Hall's Muscle Shoals-based Fame label, entering the charts with 'Tell Daddy' and 'Thread The Needle' in 1967.

The following year he signed with Atlantic and recorded a succession of solid soul hits which reached both R&B and pop charts. They included 'Looking For A Fox', 'Slip Away' (national Top Ten in 1968), 'Too Weak To Fight', 'Snatchin' It Back', 'Patches' (taken from a Chairmen Of The Board album, it reached No. 2 in Britain in 1970), 'It's All In Your Mind' and 'The Court Room'.

Mel Carter, born in Cincinnati on April 22, 1943. Carter worked with Paul Gayten's band before moving to gospel where he sang with the Robert Anderson Singers and his own group, the Carvetts. In 1960 he moved to California where Sam Cooke signed him to Derby, the label on which he brushed the Top Fifty with the romantic soul ballad, 'When A Boy Falls In Love' in 1963. More substantial hits followed on Imperial. With 'Hold Me, Thrill Me, Kiss Me' (which reached the Top Ten in 1965), 'All Of A Sudden My Heart Sings', 'Band Of Gold' and 'You You You' (all Top Fifty hits) Carter strayed towards a middle-of-the-road, singalong style which led to a durable cabaret career.

Carter and Lewis. Both born in Small Heath, Birmingham, in 1942, songwriters John Carter (John Shakespeare) and Ken Lewis (Kenneth Hawker) formed the group Carter, Lewis and the Southerners (which included Jimmy Page) in the early Sixties. Between 1962 and 1963 they were hardly off the air and had a minor hit with 'Your Momma's Out Of Town'.

In 1964 Carter and Lewis joined forces with songwriter

Perry Ford (Bryan Pugh, born 1940 in Lincoln) to provide
vocal backings – for example on the Who's 'Can't Explain'.
The trio then decided to put out their own recordings under
the name of the Ivy League and, in 1965, had a couple of
British Top Ten hits in a close-harmony style influenced by
both the Beach Boys and the Four Seasons, 'Funny How
Love Can Be' and 'Tossing And Turning', both on Picca-
dilly. Carter then left the group and was replaced with yet
another songwriter, Tony Burrows. In 1967 a completely reshaped Ivy League was augmented by one, became the
Flowerpot Men and, during the flower vogue, had a solitary
hit with a Carter–Lewis song, 'Let's Go To San Francisco'.
The following year, after the failure of the gloriously over-
produced 'A Walk In The Sky', they changed their name to
Friends in an unsuccessful attempt to halt their decline.
Meanwhile Carter and Lewis returned to session singing and
entered the lucrative world of commercials, working separ-
ately and together as producers and writers. John Carter
recently reappeared in the British and American charts as
the lead singer on the First Class's 'Beach Baby'; another
member of the 'group' was Tony Burrows.

Jimmy Castor, born on June 22, 1943 in New York, sang on
street-corners with the likes of Frankie Lymon and the Teenagers who recorded 'I Promise To Remember', a Castor
song which he had previously cut on Wing with his own
group, the Juniors: Orton Graves, Johnny Williams and Al
Casey Jr., son of the famous jazz guitarist. Castor also sang
with the Teenchords, recorded as a solo artist for Winley,
Clown, Jet-Set and Decca and played saxophone on Dave
'Baby' Cortez's 'Rinky Dink'. In 1966 he had a Top Forty
hit on Smash with a Latin calypso, 'Hey, Leroy, Your
Mama's Calling You'. After other records on Compass and
Capitol, he reached the top with a ferocious discotheque
classic, 'Troglodyte' (RCA). Subsequent discs for Atlantic,
including the aptly titled 1974 album *The Everything Man*
and the 1975 hit 'King Kong', demonstrated Castor's exceptional versatility.

Chad and Jeremy. The aura of the British public school surrounded ex-Central School of Speech and Drama students, Chad (born Dec. 10, 1943) and Jeremy (born March 22, 1944). They were polite and well-spoken and, accordingly, highly popular for a time in America. Their early material was a mixture of folk and pop which evolved into post-Byrds folk-rock and thence to post-*Sergeant Pepper* ideas expressed in the 'Progress Suite', a five-movement piece on *Of Cabbages And Kings* (Columbia, 1967), scored and arranged by Chad Stuart, who always took the weight of the musical duties leaving Jeremy Clyde to concentrate on the lyrics. Both played guitars, Chad adding a variety of keyboard and stringed instruments, and both sang. Their considerable success in America in the wake of the Beatles – they had three Top Twenty records, 'A Summer Song', 'Willow Weep For Me' (World Artists, 1964) and 'Before And After' (Columbia, 1965) – was never reflected in their native Britain where 'Yesterday's Gone' barely scraped the Top Thirty to give them their only taste of success. They went their separate ways in 1969, Chad trying his hand at writing musicals and Jeremy Clyde taking up acting. His best known performance was in *Conduct Unbecoming* in London's West End, which also marked ex-Manfred Mann singer Paul Jones's debut on the stage.

The Chambers Brothers – Lester (born April 13, 1940), Willie (March 2, 1938), George (Sept. 26, 1931) and Joe (Aug. 22, 1942) – moved to Los Angeles from Lee County, Mississippi, during the early Fifties. Their early records on Vault included magnificently rough versions of soul material like 'Your Old Lady' and 'People Get Ready'. Heavily featuring mouth-harp, these discs were acclaimed by fans of downhome blues. Augmented by ex-Manfred Mann drummer, Brian Keenan, the Brothers joined Columbia to make successful discs like 'Time Has Come Today' (No. 11 in 1968) and 'I Can't Turn You Loose'. The band's stoned black hippie image was taken up by the underground press and new white audiences. 'Shout', an ecstatic Vault re-issue, also made the charts in 1968, while 'Funky' became a Top Forty R&B hit in 1971.

Gene Chandler, sporting a top hat, cloak, and cane, shot to fame in 1962 with the ludicrous but irresistible dook, dook, dook, 'Duke Of Earl' (Vee Jay). Seemingly doomed by such an outrageous gimmick, Chandler – born July 6, 1937 in Chicago – was rescued by Curtis Mayfield who gave him further hits with some of his best songs, including 'Rainbow' (1962), 'Man's Temptation' (1963), both on Vee Jay; and 'Think Nothing About It', 'Just Be True' (1964), 'Nothing Can Stop Me' (1965) on Constellation. Based in his home-town Chicago, he continued to record successfully for the city's major black music outlets, notably Checker, with 'I Fooled You This Time' (1967); Brunswick, 'Girl Don't Care' (1967), 'From Teacher To The Preacher' with Barbara Acklin (1968); and Mercury, 'Groovy Situation' (1970), 'Ten And Two' with Jerry Butler (1971). Since 1972 he has been reunited with Mayfield on the star's own Curtom label.

Ray Charles was born Ray Charles Robinson in Albany, Georgia on Sept. 23, 1932. Blind at six – he suffered from glaucoma – he studied music at a school for the blind in Florida until he was orphaned in 1947. After a lean couple of years gigging around Florida, he moved to Seattle, Washington, and formed the Maxim Trio, blatantly based on the then commercial piano/guitar/bass sound of the Nat 'King' Cole group: Charles sang, played piano, sometimes organ, plus alto saxophone and clarinet. They cut a number of Nat Cole-type ballads and Charles Brown-influenced blues for Swingtime, displaying enough potential for Atlantic to buy up Charles's contract in 1952. It was around this time too that R. C. Robinson became 'Ray Charles' to avoid confusion with Sugar Ray Robinson, boxer-turned-entertainer.

Charles had freelanced with Lowell Fulson, Guitar Slim and Ruth Brown in between regular club and TV engagements with the trio, and the welding of this varied experience to the influence of his Baptist church upbringing resulted in a gospel-tinged 'soul' sound. He took the typical gospel rhythms, call-and-response patterns and sixteen-bar chord progressions and sang secular lyrics over them with the yelled asides, exhortations and catches in the voice of a Southern service in full swing. 'Talkin' 'Bout Jesus' became 'Talkin' 'Bout You', and even 'My Bonnie Lies Over The Ocean' and Stephen Foster's 'The Old Folks At Home' (as 'Swanee River Rock') were given the treatment, with a four-girl vocal group (the Raylettes, later 'Raelets') on responses, the melody lines recast and the 'new' songs credited to Charles.

Signed to Atlantic and making regular visits to the American charts with 'I Got A Woman', 'A Fool For You', 'Lonely Avenue', 'Hallelujah I Love Her So', etc., he also recorded several instrumental jazz albums with groups from his own band and with Milt Jackson, vibraharpist with the Modern Jazz Quartet. They featured Ray's piano style – the funkiest of blues filled out with modern jazz harmonies – and his Charlie Parker-derived alto. In 1959, only months after cutting his most basic hit – 'What'd I Say', complete with fundamental 12-bar riff and call-and-response with the Raelets – Charles recorded some sides with strings and voices, arranged by Ralph Burns. Later that year, he accepted a contract offer from ABC-Paramount, and Burns was hired to arrange the first single, 'Georgia On My Mind'; thanks to ABC's superior promotion and distribution machine, it topped the charts on both sides of the Atlantic.

At first, there were still plenty of soul/gospel rockers like 'Hit The Road, Jack' and 'Sticks And Stones', and even the *Modern Sounds In Country And Western Music* LPs were split between string and big-band backings (Volume Two had 'You Are My Sunshine', a superb holy leg-pull right out of the 'My Bonnie' bag); soon, though, sentimental ballads accounted for nearly all the singles. Selling-out wasn't involved, since Charles had always been eclectic in his choice of material, and what's more was able to produce something worthwhile in each of the idioms he tackled: some of the items with strings ('Come Rain Or Come Shine', 'Georgia', 'Take These Chains From My Heart') are among the finest

92

things he's done. It was more a question of balance, as the entire output gradually veered towards a smooth, inoffensive repertoire. Concerts became dominated by old favourites, most of them sounding very tired, but Charles's charisma, his inability to stop swinging and the odd snatch of his still spine-tingling piano ensured that there was always something to be had from a live performance. Albums like *A Message From The People*, featuring good songs delivered with conviction, were few and far between. Only one jazz LP came out during the Sixties, a big-band album with Ray on organ throughout, *Genius + Soul = Jazz*.

Whether or not Ray Charles's future work will return to the level of his greatest records, he is already acknowledged as the most important influence on the course of post-war black music. His profane mingling of secular and sacred styles proved to be the blueprint for the many varieties of soul music which dominated the R&B and often the pop charts throughout the Sixties. And when young white singers turned towards black music for inspiration in that decade, it was Ray Charles who was most influential, just as Chuck Berry's guitar style could be heard in the playing of hordes of white guitarists. Among those who have openly copied the master are David Clayton-Thomas, Righteous Brother Bill Medley, Joe Cocker, Long John Baldry and Stevie Winwood. And the wheel came full circle when Nat 'King' Cole reached the charts in 1962 with a country and western song, 'Dear Lonely Hearts', phrased unmistakably in the manner of the man who had once paid him the same compliment.

Cher, born Cherilyn Sarkasia LaPier on May 20, 1946, in El Centro, California, came to prominence in 1965 with a series of hit recordings with her husband Sonny Bono, whom she had met while singing back-up vocals on Phil Spector's sessions. She soon launched her solo career with Dylan's 'All I Really Want To Do' (Imperial), and a succession of hits followed: 'Where Do You Go' (1965), 'Bang Bang' (1966) and 'You'd Better Sit Down, Kids' (1967), all dramatically produced and arranged by Bono and Harold Battiste. A label switch to Kapp in 1971 resulted in even greater success. One of her singles, the melodramatic 'Gypsies, Tramps And Thieves' (1971), proved to be the biggest seller in the label's history and the album of the same name turned gold, as did the *Half Breed* album. Her last MCA/Kapp hit was 'Dark Lady' in 1974, after which she split with Sonny and signed with Warner Bros. to cut *Stars*, produced by Jimmy Webb and featuring her rich-voiced interpretations of songs by Neil Young, Eric Clapton and Jimmy Cliff. She also cut a disastrous single for Warner-Spector, 'A Woman's Story'. Unlike Sonny, who has disappeared from view since the duo split, Cher is still a top draw in rock and fashion circles and appears with monotonous regularity in society columns on both sides of the Atlantic.

Chicken Shack were part of Mike Vernon's Blue Horizon stable which dominated the British blues renaissance of the late Sixties. Their reputation was built on the virtuoso guitar playing of Stan Webb and the singing of pianist Christine Perfect, whose version of Etta James's 'I'd Rather Go Blind' (Blue Horizon) provided their only hit single. Following the departure of Christine Perfect to join her husband, John McVie, in Fleetwood Mac and Andy Sylvester (bass) and Dave Bidwell (drums) to join Savoy Brown, and apparently oblivious to changes in public taste, Webb continued to lead the band until 1974 when he himself joined Savoy Brown briefly for an album and a tour, before forming the Stan Webb Band.

Lou Christie, born Lugee Salo on Feb. 19, 1943, in Glen Willard, Pennsylvania, had two spasms of success both surprisingly out of time with the music scene around him. In 1963 he scored two American Top Twenty hits with 'The Gypsy Cried' and 'Two Faces Have I' (both on Roulette), reviving the dying embers of an era of high image falsetto rockers in the Jimmy Jones/Del Shannon fashion, in the year before the Beatles were to unsettle that old order of things. He returned in 1966 with the No. 1 'Lightnin' Strikes' (also a British hit), a fine rock ballad with a Motown style beat and that throwback baritone to falsetto singing that this time was set against the contemporary punk stance of the song's lyric, a conscience-ridden lad lusting after his girl. His album of that year *Lightnin' Strikes* (MGM) was another paean to the Fifties with its 'sweet side' of current covers and more interesting 'rockin' side' (all Lou Christie/Twyla Herbert originals). Lou Christie's career is strangely schizoid in this way. The Top Twenty follow-up, 'Rhapsody In The Rain', was actually banned in Britain for its too graphic sexual rhythms and 'makin' love in a storm' lyrics, despite its dated musical/ vocal dressing. Three years later Lou came up with a further hit, 'I'm Gonna Make You Mine' (Buddah), surprisingly trite after his earlier irreverent classics. He currently records on Elektra.

The Dave Clark Five were the first British group to provide a popular alternative to Merseybeat through a harsh combination of shouts and thumps that was for a time referred to as the 'Tottenham Sound'. Formed in that North London suburb in 1960, the group (who, in spite of their music, had a decidedly clean-limbed image) were Clark on drums (born Dec. 14, 1942), Lenny Davidson (May 30, 1944), Rick Huxley (August 5, 1942), Denis Payton on sax (Aug. 1, 1943) and singer Mike Smith (Dec. 12, 1943). Four chart-busters followed their first big hit, 'Glad All Over' on Columbia (Epic in America), in 1964, but their British popularity declined with a series of smash American tours/hits in the mid-Sixties. In 1968 Clark, who had always fancied himself as an actor, ploughed some of the group's fortunes into TV film production. One programme, starring Clark, was screened, but a projected series did not materialize. In the Seventies Dave Clark surfaced briefly with 'Everybody Get Together', a British Top Ten hit in 1970.

Petula Clark, born in Epsom, Surrey, Nov. 15, 1933, in little over a decade became one of Britain's biggest child stars through wartime film and radio performances. Children's songs gave way to adult ballads, and 'With All My Heart' in 1957, launched her internationally. France, her current home, adopted her as its own, especially after marriage to Claude Wolff, a young executive at Vogue Records. She continued logging up chart hits, securing her first American hit, a No. 1, with 'Downtown' in 1964. Hits have eluded her since 1968 but carefully judged television and concert appearances, and successful screen roles (*Finian's Rainbow*, *Goodbye Mr Chips*) have consolidated her worldwide status.

The Classics IV, featuring Dennis Yost, were formed in Jacksonville, Florida and subsequently moved to Atlanta in 1967 – Dennis Yost, vocals; James Cobb, guitar; Wally Eaton, rhythm guitar; Kim Venable, drums; and Joe Wilson, bass. Their first release, the No. 3 'Spooky' (Imperial), established them as a group whose soft, sincere ballads and smoothly commercial arrangements would have a built-in audience. As a session group they backed Tommy Roe, Billy Joe Royal and the Tams. While they kept coming up with strong material (most of it written by Cobb and Buddie Buie, who also arranged and produced the records), the Classics IV with a much-changed line-up continued having hits. 'Stormy', 'Traces' and 'Everyday With You Girl' were all Top Twenty entries during 1968–9. But despite large sales and an attempt in 1969 to promote lead singer Dennis Yost as a star along the lines of Bobby Goldsboro or Gary Puckett, he and the group had never created enough of an identity to pull it off. Leaving Imperial/Liberty (which had just merged with United Artists), the group resurfaced on MGM-South (a label over which their mentor, Bill Lowery, had more direct control) in 1972 with 'What Am I Crying For?', which worked its way up to No. 39. Buie and Cobb are now in the Atlanta Rhythm Section whose albums include *Dog Days* (Polydor, 1975).

Joe Cocker, born on May 20, 1944, a Sheffield gas-fitter and pub singer, first recorded a Beatles tune 'I'll Cry Instead' as Vance Arnold and the Avengers in 1963. He dropped out of music to return with pianist Chris Stainton and Denny Cordell as producer in 1967 with 'Marjorine' a minor hit which first drew national attention to his raw, anguished, powerful blues voice. The follow-up – the Beatles' 'A Little Help From My Friends' – was a British No. 1 in 1968 and a worldwide smash leading to a first album of the same name which featured Jimmy Page, Albert Lee, Stevie Winwood, and Henry McCullough, among others.

The Grease Band, comprising Bruce Rowland, Alan Spenner, and McCullough in addition to Cocker and Stainton, toured America and played Woodstock in 1969. There Cocker met Leon Russell whose 'Delta Lady' was to be his third British hit, and together with session musicians and the Grease Band an album, *Joe Cocker!*, was cut under Russell's supervision. Then Russell put together Mad Dogs and Englishmen for an American tour in 1970 when the Grease Band quit; and the tribe of over twenty musicians and singers, including the pirated Delaney and Bonnie Band, were a runaway success. A live double album (which went gold) and film resulted and Russell emerged a superstar. But Cocker, who reportedly made only $800 from the tour, retired to England after recording one more song, 'High Time We Went', a minor American hit.

In 1972, he made a disastrous comeback bid with a tour, opening in the States and closing in Australia, where repeated arrests led to his deportation. That year he released a further album, *Something To Say*, which showed a marked limitation and deterioration in his vocal powers. In 1974, he returned once more with a better album, *I Can Stand A Little Rain*, which none the less ranked below his former greatness. He began to tour again in the summer of 1974, opening with a concert in Los Angeles which ran into many difficulties. However, he persisted with live work and by March, 1975, had an American Top Ten hit with a track from the album, 'You Are So Beautiful'.

Albert Collins was born in Leona, Texas in 1930. His shuffle blues vocal and guitar style – influenced by T-Bone Walker and Gatemouth Brown – was formed in the clubs of the Houston ghetto where his career began. He has not always done himself justice on record, considering the brilliance of his live performances. The important singles – 'The Freeze' on Kangaroo in 1958 and 'Defrost' on Great Scott in 1962 (but also issued on Hallway and Smash) – sold well in the South without reaching the national charts. Under the guidance of producer Bill Hall, Collins' subsequent singles and albums for TCF-Hall, Tracie, 20th Century Fox, Blue Thumb, Imperial and Tumbleweed have achieved considerable success among white blues enthusiasts.

Judy Collins, along with Joan Baez and Joni Mitchell, is one of the three great female singers who emerged through the American folk scene in the Sixties. Born in Seattle on May 1, 1939 and originally trained as a classical pianist, she began singing in the folk clubs of Denver and Central City, Colorado, before moving east to Greenwich Village, New York. Her first album *A Maid of Constant Sorrow* (Elektra, 1961) demonstrated her exquisite, crystal-clear voice on traditional material.

As the folk scene developed, Collins managed to keep at least one jump ahead. She moved from folk to contemporary songs by up-and-coming writers. So, in 1963, she recorded Dylan tracks, and in 1966 she was the first to record Leonard Cohen's 'Suzanne'. On *Wildflowers*, in 1967, she took another step forward by including some of her own songs for the first time. By now her style had broadened to include ballads and *chanson*, and she was rightly recognized as a superb interpreter of writers as varied as Jacques Brel, Brecht/Weill, Joni Mitchell and Randy Newman. This album qualified for a gold record, as did *Who Knows Where The Time Goes* (1968), which included Stephen Stills among the backing musicians. Collins later had hit singles with 'Both Sides Now' and 'Amazing Grace', and in all her recordings retained her magnificent, clear voice.

She has been active in politics, including help in registering black voters in Mississippi in 1964. In 1974 she seemed to be drifting away from music when *Antonia: Portrait of a Woman*, a film about her classical teacher, Antonia Brico, which she helped make, was nominated for an Academy

Award. But in 1975 she returned to rock and the charts with a bang following the success of Stephen Sondheim's 'Send In The Clowns', which came from a Broadway show.

Columbia Records entered the Sixties with a healthy stable of middle-of-the-road stars (Mitch Miller, Doris Day, Andy Williams, etc.) and a string of enormously successful Broadway cast albums (*South Pacific*, *My Fair Lady*) that bode well for the future. Yet by 1966, with only the Byrds, Dylan, Simon and Garfunkel and Paul Revere and the Raiders – their best-selling rock act – and with post-Beatles rock transformed into the major concern of the record industry, things looked decidedly bleak, though the country music division was healthy and soul hits came sporadically on Okeh and Dare. While in the rock field Dylan gave them prestige, he did not sell in vast quantities and Simon and Garfunkel would not become real moneyspinners until 1968. By then, the whole problem had been solved by a mixture of good luck and good judgement when Clive Davis, the company's new president, went to the Monterey Pop Festival, saw rock's future and waved the corporate cheque book. A few years of frenzied signings later, Janis Joplin, Blood, Sweat and Tears and Sly Stone and Johnny Winter had been added to the roster, and the cash expectations of groups looking for a record contract had drastically risen. This was topped off by an advertising campaign that proclaimed 'The Man Can't Bust Our Music' and invited readers to 'Join The Revolution' – and this at a time when in Britain, the newly independent CBS's only sizeable hits were with pop groups like the Tremeloes. That said, the result of Columbia's sudden burst of activity was that by 1969, the company again was well balanced and extremely profitable, with soul the only area left to be explored.

Arthur Conley, an Otis Redding protégé born on April 1, 1946 in Atlanta, Georgia, had unsuccessful releases on Stax, Volt, and the star's Jotis label before 'Sweet Soul Music' (Atco), a Top Five hit in 1967. Originally written and recorded by Sam Cooke as 'Yeah Man', Redding and Conley's adaptation included the names of top soul stars and used a classic Memphis arrangement to create an anthem for the music that was ultimately ridiculed as a cliché-ridden parody. Conley never really recovered. After half-a-dozen smaller hits, including 'Funky Street' and 'People Sure Act Funny' (1968) he joined Capricorn Records in 1971 and hasn't had a hit since.

The Contours – Hubert Johnson, Billy Gordon, Sylvester Potts, Joe Billingslea and Billy Hoggs – were introduced to Motown's Berry Gordy by Johnson's cousin, Jackie Wilson, in 1961. The following year the frenetic 'Do You Love Me' topped the R&B charts and got to No. 3 in the national charts. It was covered in Britain by Brian Poole and the Tremeloes and the Dave Clark Five. Other distinctively hoarse dance records entered the middle reaches of the Hot Hundred, including 'Shake Sherrie', 'Don't Let Her Be Your Baby' (1963), 'Can You Do It', 'Can You Jerk Like Me' (1964), 'First I Look At The Purse' (1965), and 'Just A Little Misunderstanding' (1966). A ballad, 'It's So Hard Being A Loser' (1967), completed their chart run. Later members of the Contours included Joe Stubbs (brother of the Four Tops' Levi) and Dennis Edwards (subsequently with the Temptations).

Sam Cooke, born one of a family of eight in Chicago on Jan. 22, 1931, first sang publicly in his local Baptist church, at the age of nine, when he got together with two sisters and a brother under the name of the Singing Children. In his early teens he moved to another young Baptist group, the Highway QCs. They were coached for a while by R. B. Robinson, the baritone with a leading gospel quartet, the Soul Stirrers. When the Stirrers' lead tenor, Robert (R. H.) Harris, retired in 1950, Cooke was invited to take over, and he sang with the group until 1956.

The Soul Stirrers had already been responsible for major innovations in their field. Apart from being one of the first itinerant quartets to deal solely in hymns and modern gospel songs – rather than jubilees and spirituals – the group also singled out and emphasized the lead vocal to a far greater extent than their predecessors. They introduced a 'second lead' to fill in the tenor harmonic line and with this freedom Harris was able to develop a highly individual style of syncopated improvisation, prominently featuring his falsetto. Sam Cooke's mature vocal style built on the groundwork done by Harris.

Once he had found his feet with the Soul Stirrers, Cooke also confirmed the uniquely contemporary and exciting atmosphere the group had brought to gospel. He became the idol of thousands of young girl fans, projecting the sexuality that had always been central to gospel, but bringing to it a cool, urban sophistication. The Soul Stirrers did their first session for Specialty early in 1950, and many of Cooke's recordings with them – such as 'Touch The Hem Of His Garment' and 'Were You There' – show his pop-soul style fully developed.

In 1956 Bumps Blackwell encouraged Cooke to record some pop songs. A number of ballads were released, of which 'Lovable', 'That's All I Need To Know' and 'I'll Come Running Back To You' were the most notable, the latter a million-seller on its belated release in 1957. Initially, he recorded under the name Dale Cook to avoid offending the gospel world. (He was christened Sam Cook, and the 'e' was added to his surname during his period at Specialty.) When Blackwell added a white female vocal chorus to sweeten Cooke's recording of 'You Send Me', Art Rupe (Specialty's owner) offered to lease them the tape and release both of them from their contracts in return for forgoing their past royalties. Blackwell took the tapes to Bob Keene on whose Keen label 'You Send Me'/'Summertime' was a national chart topper and eventually sold some two-and-a-half million copies. Other major hits on Keen were 'Only Sixteen' and 'Wonderful World' in 1959.

On these early pop records, the smooth, open delivery and lyrical purity of Cooke's gospel style remained virtually intact. His singing was a little more restrained and wistful, fitting the teenage-fantasy-sentimentality of the lyrics. But the controlled passion and the adlibbed mannerisms of 'You

Send Me' – such as the wailing 'whoa-uh-oh-ah-oh' with which he extended many of the lines, giving weight to an insubstantial lyric and tune – were direct transpositions from his church style. It was a style without a clear precedent in mass popular music, and one that contrasted sharply with the dominant hot, raucous mood of rock'n'roll.

The switch to pop caused a final rift with the Soul Stirrers and they replaced him with future Stax performer Johnnie Taylor, who had also been in the Highway QCs. Cooke didn't lose touch entirely with his church music roots, however. In association with J. W. Alexander – late of the Pilgrim Travellers gospel group – he spent much of 1958–9 forming his own company, Sar Records, one of the first black-owned labels. Sar put out a series of strongly gospel-flavoured R&B hits in 1960–2, including the Sims Twins' 'Soothe Me', Johnnie Taylor's 'Rome (Wasn't Built In A Day)' and 'Lookin' For A Love' by the Valentinos – a group featuring Bobby Womack, who was not only heavily influenced artistically by his mentor but was later to marry Cooke's widow.

Meanwhile, Cooke had signed as a performer with RCA-Victor. By retaining his basic vocal style, Cooke was able to transcend the generally inflated and unsympathetic orchestral backings created by producers Hugo and Luigi, and many of his RCA performances were as influential and artistically convincing as they were commercially successful. The major hits included 'Chain Gang' (No. 2) and 'Sad Mood' in 1960, 'Cupid' in 1961, and in 1962, 'Twisting The Night Away', 'Having A Party' and 'Bring It On Home To Me', which featured ex-Pilgrim Traveller, Lou Rawls, as second vocalist. 1963 produced 'Little Red Rooster', with Ray Charles on piano and Billy Preston on organ; and in the following year came 'Ain't That Good News', 'Tennessee Waltz', 'That's Where It's At' and 'Shake'. The flipside of the latter was one of Cooke's greatest compositions, 'A Change Is Gonna Come', with its seemingly prophetic expression of the imminent upsurge in black political and social consciousness. But when the record reached the Top Ten early in 1965, Cooke was dead. He was shot at a Los

Angeles motel on Dec. 10, 1964. The court returned a verdict of justifiable homicide.

Sam Cooke's influence was enormous. He stands at the head of the entire sweet soul ballad tradition, and performers such as Otis Redding, Al Green, Smokey Robinson, Johnny Nash, and Marvin Gaye have openly borne witness to their debt to him. Part of his importance lay in the fact that, like Ray Charles, he demonstrated that an R&B artist could retain a vital relationship with the black audience while surviving in the teenage pop market and in a Las Vegas night-club context as a performer of standards. He was also a significant force in British rock, with Rod Stewart modelling his style on Cooke's and a number of groups scoring important hits with songs he made famous – including the Animals ('Bring It On Home To Me') and even Herman's Hermits ('Wonderful World').

Denny Cordell, born Dennis Cordell-Laverack in Brazil in 1942, of an English father and Brazilian mother, was sent to public school in England. In 1963–4, he worked for Saltaeb, the firm which marketed Beatles goods, and stumbled into record production by discovering the original Bessie Banks version of 'Go Now' and placing it with the Moody Blues who were contracted to Saltaeb at the time. Although Cordell was heavily involved in the production of the Moody Blues hit version of the song, production credits on the label went to friend Alex Murray who had more experience in the business. However, Cordell did produce the group's subsequent discs between 1965 and 1966 – with a notable lack of commercial success.

During this period, Cordell – a non-musician – also supervised discs by the Mark Leeman Five, Jackie Edwards and a host of obscure names before recording the Move's early hits, starting with 'Night Of Fear' late in 1966. He also recorded Georgie Fame's No. 1 hit, 'Getaway', and follow-ups such as 'Sunny' and 'Sitting In The Park'. However, his golden moment came with his production in 1967 of 'A Whiter Shade Of Pale' by Procul Harum. Shortly after, EMI allocated to him their old Regal-Zonophone label for which he

103

produced the Move ('Flowers In The Rain'), Procul Harum ('Homberg') and Joe Cocker ('With A Little Help From My Friends').

Teaming up with Leon Russell in 1969, Cordell achieved tremendous success with Joe Cocker in 1969–71. Since then he has administered Shelter Records from its base in Russell's hometown of Tulsa, Oklahoma.

Country Joe and the Fish began life as a jug band in Berkeley, California, in 1965. Joe McDonald (born Jan. 1, 1942 in El Monte, California) wrote their lyrics, drawing his material from the current political talking points of Berkeley, and also from the social life and drug experimentation there. The songs were powered by the Fish's acid-rock sound, particularly Barry Melton's fluid guitar work. Their first album (produced by Sam Charters on Vanguard), aptly titled *Electric Music For The Mind And Body* (1967), successfully integrated love songs ('Grace'), political skits ('Superbird'), social satire ('Not So Sweet Martha Lorraine') and drug songs ('Flying High'). McDonald's sharp lyrics were influenced by the political songs of Guthrie and Dylan and the Fish's sound was more disciplined and melodic than other psychedelic West Coast groups.

Their second album in 1967 had a less optimistic feel, and featured McDonald's insanely catchy, suicidal, Vietnam marching song, 'I-Feel-Like-I'm-Fixin'-To-Die Rag', as the title track. The Fish were still impressive as a musical combo, and their Indian instrumental, 'Eastern Jam', displayed Melton's guitar work at its most high-powered. However, Country Joe and the Fish, never the most stable of groups, subsequently went through personnel changes and recurrent break-ups. McDonald, the central figure, alternated between dominating the group and despairing of them. Their recordings only occasionally recaptured the power of their first two albums – the Vietnam song, 'An Untitled Protest' on *Together* (1968), the drugs and death warning on 'Crystal Blues', and the optimistic rebirth described in 'Here I Go Again'. In 1970, they split up for the final time, accurately reflecting the fragmentation of the youth/drugs/protest society that spawned them. Joe McDonald has since pursued an interesting solo career.

Don Covay, born in Orangeburg, South Carolina, in March, 1938, son of a Baptist preacher, received his musical grounding in a family gospel quartet, the Cherry-Keys, formed when the Covays moved to Washington. He entered the secular field at high school in his mid-teens, joining the Rainbows after they had hit locally with 'Mary Lee' (Red Robin) in 1955.

Don's solo career began when Little Richard played Washington in 1957 – he hustled a job as warm-up vocalist on the show, and Richard was sufficiently impressed to record him (as 'Pretty Boy'). Atlantic issued his 'Bip Bop Bip' in 1957. Don soon reverted to his own name, label-hopping to Sue, Columbia, Epic, RCA and Big Top before scoring a regional hit in 1961 with 'Pony Time' (Arnold). 'Popeye Waddle' was a 1962 hit on Cameo – another stereotyped Philadelphia dance disc, but items on Parkway and Landa were ignored. In 1964 Covay and his Goodtimers group signed to Rosemart and immediately reached the Top Fifty with the atmospheric, bluesy 'Mercy Mercy'. Rosemart was distributed by Atlantic, who then took over his contract, but despite recording in various styles and locations, his only other hit in the Sixties was 'Seesaw' (1965).

An unsuccessful attempt to regain hit status in a blues idiom came in 1970, and the following year Covay signed with Janus, moving to Mercury in 1972 as A&R director/performer, soon attaining chart status with 'I Was Checkin' Out, She Was Checkin' In', a searing soul ballad, followed by the highly acclaimed *Superdude 1* album and a further hit single, the dynamic gospel-soul 'It's Better To Have And Don't Need'. A prolific and most successful songwriter, Covay was a Grammy nominee in 1968 when his 'Chain Of Fools', sung by Aretha Franklin, was a No. 2 American hit.

The Cowsills were dubbed 'America's First Family Of Music' after their million-selling first release, 'The Rain, The Park And Other Things' (MGM, 1967). However, the pop harmony sound of the Cowsills – Bill (born Jan. 9, 1948), vocals; Bob (Aug. 26, 1949), vocals; Barry (Sept. 14, 1954), bass; and John (March 2, 1956), drums – soon floundered. A complete family unit, the group was managed by Pa Cowsill, another son was road manager, yet another looked after the sound equipment, while Ma (Barbara) sang with her boys on occasion, as did Susan, the youngest – eight in 1967. Unlike the Osmonds, the Cowsills never found a way of capitalizing on the image possibilities they presented and within two years their chart career was over, brought to an end with their second million-seller, 'Hair' (1969), after which Bill, who had rearranged the song for the group, left to pursue a solo career.

Cream, recognized in retrospect as the original 'supergroup', was a trio formed in the summer of 1966 when Eric Clapton left John Mayall's Blues Breakers with a reputation as Britain's finest blues guitarist and teamed up with two former members of the Graham Bond Organization, Ginger Baker (drums) and Jack Bruce (bass), who, after being bullied out of the Organization by Baker, had spent the previous six months languishing in pop with Manfred Mann – he played on 'Pretty Flamingo' – and getting his kicks staging harmonica battles with Paul Jones. Their pedigree in British blues was immaculate, their individual technique superb, and, having all had to fight for prominence in egocentric line-ups, they possessed a rare equilibrium.

In contrast to the heavy, blues-oriented performances of their early live work, the group's first single, 'Wrapping Paper' (Reaction, October 1966), was emphatically low-key and flopped. But 'I Feel Free' and the more stylistically characteristic *Fresh Cream*, released in December that year, both made the charts. On stage their forte became extended improvisation, and following *Disraeli Gears* (1967) – like the first album a studio production – their albums juxtaposed long, live work-outs of mainly blues material with shorter studio songs, usually by Jack Bruce and Pete Brown, such as 'White Room' and 'Politician' on *Wheels Of Fire*.

Since the group had been spending much of their time in

106

America, where their impact on audiences generally ignorant of the first wave of British blues had been greater than at home, the 'Live At The Fillmore' set on the double *Wheels Of Fire* (Polydor, 1968) was a revelation to the many British fans who had never seen them on stage. Although the energy of 'Spoonful' and Baker's drum feature, 'Toad', became dissipated over a quarter of an hour; the reworking of Robert Johnson's 'Crossroads' was a startling demonstration of Cream's considerable qualities with its stunning solo by Clapton urged on by Bruce's constantly challenging bass patterns and Baker's restless drumming.

Apparently at a peak of creativity and universal popularity, but privately dissident, they announced their intention to split, which they did at the end of 1968. *Goodbye* (Polydor, 1969), included, besides some of their best live work, their third and final hit single, 'Badge', written by Clapton and George Harrison. At their best masters of blues interpretation and rock musicianship, at their worst purveyors of empty virtuosity, Cream's influence was two-fold – they encouraged the worst excesses of heavy self-indulgence as well as inspiring individual expression. As if to emphasize the fact that the group had broken up before exploring their full potential, their recordings were subsequently repackaged in seemingly endless permutations.

The Critters' initial claim to fame was in recording 'Younger Girl', a John Sebastian song from the first Spoonful album. This, and the Top Twenty follow-up, 'Mr Dieingly Sad', were both substantial hits in 1966. The group – Chris Darway, autoharp; Kenny Corka, bass; Jeff Pelosi, drums; Bob Spinella, organ; and guitarist Jim Ryan, who also arranged some of their material – recorded for Kapp. Their first album, *Younger Girl*, was a delightful summery disc in 1966. They made a second for Kapp, *Touch 'n' Go*, and a final album, *The Critters*, for Project Three, the label set up by the production company responsible for their earlier albums. After the split, inevitable once the wake of their hits had subsided and their easy folk rockin' style became outmoded, Jim Ryan later worked with Carly Simon.

Steve Cropper played permanent under-secretary to the Sixties' changing guitar heroes, but has shunned the glare of solo superstardom to make his mark in his Memphis studio, TMI. Working on most of Stax's biggest hits as arranger/co-writer, he cut into the heavy Memphis beat with clean, incisive licks that made him the most distinctive accompanist of the era.

Born in Willow Spring, Missouri on Oct. 21, 1941, by the age of sixteen he was in Memphis where he formed a high-school band, the Mar-Keys, and had his first composition, 'Flea Circus', recorded by local hitmaker Bill Justis. 'Last Night' (1961) and other releases by the Mar-Keys on the embryo Satellite/Stax labels led to further instrumentals by various permutations of house musicians (the Triumphs, the Van-Dells, Booker T and the MGs) each featuring Cropper. It was for his work with the latter quartet that he became widely known, but like the rest of the group his contribution to the growth of Stax was most fully realized supporting the company's vocal stars. For several years he could be heard on nearly every track cut at the McLemore Avenue studios, as well as collaborating on many of their most famous recordings with Eddie Floyd ('Knock On Wood', 'Raise Your Hand'); Don Covay ('See Saw', 'Sookie Sookie'); Wilson Pickett ('In The Midnight Hour', 'Don't Fight It', '634-5789' – written with Floyd, 'Niney-Nine-And-A-Half Won't Do'); and Otis Redding ('Mr Pitiful', 'Fa-Fa-Fa-Fa-Fa', 'The Dock Of The Bay').

When the company expanded and the old corps dispersed, Cropper stayed in Memphis as a freelance jack-of-all-trades and producing for his own TMI label. In 1969 he recorded a pleasant solo album, *With A Little Help From My Friends* (Volt).

The Crystals, formed on a semi-pro basis in 1961, were all Brooklyn schoolgirls – Dee Dee Kennibrew, Dolores 'La La' Brooks, Mary Thomas, Barbara Alston and Pat Wright. It was this quintet which recorded 'There's No Other' for Phil Spector's Philles label in 1961 and registered an American Top Twenty hit. Their follow-up, 'Uptown', reached the American Top Ten early in 1962 but their third disc, 'He Hit Me' was withdrawn shortly after release following objections to its title, whereupon Spector issued the classic 'He's A Rebel' which topped the American charts in November, 1961 and ushered in the so-called 'Spector Sound'. Ironically, 'He's A Rebel' did not feature the real Crystals but an LA session group led by Darlene Love, who also sang on the successful follow-up, 'He's Sure The Boy I Love'. In 1962, Mary Thomas left the group which continued as a quartet but featured on their two biggest sellers, 'Da Doo Ron Ron' and 'Then He Kissed Me'.

By 1964, Spector had dropped the Crystals, by then a fading chart force, from his roster and they went on to record two unsuccessful Motown-styled singles for United Artists.

Mike Curb, born in Savannah, Georgia on Dec. 24, 1944, was once touted as the 'Boy Wonder' of the record business. At the age of 25, he was appointed President of MGM Records in 1968. Prior to that, he had been extremely active for over five years as a Los Angeles producer and songwriter. His talent was for finding musicians on the street, turning them into studio groups overnight, and leasing masters to a variety of labels. All this was done under the banner of Sidewalk Productions, who provided many recordings for the Tower label, and also released quite a few on Curb's own Sidewalk label. Notable among these were early tracks by the Mugwumps, the Electric Flag, the Stone Poneys, and Davie Allan and the Arrows.

More than anything else, however, Curb was known for assembling soundtrack albums (using mostly the same groups who recorded for Sidewalk) for American International Pictures, a leading maker of so-called 'youth exploitation' movies. Curb's soundtracks included *Riot On Sunset Strip*, *Psych-Out*, *Teenage Rebellion*, *Mondo Hollywood*, *Freakout U.S.A.*, and *The Wild Angels*. Through A-1, he became involved with Transcontinental Entertainment Corp, for whom he acquired and ran a number of small labels, all of which were discontinued when he joined

MGM. He lasted three or four years at MGM, but failed to bring the ailing label the 'youth image' they'd hoped for.

The Cyrkle began life as the Rondells, a New York singing group spotted and subsequently renamed by the Beatles' manager, Brian Epstein, who then exposed them nationally in America through a supporting slot on the Beatles' 1966 tour there. Group members, Tom Dawes (born July 25, 1944), Don Danneman (May 9, 1944) and Marty Fried (1944) – later joined by Michael Losekamp (1947) – had a light, friendly sound, not unlike Gary Lewis and the Playboys. Their first release, the Paul Simon composition, 'Red Rubber Ball' (Columbia) was an American No. 1 in 1966. Produced – and frequently joined – by John Simon, they had a second Top Twenty record with 'Turn-Down Day' and several good, but decreasingly successful, follow-ups.

Cyril 'Squirrel' Davies, born in Denham, Bucks., in 1932, was a panel-beater by day and played banjo in jazz and skiffle outfits before opening the London Blues and Barrel-house Club with Alexis Korner in 1955. After switching to harmonica, he worked with Korner backing Ottilie Patterson, and in 1961 the two formed Blues Incorporated. His hatred of saxophones led him to quit in November, 1962, to lead his own Muddy Waters-style band and he converted Screaming Lord Sutch's Savages, who included Nicky Hopkins on piano, into his R&B All-Stars, adding a black vocal trio, the Velvettes, and Long John Baldry for 'Country Line Special'/'Chicago Calling' (Pye), his best-remembered single in 1963. Little more than a year later on Jan. 7, 1964, Davies collapsed and died.

Billie Davis, the British soul singer who barely survived an accident-prone career, was born Carol Hedges in Woking, Surrey, in 1945. She was groomed for stardom by Robert Stigwood, teamed with Mike Sarne for 'Will I What?', and then allowed to go solo for 'Tell Him' (Decca), which became her sole hit in 1963. Immediately afterwards, she met ailing ex-Shadows bass guitarist Jet Harris and began a long, over-publicized relationship. Throughout the Sixties she persevered for further hits, graduating from pop to soul and reaching maturity in 1967 with her powerful version of 'Angel Of The Morning'. Her talents have long been acclaimed in Europe but her full potential has yet to be realized.

The Spencer Davis Group, originally the Spencer Davis Rhythm and Blues Quartet, were a pioneer Birmingham R&B group comprising brothers Stevie Winwood, guitar, keyboards and vocals (born May 12, 1948) and Muff Winwood, bass (June 15, 1945), Pete York, drums (Aug. 15, 1942), all from trad jazz backgrounds, and Spencer Davis, guitar (July 17, 1942), a folk-blues performer. The keynote of the group was Stevie Winwood's amazingly mature and strong blues voice, perfect for their material culled from black American sources, e.g. Sonny Boy Williamson and Bo Diddley.

Discovered in Birmingham by Chris Blackwell in 1964, they recorded unsuccessfully for Fontana throughout 1964 and 1965 until two songs by Jamaican singer, Jackie Edwards, propelled them into the charts. The first 'Keep On Running' made No. 1 in December, 1965 and was distinctive among British R&B for Winwood's voice and Muff's prominent, compulsive bass. Similar hits followed in 1966 with 'Somebody Help Me', 'When I Come Home' and 'Gimme Some Loving' – their first American Top Ten record – while the group toured R&B clubs and played all-nighters throughout Britain, culminating in their last hit, 'I'm A Man', a Stevie Winwood composition in February, 1967.

In early 1967, both Winwoods left, Stevie to found Traffic, Muff to work for Chris Blackwell's Island Artists, and since then Davis, who was largely a figurehead, has kept various groups together under the same name without ever achieving another chart success.

Dave Dee, Dozy, Beaky, Mick and Tich took its name from the nicknames of its members: David Harman (born 1943),

Trevor Davies, John Dymond, Michael Wilson and Ian Amey, all born in 1944. When they arrived in London from Salisbury to record 'No Time' in 1965, they sported a comic image, but this was dropped when success arrived at the end of the year with 'Hold Tight' on Fontana and, by 1967, they were leaders of fashion. Their hits (driving disco fodder written by their managers Howard and Blaikley) numbered almost a dozen and made them the most prolific chart-toppers of the period. In 1969 Dave Dee left to become an actor, failed, and returned in 1973 as A&R chief of Atlantic Records' London office.

Desmond Dekker, born in Jamaica, came to prominence in 1967 when '007' (Pyramid), a disc glorifying the rude boy era, climbed into the British singles charts. It was a light, infectious rock-steady number with a catching melody and he continued in similar vein with more than twenty consecutive chart-toppers in Jamaica, including 'Hey Grandma' and 'Music Like Dirt', before 'The Israelites' gave him a second British hit, climbing to No. 1 in April, 1969 and to No. 10 in America on Uni. Sung in a mixture of English and Creole patois, it was immensely popular and paved the way for further reggae chart entries, 'Return Of Django' and 'The Liquidator'. A follow-up, 'It Mek', was almost as successful and the following year he had his fourth British hit with 'You Can Get It If You Really Want', before fading via poor material. Re-released in 1975, 'The Israelites' was a hit again.

Sugar Pie De Santo, a diminutive but fiery R&B singer whose exciting stage presence has rarely been captured on record, was discovered by Johnny Otis in the mid-Fifties. She recorded for Federal and Aladdin before scoring regional hits on Check and Veltone, touring with the James Brown revue in 1960. Four years later she achieved national success with 'Slip-In Mules' (an answer to 'Hi-Heel Sneakers') and 'Soulful Dress'/'Use What You Got' on Checker – the only records to do her justice. Later issues on Cadet, Brunswick, and Soul Clock were poor, but her recent Jasman sides have been bluesier and better.

Jackie De Shannon has been called the Ellie Greenwich of California – an apt description of this singer/songwriter who was responsible for an impressive number of great tunes recorded by herself and others, throughout the mid-Sixties and early Seventies. Born in 1944 in Hazel, Kentucky, she started as a writer for the Kalin Twins and Brenda Lee ('Dum Dum') amongst others before she began recording in 1960 with a group called the Nomads, and soon was signed to Liberty where she released many singles and albums. Working with arranger Jack Nitzsche and other songwriters, including Sharon Sheeley and Randy Newman (she co-authored some of his first songs), De Shannon's songs were covered widely, particularly by English groups like the Searchers whose early hits included her 'Needles And Pins' and 'When You Walk In The Room'. Her own biggest hits were 'What The World Needs Now Is Love' (Imperial, 1965), and 'Put A Little Love In Your Heart' (Imperial, 1969), both Top Ten records. In 1972, she moved to Atlantic Records, where she released two fine solo albums, before moving on to Columbia for the powerful but commercially unsuccessful *New Arrangement* (1975).

The Deviants, originally the Social Deviants back in 1967, were a community band led by Mick Farren, then working at *International Times* and the first London 'underground' club, UFO. They came together for a series of 'total assault' gigs in the early underground clubs and for free concerts. After drummer Russ Hunter joined, the band moved on to a more semi-pro basis but the other musicians were less committed and the Social Deviants broke up. Farren and Hunter put together a new band, the Deviants, producing, pressing and distributing their first album themselves. *Ptoof* was on the Underground Impressarios label and was just sold through *It* and *Oz*, notching up 8,000 in sales before Decca subsequently re-released it. A more stable line-up completed by bass player Duncan Sanderson and guitarist

Paul Rudolph recorded a second album, *Disposable*. The group originally was heavily – if anarchically – political but changed later to a policy of simply trying to create a good-time atmosphere on stage. They were never a very accomplished musical outfit, the family ideal outweighing their development as musicians. In 1968, during a vast American tour, they called it a day with Hunter, Sanderson and Rudolph joining Twink (late of the Pretty Things), whom they had backed on a solo album, to form the Pink Fairies. The Fairies had a similar spirit but greater musical ambition, an ambition that was to remain unfulfilled.

The Dixie Cups – Barbara Ann Hawkins (born 1943), Rosa Lee Hawkins (1944) and Joan Marie Johnson (1945) – were discovered at a New Orleans talent contest by bandleader Joe Jones. They were still attending Southern University when 'Chapel Of Love' – a song originally written for the Ronettes by Phil Spector and others – reached the top of the charts on Red Bird in 1964. Four other hits followed: 'People Say', 'You Should Have Seen The Way He Looked At Me', 'Little Bell' and the semi-traditional New Orleans chant 'Iko Iko'. When Red Bird folded in 1966, the group recorded for ABC/Paramount without success.

Tom Donahue, known as 'Big Daddy' because of his size, was born May 21, 1928, in South Bend, Indiana. Donahue started as a deejay with WTIP in Charleston, Virginia, and then became Philadelphia's top disc jockey at WBIG in the Fifties before leaving for San Francisco in 1961. By 1964, while working at KYA along with another disc jockey, Bob Mitchell, he promoted the Cow Palace shows and the Beatles' and Rolling Stones' appearances there. In the same year as they set up Autumn records, using the KYA studios to record in, they had a national hit with their second release, Bobby Freeman's 'C'mon And Swim'. Sylvester 'Sly' Stewart joined the company as arranger and producer and even recorded some songs himself. Donahue himself recorded such bands as the Beau Brummels, the Charlatans, the Great Society, even the Grateful Dead and, in fact, negotiated the Airplane's recording contract. However, for various reasons – mostly financial – Autumn records never took off and folded in 1966.

Donahue's involvement with the San Francisco music scene was total. In the summer of 1965 he opened a North Beach club, Mothers, with the help of Mitchell where they put on outside bands like the Byrds and the Lovin' Spoonful. Mitchell died in 1966, but Donahue continued in his various roles as deejay and producer. In 1968, after the demise of Autumn records, he left KYA and set up the revolutionary KMPX-FM station and later KSAN-FM. Among the various groups that he managed were Stoneground, the Fast Bucks and Bad Rice. If not as well remembered as Bill Graham, Donahue – who died on April 28, 1975 – epitomized the early San Francisco approach to music.

Donovan, born Donovan Leitch on May 10, 1946, in Glasgow, started as one of the hundreds of early-Dylan imitators who flourished in the British folk clubs in the mid-Sixties. Appearances on the television show *Ready, Steady, Go* – with a guitar sticker proclaiming 'This Machine Kills', omitting the vital word 'Fascists' from the slogan originally coined by Woody Guthrie – led to a contract with Pye, and his first hit, 'Catch The Wind' (1965). His style was so similar to Dylan's that the British folk scene was unsure how to react.

Donovan then switched from Dylan to flower power, which by 1966 was blossoming across the Atlantic. With their soft-rock backing, and rhythmic, trance-like tunes, his songs 'Sunshine Superman' (1966) and 'Mellow Yellow' (1967) brilliantly captured the mood of the new movement, and both became million-sellers. The resulting album, *Sunshine Superman* (1967), which included 'Young Girl Blues' and 'Hampstead Incident' amongst others, and was produced by Mickie Most, saw Donovan at his observational best and was a deserved classic. Donovan moved on – or off – to publicly renounce drugs, take up with Eastern mysticism and then leave Mickie Most in the search for a musical identity. Along the way he has recorded an album of children's songs (*HMS Donovan*, 1971), and interrupted his cosmic philosophizing for a study of spacemen's toilet arrangements ('The Intergalactive Laxative', on *Cosmic Wheels*, 1973). In 1974, he wrote a theatrical stage show *7-Tease*, that dealt with the fate of hippy mind-searching and drugs. The accompanying album, produced by Norbert Putnam in Nashville, showed he was still developing – this time as a mainstream rock balladeer. Fashionable as it has become to dismiss Donovan, it's worth remembering that he gave the Sixties some of their best songs – and he's far from finished.

The Doors came together in Los Angeles in 1965 when Jim Morrison, would-be poet (born in Melbourne, Florida on Dec. 8, 1943) met keyboard player Ray Manzarek (born in Chicago on Feb. 12, 1935) in the film-making department of UCLA. They subsequently teamed up with ex-jugband guitarist Bobby Krieger (born in Los Angeles on Jan. 8, 1946) and drummer John Densmore (born in Los Angeles on Dec. 1, 1945). They borrowed their name from William Blake (via Aldous Huxley) – 'If the doors of perception were cleansed/All things would appear infinite' – and Morrison's lyrics and performances concentrated on acting out images and obsessions from his own poetry.

After performing as a support band around L.A., the Doors succeeded in being fired from their most important booking, at the Whiskey A Gogo, for performing 'The End', a semi-spoken, semi-improvised musical melodrama filled with apocalyptic imagery and Freudian references: 'Father, I want to kill you/Mother, I want to . . . (piercing shrieks) . . !' Their show was rather too dramatically convincing for current tastes. However, Jac Holzman of Elektra Records had seen them in action, and rewarded their daring with a lucrative contract. Their debut album, *The Doors* (1967), featured a lengthy rendition of 'The End', and 'Light My Fire', an extended, rhythmically tough but melodic invitation to erotic ecstasy. An edited version of this became a No. 1 single. Other successes on the album were 'Break On Through (To The Other Side)' which succinctly expressed the Doors' philosophy, and 'Soul Kitchen', a catchy account of mind/body alienation.

The Doors album worked because the instrumental energy packed enough power to sustain Morrison's dramatics – he projected an image halfway between street punk and depraved poet. The second album, *Strange Days* (1967), smoothed the rough edges off their music and contained their most carefully crafted work. Themes of alienation pervaded the album from the bizarre cover photo, via the haunting ballad, 'People Are Strange', to the lengthy concluding statement 'When The Music's Over' which tied the apocalyptic mood of 'The End' to more specific concerns – the Vietnam war, ecological awareness, and the almost magical significance of rock music. The rich imagery of Morrison's songs, Manzarek's classical/rock keyboards, Krieger's versatile guitar, and Densmore's dense drumming combined to create the musical energy to sustain their pretensions. Live, the Doors' music was a full-scale attempt at electronic, musical ritual, centring around Morrison's skin-tight leather theatricals.

1968 saw another No. 1 single, 'Hello I Love You', and the album *Waiting For The Sun* which carried the Doors further into political poses, and caused them problems. To 'underground' fans their politics appeared shallow. To promoters and police, their performance of songs announcing 'They've got the guns but we got the numbers!' coupled with Morrison's incitements to sexual frenzy, spelled trouble. It culminated in Morrison's arrest for allegedly exposing himself on stage in Miami, in March, 1969. The mood of liberation and psychic exploration which gave the Doors their context for performing, had crumbled, and the Doors' musical ritual began to look absurd and over-inflated. Morrison reduced the number of live performances they gave, and his final recordings, *Morrison Hotel* (1970) and *L.A. Woman* (1971), returned to the earthy roots of R&B. The music was tight and beautifully performed, possibly the Doors' best, but seemed somewhat perfunctory. Finally, Morrison left for Paris to concentrate again on poetry, and there he died – suddenly and rather mysteriously – in July, 1971. Without him, the Doors recorded two further albums, demonstrating their musical excellence, but lacking a clarity of focus without Morrison. They disbanded in 1973.

The Doors were probably the group who most successfully carried 'underground' music beyond an audience of freaks and students to a mass teen market – they had six Top Twenty singles. At his peak, Morrison successfully combined Presley's physical magnetism with highbrow, intellectual restlessness, claiming Céline and Camus as his major influences. Morrison's charisma, and their chart success, earned them a huge audience while their music explored the mysteries, totems and taboos of contemporary America.

Lee Dorsey, born in New Orleans on Dec. 24, 1924, enjoyed worldwide success in the mid-Sixties with a series of jaunty dance records on Amy. Beginning with 'Ride Your Pony' in 1965, Dorsey reached No. 44 with 'Get Out Of My Life, Woman', No. 8 with 'Working In The Coalmine' and No. 23 with 'Holy Cow'. The last two were Top Ten hits in Britain on Stateside. Formerly a boxer and US marine, Dorsey first came to national prominence in 1961 when the infectious 'Ya Ya' was a No. 7 hit for Bobby Robinson's Fury label, with 'Do-Re-Mi' as the carefully calculated followup. The company collapsed and Dorsey moved to the Marshall Sehorn–Allen Toussaint team, with the latter producing his hit recordings. Later singles were unsuccessful and in 1970 Dorsey signed with Polydor to make a concept album called *Yes We Can*, again produced by Toussaint. He remains active within the New Orleans music scene.

Tom Dowd, a pioneer in the development of recording techniques, started as an engineer for Atlantic in 1948. The clarity of many hit records for Joe Turner, Ray Charles and others was much envied by rival companies. Among independent record companies, Atlantic led the way in the use of stereo and eight-track recorders, on which Dowd worked with Leiber and Stoller for the Coasters' and the Drifters' hits. He was equally influential at the Stax studios where he engineered sessions by several of the major Memphis soul artists in the Sixties. Eventually, he became a fully-fledged producer, working with the Young Rascals, Aretha Franklin, Eric Clapton and Rod Stewart.

Julie Driscoll, born on June 8, 1947 in London, was working as producer Georgio Gomelsky's secretary and Yardbirds fan club administrator in 1965 when her employer suggested she would ideally complement Long John Baldry and Rod Stewart in Steampacket, which also included an expanded Brian Auger Trinity. When first Stewart, and then Baldry, left a year later and Steampacket folded, 'Jools' stayed on to front Auger's band, gaining attention as much for her appearance as her vocal ability. They had an international hit single in 1968 with Dylan's 'This Wheel's On Fire' on Gomelsky's Marmalade label and it was on a subsequent American tour that she quit. She virtually retired, emerging occasionally to sing with her husband, jazz pianist Keith Tippett's massive experimental band, Centipede.

Bob Dylan was born Robert Allan Zimmerman in Duluth, Minnesota, on May 24, 1941. At high school in nearby Hibbing, he played briefly in a rock'n'roll band, and then attended the University of Minnesota at Minneapolis for a year. Here Robert Zimmerman became Bob Dylan the folk singer, who set out to make his name in the mecca of the folk scene, New York's Greenwich Village. He was determined to become a 'famous folk singer' and consequently he trimmed his sails and ignored many of the other musical influences of his teenage years. On the first few albums he cut after veteran producer John Hammond signed him to Columbia in 1961, there was little evidence of his love for Hank Williams or Chuck Berry – though occasionally he let slip an Everly Brothers riff. Instead, Dylan's music was very much in the mainstream of the folk revival. And it was good, sometimes brilliantly so. He quickly became known as the most talented of the young writers (like Phil Ochs and Tom Paxton) whose songs became anthems for the white students involved in the civil rights and anti-war movements. There were protest songs like 'Blowin' In The Wind' and 'A Hard Rain's Gonna Fall', love songs like the traditional 'Corrina' and the traditionally based 'Girl From The North Country' and funny songs like the various renditions of 'I Shall Be Free'. The tunes were relatively simple (often lifted from traditional folk material), and his technical ability (both singing and playing the guitar and harmonica) was, in the field of folk music, primitive. But the impact was unusually hard-hitting – Dylan was creating a mood, and the scenarios he was painting needed no sophistication. The voice, the guitar playing and the sometimes vicious harp sounds, helped set the tone in which his stories could unfold and hit home. There was nothing more moving in the world of the Cuban missile crisis and CND than to listen to Dylan singing 'Masters of War' and 'Hard Rain'. He quickly became a spokesman for a generation of students and activists.

It was in this period (1961–4) that Dylan became the hero of the folk set and the radicals, but in the wider world of pop music his songs were known only in the versions of others, notably those of Peter, Paul and Mary. All that changed for two reasons. First, his typecasting as a radical guru began to irritate him, and the irritation showed in his songs, notably on the fourth album, *Another Side Of Bob Dylan* (1964). The seminal track, 'My Back Pages', found Dylan railing against 'the lies that life is black and white' and commenting on his earlier firm commitment that 'I was so much older then, I'm younger than that now'. Second, and more important, was the revolution in British pop around 1963 and 1964. Dylan reportedly 'jumped out of his car seat' when he first heard the Animals singing his version of the traditional 'House of the Rising Sun' because of the sheer brashness of the adaptation. It opened his eyes to a new musical world, and made him realize that it was possible to express his love for Chuck Berry and Woody Guthrie at the same time. His next album was called *Bringing It All Back Home*, a subtle reference to his admiration for the way in which the British artists had revived his own interest in American rock'n'roll. One side of the album was devoted to rock songs, with a Rolling Stones riff on every other one of them. 'I have given up the struggle for perfection', he acidly noted on the sleeve, and his music leapt along joyously and uninhibitedly, romping through 'Subterranean Homesick Blues', a direct descendant of Chuck Berry's 'Too Much Monkey Business'.

Dylan's switch in direction had caused a few missed heartbeats among his erstwhile followers, but at least the album had another side to it, which included 'Mr Tambourine Man' and the almost political 'It's All Right, Ma'. But the concerts he gave during 1965–6, beginning with his performance with the Paul Butterfield Blues Band at the Newport Folk Festival, divided his audience dramatically, and Dylan became a rock idol virtually by default, the success of 'Like A Rolling Stone' – it reached No. 2 in 1965 – more than compensating for the lost purist folk audience. The albums of this period – *Highway 61 Revisited* and the double *Blonde On Blonde* – represent the pinnacle of Bob Dylan's recording career. The musicians he worked with – Al Kooper, Robbie Robertson and Nashville sidemen like Charlie McCoy and Kenny Buttrey – were perfect choices to carry through the fusion of the various styles Dylan had absorbed over the years. Musically, the songs were still constructed simply, using well-worn chord sequences, but they were often longer, more flowing and with Kooper's lush organ sound the effect of, for instance, 'Queen Jane Approximately' and 'Like A Rolling Stone', was magisterial. And Dylan's lyrics were still centrally important, though now linear coherence had collapsed before the rush of rich, myriad images. Their landscape was now an interior one, with the power and special logic of dreams. Sometimes ('Tombstone Blues', 'Desolation Row') they were peopled with historical figures in strange conjunctions, elsewhere they were intensely lyrical with archetypal images from blues or country music transformed in Dylan's intense inner visions of the urban nightmare ('Visions Of Johanna' and the twelve-minute 'Sad Eyed Lady Of The Lowlands'). And Dylan's zany, deadpan humour was still in evidence on 'Rainy Day Women' and 'Leopard Skin Pill Box Hat'.

Dylan's own lifestyle was accurately reflected in the kaleidoscopic chaos of the songs he was writing, and he seemed to be driving himself onwards at a terrifying pace (*Highway 61* and *Blonde On Blonde* – three albums in all – were released in the space of a few months). 'He'll be a legend,' said Pete Seeger, 'if he doesn't blow up first', and the sense of impending implosion was especially strong in the cathartic performances of his 1966 tour with the Hawks (later to become The Band).

In August, 1966 Dylan's career was abruptly interrupted by a motorcycle smash and he vanished from public view for two years. His presence, though, was everywhere, from the posters in every head shop to constant press rumours of his imminent return and bootleg recordings of concerts, like the famous 1965 Albert Hall show in London, were distributed widely, filling the gap in his official releases. Paradoxically, his silence caused his mystique to grow and Dylanologists of varying degrees of credulity and sanity flourished. For a period during 1967 Dylan lived in Woodstock with The Band – his 1965–6 touring group – and his musical development continued in this secluded atmosphere. The recordings made at this time (which soon became available in bootleg form) were tortured probings into Dylan's post-King of Rock and Roll mind. Some songs were hilariously funny drunken ravings ('Please Mrs Henry', 'Million Dollar Bash'), but the overall mood, set by the more sombre of the numbers, was penitent and full of an ominous sense of foreboding. On 'Tears of Rage' and 'Too Much of Nothing' he seemed to feel overwhelmingly guilty for his past and sorry for those he had – admittedly unwittingly – led. On 'I Shall Be Released' and 'Wheel's On Fire', he seemed aware, vaguely and subconsciously, of an imminent explosion which might or might not be a kind of liberation. The songs prove an unnerving experience to listen to, but on the simple emotional level they are the most personal and moving of all of Dylan's songs. There is none of the detachment which characterizes most of his previously issued work, none of the confidence and none of the arrogance – he sings them ·

122

plaintively and rawly, occasionally aided by Richard Manuel's harmony lines. *The Basement Tapes*, the title given to the bootleg album which contains all of his tracks recorded with The Band in 1967, is the most atmospheric and the most direct Dylan album. And if *Sergeant Pepper* and *Blonde On Blonde* are the finest celebrations of the optimism of the new Sixties counter-culture, *The Basement Tapes* is the crucial expression of the other side of that optimism. In that respect it must rank as the forerunner of a whole series of major Seventies records which have eschewed utopian statements in favour of explorations of the prevailing nightmare. Finally, in 1975, the tapes were officially released on Columbia, eight years after they were made.

Dylan presented a new stance to the public at large with the release of *John Wesley Harding* in 1968. In marked contrast to the prevailing trend toward complexity (musical and lyrical), the songs were direct and simple ('The key', Dylan cryptically remarked in the sleeve note, 'is Frank'), and continued to explore themes of guilt and self-doubt. But the last two tracks, 'Down Along The Cove' and 'I'll Be Your Baby Tonight', pointed towards the mellower tone of the two country albums which followed, *Nashville Skyline* (1969) and *Self Portrait* (1970). These albums brought Dylan his first real critical attacks since the move into rock in 1965. He was accused of a retreat into the banality and sentimentality of country music, while *Self Portrait*, a double album of other people's songs, was said to be mere self-indulgence. In fact, this was yet another instance of the emergence of an early musical influence on Dylan: his friendship with Johnny Cash, who duetted with him on 'Girl From The North Country' on *Nashville Skyline*, dated from the early Sixties. The albums marked the beginning of an important rapprochement between rock and country music as many artists, from the Byrds to Joan Baez, followed him in recording in Nashville. They were, however, the last of Dylan's albums to have that pioneering effect. In the Seventies, he has played a minor role in the development of rock and his records have sometimes been diffuse and uneven. On *New Morning* (1970) and *Planet*

Waves (1973) he often sounded contrived and even hackneyed, often presenting the persona of a conventional family man far removed from the acute and acerbic love songs of earlier years. *Pat Garrett And Billy The Kid* (1973) was a soundtrack album containing one classic song ('Knocking On Heaven's Door'). *Blood On The Tracks* (1975), in contrast to the preceding albums of the Seventies, saw Dylan in a more questioning mood, with songs like the embittered 'Idiot Wind', the cryptic 'Lily Rosemary, And The Jack Of Hearts', and the deceptively gentle 'A Simple Twist Of Fate'. A similar feeling was evident on 'Hurricane' (1975), the story of Reuben Carter's wrongful imprisonment.

Dylan was still receiving the kind of attention he had attracted in the previous decade. His fragmentary, surrealistic novel, *Tarantula*, was published in 1971, he played a cameo role in Sam Peckinpah's *Pat Garrett* movie and his few public appearances (the Bangladesh concert, the Woody Guthrie memorial event) foreshadowed the enormous response to his 1974 American tour with The Band. Over six million applications were made for tickets, and the resulting live album, *Before The Flood*, found both Dylan and The Band returning to their greatest songs of earlier years in a powerful way. That record and *Planet Waves* appeared on Asylum (Island in Britain), the label to which Dylan had moved when his Columbia contract ran out. The relationship with Columbia had been stormy, particularly after the two-year lay-off and the emergence of the brash Clive Davis as chief executive. He seemed to personify the image of the corporate music business, while David Geffen of Asylum had apparently grown with his artists. Columbia then released the appalling *Dylan* (1974), a cynical collection of outtakes, of interest only to the (many) Dylan fanatics. In the event, the relatively low sales of *Planet Waves* led in 1974 to a re-signing with Columbia for a further five-year period.

The mid-Seventies found Dylan presenting himself as a musician among his peers on the Rolling Thunder Tour (with Joan Baez and others), but inevitably bedevilled by rumour and the intense scrutiny of Dylanologists like the indefatigable A. J. Weberman, always ready with accusations of pro-Israeli sympathies or 'revelations' about his private life. This was perhaps inevitable because his recorded output from *Bob Dylan* in 1961 to *Nashville Skyline* in 1970 represented the work of the greatest individual rock talent of the decade. In one stunning period during 1965, the charts were topped by a succession of records directly bearing the Dylan trademark: 'Mr Tambourine Man' by the Byrds, 'Satisfaction' by the Rolling Stones, 'I Got You Babe' by Sonny and Cher, 'Help' by the Beatles and 'Eve Of Destruction' by Barry McGuire. Without Dylan, the Sixties would have taken a different route: there would have been no *Sergeant Pepper*, no *Beggar's Banquet*, no *Music From Big Pink*. That was the level of his impact. It did much to mould the sensibility of a whole generation in industrialized countries, and to understand the Sixties no future chronicler will be able to ignore the music of Bob Dylan.

The Easybeats – George Young (born Nov. 6, 1947), Gordon Fleet (Aug. 16, 1945), Dick Diamonde (Dec. 28, 1947), Harry Vanda (March 22, 1947) and Little Stevie Wright (Dec. 20, 1948), all the sons of parents who later emigrated to Australia – were the top local group in Australia by mid-1966, having had four chart-toppers in less than a year. That summer, they went to Britain to record 'Friday On My Mind' and conquer the world. Written by Young, the rhythm guitarist, and Vanda, the group's singer, it was a worldwide hit, reaching No. 6 in Britain, No. 16 in America and No. 1 in Australia – for eight weeks!

Failure to match the success of that single – still one of the best-ever expressions of teenage frustration with the nine-to-five routine – caused them to change their style in an attempt to accommodate new audiences. Their album *Vigil* (United Artists) was accordingly a curious mixture of easy-listening type songs like 'Can't Take My Eyes Off You', material like 'Hit The Road Jack' and pseudo-psychedelic songs such as 'We All Live Happily Together'. Two tracks taken from that album, however, did become minor hits in Britain – 'The Music Goes Round My Head' and 'Hello, How Are You' – and a further record, 'St Louis'

(Rare Earth) was a very small hit in America in 1969. The band broke up in 1970 when Vanda and Young left to form their own group, first Band of Hope, and then the Marcus-Hook Roll Band in 1972 which released one fine, unsuccessful single, 'Natural Man' (Regal-Zonophone) before they finally called it a day, returning to Australia to work as producers.

Donnie Elbert, whose distinctive – and influential – use of falsetto took 'What Can I Do' into the lower reaches of the Hot Hundred on DeLuxe in 1957, has recorded for many labels. They include Vee Jay, Red Top, Jalynne, Cub, Parkway, Checker, Gateway (songs like 'A Little Piece of Leather' were popular in London clubs), Atco and, in Britain, New Wave and CBS. On his return to America, Elbert reached the Top Twenty with 'I Can't Get Over Losing You', on Rare Bullet, in 1970. A disco revival of the Supremes' 'Where Did Our Love Go' (recorded in London in 1969 but turned down by various record companies) was a Top Ten hit on All Platinum in 1971. More recently, Elbert has recorded for Avco.

Electric Flag was to be an 'American Music Band': Mike Bloomfield, the great white hope of the blues guitar; Nick (the Greek) Gravenites, the gifted Chicago singer-composer; Buddy Miles, the behemoth black soul drummer; and a full horn section. Their Stax-styled soul and South Side Chicago blues, seasoned with a dash of psychedelia and electronics, was brash and flashy, thunder and lightning.

Their debut before an uncritical audience at the Monterey Pop Festival in 1967 was widely acclaimed, as were subsequent live appearances. Inexplicably, their first LP (*A Long Time Comin'* on Columbia) earned only mild praise from critics, but it certainly justified the Flag's tremendous reputation. A victim of hard drugs and clashing egos, the band disintegrated almost as quickly as it had burst on to the scene; a second album by a Miles-led Flag was a pale shadow of the first, and that was it until a spotty 1974 re-union LP for Atlantic.

The Electric Prunes (Jim Lowe, Ken Williams, Mark Tulin, Preston Ritter, and 'Weasel') recorded in Los Angeles from 1965 to 1969. Their No. 11 hit, 'I Had Too Much To Dream (Last Night)' (Reprise, 1966), was a minor punk-rock classic, chiefly because of Dave Hassinger's production gimmickry. He took advantage of the latest technological advances in fuzz and reverb to create a sound that was 'freaky' without being too blatantly underground. They had one follow-up hit, 'Get Me To The World On Time' but kept recording for several years, producing two of the first 'concept' albums, *Mass in F Minor* and *Release of an Oath* (Reprise), both written and arranged by David Axelrod. By their fifth and final album, *Just Good Old Rock and Roll* (Reprise, 1968) none of the original members remained in the group.

Elektra Records. The Elektra Record Company, one of the most respected labels for musical tastes and policy throughout the Sixties, was founded in October, 1950 by Jac Holzman with an initial budget of $600. The company grew from Holzman's twin fascinations with engineering and music, and was originally run from his dormitory at St John's College in New York State.

For the first five years of its existence, Elektra released around thirty obscure albums catering to minority tastes. But, in 1955, a turning point occurred when Josh White, a folk blues singer, and Theodore Bikel, a purveyor of multilingual folk songs who later featured in Frank Zappa's film, *200 Motels*, were signed to the label and gave the company some commercial appeal. At this time, budgetary restrictions confined Elektra to recording folk singers, as recording costs for such artists were very limited, and among other early artists on the label were Oscar Brand, Ed McCurdy and Bob Gibson. The earliest Elektra artist who remains significant in the Seventies is Judy Collins, who was signed to the label in the early Sixties. Other familiar folk singers of the time who started their careers on Elektra include Tom Paxton and Phil Ochs, who were quick to follow the lead established by Bob Dylan. Holzman's desire to extend the breadth of Elektra's catalogue led to a number of 'project' albums, and among the artists who contributed tracks to such a collection as *The Blues Project* were Dave Van Ronk, Geoff Muldaur, Eric Von Schmidt and Koerner, Ray and Glover, the last named of which produced the first white blues-type albums for Elektra. The pianist on Von Schmidt's tracks was Bob Dylan, working under the alias of Bob Landy. Others in the 'project' series included such latter-day artists as Peter Rowan, Richard Greene, David Blue and Richard Fariña, while an intended 'Electric Guitar Project', which was finally released as *What's Shakin'*, featured Paul Butterfield, Mike Bloomfield, the Lovin' Spoonful, Eric Clapton, Stevie Winwood, Tom Rush and Al Kooper.

Paul Butterfield was the first fully electric artist to sign to the label, and after the success enjoyed by the Butterfield band, a near-miss at signing the Lovin' Spoonful, and a couple of early tracks with the Byrds, Holzman entered the field of rock. Signings included Love, the Doors, Tim Buckley, Tom Rush, Clear Light, Earth Opera, the Dillards, Lonnie Mack, Fred Neil, the Incredible String Band, the Stooges, the MC5, Nico, David Ackles, and Rhinoceros, who are all either famous in their own right, or whose members subsequently formed part of such bands as Crosby, Stills and Nash, the Mothers of Invention and Sea Train. Later signings, such as the New Seekers, together with a flock of English material purchased for America, tended to subvert the label's image 'quality', but more recently artists like Carly Simon, Mickey Newbury, Harry Chapin and Bread have gone some way towards restoring that image.

In August, 1973, Jac Holzman was appointed senior vice-president of Warner Communications Inc., and relinquished his post as president of the record company which he had single-handedly built during its 23-year history, handing over his duties to David Geffen, who merged Elektra with his own company, Asylum Records, under the corporate banner of Warner Communications.

The Elgins had a series of small hits during 1966: 'Put Yourself In My Place', 'Darling Baby' and 'Heaven Must Have Sent You'. Johnny Dawson, who had sung on records by the Emeralds (on the States label) and the Downbeats (Backbeat/Peacock) changed his group's name to the Elgins when they signed with Motown's VIP label. Besides Dawson, the group included Norman McClean, Cleotha Miller, Saundra Edwards and Robert Fleming. By the time 'Heaven Must Have Sent You' entered the British Top Ten in 1971, their main lead singer, Edwards, had been replaced by Yvonne Allen, previously lead vocalist with the Donays, whose 'Devil In Her Heart' had earlier been revived by the Beatles.

Jack Elliott, a colourful archetype of the American folksong rambler 'citybilly', was born in Brooklyn in 1931. He so thoroughly absorbed rural speech, manners and performing styles that he typified the American Everyman from Everywhere. As a teenager, he became Woody Guthrie's friend, disciple, travelling companion and interpreter. Guthrie once said of him: 'Jack Elliott sounds more like me than I do.' While mostly identified with the Guthrie songbag, wit and lifestyle, Elliott also mastered the idioms of Jimmie Rodgers and Hank Williams. An important influence on Dylan, perhaps his most successful recording, apart from the Guthrie material, was Jesse Fuller's 'San Francisco Bay Blues'. Working in England and France in the late Fifties, Elliott introduced American folk and country and western music to a vast European following. His audiences on both sides of the Atlantic also rollicked in his Will Rogers-style folksy anecdotage and corn-fed humour. A major interpreter of warmth, charm and undeniable musical identification with the silent greats.

Shirley Ellis, born in New York in 1941, was managed by her husband, Lincoln Chase, composer of several rock'n'roll

129

standards including 'Such A Night' for the Drifters and 'Jim Dandy' for Lavern Baker. His own career as a singer with records on Decca, Liberty, Splash, Dawn, Columbia, RCA-Victor and Swan, ceased when he married Shirley Ellis. Chase composed three soul-flavoured nursery-rhyme novelty numbers for her – 'The Nitty Gritty', 'The Name Game' and 'The Clapping Song'. All reached the Top Twenty on Congress during 1963–5. Despite smaller hits for Congress and Columbia (including 'Soul Time' in 1967) she has since retired.

Lorraine Ellison recorded for Gee and with the Ellison Singers for Savoy's gospel label, Sharp, before her first minor R&B hit, 'I Dig You Baby' on Mercury in 1965. A contract with Warner Bros./Loma led to the Jerry Ragavoy production of 'Stay With Me'. Nothing else on her three Warner Bros. albums had anything like the almost neurotic depth of emotion on this piece of deep soul. Critics and R&B buffs adored it, but the single only just made the Top Sixty in 1966. 'Heart Be Still', written by Ragavoy and Bert Berns, also entered the charts, while Ellison's compositions with Sam Bell of the Enchanters have been recorded by numerous Philadelphia-based soul singers, including Howard Tate, Garnet Mimms and Linda Jones.

Brian Epstein, born on Sept. 19, 1934, was the son of a Liverpool department store owner. After a year's National Service in the Army (he was discharged as mentally and emotionally unfit), Epstein spent a year at the Royal Academy of Dramatic Art in London. He returned to Liverpool in 1957 to take charge of the record department of the family store, North End Music Stores (NEMS), where he surprised himself and everybody else by being a great success. He prided himself on following up customers' enquiries, which included a request for 'My Bonnie' by the Beatles, on Oct. 28, 1961 – the date is recorded faithfully in Epstein's autobiography, *A Cellar Full Of Noise* (1964).

In search of the record, he discovered that the group were playing at the nearby Cavern Club where he watched their act several times. Despite warnings about their unreliability from Alan Williams, the group's ex-manager, Epstein signed them to a contract. He was attracted by their 'very considerable magnetism' which reawakened his own creative yearnings. Epstein's percentage as manager was 25, and by the middle of 1962 he had signed them for recording to EMI's Parlophone label, under the supervision of George Martin.

After the Beatles' meteoric success, NEMS Enterprises (Epstein's management company) signed other Liverpool acts: Gerry and the Pacemakers, Billy J. Kramer and the Dakotas, the Big Three, Cilla Black and Tommy Quickly, of whom only Gerry Marsden and Cilla lasted as major artists beyond the beat boom itself. Epstein devoted himself primarily to the Beatles, however. He cajoled them into stage suits and their mop-top image; he manoeuvred drummer Pete Best out and Ringo in; he masterminded their tours, where his attention to detail and protectiveness was most called for. But by August, 1966, the group themselves were tired of the show business aura Epstein had done so much to create around them. They ceased touring and he found himself redundant. He took some interest in the pop-folk group, Cyrkle, and in American folk singer Eric Andersen, but was hard hit by the growing distance between his original protégés (especially Lennon) and himself. On Aug. 27, 1967, when the Beatles were meditating with the Maharishi Mahesh Yogi in Wales, Brian Epstein died, alone, in his London flat from an overdose of sleeping pills. The coroner's verdict was accidental death.

The Equals, whose reputation rests almost entirely on the success of 'Baby Come Back' (President), a European million-seller and British No. 1 in 1968, had originally recorded the song in late 1966 as a B-side. Although they had only two more hits over the next three years, the original personnel – the twins, Dervin and Lincoln Gordon, vocals and guitar respectively (born June 29, 1948); Eddie Grant, lead guitar (March 5, 1948); Pat Lloyd, guitar (March 17, 1948); and John Hall, drums (Oct. 25, 1947) – stayed together until Grant left to pursue a solo career in 1971. His replacement,

131

Jimmy Haynes, was in turn replaced by Dave Martin in mid-1973. Neil McBain took over from Hall early in 1975.

Betty Everett, born in Mississippi in 1939, recorded unsuccessfully for Chicago labels Cobra, One-derful, and C.J. before scoring national hits on Vee Jay with catchy pop songs – 'You're No Good' (1963), 'It's In His Kiss (The Shoop Shoop Song)', 'Getting Mighty Crowded' (1964), and a romantic duet with Jerry Butler, 'Let It Be Me'. After the company's collapse and an inauspicious year with ABC-Paramount, she surfaced with 'There'll Come A Time' (1968) and others on UNI, and has remained a consistent name in the soul charts, recording for Fantasy since 1970.

The Exciters – Brenda Reid, Carol Johnson, Lillian Walker, and Herb Rooney from Jamaica, New York – first recorded for United Artists in 1962. Leiber and Stoller's production and Teacho Wilshire's arrangements employed the ethereal strings, marimba and tom-tom *baion* beat of earlier Drifters records. The potent, soulful songs were supplied by Bert Berns, Van McCoy and Burt Bacharach and included 'Tell Him' (a 1962 Top Ten hit), 'He's Got The Power', 'Get Him' and 'Do Wah Diddy', covered in Britain by Manfred Mann. The Exciters had smaller hits with 'I Want You To Be My Baby' (on Roulette in 1965), 'A Little Bit Of Soap' (Bang, 1966) and 'You Don't Know What You're Missing' (RCA, 1969). After other records on the Today label, Johnson and Walker were replaced by Ronnie Pace and Skip McPhee.

John Fahey, the noted folk/blues/classical guitarist, was born on Feb. 28, 1939, and grew up at Takoma Park, Maryland. He learnt guitar at 13, inspired by the records of Blind Willie Johnson and other blues guitarists and later went on to study folklore and mythology. This led to his rediscovering such major bluesmen as Bukka White, Skip James and Charley Patton – about whom he wrote a book, *Charley Patton*. Interestingly, Canned Heat came together through mutual acquaintance with Fahey. At the same time he set up his own unpredictable record label, Takoma Records, which released a variety of ethnic albums, including some by Fahey himself. In 1967, he signed with Vanguard, cutting one album a year until he quit the company in 1969 and signed with Reprise. However, his best albums came from the early Takoma period, the most famous being *The Transfiguration Of Blind Joe Death*. He recorded two albums for Reprise, *Of Rivers And Religion* and *After The Ball*, both combining acoustic guitar pieces with instrumentally augmented ventures into vintage Dixieland. Well received by critics, they didn't sell in any vast amounts and sales-hungry Reprise dropped Fahey in 1974.

Fairport Convention are best known as the first exponents of British folk-rock, though during the various line-ups (at least nine in as many years) the band has veered through American West Coast music to the highly original songs of Richard Thompson and Sandy Denny (born on Jan. 16, 1947). The original Fairport band was formed in 1967, played Dylanish, Byrdish, Butterfieldish material in London's 'underground' clubs, and gloried in being the scruffiest outfit in town. The founding line-up was Richard Thompson, Simon Nicol (guitars), Ashley Hutchings (bass), Martin Lamble (drums) and Judy Dyble – later augmented with Ian Matthews as additional singer.

Only with the arrival of Sandy Denny from the folk-club scene after Dyble's departure did a British traditional element creep in : 'Nottamun Town' and 'She Moves Through The Fair' on their second album, *What We Did On Our Holidays* (Island, 1969), were the first-ever British folk-rock tracks. Denny's exquisite voice and the discreet muted backing ensured they were a success. Two albums later, with *Liege and Lief*, the band concentrated on what they called a 'folk-rock project'. By now the line-up had changed again : Lamble had been killed when the band's van crashed and Dave Mattacks had taken over on drums; Matthews had left, and one of the folk scene's finest instrumentalists, fiddler Dave Swarbrick (born April 5, 1941) had joined. *Liege and Lief* (1969) was a milestone, for the Fairports now used all-out amplification, with long instrumental workouts, on lengthy narrative ballads. The music was loud, electric and exciting, yet the narratives and the strong folk melodies still came across. Inevitably for the Fairports, more splits followed. Sandy left for a solo career, and Ashley left to found Steeleye Span, Dave Pegg (born Nov. 2, 1947) taking his place on bass. The band was still excellent, thanks largely to Richard Thompson's guitar work, and the musical approach began to veer away from folk to include more of his songs. After *Full House* (1970), Thompson left and the band began to lose its musical direction. A folk-rock 'concept album', *John Babbacombe Lee* (1971), was a partial success but lacked musical guts. The decline continued with Simon Nicol's departure, and reached rock-bottom with *Rosie*. From 1973 onwards, after yet more changes in personnel, the band began to regain the old excitement. When Sandy Denny rejoined in 1974 it was clear that the Fairports could again be a major force in British rock. By now they had progressed to a very varied musical format, with Sandy's fine, moody ballads interspersed with Swarbrick's fiddle jigs, traditional songs, and new material from the rest of the band, as exemplified on the fine *Rising For The Moon* (1975).The line-up in the summer of 1975 was Sandy Denny (vocals, piano); her husband, Trevor Lucas (vocals, guitar, born Dec. 25, 1943); Jerry Donahue (guitar, born Sept. 24, 1946); Dave Swarbrick (vocals, fiddle, mandolin), and Dave Pegg (bass). After Dave Mattacks' departure, Bruce Rowland joined as drummer.

Marianne Faithfull, born in Hampstead, London, in 1946, was an ex-convent schoolgirl discovered by Andrew Oldham at a party. He asked her to record a Jagger–Richard composition, 'As Tears Go By'. Her plaintive, cultured folky tones made a refreshing change in 1964, and the record (plus three follow-ups) made the charts. She then absented herself to have a baby. In 1967 her notorious affair with Mick Jagger tarnished her pure image, but initially furthered her new career as an actress. She appeared in Chekhov and several films, but after her break with Jagger, her personal life was disrupted by drug problems. Eventually she recovered to make occasional appearances on the London stage.

Georgie Fame was the professional name given to Clive Powell, born in Leigh, Lancashire, on June 26, 1943, by impresario Larry Parnes when he led Billy Fury's backing group, the Blue Flames. The group – Fame (piano), Colin Green (guitar), Tex Makins (bass) and Red Reece (drums) – stuck together after leaving Fury and made their first appearance at London's Flamingo Club on a Sunday afternoon session early in 1962.

Augmented by a tenor saxophone (first Al Watson, then Mick Eve), the Blue Flames were given a residency at the Club's Saturday all-nighter session. John McLaughlin replaced Green that summer and, in November, Fame radically altered the group's sound when he bought a Hammond organ and Leslie speakers. However, the biggest change in the Blue Flames' music was prompted by the club's predominantly black audience – a mixture of American GIs on weekend leave and West Indians – who introduced Fame to his major influence, Mose Allison, and the beginnings of soul and ska. Green returned in place of McLaughlin and the line-up was expanded to include John Marshall (baritone sax), Eddie Thornton (trumpet), Cliff Barton (bass) and Speedy Acquaye (congas), although personnel changed frequently. Apart from two instrumental singles for the small independent R&B label, Fame's first release was a live album, *Rhythm And Blues At The Flamingo* (British Columbia, 1964), and he recorded a second before 'Yeh Ych' made No. 1 in January, 1965. Subsequent hits launched him on a solo career and allowed him to achieve his ambition to sing with big bands. He broke up the Blue Flames in September, 1966 (drummer Mitch Mitchell joined Jimi Hendrix), recorded *Sound Venture* (Columbia, 1966) with the Harry South Band, won jazz polls, and the following year appeared at the Albert Hall with Count Basie. His biggest hit, 'The Ballad Of Bonnie And Clyde', marked the nadir of his artistic career at the end of 1967. He later partnered Alan

Price, mainly for television and cabaret work, but the sum of their talents proved less fruitful than the parts. In 1974, he re-formed a large and unwieldy Blue Flames and recorded *Georgie Fame* (Island).

Richard and Mimi Fariña were a singer-songwriter couple who irradiated the mid-Sixties with distinctive, gentle folk-rock songs of love and social commentary. Born in 1937, Richard married Mimi (born 1945), Joan Baez's sister, in 1963 in Paris. Richard was emerging as a promising novelist (*Been Down So Long It Looks Like Up To Me*) and songwriter when he was killed in a motorcycle accident near Carmel, California, on April 30, 1966, on his wife's 21st birthday. Mimi has since been an actress, solo singer and songwriter.

Fariña, of Irish-Cuban descent, played dulcimer; his wife played guitar and both sang in warm harmony. They attracted national attention at the 1965 Newport Folk Festival, playing in the rain to a mesmerized audience. While very much derivative of Dylan and Joan Baez, the duo established a new quality of swinging folk-rock that was 'pure' enough to appeal to traditionalists. Their approach towards topical material was fresh and without clichés. Three albums were issued by Vanguard, *Celebration For A Grey Day*, *Reflections In A Crystal Wind* (1965) and *Memories* (1968). Better known songs include 'Pack Up All Your Sorrows', 'Hard-Lovin' Loser', 'House Un-American Blues Activities Dream'.

Chris Farlowe, born John Deighton in London on Oct. 13, 1940, began his career as teenage leader of the John Henry Skiffle Group which won the All-England Skiffle Championship. As Chris Farlowe he fronted the Thunderbirds, whose personnel included Albert Lee (guitar) and Dave Greenslade (organ), singing rock'n'roll and – by 1962 – a brand of R&B that landed them a residency at London's Flamingo Club.

Prior to the patronage of Mick Jagger and Keith Richard, which brought him a No. 1 international hit in the summer of 1966 with 'Out Of Time' (Immediate), he had no chart success though he recorded two cult singles, the mods' anthem, 'Buzz With The Fuzz' (Columbia, 1965) and a version of 'Stormy Monday Blues' (Sue, 1965) as Little Joe Cook which fooled some British blues enthusiasts into thinking he was black. The hit changed his style, pulled him out of the clubs where his following was strongest, and led to the break-up of the Thunderbirds. He reorganized the group as a trio with Lee, Pete Shelley and Carl Palmer in 1967 and kept them together for a year. Later, he rejoined Greenslade in Colosseum, and three months after the band's split in November, 1971, joined Atomic Rooster. He temporarily quit rock in 1973 to pursue his business interest in Nazi memorabilia. He has never been able to find a satisfactory showcase for his powerful, bluesy voice and informal style outside of the Thunderbirds and the London R&B club circuit of the mid-Sixties. Accordingly, when he returned to performing in 1975 it was as part of a band (which included Albert Lee), and his first album was a live recording, *The Chris Farlowe Band, Live* (Polydor).

Wes Farrell, born in New York in 1940, has been one of the most successful backroom boys in American pop in the Sixties and Seventies. His association in the late Fifties with R&B producer Luther Dixon and with Bert Berns led to several co-written compositions for soul artists, notably the Shirelles. He joined Roosevelt Music in 1961, hiring then unknown writers like Neil Diamond and the Feldman-Goldstein-Gottehrer team.

By 1963, Farrell's own songs, including 'Come A Little Bit Closer' (Jay and the Americans), and two with Bert Berns – 'Goodbye Baby' (Solomon Burke) and 'My Girl Sloopy' (the Vibrations) – were reaching the charts. 'Sloopy' became a Cuban-soul standard with other hit versions by Little Caesar and the Consuls, the McCoys (as 'Hang On Sloopy') and Ramsey Lewis. By 1967 Farrell's publishing organization was cleaning up in the bubblegum/teenybop field. The Cowsills, Beacon Street Union, Brooklyn Bridge and Every Mother's Son were among the groups whose discs he produced and leased to big labels, particularly MGM. He

137

was also the creator of the Partridge Family and his Chelsea and Roxbury labels (formed in 1972) have had a number of disco hits.

José Feliciano, blind since his birth, born on Sept. 10, 1945, in Puerto Rico, grew up in New York's Harlem. Always fascinated by music, at 18 he dropped out for a life in Greenwich Village coffee houses like the Café Id. His residency there led to an RCA contract, a single 'Everybody Do The Click' and album *The Voice And Guitar Of José Feliciano* in 1964. He showed a diversity of style – rock'n'roll, R&B and native Latin influences. Spanish language recordings propelled him to spectacular success in Central and South América and later in America and Europe with 'Light My Fire', 'California Dreamin'' and the *Feliciano* album in 1968. The originality and freshness of his arrangements and interpretations have lost their impact through years of repetition of a tried formula. He has a natural warmth of performance, but his work in the Seventies, even *Compartments* (1972) with Steve Cropper, remains trite.

Festivals. They were an established part of the jazz and folk worlds long before the first rock festival, at Monterey, in 1967. The annual events at Newport, Rhode Island, were the most prestigious concerts for jazz musicians and folk singers in America. A similar festival in Britain, organized by the National Jazz Federation, became a platform for the new R&B and rock groups of the mid-Sixties and saw the Yardbirds and the Who amongst others, performing alongside jazz musicians.

Monterey was set up by Los Angeles music mogul, Lou Adler, with two musicians, Paul Simon and the Mamas and Papas' John Phillips. Its purpose was to present the 'new music' of the mid-Sixties in an appropriate setting. Its immediate inspiration came from the open-air concerts in San Francisco, notably the famous Human Be-In of January, 1967. Featuring Jimi Hendrix, the Who, Janis Joplin, Jefferson Airplane, Otis Redding, Ravi Shankar and others, Monterey set the pattern for what was to follow, not least in the fact that it was both filmed and recorded, though the live album didn't appear.

During the next three years about 30 festivals were held in America, attended by an estimated 2½ million people. Woodstock's 450,000 attendance was not exceeded until 1973, when 600,000 turned up at Watkins Glen, Indiana, to hear the Allman Brothers, The Band and the Grateful Dead. But that was only a one-day event, unlike the major festivals of the Sixties when most of the audience would camp out for up to a week.

A hippie mystique developed around the rock festivals, and anthems were written about them by Joni Mitchell and Eric Burdon. They were, it was said, the prototype communities of a new society, evidence that 'we' were going to spread the gospel of peace and love all over the nation. It was true that many festival-goers had to practise self-help over food, shelter and sanitary facilities since, in most cases, the provision made by the organizers was hopelessly inadequate. Yet the audiences were also at the mercy of the elements, and baking sun or torrential rain could make a festival site bear more than a passing resemblance to a refugee camp.

There were also large sums of money involved. Festivals were a promoter's dream, since they could accommodate ten times the audience of the largest hall. And even if only a minority of those attending actually paid to get in (as was often the case), there was always the future income from film and record rights. The promoters of Woodstock, for instance, sold $1.4 million worth of tickets, and paid the artists a total of $150,000, according to an investigation by *Variety* magazine. Even though the cost of preparing the site was massive, the profit margin was undoubtedly enormous.

The festival boom died down with the arrival of the Seventies. Promoters were increasingly harried by authorities worried about civil disorder and radicals who felt festivals should be free and tried to make them so – like those at the Isle of Wight Festival in 1970 (starring Dylan and The Band) who occupied a hill overlooking the stage. Also, the philosophy which had fuelled the major events had suffered a fatal blow at the Altamont Raceway in 1969, when a young black was knifed by Hell's Angels in front of the stage on which the Rolling Stones were performing. However, festivals spawned a new PA technology which led to regular concerts by superstars in outdoor (usually sports) arenas to audiences far bigger than any auditorium could hold, thereby permanently removing successful artists from relatively 'intimate' concert halls.

The Fifth Dimension were spawned in Los Angeles where Florence LaRue Gordon and Marilyn McCoo were born in 1943 and 1944 respectively. The three male members – Billy Davis Jr., Lamont McLemor (born 1939) and Ron Townson (born 1933) came from Louisiana. First known as the Versatiles, then the HiFis, they were touring as part of the Ray Charles Revue when they met manager Mark Gordon, who signed them to Johnny Rivers' Soul City Records. They adopted their now familiar name in 1967. Their novel, soul-flavoured harmony work, combined with the then unknown Jim Webb's songs and Bones Howe's arrangements and production, captured public imagination with 'Up, Up And Away' and polished albums like *Magic Garden* and *Stoned Soul Picnic*. After 'Aquarius' in 1970, they became increasingly soulless, sophisticated and slick. The showbiz rot had set in and with it came an end to their excitement and exuberance.

Wild Man (Larry) Fischer was a common fixture on Los Angeles' Sunset Strip from 1965 on. Born in 1945 he was a freak among freaks, known for his unique approach to panhandling: in return for a nickel or a dime, he'd make up and sing you a song on the spot, usually a free-association wonder based on some old Fifties standard. A genuine kook, he fell in with Frank Zappa and the GTOs (Girls Together Outrageously), and cut an album of his songs, *An Evening With Wild Man Fischer* (Bizarre, 1969), under Zappa's direction. Since then he's had a loyal cult following, and he spends his time wandering around the country singing for them. His first record in six years was a 1975 single which promotes a Los Angeles record store.

Fleetwood Mac, originally Peter Green's Fleetwood Mac, played its first engagement on Aug. 12; 1967, as part of the National Jazz and Blues Festival. As a result of their appearance, they were signed to a recording contract with Blue Horizon records. Fleetwood Mac then consisted of Peter Green, vocals/guitar (born Oct. 29, 1946); Jeremy Spencer, vocals/slide guitar (July 4, 1948); John McVie, bass (Nov. 26, 1945); and Mick Fleetwood, drums (June 24, 1947). *Fleetwood Mac* (Blue Horizon, 1968) reached No. 1 and stayed in the charts for almost thirteen months. This was followed by 'Black Magic Woman' and the bluesy 'I Need Your Love So Bad', both of which were minor British hits.

Shortly after, Peter Green's friend, guitarist Danny Kirwan (born May 13, 1950), was recruited into the Fleetwood Mac line-up. A month later the band cut their million-selling single, 'Albatross' – a British Top Five hit again when it was re-released in 1973. In August, 1969, Fleetwood Mac signed with Reprise, continuing their hit formula with 'Oh Well' and 'The Green Manalishi' in addition to two top-selling albums, *Mr Wonderful* and *Then Play On.* After 'The Green Manalishi', Peter Green quit the band, and his place was taken by John McVie's wife, Christine Perfect, formerly of Chicken Shack. The band was now very much aware that they had to find a new direction without their former leader, and recorded several new songs for the hit album *Kiln House* (1970) and their passport to the States.

In February, 1971, while in America, Jeremy Spencer disappeared and was later found to have joined a Los Angeles religious cult, the Children Of God. Ironically, as California took Jeremy away, it also provided a replacement in guitarist Bob Welch. The group's next album, *Future Games* (1971), ushered in a new era. They had left behind the 12-bars that initially made their name, but the blues in its root form remained a major influence. In mid-1972 guitarist Bob Weston joined the band, creating a more complex overall sound. The subsequent *Penguin* and *Mystery To Me* (1973) involved further musical exploration. In 1973, the group decided to settle permanently in America – but without Weston. A year later they released *Heroes Are Hard To Find*, their first album made wholly in America, but by early 1975 had once again changed the line-up. Lead guitarist Bob Welch left the group to concentrate on production work, and was replaced by San Franciscans Lindsey Buckingham (vocals, guitar), and girl vocalist, Stevie Nicks, who previously worked as a duo. The group now spend all their time recording (*Fleetwood Mac*, 1975) and touring in the USA.

Eddie Floyd, born in Montgomery, Alabama on June 25, 1935, moved to Detroit in his teens, where he sang from 1956 with the Falcons, the vocal group whose impassioned gospel style anticipated soul music. He was the group's featured soloist on their Mercury records, but left in 1962 to pursue a solo career. He recorded for Lupine, Atlantic, Safice (a label he formed with Al Bell and Chester Simmons) and Stax, with whom he still records.

His first hit, 'Knock On Wood', topped the R&B charts and reached the national Top Thirty. It remains a discotheque classic. Other Memphis soul hits included 'Raise Your Hand', 'I Never Found A Girl', 'Bring It On Home To Me' (Top Twenty in 1968), 'I've Got To Have Your Love', 'Don't Tell Mama' and, in 1970, 'California Girl'. Floyd's own compositions have been recorded by Wilson Pickett, Otis Redding and Solomon Burke.

Folk Revival (America). The unparalleled revival of interest in folk music that began about 1958 in America involved considerably more than a change in music tastes. It was also a political and social movement, a search for an alternative culture, and the start of a 'back-to-the-country' movement that has still not run its course. 1958 marked the start of the revival, for in that year the Kingston Trio had a chart hit with the unlikeliest sort of song, 'Tom Dooley', a traditional murder ballad. But it caught the popular imagination and set out the twin directions the revival would take – on one hand, traditional music and performers were discovered and lionized, while on the other, an upsurge of city and college-based performers worked in folk style or neo-folk style. The folk revival brought into the popular mainstream of American music a different beat; music of earnest simplicity; meaningful lyrics; ancient story-songs and modern protest-topical commentaries.

An earlier major folk revival had happened during World War II, in the spirit of the New Deal and anti-Fascist populist movement. Two giants of that period, Leadbelly, the black Texas powerhouse, and Woody Guthrie, the white Oklahoma Dust Bowl bard, left a legacy that the post-1958 revival developed. The strongest link between the two revivals was Pete Seeger, who, with the Almanac Singers, the Weavers, and then on his own, is regarded as the 'father' of the folk revival. Several other older performers set the stage for the new revival, among them Harry Belafonte, Burl Ives and Josh White: sophisticated interpreters with roots out in the country. The success of the Kingstons sparked other group efforts. Among them were the Limeliters, Brothers Four, Chad Mitchell Trio, Tarriers, Rooftop Singers, and the Highwaymen. Shaped in the image of both the Kingstons and the Weavers were Peter, Paul and Mary, the dominant folk group of the 1960s.

Other new interpreters emerged: Odetta with her rich voice; Judy Collins and Joan Baez; Bob Gibson, Eric Weissberg and Billy Faier explored instrumental virtuosity; Dave Van Ronk, Eric Von Schmidt and John Hammond Jr., showed that white city boys could empathize with the blues. Jack Elliott kept Woody's style vibrant. Soon, it wasn't enough to do the songs of the country stylists, but the recordings and the rural performers themselves were rediscovered. City audiences marvelled at the blues of Robert Johnson, John Lee Hooker, Muddy Waters, Lightning Hopkins, Sonny Terry and Brownie McGhee, the Rev. Gary Davis and black songsters like Mississippi John Hurt and Mance Lipscomb. The white rural ballad tradition came alive again, too, unearthing great ballad-singers like Roscoe Holcomb, Frank Proffit, Horton Barker, Mother Maybelle

Carter, Sarah Ogan Gunning. The Citybilly trio, the New Lost City Ramblers, revived old string-band sounds, while a succession of able urban bands, like the Bluegrass Boys and the Charles River Valley Boys pointed in the direction of that virtuoso bluegrass style pioneered by Bill Monroe and such famous alumni as Earl Scruggs and Lester Flatt.

The settings for the great revival were many, but coffee-houses and campuses seemed especially suitable for folk song. Regional and college folk festivals abounded, while the annual Newport Folk Festivals became national extrava-ganzas, the meeting of the hip new with the dedicated old. Some folk festivals had a quasi-religious feel, invested with high purpose, brotherhood and ethical content, through and beyond the music. Recordings proliferated, on specialist labels like Folkways, Vanguard, Prestige, Elektra, but soon every major label also had its folk roster. When the music business got into the revival, there was a dilution of material, but a broadening of the audience. The TV hootenanny show, embattled and unbalanced, turned the revival for two years into a craze. Around 1964, the heat cooled as rock and the Beatles arrived, and Dylan and the Byrds explored folk-rock. But the revival had discovered great music and tradi-tions, and the rediscovery continued in myriad ways and with many voices.

Wayne Fontana, best remembered for his mid-Sixties hits with the Mindbenders, was born Glyn Ellis in Manchester in 1947. He started playing in a school skiffle group, the Velfins, later forming Wayne Fontana and the Mindbenders. Their first record issued in June, 1963 on Phillips' Fontana label, was a cover of Bo Diddley's 'Road Runner'. A year later, they scored their first chart success, hitting the No. 2 slot with Major Lance's 'Um Um Um Um Um Um'. But it was the subsequent 'Game Of Love' (1965) that brought the group world wide acclaim. It reached No. 1 in America, Can-ada and Australia, and No. 2 in Britain. Later singles failed to click, however, and the group split in February, 1966. As a solo act, Fontana made the charts with 'Come On Home' and 'Pamela Pamela', which reached No. 11. Fontana still tours America fairly frequently, working with various rock 'n'roll revival shows.

The Fortunes, from Birmingham, were British Decca's first provincial signings along with the Rockin' Berries. Both had a strong commercial strain and not surprisingly outlived most of the other, highly derivative, Birmingham beat groups by becoming typical Northern cabaret mainstays after the flow of hits was over.

The Fortunes – Glen Dale, vocals, guitar; Barry Pritchard, vocals, guitar; David Carr, keyboards; Rod Allen, bass guitar; Andy Brown, drums – were a strong harmony group far removed from the cut-and-thrust R&B scene. Their early reputation rested on their recording of 'Caroline', the theme song for the pirate radio station and thus heard daily. In 1965, they had three British and American chart hits, 'You've Got Your Troubles', 'Here It Comes Again' and 'This Golden Ring' – all pleasant, totally inoffensive examples of British pop, though they earned more money by recording 'It's The Real Thing' for Coca Cola. After a stream of personnel changes they re-emerged as a chart force in 1972 with two British Top Twenty records, 'Freedom Come Freedom Go' and 'Storm In A Teacup'. It might still have been 1965 for all their style had changed.

Fred Foster was already established in the Nashville Music scene when he formed Monument Records in 1958. Immediately, he achieved popular success with country artist Billy Grammer, whose 'Gotta Travel On' reached No. 4. Grammer followed up with Pee Wee King's 'Bonaparte's Retreat'. Foster had further hits with other country artists, Dick Flood and Jack Eubanks and the black vocal group, the Velvets, until he found a star to cement his success.

This was former rocker Roy Orbison, whose internationally famous lachrymose ballad style was developed with Foster at Monument into hits of the early Sixties like 'Uptown' (the first in 1960), 'Only The Lonely', 'In Dreams', 'Running Scared' and 'Pretty Woman'. Boots Randolph tasted success in the mid-Sixties with the instrumental 'Yakety Sax', and

Foster was joined by Billy Swan, later a recording star himself, as a producer. In 1969, Monument launched Tony Joe White from the Southern swamps and ushered in an era of laid-back country soul with 'Polk Salad Annie'.

The Foundations were launched in October, 1967, with a million-selling single, 'Baby Now That I've Found You' (Pye), written and produced by Tony Macaulay. The group – Clem Curtis, vocals (born Nov. 28, 1940); Tony Gomez, organ (Dec. 13, 1948); Eric Allandale, trombone (March 4, 1936); Pat Burke, saxophone (Oct. 9, 1937); Mike Elliott, saxophone (August 6, 1929); Alan Warner, guitar (April 21, 1947); Peter Macbeth, bass (Feb. 2, 1943) and Tim Harris, drums (Jan. 14, 1948) – had a string of hits over the next 18 months, including a second million-seller with the Macaulay-D'Abo composition, 'Build Me Up Buttercup', in 1968. That year Elliott left and Curtis was replaced by Joey Young. Following an unsuccessful period, the group broke up late in 1970. A different line-up later appeared under the same name.

The Fourmost – Brian O'Hara (lead guitar, born March 12, 1942); Mike Millward (rhythm, May 9, 1942); Billy Hatton (bass, June 9, 1941); and Dave Lovelady (drums, Oct. 16, 1942) – had previously been known as the Four Jays and Four Mosts until manager Brian Epstein changed their name. They were supplied with two lightweight Lennon and McCartney songs for their first two singles ('Hello Little Girl' and 'I'm In Love') but neither did as well as 'A Little Lovin' ' which got to No. 6 in 1964. The group were part of the more showbiz-oriented axis of Merseybeat (Gerry Marsden, Cilla Black, etc.) and soon a long variety engagement at the London Palladium led to a career in cabaret.

The Four Seasons were the most successful and influential of all the East Coast vocal groups, wtih Frankie Valli's piercing falsetto as their trademark. The original quartet was Valli (born Francis Castellucio in Newark, New Jersey, in 1937), Nick Massi (Newark, 1935), Tommy DeVito (Bellville, New Jersey, 1936) and his brother Nick. Originally known as the Variatones, they signed to RCA as the Four Lovers in 1956, having a small hit with 'You're The Apple Of My Eye'.

In 1960, Valli met Bob Crewe of Swan Records, who signed the group as session singers and players. He also began to write songs for them with new member Bob Gaudio, who had replaced Nick DeVito. Success came in 1962 with two million-sellers, 'Sherry' and 'Big Girls Don't Cry', on Vee Jay. For the next four years they had an unbroken series of hits, including a further No. 1 in 'Rag Doll' (American Philips). Making use of all the effects of uptown R&B production techniques under the guidance of Crewe, their style was based on that of Fifties groups like the Diamonds and Maurice Williams and the Zodiacs: essentially a white interpretation of a black sound. The group became officially known as Frankie Valli and the Four Seasons when Bob Gaudio joined, although they also recorded a version of Dylan's 'Don't Think Twice' under the pseudonym of the Wonder Who in 1964, just to prove that their records were not selling on the strength of the name alone. The record reached the charts at the same time as 'Let's Hang On' and Valli's solo release, 'You're Gonna Hurt Yourself', were in the Top Ten.

Refusing to change their style when the Beatles threatened their status, they maintained a healthy following throughout the latter half of the Sixties, although they failed to match the success of their earlier recordings. In 1968, they attempted to go progressive with an album called *Genuine Imitation Life Gazette* but its relative failure led indirectly to Bob Crewe breaking off his association with the group and to Gaudio taking over the role of producer. Litigation with Philips left the group with no recording outlet for a couple of years, until moving to the West Coast, they helped launch Motown's subsidiary label, Mo-West. Valli developed a concurrent solo career by concentrating particularly on the middle-of-the-road market which came to fruition in the mid-Seventies with records like 'My Eyes Adored You' (Private Stock, 1975).

The Four Tops were originally the Four Aims, formed in their hometown of Detroit in 1953 by Levi Stubbs, Renaldo Benson, Lawrence Payton and Abdul Fakir. 1975 saw the group recording successfully on Warner Bros. In 1956 they signed with Chess as the Four Tops, recording one unsuccessful single.

The late Fifties were spent playing endless club and cabaret dates in a variety of musical styles, and they spent some time touring with Billy Eckstine's roadshow before John Hammond signed them to Columbia in 1962. Singles on Columbia and Riverside didn't sell, but attracted the attention of Berry Gordy whose Motown organization was growing rapidly. He signed them in 1964, initially assigning them to his short-lived Workshop jazz label, but actually releasing their first disc, 'Baby I Need Your Loving', on Motown. This atmospheric, storming beat ballad was a Top Twenty smash, and began a sequence of 28 chart entries over eight years (a reissued Columbia track even sneaked a small hit), largely comprising mid-tempo ballads with a heavy beat, and often written by the prolific trio of Lamont Dozier, Brian and Eddie Holland. Their first chart-topper was the 1965 million-seller 'I Can't Help Myself', while in 1966 'Reach Out, I'll Be There' was a transatlantic No. 1. This track in particular shows how far and how fast Holland, Dozier and Holland, the Four Tops and Motown, had developed in just two years. The instrumentation – flutes, oboes and Arab drums – was unusual, pointing to future developments in soul. Similarly, Stubbs' dramatic and imaginative lead vocal galvanizes the lyric. Moreover, the song was the first of a sequence of equally dramatic hits, including 'Standing In The Shadows Of Love', 'Bernadette' and '7 Rooms Of Gloom' (1966–7). However, despite further hits on Motown in 1972, the group moved to Dunhill, enjoying an immediate Top Ten hit with 'Keeper Of The Castle'. Under the wing of a new writer/production team, Dennis Lambert and Brian Potter, they have continued to prosper.

Kim Fowley, an American singer, producer and composer (born Los Angeles on July 27, 1942) became involved in music in high school, working with schoolmates Gary Paxton and Skip Battin, producing groups he assembled from kids picked at random on the street. Some of the groups he wrote and produced for were the Jayhawks ('Stranded In The Jungle'), the Paradons ('Diamonds And Pearls'), B. Bumble and the Stingers ('Nut Rocker'), the Innocents ('Honest I Do'), Skip and Flip ('Cherry Pie'), and the Hollywood Argyles ('Alley Oop'). In the early Sixties he was involved with the Rivingtons ('Papa Oom Mow Mow'), and Paul Revere and the Raiders. In addition, there were dozens of records either written, produced or sung by Fowley released on countless local labels – and many on his own Living Legend label.

He spent 1965 in England, working with a number of acts who later achieved fame, among them the Rockin' Berries, P. J. Proby, the Soft Machine, Cat Stevens, Dave Mason and Jim Capaldi. Back in America, he joined the Mothers for their first album, then returned to solo work. Currently he confines his activities to songwriting (in the last two years his songs have been recorded by the Byrds, New Riders, Leo Kottke, Emerson Lake and Palmer, Sir Douglas Quintet, Masters of the Airwaves, Blue Cheer, REO Speedwagon, Helen Reddy and others), publishing and talent spotting. None the less, precisely what Fowley did for the various people whose careers he has been 'involved' in has always been unclear – and indeed often his 'involvement' has been disputed. That said, musically, Fowley has an undeniable talent for novelty songs and uncomplicated teenage anthems. His six albums – such as *Outrageous* (Imperial, 1968) and *International Heroes* (Capitol, 1973) – are noted for their satiric qualities, while the hundreds of singles he's been involved in have inspired a cult following.

Inez and Charlie Foxx, a sister/brother team from Greensboro, North Carolina, first hit with the million-seller 'Mockingbird' (1963) – a bouncy adaptation of a children's song. Other gimmicky records on the Symbol label ('Hi Diddle Diddle', 'Hurt By Love') gave little hint of Inez's fine, emotive voice. Writer/producer Charlie (born on Oct. 23,

1939) also contributed background chants and the energetic parts of their stage routine. Later releases on Musicor/Dynamo were better, particularly 'I Stand Accused – Guilty' (1967), although their biggest hit, 'Count The Days', was similar to their earlier work. Since 1969, Inez – born Sept. 9, 1942 – has performed solo, recording in Memphis for the Stax and Volt labels.

Aretha Franklin, like Ray Charles before her, exorcized her own personal demons through the ecstasy of gospel emotion initially on recordings that gained her much respect but limited success, before eventually finding the formula to seduce an international, multi-racial audience. Ironically it was Atlantic, the company that lost Charles just before his breakthrough, who guided Aretha to stardom. But in the years between their handling of the two performers, times had changed. Whereas Charles was not accepted by a mass audience until he'd disguised his black roots with a liberal coating of whitewash, it was precisely by rejecting ambiguous compromise that Aretha emerged as a major name.

Unlike Charles, who had adopted gospel phrasing to give his blues new expression, Aretha was a true daughter of the church. Born in Memphis on March 25, 1942, one of six children of the Reverend C. L. Franklin, she was raised in Detroit surrounded by the ballyhoo of her father's success. A wealthy and, by all accounts, devastating Baptist preacher, he held sway over a large and devoted congregation; commanded pop star fees on his crusading personal appearances, and recorded a whole library of religious albums for Battle (Detroit) and Chess (Chicago). The Franklin home was open house for the top black personalities of the day. In particular, the two reigning gospel queens, Mahalia Jackson and Clara Ward, were close friends who helped to mould the young Aretha. By the age of nine, she was singing in her father's choir; at twelve, she was the star soloist; and then, in 1956, the fourteen-year-old protégée began cutting solo recordings for Chicago labels JVB and Checker. After four years of recording straight gospel, heavily influenced by Clara Ward, Aretha was encouraged by Sam Cooke to follow his switch to commercial success. In 1960, she left her father and settled temporarily in New York where she was signed to Columbia records by John Hammond.

In six years Columbia tried many settings for Aretha's emotive vocal style, but with every change of direction they were always one step out of tune with the times. Following her initial bluesy sides, she attacked showbiz standards; a collection of Dinah Washington's hits; other artists' pop chart entries; after-hours jazz ballads; and a few originals that were arranged in a Columbian approximation of soul music. Although she scraped the charts half a dozen times (notably 'Rock-A-By Your Baby With A Dixie Melody', 1961, 'Don't Cry Baby', 1962, 'Runnin' Out Of Fools', 1964) and survived the endless round of night clubs, it was an abysmal waste of talent, akin to RCA's persistent attempts to make another Sammy Davis Jr. out of Sam Cooke.

In November, 1966, she found a more sympathetic home at Atlantic records. Supervised by the company's veteran producer Jerry Wexler, she was recorded at the Muscle Shoals studio in Alabama, just simply wailing her heart out over a beautifully economic backing. The stunning result, 'I Never Loved A Man (The Way I Love You)', went straight to the top of the soul charts, hit the Top Ten, and sold a million. There followed a string of equally convincing performances ('Respect', 'Baby I Love You', 'Natural Woman', 'Chain Of Fools', 'Since You Been Gone', 'Think'), each as enthusiastically received as the first. By the end of 1968 Wexler had twice been acclaimed 'Producer Of The Year' and Aretha was being showered with gold records and effusive rhetoric.

The next two years were not so golden. Disturbed by the pressures of success and suffering the pangs of a broken marriage to manager Ted White, Aretha seemed confused. Many of her recordings lacked the intensity of the previous hits and her stage shows were similarly disappointing. Not only was her ponderous road band unable to match the excellent studio musicians, but audiences were less than delighted by her alarming tendency to break into a hearty rendition of 'There's No Business Like Show Business'. By the autumn of 1970 she had remarried, scrapped the large band in favour of a tighter combo led by King Curtis, and begun to pull out of the trough. A successful appearance at New York's Philharmonic Hall in December of that year which had critics proclaiming 'Aretha returns to life', and her superb interpretation of Ben E. King's 'Don't Play That Song', seemed to prove it. The following spring a confident self-portrait, 'A Brand New Me', preceded a triumphant concert at Fillmore West in San Francisco (recorded, and released on album). The Queen of Soul was back on top. Since then she has firmly established herself as the leading black female entertainer – not quite as relevant to younger audiences as the new heroines like Millie Jackson, and perhaps a little too fond of reworking other people's hit songs, but still a unique and influential vocalist who can pack the concert halls of Europe while whupping all those funky bands in the soul charts. (Indeed, she has achieved more No. 1 soul hits than everyone except James Brown.)

In the spring of 1972, before the congregation of the Temple Missionary Baptist Church in Watts, Los Angeles, Aretha joined with gospel star James Cleveland and the Southern California Community Choir to record the benefit concert that was later released as *Amazing Grace*. Clearly moved by his daughter's performance, the Reverend C. L. Franklin had no doubts about the true strength of her talent. 'If you want to know the truth, Aretha has never left the church. If you have the ability to feel, and if you have the ability to hear, you know that Aretha is still a gospel singer.'

Dallas Frazier is one of several white Southerners whose songs are more successful on other people's records than on his own. Frazier's personal style tends to be too much like R&B for country fans and too country for black record-buyers, and yet set apart from the pop mainstream. Born in Spiro, Oklahoma in 1939, he moved with his family to Bakersfield, California in 1950. Two years later, he won a Ferlin Husky-sponsored talent contest and went on to record children's novelty songs for Capitol. By 1957 he had stopped imitating Mel Blanc but still read comics, as one of his first compositions, 'Alley Oop', showed. It topped the American charts, recorded by the Hollywood Argyles, a motley collection of Los Angeles record people including Sandy Nelson, singer Gary Paxton and Frazier himself.

After various records for Jamie, Musikon and Mercury, Frazier moved to Nashville and rejoined Capitol, for whom he cut some powerful R&B sides of which 'Elvira' (No. 72 in 1966) was the best. He had clearly listened to all sorts of music, but rockabilly and West Coast R&B seemed to have the most influence on his vocals. The street-argot eloquence of his best lyrics rivalled the writing of Jerry Leiber. Some of Frazier's notable compositions include 'Ridin' Hood' (the Coasters), 'Mohair Sam' (Charlie Rich) and 'The Son Of Hickory Holler's Tramp' (O. C. Smith). In the late Sixties, he recorded for RCA-Victor and consolidated his position in the country field with a colossal number of slushy pop and C&W ballads for Jerry Lee Lewis, Henson Cargill, Jack Greene (the original version of 'There Goes My Everything'), Charlie Pride, Elvis Presley and others. His own records were invariably of greater interest. 'California Cottonfields' (later recorded by Merle Haggard) was outstanding. It told the story of his daddy's move from the Mid-West to the 'Promised Land': a three-minute sound-picture from *The Grapes Of Wrath*.

John Fred and his Playboy Band. Born in Baton Rouge, Louisiana, on May 8, 1941, John Fred had a minor hit in 1959 with 'Shirley' (Montel) and for years led one of the most popular touring bands, the Playboys (Ron Goodson, Tommy Dee, Andrew Bernard, Harold Cowart, Joe Micelli, Charlie Spinoza and Jimmy O'Rourke), in the Louisiana/East Texas region. The group's big break came when the Fred-Bernard composition, 'Judy In Disguise (With Glasses)' became a worldwide hit in 1967. A bubblegum derivative of the Beatles' 'Lucy In The Sky', it proved to be John Fred's only substantial hit. He is still one of Louisiana's most respected singers and bandleaders.

Freddie and the Dreamers arrived from Manchester early in the beat boom. Freddie Garrity (born Nov. 14, 1940); Pete Birrell, bass (May 9, 1941); Roy Crewsdon, guitar (May 29, 1941); Bernie Dwyer, drums (Sept. 11, 1940) and Derek Quinn, lead guitar (May 24, 1942) performed happy-go-lucky songs while posturing and leaping about. Pint-sized Freddie had been a milkman before the group passed a BBC audition in 1963. They appealed to a much younger audience than their contemporaries and, after seven hits on British Columbia – including 'I'm Telling You Now' (an American No. 1) and 'You Were Made For Me' – became increasingly involved in children's entertainment. They broke up at the end of the Sixties but Freddie and Pete Birrell remained together to star in the long-running children's TV series *Little Big Time*.

The Fugs were both the extension of the Beat poets into rock and the first of a line of New York bands who made outrage their stock in trade. Founded by poets Ed Sanders, Tuli Kupferberg and Ken Weaver, the group was signed by the avant-garde jazz label, ESP, in 1965. Their three albums for the company show a progression from musically crude political chants like 'Kill For Peace' and versions of William Blake poems to drugs and sex songs like 'New Amphetamine Shriek' and 'Coca Cola Douche'. The Fugs were signed by Reprise in the hippie atmosphere of 1967 and went on tour, augmented by genuine musicians including bassist Charlie Larkey and guitarist Stefan Grossman. Their three albums for Reprise brought them a cult following which survived the group's demise at the end of the Sixties.

The Bobby Fuller Four, a quartet from El Paso, played Texas rock'n'roll. They welded their own rough-hewn vocal harmonies to the loose, loping West Texas rhythms and scored twice in 1966 with Sonny Curtis' 'I Fought The Law' and with Buddy Holly's 'Love's Made A Fool Of You' on Mustang. But success was short-lived. Within months, Bobby died in a freak car accident. His brother, Randy, stuck around to make a couple of singles, but soon joined De-Wayne Quirico and Jim Reese back in Texas and obscurity.

Marvin Gaye, born in Washington, D.C., on April 2, 1939, received his musical grounding singing in the choir and playing organ at the Washington church where his father was minister. His career in the popular field began when he won the school talent show: the show was judged by Harvey Fuqua and Marvin won singing his song 'Ten Commandments Of Love'.

At his father's instigation he enlisted in the USAF on graduation, but was soon demobbed on psychological grounds. He immediately renewed his friendship with Fuqua, singing in the Moonglows in the twilight of their career, including their 1959 Chess release 'Mama Loocie'. In 1960 Gaye and Fuqua moved from Chicago to Detroit, where Fuqua formed his Harvey and Tri-Phi labels, beginning an association with the Gordy family. Berry Gordy had recently formed the fledgeling Motown Corporation which soon engulfed the Fuqua labels, while Berry's sisters, Gwen and Anna, were soon married to Harvey and Marvin respectively. Berry heard Marvin sing at an informal party in Detroit, and signed him to the Tamla label in 1961.

Marvin's first three releases meant little, but the fourth, 'Stubborn Kind Of Fellow', a crisp, mid-tempo beat ballad with gospel chanting by the Vandellas in the background was a Top Fifty hit late in 1962, starting a run of some 28 Top Fifty hits over the next ten years, ten discs reaching the Top Ten, peaking with the chart-topping 'Heard It Through The Grapevine' in 1968. Much of Marvin's material was in the beat ballad idiom, ideally suiting his soft tenor voice. There were some notable exceptions – the rasping 'Hitch Hike' dance song (his second hit, in 1963); the storming 12-bar blues format gospel rocker 'Can I Get A Witness' (later in 1963); a similar, if less frantic 'You're A Wonderful One' (1964) and the powerful Bo Diddley-beat 'Baby Don't You Do It' (1964). In 1964, Marvin was teamed with Mary Wells for a duet album, both sides of the spin-off single making the Top Twenty, but the success was short-lived since Mary Wells quit Motown for 20th Century soon after. A partnership with Kim Weston followed, yielding a 1967 Top Twenty hit 'It Takes Two', but then Kim Weston left for MGM.

The beautiful Tammi Terrell was Marvin's third distaff partner, beginning in 1967, and this time the combination was more permanent, scoring ten Hot Hundred entries – four of them Top Ten – over three years. But this pairing was tragically terminated in 1970 when Tammi died after undergoing several operations on a brain tumour. Tammi's death had a profound effect on Gaye: his mid-1970 hit was aptly entitled 'The End Of Our Road', following which he quit touring and spent many months reshaping his recording career, resurfacing in 1971 with the deeply introspective 'What's Going On', 'Mercy Mercy Me (The Ecology)', and 'Inner City Blues' in a subdued, philosophical vein, vastly different from his Sixties teen-ballad hits. During 1972 he wrote the soundtrack for 20th Century-Fox movie *Trouble Man*, and the title single brought him another Top Ten hit, while in May 1972 he returned to stage appearances following which a musically excellent and critically acclaimed 'live' album was issued. Gaye's success with such diverse projects as the *What's Going On* song cycle and the three-million seller, 'Let's Get It On', demonstrate his importance within contemporary black music, while his independent attitude towards recording forced Motown to allow other artists, including Stevie Wonder, more freedom in the studio and to treat albums as more than 'two hits and 10 fillers'.

Bobbie Gentry, born in Chickasaw County, Mississippi on July 27, 1945, was a Las Vegas night-club dancer before taking the pop charts by storm in 1967 when 'Ode To Billie Joe' made No. 1 on Capitol. Following up with songs like 'Okolona River Bottom Band', 'Mississippi Delta' and 'Chickasaw County Child', she became a TV favourite even before teaming with Glen Campbell. Her individualized statements of Deep South living were not only successful in their own right but, combined with her other talents, were a publicist's dream and even gained her a solo TV series in Britain.

The Gentrys were Memphis, Tennessee's answer to the
156

British-inspired beat scene of 1965. After several months of playing local clubs, talent competitions, teen fairs and even Ted Mack's Amateur Hour, the group (Larry Raspberry, Larry Wall, Jimmy Johnson, Bobby Fisher, Pat Neal, Bruce Bowles, Jimmy Hart) was signed to the local Youngstown label. Their second single, 'Keep On Dancing' – revived by the Bay City Rollers in 1971 – was picked up by MGM and was a Top Ten hit in September of 1965. It was a period classic, one of those songs dedicated to and designed for dancing, mentioning all the top dances of the day and filled out with a solid beat and punk organ sound reminiscent of some of the tougher Texas groups of the time. Like most groups of this era who were favoured with one phenomenal hit, they were never able to follow it up, although they made a fairly strong comeback in 1970 with 'Why Should I Cry' and 'Cinnamon Girl' on the newly reactivated Sun label. In 1973, Larry Raspberry launched his own group, the High-steppers, currently doing well on Stax. The rest of the Gentrys now record for Capitol.

Gerry and the Pacemakers – Gerry Marsden (vocals, guitar, born Sept. 24, 1942), Les Maguire (piano, Dec. 27, 1941), Les Chadwick (bass, May 11, 1943) and Freddie Marsden (drums, Nov. 23, 1940) – were the second group to be signed by Brian Epstein, in 1962. Like the Beatles, they recorded for Parlophone and were produced by George Martin. Their first album, *How Do You Like It?* showed they were well-schooled in rock'n'roll and R&B standards, but as a singles group they emphasized Gerry Marsden's cheeky chappie image. Each of their first three records went to No. 1 in Britain, and the first two (Mitch Murray's 'How Do You Do It?' and 'I Like It') also made the American Top Twenty. The third was the *Carousel* ballad, 'You'll Never Walk Alone', which was quickly adopted by Liverpool soccer fans and later by fans of every other team in England. The hits continued into 1965 and included the theme song from a movie, *Ferry Cross The Mersey*, in which the group starred. Soon after, the Pacemakers split up, with Gerry going on to a career as a television and cabaret entertainer.

The Godz, four New Yorkers – Jim McCarthy, guitar, vocals; Larry Kessler, guitar, viola, vocals; Jay Dillon, psaltery, autoharp, keyboards; Paul Thornton, drums – with their first album, *Contact High*, 1967, simultaneously produced the ultimate New York album of the period and possibly the worst ever recorded. However, their albums aren't simply good because they are bad (i.e. kitsch); they worked hard to achieve that low level, following the anarchic course set by their ESP label cohorts, the Fugs. Only ESP would have let them into the studios again (*Godz Two* and the less audacious *The Third Testament*). The first two are severe amusical romps, of wailing unharmonic vocals, avant-garde solos and grinding fiddle. 'Squeak' and 'White Cat Heat' display their talents best and may hold the secret to the ultimate riot control weapon.

Barry Goldberg began playing piano in the late Fifties in Chicago, sitting in with bluesmen like Otis Rush, Muddy Waters and Buddy Guy and becoming well established in the South Side clubs. In 1965, he played with Bob Dylan on the controversial electric set at the Newport Folk Festival. He'd been enticed there by Michael Bloomfield, with whom he'd played occasionally in the Butterfield Blues Band. On his return to Chicago he set up the Goldberg-Miller Blues Band (also known as the Third World War Blues Band) with Steve Miller, recording an album, *Blowing My Mind*, in 1966, though Steve Miller had already left for San Francisco by the time of its release. A much respected player, Goldberg has never made a really worthwhile album despite surrounding himself with fine and willing musicians like Duane Allman, Harvey Mandel (who had replaced Miller in the Blues Band) and Mike Bloomfield on albums like *Two Jews' Blues* and *Blasts From My Past* (Buddah, 1968 and 1969 respectively). Bloomfield enticed him to California when he set up the Electric Flag in 1968. Eventually he made the switch from being purely a keyboard player to a self-contained singer, musician and writer, and in 1973 he produced his most pleasing album, *Barry Goldberg*, at Muscle Shoals and worked on Gerry Goffin's solo album, *It Ain't Exactly Entertainment* (Adelphi).

Goldie and the Gingerbreads. Britain had seen a girl drummer, Honey Lantree of the Honeycombs, and a bass player, Megan Davies of the Applejacks, but the arrival of the all-girl band, Goldie and the Gingerbreads, led by Goldie Zelkowitz, struck an immediate vein of publicity. In America, all-girl bands were more commonplace and they never had the same impact there in their two years together. But, in Britain in 1965, out on the road on a series of package tours and one-nighters they enjoyed considerable renown. Singles like 'Can't You Hear My Heartbeat' and 'That's The Way I Love You' gave them minor hits but their real strength (novelty appeal aside) was that they could really play. Publicity stories of the day had leading British musicians watching from the wings *because* they were so good. By 1969, having returned to America, the band had folded. Goldie became involved with a jazz group which evolved into the ten-piece, otherwise male, Ten Wheel Drive. The other Gingerbreads formed the nucleus of the eight-piece all-girl Isis. Goldie herself made a couple of albums as Genya Raven and more recently as Goldie Zelkowitz.

Bobby Goldsboro displays a clean-cut image of youthfulness, and he has been responsible for many heavily recorded pop and country songs. Born in Florida, on Jan. 18, 1941, he worked for some time as a guitarist with a variety of rock studios locally before joining Laurie Records in 1962, when he scored a minor hit with 'Molly'. In 1964, he joined United Artists, where he was produced by Bob Montgomery, and his 'See The Funny Little Clown' made the Top Ten. In 1968, he finally hit No. 1 with 'Honey' (a hit again in Britain in 1975). Lately he has aimed more at the mainstream country-pop market.

Giorgio Gomelsky, one of a handful of promoters who saw the early potential of British R&B, started Sunday night sessions at the Station Hotel, Richmond, giving the Rolling

Stones a residency in February, 1963. His reluctance to bind the group to a written managerial contract allowed Andrew Oldham to sign them up, and he was more careful with the group who took over the Stones' residency, the Yardbirds. He went on to manage other Crawdaddy club bands, including the Brian Auger Trinity and the T-Bones, and created Steampacket in 1965. He subsequently formed his own Marmalade record company with Polydor Records, but despite the international success of Julie Driscoll and the Brian Auger Trinity with 'This Wheel's On Fire' in 1968, the label was short-lived and he left England for France to establish an 'alternative' circuit for groups like Gong and Magma (whom he also managed). A series of albums cut from tapes in his possession appeared on the French BYG label under the collective title of *Rock Generation* and featured material by groups with whom he had been involved in London – though not the Stones. He set up Utopia Records in 1975.

Lesley Gore, born on May 2, 1946, in Tenafly, New Jersey, was one of the few singers to emerge in the 1962–5 'girl group era' who survived into the late Sixties, mainly on the strength of her material, style and the large following generated by the string of seven straight Top Ten records that started her career. Her first hit was the No. 1, 'It's My Party' (Mercury, 1963), followed by an answer to that, 'Judy's Turn To Cry' and then 'She's A Fool' and 'You Don't Own Me', which she also sang in a stunning performance in *The T.A.M.I. Show.* These records shared certain key elements: strong productions, impassioned, crying vocals, and the themes of teenage love triangles. 'That's The Way Boys Are' and 'Maybe I Know' followed in the same vein, but later hits such as 'Look Of Love', 'Sunshine, Lollipops And Rainbows' and 'California Nights' found her moving towards more of a mainstream pop sound. After ten years with Mercury, she signed with Motown in 1972 and then A&M in 1975.

Graham Gouldman, formerly with Manchester group, the

160

Mockingbirds, wrote hits for several British groups of the mid-Sixties. 'Listen People' was a Top Ten hit in America for Herman's Hermits in 1966, and Gouldman also provided the group with 'No Milk Today' and 'East-West'. The Hollies recorded 'Bus Stop' and 'Stop Stop Stop', songs which showed Gouldman's eye for unusual settings for conventional pop love lyrics. He also had three hits writing for the Yardbirds ('For Your Love', 'Heart Full Of Soul', 'Evil-Hearted You') before moving to New York to work in the Kasenetz-Katz bubblegum music organization. Returning to Britain in 1969, he began working with Lol Creme and Kevin Godley, cutting an unreleased album for Giorgio Gomelsky's ill-fated Marmalade label. That association was to provide the basis for 10cc, the group formed by the trio and Eric Stewart in the Seventies.

Bill Graham, who oscillated from business manager of the San Francisco Mime Troupe to promoter of Bob Dylan's 1974 American tour, is one of the few people who outlasted the San Francisco boom of 1967–9. Starting with a couple of benefits for the Mime Troupe in 1965–6, Graham slowly moved into full-time promotion. 1966 saw him looking after the Fillmore and temporarily managing the Jefferson Airplane; 1968 looking after the Fillmores West and East plus a record label (Fillmore, of course) that soon folded. By now he had a virtual monopoly of promotions in the Bay Area and was beginning national promotions. Always outspoken, Graham was often accused by the San Francisco 'head community' of being nothing more than a dollars and cents man. However, his continued involvement in live music and his reputation of being a tough, but fair, businessman demonstrates that his interest in music is more than merely mercenary.

Davy Graham, born in 1940 of Scottish-Guyanese parents, became the largely unrecognized father of the British 'folk baroque' guitar style. As an itinerant musician in Europe and North Africa, he absorbed jazz, folk, Arab and Indian influences, and blended them all in his playing. His experiments with Alexis Korner on *3/4 A.D.* (1961) and then with folk singer Shirley Collins on *Folk Roots, New Routes* (Decca, 1965) were largely ignored because they were so far ahead of their time – but they pointed to a whole variety of eclectic styles that were to come. Illness in the late Sixties affected his career, but by the mid-Seventies he had recovered and was back playing on the folk circuit.

Grass Roots have been one of the most enduring hit singles groups of the past decade. Their first records came out in 1966, at the height of folk-rock, and were in fact written and performed by P. F. Sloan and Steve Barri for the first year. The No. 28, 'Where Were You When I Needed You' was their biggest hit during this period. By 1967, a real group had been assembled – Warren Entner, vocals, guitar; Rob Grill, vocals, bass; Ricky Coonce, drums and Creed Bratton, guitar – and 'Let's Live For Today', a cover of an Italian hit by the Rokes, was a Top Ten hit. From there, the Grass Roots were launched on a series of hits that included 'Things I Should Have Said', 'Midnight Confessions', 'Bella Linda', 'I'd Wait a Million Years', 'Heaven Knows', 'Temptation Eyes', 'Sooner or Later', 'Two Divided By Love', continuing to the present.

The Grateful Dead had their origins in Mother McCree's Uptown Jug Champions, late in 1963. The Jug Champions were: Jerry Garcia, guitar, banjo, vocals (born Jan. 1, 1942); Pigpen (Rod McKernan), harmonica, piano, vocals (Sept. 8, 1945); John 'Marmaduke' Dawson, guitar, vocals (later of the New Riders); Bob Matthews, guitar, vocals (later a member of the family as recordings and equipment man); and Bob Weir, jug and kazoo (Oct. 16, 1947), then a guitar novice taking lessons from Jorma Kaukonen. Work was scarce for the Jug Champions until Dana Morgan, owner of a music store where Garcia had worked, provided the equipment for them to become an electric band, the Warlocks. Dawson and Matthews had left to be replaced by Bill Sommers (actually Kreutzmann – born on April 7, 1946) and Morgan himself, on bass. He was quickly replaced by Phil Lesh (March 15,

1940) then a musician of classical leanings, who took a two-week crash course in bass playing to complete the now familiar Dead line-up.

The Warlocks played their first date in July 1965 and dealt in pretty straight rock'n'roll until they collectively started taking acid. The sets immediately became more diffuse, stretching out the numbers and increasing the volume. This led to the Dead's involvement with the Pranksters, typified by the Acid Tests and culminating in the Ken Kesey-organized Trips Festival. By now the Warlocks had become the Grateful Dead, the name itself the outcome of an evening of stoned lexicology, and were already the nodal point of a family of musicians – they acquired a second drummer, Mickey Hart, in the summer of 1967, and keyboard player Tom Constanten, a friend of Lesh's, was intermittently with the group – associated sound and light show operatives, road crew, wives, friends and children. The family included designer Rick Griffin, lyricist Robert Hunter and *engineer* Owsley. Owsley's role was threefold; he was a chemist of highly potent LSD, an electronics wizard who supervised the building of their impeccable sound system and, for a while, their financial benefactor.

The family grew after they moved to 710 Ashbury, San Francisco, and with it grew the myth surrounding them and the 'Frisco scene. This phenomenon was about to explode in a blaze of publicity with the Dead at its centre in their communal Haight Street house, playing for free in the park and with Garcia (Captain Trips) – despite his denials – as a kind of guru figure. Finally, the Dead signed with Warner Bros. Their first three albums – *Grateful Dead* (March, 1967), *Anthem To The Sun* (August, 1968) and *Aoxomoxoa* (June, 1969) – were charged with the group's presence and multi-directional consciousness, but never had the commercial possibilities of the Jefferson Airplane's early albums. They ended up over 100,000 dollars in debt to Warners, as well as owing them an album. The essence of the Dead had always been their phenomenal live show, and finally on *Live/Dead* (1970) they allowed people outside 'Frisco a glimpse of the band's real power. They were also by now touring more widely than ever, including a first European visit.

Success came with the realization of their studio capabilities on two stylish country-rock albums, *Workingman's Dead* and *American Beauty* in 1971, on which they showed, for the first time, a previously undeveloped vocal strength. Garcia, Weir and Lesh sounded like a rough and ragged, less sterile Crosby, Stills and Nash. Similarly, lyricist Robert Hunter made the transition from the complex word patterns of 'Dark Star' to the simplicity of 'Uncle John's Band'. The tighter Dead had achieved a synthesis of Haight Street freeness and country-rock precision and discipline. It was amply illustrated on their next album, another live double set, *Grateful Dead*, winning them their first gold album. This was followed by a dangerous period of over-exposure. Jerry Garcia, in particular, played countless sessions. Three members of the group made albums in 1972 – Jerry Garcia (*Garcia*), Bob Weir (*Ace*), and the soon-to-leave Mickey Hart (*Rolling Thunder*) and the Dead themselves celebrated their two-month European tour with a triple live album, *Europe '72*. Though beyond their control, the Dead additionally fell foul of a mixed spate of bootlegs and some weak early live recordings dredged up from 1966 on MGM.

The group, however, rode it all out. The death of Pigpen in March, 1973, was obviously a deeply felt setback but he had been ill for over a year with a serious liver disease, and a keyboard player, Keith Godchaux, had already been added to the group. He gave a fresh impetus to the band at a time when they were flagging, and his wife Donna sang with them from time to time. The Dead were also taking care of business: they set up their own record company, Grateful Dead Records, on which their latest studio albums, *Wake Of The Flood* and *From The Mars Hotel* appeared, and Round Records on which they released the less commercial albums of the Dead family. They also developed complementary fields. Today their 150-member family runs the Fly By Night travel company, Out of Town Tours, a booking agency, Ice Nine Publishing Company, a recording studio, and more besides.

Perhaps the secret of the Dead's prolonged life is that all

164

the individual members are free to involve themselves in a variety of projects – exemplified in Jerry Garcia's many ventures, notably the spin-off band, the New Riders of the Purple Sage, now a completely separate unit. This, combined with the astute business sense of their current manager, John McIntire, has given them a great stability. The remarkable history of the Grateful Dead, from jug band to social institution – 'what a long, strange trip it's been' – is a testament to the power of the hopes and ideals that were pinned to rock's mast in the heady days of 1966–7. None the less, however naive and aimless their endless jamming may appear on occasion, it's the Dead's music, far more than the organization of their business affairs, that has shown them consistently struggling to develop those ideas. Certainly, no other group, outside of those heavily influenced by jazz, has introduced as much *structured* free-form music into rock. Never as reflective as Country Joe (and the Fish) or as anarchic as Jefferson Airplane, the Dead are none the less *the* representative San Franciscan band.

Owen Gray, born in Jamaica, was a classic reggae singer, barely changing his style through the years, but always abreast of the trends. Popular from the very outset of his career with discs like 'Sinners Weep' and 'No Good Woman', he continued to cut material of the highest quality. 'Millie Girl', 'Darling Patricia' and 'Tree In The Meadow' were extremely popular ska discs, while his faultless 'Girl What You Doing To Me' was among the best of the early reggae sounds, skirting the British charts in 1969. In the Seventies, Island Records were promoting him on commercial reggae cuts including John Lennon's 'Jealous Guy'.

Peter Green, the founder and original lead guitarist of Fleetwood Mac, was born in Bethnal Green, London on Oct. 29, 1946. On leaving school, Green played with various semi-pro bands before joining Rod Stewart, Peter Bardens and Beryl Marsden in the 1966 club band, Steampacket. His big break came later that same year when he replaced Eric Clapton in John Mayall's Bluesbreakers. Influenced by both

B. B. and Freddie King, Green's reputation as a guitarist soon grew and he was heavily featured on Mayall's 1967 album *A Hard Road*. After a year with the Bluesbreakers, he left to form Peter Green's Fleetwood Mac. Green was responsible for writing most of their biggest hits including the multi-million seller instrumental 'Albatross', 'Oh Well', 'The Green Manalishi', 'Man Of The World' and 'Black Magic Woman', which was covered in later years by Santana. Green left Fleetwood Mac in May 1970, following a traumatic illness, from which he is still recovering.

Greenwich Village, Manhattan's Latin Quarter, a few square miles of turf below New York's 14th Street, has long been a magnet for provincials seeking personal freedom and the artistic life. In the middle Sixties, the section turned middle-class and the bohemians went West in droves, whilst their successors, the hippies, populated the adjacent East Village.

Jazz clubs and ethnic music abounded and, later, rock got firm roots in the East Village. Folk music was always in its natural environment in and around 'The Village'. Annual folk song and dance festivals near the fountain below Washington Arch date back to the Thirties. Since then, outdoor Sunday hootenannies have brought together singers, pickers and fiddlers the way London's Speaker's Corner magnetizes opinion-hawkers. Village radical politics and lifestyles attracted folkniks of every description. Woody Guthrie, Pete Seeger and The Almanac Singers lived there in World War II on West Tenth Street. Josh White and Billie Holiday got their start at Café Society Downtown at Sheridan Square, while Harry Belafonte began at the Village Vanguard. The Village Gate carried on that tradition as a major centre for folk and jazz.

In the heat of the folk revival, after 1960, small clubs mushroomed with folk singers. Gerde's Folk City, the Gaslight, the Bitter End, the Café Wha? and the Thirdside offered a continuing stream of talent. Coffeehouses were especially important locations for mobile singer-guitarists. Nearly every established folk singer, from Paxton to Ochs to

Peter, Paul and Mary to Dylan got their major impetus and developed an audience in The Village. Although young talent was often exploited by club and coffeehouse managements, the venues were unequalled as an incubator for successful performers. The gloss and the charm have since worn thin, but Greenwich Village still stands as a national campus for students and practitioners of the alternative culture.

Woody Guthrie, probably the most influential single figure in American folk music – was born in Okemah, Oklahoma on July 12, 1912, and left a legacy of a thousand songs, several books, hundreds of articles, folk poems and essays, and a lifestyle that still impels young hopefuls to pack bedrolls and guitars, don boots and hit the road to discover the real and gritty world at the end of the dusty highway.

Woody was really too short to be a giant, too lean and delicate-faced to be a hero, terribly ungrammatical to be a poet, with too flat and nasal a little voice to be considered a great singer. Yet Woodrow Wilson Guthrie was all those: a giant of humanism, a hero of the American little man, a major folk poet and a singer and composer of some of the country's greatest songs: for instance, 'Pastures Of Plenty', 'Deportees', 'Hard Traveling', 'Dust Bowl Refugees', 'This Land Is Your Land' and 'So Long, It's Been Good To Know You'. Guthrie has been called 'America's best contemporary ballad composer', 'the best folk ballad composer whose identity has ever been known', a 'rusty-voiced Homer' and 'an influence on America as great as Walt Whitman'.

As with Whitman, Thomas Wolfe, Carl Sandburg, and, later, Jack Kerouac, the Guthrie vision of America was a heady one, intoxicated with the breadth and richness, the variety and promise of the American soil and character. He would pile up his images upon each other like a drunken mason building a dream house. His early years were recounted in his brawling 1943 autobiography, *Bound For Glory*, most notable for its portrait of rural hardship in the great Depression. Fragmentarily, Guthrie's story runs like this: Born in Oklahoma in 1912; childhood in a boom town; life on the road into Texas; the agonies of the Dust Bowl refugees; the lure and heartbreak of California; daily radio shows for a dollar a day on Los Angeles' WKVD; friendships with Will Geer, the actor, and Cisco Houston, folk singer; trips to migrant labour camps; the trek East and contact with the Left-oriented folk movement; Library of Congress recordings for Alan Lomax (released commercially later by Elektra); the singing with Hally Wood and Burl Ives and The Almanac Singers, who included Sis Cunningham and Gordon Friesen, who later edited *Broadside* magazine; restless trips back and forth across the continent with Pete Seeger; recording *Dust Bowl Ballads* for Victor, and the beginning of extensive recordings for Stinson and Folkways; deep involvement with the trade-union movement; writing columns for *The People's World*; the marriages and divorces and the children; the death in a fire of his daughter, Kathy Ann; the birth of his son, Arlo. And through it all, the writing, adapting, rewriting and arranging of songs out of the Carter Family songbook, out of country standards, out of hymns and union song traditions, the reawakening in a contemporary vein of an old tradition.

In the late Forties, Woody fell prey to the degenerative nerve illness that had killed his mother, Huntington's chorea. Gradually, his pen and voice were stilled. Then began the endless years in Eastern hospitals, where his limbs shook convulsively and uselessly, where he could barely talk or show recognition. On Oct. 3, 1967, with no possible hope for an end to nearly two decades of suffering, he died. Through the efforts of Harold Leventhal, his longtime agent, and Bob Dylan, his best-known disciple, memorial concerts were held on both coasts, involving most of the leading figures of American folk music. It was a testimony to the key importance of Guthrie to the folk movement.

Buddy Guy, born in Lettsworth, Louisiana on July 30, 1936, was one of the younger generation of 'Chicago' bluesmen. George 'Buddy' Guy learned his blues from records by Lightning Hopkins, John Lee Hooker, etc., on the radio, experimenting on a home-made guitar before his father bought him a real instrument. He played in Big Poppa Tilley's group, touring Louisiana backing Excello artists like Slim Harpo, and recorded for Ace in Baton Rouge, before migrating to Chicago in 1957. He played Chicago clubs for some while before signing to Artistic in 1958. There he met Willie Dixon. Artistic folded under violent circumstances in 1959 and Dixon took Guy to Chess, where his first session yielded the renowned 'First Time I Met The Blues', performed in Guy's characteristic style – high-pitched, near-hysterical vocal and a biting, penetrating guitar. He had an R&B chart hit with 'Stone Crazy' in 1962, worked steadily as a name act and sessioneer for Chess until 1968, and has subsequently recorded for Blue Thumb, Vanguard and Atco.

Rick Hall, a leading independent producer/arranger/engineer, was responsible for a solid string of hits from Muscle Shoals, Alabama. Born Jan. 31, 1932 in Mississippi, Hall progressed from session musician at Hi studios in Memphis to a songwriting partnership with Billy Sherrill. In 1961 he opened his own Fame studios near Muscle Shoals, and cut his first hit, Arthur Alexander's 'You Better Move On'. By 1964 Hall had formed his own record label, Fame – distributed by Vee Jay – and scored an immediate chart success with Jimmy Hughes' 'Steal Away'. That same year Buddy Killen used the studios to produce Joe Tex's million-selling 'Hold What You've Got'.

When Vee Jay went bankrupt in 1965, Hall switched outlets to Atlantic and recruited a regular unit of studio musicians – Jimmy Johnson (guitar), Norbert Putnam, Albert Lowe and David Hood (bass), Roger Hawkins and Jerry Corrigan (drums), Spooner Oldham and David Briggs (keyboards), Chips Moman, Eddie Hinton and Duane Allman (guitars). Later session men included Barry Beckett and Tommy Cogbill. The studio quickly gathered attention with hits like Percy Sledge's 'When A Man Loves A Woman', Wilson Pickett's '634-5789' and Aretha Franklin's 'I Never Loved A Man (The Way I Loved You)'. Other Fame hits include Wilson Pickett's 'Hey Jude' and Clarence Carter's

'Patches'. The studios were also used by such artists as Boz Scaggs, Ronnie Hawkins, Bobbie Gentry and Cher.

In 1967, Moman and Cogbill left Hall to launch their own AGP studios in Memphis, eventually recording Elvis Presley, the Box Tops and King Curtis. A year later, Hall withdrew his Fame label from Atlantic following a disagreement over advances and signed a new deal with Capitol, although still continuing to produce his protégé, Clarence Carter. Dissatisfied with the new set-up, Johnson, Beckett, Hood and Hawkins quit in 1968 to open their own studio, Muscle Shoals Sound, picking up the Atlantic projects. Hall wound up Fame Records in 1974, but still continues to work out of his studio with artists like the Osmonds, Paul Anka, Mac Davis, Travis Wammack and Candi Staton.

Johnny Halliday, once rumoured to be American, was born in Paris on June 15, 1943 as Jean-Philippe Smet. In France and elsewhere on the Continent he had few rivals – not even leading British rock'n'rollers could match him – and was as big as Presley. His main rival was Vince Taylor who, though British, was comparatively unknown in his home country.

Halliday covered all the leading American and British hits, a practice generally referred to as 'ye-ye' in France, even visiting British studios and Memphis to get the sound right for the French market. His multi-lingual version of 'Let's Twist Again' ('Viens Danser Le Twist') was a million-seller for him in 1961. A spectacular performer at his peak in the pre-Beatles Sixties when he frequently caused riots, Halliday was the first to credit the role of his manager, his elder stepbrother, Lee, and the excellence of his backing group, the Golden Stars. A typical album, *Johnny Halliday Sings America's Rockin' Hits* (1962), reveals him to be much better than British exponents of the cover-version syndrome. He never actually had a hit in Britain or America, not for want of trying or through any real deficiency on his part. In France, paralleling Cliff Richard, he has always remained sufficiently in touch with trends to have survived gracefully, and well rewarded, over fifteen years of rock.

John Hammond, born into a wealthy middle-class family on Dec. 15, 1910, in New York City, was educated at Yale and studied classical music at Juilliard. Best known for using his money, position, pen and energies in the cause of mainstream jazz in the Thirties, his career spans American popular music from Bessie Smith to Bob Dylan.

As a writer, he was involved with *Melody Maker* and *The Gramophone* in Britain, *Down Beat* in America, contributed pieces on race relations to several publications, and was for a time vice-president of the National Association for the Advancement of Colored Peoples. As an impresario, he presented black bands at his own theatre and organized integrated recording sessions and tours at a time when they were unheard of. In various executive positions with a number of labels, he offered recording opportunities to Count Basie, Teddy Wilson, Billie Holiday, Lester Young, Charlie Christian and several boogie pianists including Meade Lux Lewis. In 1938 and 1939, Hammond presented the 'From Spirituals to Swing' concerts at Carnegie Hall, featuring varied line-ups including Young, Christian, Benny Goodman, Big Bill Broonzy and Sonny Terry. Robert Johnson was booked for the first concert, but was killed a few weeks before the date; years later, Hammond was involved in the preparation of the classic Columbia LP *Robert Johnson, King Of The Delta Blues Singers*, and in the early Sixties produced the comeback album by Son House, whose Thirties records had influenced Johnson.

Although Hammond has been associated with some of the greatest names in jazz, none were well-known when he first heard them, and he continued to back his own personal taste through the Sixties, persuading Columbia to sign Aretha Franklin and Pete Seeger, and negotiating a particularly lucrative deal for Bob Dylan who was known in the company as 'Hammond's Folly' before his records began to sell. He produced Dylan's first Columbia album in 1962 and signed Bruce Springsteen to the label in 1973.

John Hammond Jr., now known as John Paul Hammond, has been the most constant of the white blues singers who

171

emerged in the early Sixties. Born in 1943, the son of the renowned Columbia Records A&R executive, he inherited his father's enthusiasm for the country blues of Robert Johnson and others. After cutting a folk blues album for Vanguard, Hammond formed an electric band in 1964, recording an album for Leiber and Stoller's Red Bird label which featured Robbie Robertson, then of the Hawks, on guitar. The record was not released until 1968 when Atlantic bought the tapes. Since then, Hammond has continued singing and playing guitar and harmonica, while cutting occasional albums, including *Triumvirate*, with Dr John and Mike Bloomfield in 1973.

Tim Hardin was born in Eugene, Oregon in 1940. Now resident in Britain, his musical career began soon after his discharge from the US Marines in 1961, when he became part of the folk movement in Boston's many folk clubs.

By the time he released his first Verve album, in 1966, his style was maturely formed, owing more to jazz and blues than folk. He used his emotionally charged voice as a musical instrument and his first two albums – *Tim Hardin 1* and *2* – contain a clutch of subsequent standards, 'Reason To Believe', 'Misty Roses', 'If I Were A Carpenter' and 'Lady Came From Baltimore' among them. His fame spread when Bobby Darin had a Top Ten hit with 'Carpenter' in 1966 (ironically, Hardin has had only one Hot Hundred entry himself, and that was with Darin's 'Simple Song of Freedom' in 1969).

The third Hardin album consisted of forgotten tapes recorded when he was 22, showing the strong blues influence in his early work. Following a live concert album, Hardin left Verve for Columbia for whom his first album was the ambitious *Suite For Susan Moore And Damion* (1969), a thematic album dedicated to his wife and child and incorporating poetry. *Bird On A Wire*, consisting of other writers' songs, followed in 1971 and the unsatisfactory *Painted Head* in 1973. His British contract with GM has produced *Nine* (1974) to date, in which year Verve repackaged his first two albums. Hardin's career has been bedevilled with ill-health and 'bad advice'; nevertheless he produced some of the most distinctive music of the Sixties.

Harpers Bizarre – Ted Templeman (born Oct. 24, 1944), Dick Scoppettone (July 5, 1945), Eddie James, John Peterson, Dick Yount – originally started out in the San Francisco Bay area in 1963, playing imitation surf music as the Tikis. Four years later they signed with Warner Bros., had a Top Twenty hit with Paul Simon's 'The 59th Street Bridge Song' and cut their first album, *Feelin' Groovy*, arranged by Leon Russell and considered a classic in mid-Sixties soft rock. Their five-part harmonies were an extension of the harmonic style used by sophisticated vocal groups like the Hi-Los and the Four Freshmen in the Fifties. Harpers are also remembered for their revival of songs from the Thirties and Forties, notably their extraordinary Top Fifty versions of Cole Porter's 'Anything Goes', featuring Van Dyke Parks on piano, and Glenn Miller's 'Chattanooga Choo Choo'. The group split in 1970 after completing four albums and numerous singles for Warners. Templeman now works as a Warner Bros. house producer for artists including Van Morrison and the Doobie Brothers.

Richie Havens, born in New York on Jan. 21, 1941, became an underground star in the late Sixties through his idiosyncratic guitar playing and singing. Havens had been a part of the Greenwich Village folk scene as early as 1962, one of the few black singers in a mainly white idiom, although his early gospel singing experience contributed to his later style. Rather like José Feliciano, Havens' particular talent was to transform well-known songs by other artists into an instantly recognizable, personal sound, based on the insistent acoustic rhythms of his E-chord open-tuned guitar and a gruff, but soft, singing voice. By the early Seventies he had cut a dozen albums, the most outstanding being *Richard P. Havens 1983* (Verve, 1968), which included sensitive renderings of 'Strawberry Fields Forever', 'She's Leaving Home' and 'I Pity The Poor Immigrant'. The high point of his career was his Woodstock appearance in 1969. His only Top Twenty record was 'Here Comes The Sun' (Stormy Tempest) in 1971.

Lee Hazelwood, born in 1929 in Mannford, Oklahoma, went to Southern Methodist University before the Army took him to Korea. On his discharge in 1953, he became one of the most popular deejays in Phoenix, Arizona, where he broadcast C&W music locally. In 1955, he branched out into songwriting and began dabbling in record production after experimenting in his radio studio. His production of 'The Fool', by Sanford Clark, sold 800,000 copies on Dot Records in 1956 and Dot subsequently signed him as a record producer for a year, but he failed to make another hit.

In 1957, he teamed up with entrepreneur Lester Sill and they formed the Jamie label in Philadelphia with a distributor and Dick Clark of *Bandstand* fame. Through *Bandstand*, they launched Duane Eddy with the 'twangy' guitar sound which made him a star. In three and a half years, Hazelwood sold 20 million Duane Eddy records which despite their crass commerciality were the earliest 'sound' productions in rock.

In 1961, Hazelwood and Sill formed the Gregmark label which scored with Phil Spector-produced records by the Paris Sisters (Sill and Hazelwood had earlier run two less successful labels called Trey and East-West). They parted company in 1962 and Hazelwood formed an unsuccessful label, Eden. In 1964, he left the business but the following year, Jimmy Bowen at Reprise asked him to produce the bubblegum trio of Dino, Desi and Billy for whom he produced four consecutive hits. He also began recording Nancy Sinatra at Reprise and established her as a potent chart-force with 'These Boots Are Made For Walkin'' and recorded countrified duets, like 'Jackson', with her. In the late Sixties, he ran his own LHI label in Hollywood but lack of success ended the project. Always something of a bohemian, Hazelwood – now in semi-retirement – commutes between homes in Sweden, Paris and Los Angeles.

Roy Head, born in Three Rivers, Texas on Sept. 1, 1941, formed his group, the Traits, in 1958. His first records were for TNT and Renner under the direction of Huey Meaux. Subsequent discs, mainly R&B revivals, were leased to Scepter/Wand. In 1964, Head signed with Backbeat, the label on which 'Treat Her Right' reached No. 2. The funky rhythm and tightly knit brass arrangement gave Head the reputation of a blue-eyed soul brother, but the singing and guitar-work on later records, like 'Apple Of My Eye', 'My Babe', 'Wigglin' and Gigglin'' and 'You're Almost Tuff', showed him to be a latent rockabilly performer of considerable accomplishment, as was his lesser-known brother, Don. But despite a dynamic, rubber-legged stage act and equally fine singles on Mercury, Dunhill and other labels, Head was unable to do more than grace the lower reaches of the country charts during the mid-Seventies.

Bobby Hebb, born in Nashville on July 26, 1941, played the Grand Ole Opry at the age of 12 and moved to Chicago in the early Fifties where he sat in with Bo Diddley, on spoons. In 1961, he recorded for Battle with Sylvia Shemwell (later of the Sweet Inspirations) as Bobby and Sylvia. Many other records followed on FM, Rich, Smash and Boom. Hebb achieved his first major success in 1966, when 'Sunny' on Philips reached No. 2 in America and No. 12 in Britain. His brother, Hal (a member of the Marigolds, an Excello recording group) had died on the day following President Kennedy's assassination, and both events were said to have inspired the song's melancholic lyric. His later Philips records, 'A Satisfied Mind', 'Love Me' and especially 'Love Love Love', made him a firm favourite on the British Northern soul scene by 1973, when he was recording for a new label, GRT.

Jimi Hendrix, born James Marshall Hendrix on Nov. 27, 1942, in Seattle, Washington, rose from a poor black background to become at once the fêted genius of the electric guitar and a victim of the destructive forces of the recording industry in the late Sixties. Hendrix taught himself to play guitar while still at school, and listened avidly to the re-

175

corded work of Southern-born bluesmen from Robert Johnson to B. B. King. In 1961, he enlisted in the US Paratroopers, played in military clubs and met bass-player Billy Cox, whose musicianship and friendship Hendrix was to call on years later when under great pressure at the height of his career.

Returning to civilian life, Hendrix worked on various tours of the South, backing up his idol B. B. King, Sam Cooke and many others after a brief spell in a band, the Flames. He then worked for Little Richard and Ike and Tina Turner before moving to New York City. After trying to support himself playing behind the Isley Brothers, King Curtis and others on the limited black club circuit, he met entrepreneur Ed Chalpin, who signed him to a management and recording deal and made him lead-guitarist in Curtis Knight's band. Hendrix's already extraordinary gifts as a guitarist were recognized by Chas Chandler, originally the Animals' bassist, and he brought Hendrix to England at the end of 1966.

In London, the Jimi Hendrix Experience was formed – a three-piece band of astonishing power – with Hendrix on lead-guitar and vocals, Noel Redding (bass) and Mitch Mitchell (drums). Hendrix was an overnight sensation. He caught the attention of the élite of British pop society (Eric Clapton and Pete Townshend reportedly went to every club gig Hendrix had in London that winter). By the summer of 1967, he had done a successful tour of Britain, Germany and Scandinavia, and had record success with 'Hey Joe' and 'Purple Haze' and the album *Are You Experienced?* (on Track). On Paul McCartney's insistence, he was lined up for the Monterey Festival where his performance made him a star. Getting 'thrown off' a follow-up tour of America headed by the Monkees perfected the Hendrix image of a wild black anti-hero. A black freak was good music-press copy and Hendrix had developed a highly charged, controversial stage-act that included a pretence at sexual assault upon his amplifiers and sometimes setting his guitar on fire. Yet it was noticeable that his audience was almost entirely white. While it was one of Hendrix's achievements that he became the first black star to win a mass white audience, he was to find himself, by 1969, under heavy political pressure to forge a solidarity with black Americans. It was a pressure he didn't understand in political terms and which caused him much strain and difficulty.

In commercial terms, 1968 was his most successful year – gold albums (*Axis Bold As Love*, 1967, and *Electric Ladyland*), massive earnings from concerts, undisputed superstar status – and in terms of his development as a musician. He was, by the end of the year, considered light-years ahead of all other 'progressive rock' guitarists, with a unique style of keening, soaring, imaginative leaps rooted in a strong melodic sense and an earthy blues feel. Miles Davis even considered that Hendrix would become a great jazz player, so wide, it seemed, was the scope and experimental urge in his playing. But as his success increased, so did personal and professional problems. In January, 1968, he spent a night in jail after a violent row with Noel Redding, a sign of their rapidly deteriorating relationship. A month later, on his second and headlining American tour, Hendrix renounced all the showbiz gimmickry of his stage act and played his complex music straight. The reception was hostile, and Hendrix's attempt to ride out this response was not helped by having to fulfil a schedule of 54 dates in 47 days while living out a chaotic round of encounters with groupies and drugs. He lost a lot of weight and became convinced that his management were mishandling his earnings.

Despite the sustained magic of his name among the public, 1969 was an even more corrosive year. Chas Chandler was eased out of Hendrix's management; the Jimi Hendrix Experience broke up; a Toronto drugs bust hung over the star throughout the year; his money was poured, at times it seemed hopelessly, into his dream-studios, Electric Ladyland in New York; his personal life was even more anarchic; and he came under enormous political pressure to aim at black audiences and form an all-black band. His live appearances were fewer, though in July, 1969, he played at Newport, using Mitch Mitchell but bringing his old friend, Billy Cox, in on bass. A month later he played the Woodstock Festival – the last high of his career. His all-black Band Of Gypsies finally came together in December, but Hendrix was bewildered and highly dissatisfied with the band's debut. At the follow-up gig at Madison Square Garden, in January, 1970, Hendrix walked out on 19,000 people in the middle of the second number. It was the end of the Band Of Gypsies.

Hendrix went back to using Mitch Mitchell and Billy Cox (the Band Of Gypsies had been Hendrix, Cox and Buddy Miles); he filmed in Hawaii; he played more concerts; he recorded at the now open Electric Ladyland studios; and, in August, he left America – for the last time – to play at the Isle of Wight Festival. His performance received a poor critical reception, though in retrospect it was at times controlled, moving and full to straining-point with ideas and power. The European tour that followed was cut short, and Hendrix returned to England alone in mid-September. On Sept. 18, 1970, he died, suffocating on his own vomit.

Many consider that Hendrix's death came at a time when his creativity was already waning. In the best sense a simple person who didn't realize, until too late, that rock stars need to protect themselves against the ravages of their profession, he had no idea how to erect such protective barriers. It is hard to claim that his creativity was declining in the light of his 1970 work, and it is unfortunate that one measure of how profoundly important his music was in its impact has led to the barrel-scraping for material since issued to cash in – only Alan Douglas's *Crash Landing* compilation (Polydor, 1975) is worthy of Hendrix's name. Musically, his influence has proved a dangerous one for his many followers. The virtuoso technique and the fluent imagination to which it was harnessed have resulted too often in more emulation rather than inspiration. That, in itself, is an indication of his power and stature.

The Herd were an early attempt at artistic respectability by hit songwriters Ken Howard and Alan Blaikley after their pop successes with the Honeycombs and Dave Dee, Dozy, Beaky, Mick and Tich. Peter Frampton (vocals, guitar), Andy Bown (keyboards), Gary Taylor (bass), Andrew Steele (drums) performed their self-consciously serious songs

178

behind an image that was the embodiment of 1968 chic. Their three hit singles which came complete with giveaway titles like 'From The Underworld' and 'Paradise Lost' (Fontana), were pretty but as pop-oriented as that of DDDBMT. Frampton soon left to form Humble Pie and the group collapsed.

Herman's Hermits – originally the Heartbeats – were far from being the leading Manchester group when Mickie Most singled them out to record. Manchester then boasted a considerable number of better musical units, with greater local followings, but it was the potential image that Most detected in Peter Noone (born Nov. 5, 1947), the group's boyish singer. The rest of the group – Derek Leckenby, guitar (May 14, 1946); Keith Hopwood, guitar (Oct. 26, 1946); Karl Green, bass (July 31, 1946); and Barry Whitwarn, drums (July 21, 1946) – were almost superfluous. They didn't even play on most of the group's hits.

Herman's Hermits' first British single, 'I'm Into Something Good' in August, 1964, took them to No. 1. More importantly, it established them, if gently, in America. Subsequent British releases over the next three years gave them ten Top Twenty hits, but their easy rocking style had only intermittent appeal and few were sizeable.

In America, their timing was perfect: by 1965 many of the other early British beat groups were already spent forces and Herman's arrival with the classic 'little boy' and 'British' persona allowed him to clean up. The group was also solidly 'good time' when much of the other current British product was aggressively R&B-flavoured and accordingly jogged its way straight into America's hearts with eleven Top Ten hits, including two No. 1s, 'Mrs Brown' and 'I'm Henry VIII I Am'. Despite a flagging following in America and Britain, the group stayed together until 1970 when Herman went solo under his real name – though he did team up with the group again for Richard Nader's 'English Invasion Revival' in 1973. The Hermits later remained in America while Peter Noone carried on, still associated with Micky Most, and recording for his Rak label.

Holland, Dozier and Holland. During the mid-Sixties, a period known to some as the 'golden age of Motown', a vast percentage of the product emanating from the Detroit studios bore the composer and production credit legend 'Holland-Dozier-Holland'.

Lamont Dozier was born in Detroit on June 16, 1941, and raised in a musical environment; both parents sang and he joined his church choir at an early age. He made his recording debut at 15, with the Romeos, on the local Fox label in 1956, but the group soon split and Lamont went to New York, where he married and took a regular job. 1958 saw him back in Detroit, however, where he met Berry Gordy through a childhood friend, Ty Hunter, who was signed to Anna Records. He started a solo recording career as Lamont Anthony on Anna and Melody, meeting little success, but as the Motown Corporation began to grow, so did Lamont's song writing prowess, and in 1961 he met up with Brian Holland, then producing for the company with Robert Bateman – they'd produced the Marvelettes' 'Please Mr Postman'. Bateman left Motown, suggesting that Dozier team with Brian. Thus Holland and Dozier became a regular writing and production team, at which time Brian's brother, Eddie, was a hit artist with the company.

Eddie Holland, born in Detroit on Oct. 30, 1939, dropped out of college to work for Berry Gordy's music publishing company, where he would sing demos of Gordy's songs, and later collaborated as a writer himself. Impressed with Eddie's voice, Gordy signed him as an artist, with initial discs leased to United Artists. Soon afterwards Motown was formed, and Eddie's first release was 'Jamie', a heavily orchestrated beat ballad with a vocal style identical to Jackie Wilson (for whom he'd sung demos). It was a Top Thirty hit in 1962. Three of his next eight discs were small hits, by which time Eddie had teamed up with his brother and Lamont Dozier to write and produce. Brian, born in Detroit on Feb. 15, 1941, was introduced to Berry Gordy by Eddie, and Gordy coached him as a writer and producer up to the time of the trio's collaboration.

From 1962, almost everything the trio touched turned to

gold as they wrote and produced a long succession of hits for the Supremes, Temptations, Four Tops, Marvin Gaye, Martha and the Vandellas and the Isley Brothers as well as less renowned groups and performers within the Motown Corporation. However, passing years created some friction between them and Gordy, and in 1968 they quit Motown to form their own company with twin labels Invictus and Hot Wax.

In May, 1969, the trio were legally restrained from operating pending a lawsuit in which Motown alleged breach of contract, but the matter was settled out of court, and Invictus/Hot Wax rapidly accrued success as Chairmen of the Board, Freda Payne and Honey Cone soared into the Top Ten, the latter gaining the company's first chart-topper with 'Want Ads' in 1971. Brian and Lamont returned to active recording themselves, scoring pop and R&B hits as a duo in 1972/73, but Lamont quit the Hollands in 1973 to sign as a solo act with ABC on the recommendation of his longtime friends, the Four Tops, and proceeded to record some fine albums with related hit singles.

The Hollies – Allan Clarke (born April 15, 1942), Graham Nash (Feb. 2, 1942), Don Rathbone, Eric Haydock and Tony Hicks (Dec. 16, 1943), were formed in 1962 as an amalgamation of two other Manchester groups, the Deltas and the Dolphins. Their first two singles, 'Ain't That Just Like Me' (Parlophone) and 'Searchin' ', were two old Coasters' numbers and while the latter made the Top Twenty in 1963, it was 'Stay' (the Maurice Williams and the Zodiacs number) which started their string of chart entries that, amongst British groups, only the Beatles can rival.

Without being as accomplished musicians or songwriters as the Beatles, and lacking a strong image, the Hollies' success was based on their knack of choosing commercial songs and their unmistakable way of singing them; Clarke's voice and Nash's tight harmonies were inimitable. After successes with 'Just One Look', 'Here I Go Again', 'We're Through' (1964), 'Yes I Will', 'I'm Alive' (their first British No. 1), 'Look Through Any Window' (1965), they had their first relative failure with a cover of George Harrison's 'If I Needed Someone', which only just scraped into the British Top Twenty. After 'I Can't Let Go' (a No. 2 in early 1966) Eric Haydock left the group to be replaced by ex-Dolphins' bassist Bernie Calvert (Sept. 16, 1944) and in the meantime Jack Bruce played bass on the 'After The Fox' session. This period, prior to the departure of Graham Nash, saw the group at their peak. They were masters of the singles medium and their lyrics – they were writing their own songs by now – without ever being as outrageously gimmicky as Dave Dee and company, for example, were carefully constructed vignettes describing people and situations that had a real charm and humour of their own – 'Bus Stop' (the song that finally established them in America, on Imperial), 'Stop, Stop, Stop' (1966), 'On A Carousel', 'Carrie Anne', 'King Midas In Reverse' (1967) and 'Jennifer Eccles' (1968).

None the less, the Hollies' success lay almost exclusively in the singles market. Although their first album, *Stay With The Hollies* (Parlophone, 1964), sold well, their subsequent album releases never matched their singles sales. It was possibly their lack of image and uniformity of style that resulted in their missing the psychedelic flower-power boom of 1967. Tony Hicks was phased out of the group at a time when the guitar was just becoming fashionable. None the less, the albums of that year, *Evolution* and *Butterfly*, still contain superb examples of the much-overlooked songwriting team of Clarke, Hicks and Nash.

At this stage, the group lost something of its direction and finally Graham Nash, having already expressed his dissatisfaction with 'Jennifer Eccles' ('I want to make records that say something'), decided to quit. Ex-Swinging Blue Jean, Terry Sylvester (born Jan. 8, 1945), replaced Nash but something of the balance of the Hollies was destroyed. They still chose their singles skilfully – often with better results in America than Britain, e.g. 'Long Cool Woman' – but they could never decide on albums whether they were still a pop group or a rock band.

In 1971, Clarke, too, left them to pursue a more fashionable career as a solo artist. He made three albums that failed to establish him and as Michael Rickfors, his replacement, did nothing spectacular for the band, Clarke rejoined in 1973. Since then, happier with a pop identity, they have been very successful once more with even smoother productions, such as 'The Air That I Breathe' (1974).

Brenda Holloway, born on June 21, 1946 in Atascadero, California, studied classical violin before signing as a singer to Motown for whom she recorded the classic slow soul ballad 'Every Little Bit Hurts', which featured the piano of Lincoln Mayorga and, more importantly, was the company's first West Coast-produced hit: it reached No. 13 in 1964. Lesser hits included 'When I'm Gone' and her own composition, 'You've Made Me So Very Happy', later a much bigger success for Blood, Sweat and Tears. She retired in the late Sixties, returning only for occasional sessions with Joe Cocker and records with discotheque heroes, the San Remo Strings.

Jac Holzman founded Elektra Records in 1950 and remained its chief executive until 1973. Trained as an engineer, Holzman at first ran virtually a one-man operation, recording folk singers like Jean Ritchie and Theodore Bikel, who had been blacklisted in the early Fifties. The company grew with the folk revival and Holzman recorded Judy Collins, Tom Paxton and the Paul Butterfield Blues Band among many others. Elektra's sister label, Nonesuch, also developed its catalogue of classical and ethnic recordings. During the Sixties, Holzman gradually shifted his attention from East Coast folk to West Coast rock, signing Los Angeles groups Love and the Doors. In the Seventies, Carly Simon and Bread were successful Elektra signings, though by this time the exclusive mystique which had attached to the label in earlier years had all but disappeared. In 1970, the company was taken over by the Kinney Corporation and three years later grouped together with Asylum Records as a division of the massive Warner Communications Inc. The new operation was headed by Asylum's David Geffen, while Holzman became senior vice-president of the parent company, in charge of developing quadraphonic sound systems.

Earl Hooker, the most highly regarded blues guitarist based in Chicago in the Sixties, was born in Clarksdale, Mississippi on Jan. 15, 1930. Influenced by Robert Nighthawk, his first records were for Rockin' in 1952. Other singles – mainly instrumentals in a characteristic single-note slide guitar style – appeared on King (1953), Bea and Baby (1959), Chief (1960), C.J., Age and Checker. Hooker's theme tune, 'Blue Guitar' became a familiar sound on Chicago's South Side, while albums on Cuca, Arhoolie, Bluesway and Blue Thumb brought him to the attention of a wider audience before he died of tuberculosis on April 21, 1970.

John Lee Hooker, a leading pioneer of the mid-Sixties blues boom, was born on August 22, 1917, in Clarksdale, Mississippi. He moved to Memphis in his teens and started playing guitar with bluesmen like Robert Nighthawk. In 1943 he moved to Detroit, where five years later he signed to the Modern label. His first session produced the million-selling single 'Boogie Chillen', featuring just Hooker's vocals and throbbing electric guitar. It was an excellent introduction to his hypnotic, Afro-American rhythms which have since become his trademark. He followed-up with 'Driftin'' and 'Hobo Blues' – two more unaccompanied numbers. Hooker's recorded output was enormous. He cut hundreds of sides during the Fifties; although contracted to Modern, he recorded under such pseudonyms as Texas Slim and Johnny Williams for Chess, King, DeLuxe and Chance.

In 1955 Hooker officially switched labels to the Chicago-based Vee Jay company, where he made some of his best sides. They included 'Maudie', 'Crawlin' King Snake', 'Tupelo', 'Birmingham Blues' and 'I'm In The Mood', which was a huge R&B hit for him when he re-recorded it for Modern in 1951. By then he was recording regularly with a backing-group, usually with Eddie Taylor on bass guitar. As the Sixties progressed, Hooker's sound became even more urbanized, often featuring a horn section and girl singers.

This period produced his biggest hits – 'Boom Boom' and 'Dimples', which was even a minor success in the British pop charts in 1964. Many rock bands have covered Hooker songs including the Animals ('I'm Mad Again') and the J. Geils Band ('Serve You Right To Suffer').

Mary Hopkin. While watching TV's *Opportunity Knocks*, Twiggy took a liking to an angelic-looking Welsh folk singer named Mary Hopkin, and recommended her talents to Paul McCartney. He signed her to Apple, and wrote and produced her first record, 'Those Were The Days'. Instantly hummable, strikingly arranged, and beautifully sung, it zoomed to the top of the charts in 1968. Apple promoted their star (born in Pontardawe, Glamorgan, on May 3, 1950) as a paragon of chapel-bred virtue, and she was consequently maligned in the press. This did not prevent her from achieving further hits over the next year; but the crunch came when she was sent out on the road and revealed her lack of stage presence.

Ken Howard and Alan Blaikley were, after Micky Most, the most successful British pop operators of the mid-Sixties. They came into the business from an intellectual background (university and the BBC) but their first success was with the Honeycombs, a straightforward pop group whom they discovered in a pub in London's Balls Pond Road and took to No. 1 in 1964 with 'Have I The Right' (on Pye). In America it reached No. 5 on Interphon. The Honeycombs split after a couple of follow-ups and Howard and Blaikley turned their attention to Dave Dee, Dozy, Beaky, Mick and Tich, for whom they wrote ten successive Top Twenty hits, on Fontana, between 1966 and 1968.

The secret of DDDBMT's success was not the songs as such (clever variations on a basic beat, lots of innuendo – 'Bend It' was the best) but the image Howard and Blaikley created for them: flash, young, sexy, noisy. DDDBMT were the pop expression of mod teenage culture: calculated rebellion, safe but never family entertainment. By 1968 this teenage generation had grown up and Howard and Blaikley

had to change tack: they gave DDDBMT more sophisticated songs (notably 'Legend Of Xanadu', their only No. 1)
and responded to 1967 with the Herd's 'From The Underworld' (Fontana), an elaborate arrangement of hippy clichés.
They continued with both groups but by the Seventies their
time was over and their attempts to get into rock (Flaming
Youth's concept album, *Arc,* Matthew's Southern Comfort's
first LP) had critical but not popular success.

   Howard and Blaikley wrote 17 Top Twenty singles in their
time but their importance was not musical (only 'I've Lost
You' had lasting appeal – Elvis made it a hit in 1970) but
commercial: they were among the first British businessmen
to take teenage pop seriously.

Howlin' Wolf, one of the best-known names in post-war
blues, was born in Aberdeen, Mississippi, on June 10, 1910,
as Chester Burnett. He learnt guitar (and his guttural
'howlin'' vocal style) from country bluesman Charley Patton and harmonica from Sonny Boy Williamson (Rice
Miller). In 1948, Wolf was spotted performing in a Memphis
club by Ike Turner, who subsequently signed him to the
Modern label. Rival sessions with other companies followed,
and he was recorded by Sam Phillips for Sun and eventually
by the Chess brothers.

   Wolf's 270lb. frame and aggressive demeanour became
well-known in the blues clubs of Chicago, his often sug-
gestive stage-act blending perfectly with his choice of songs
– usually reflecting either infidelity or sexual prowess. All his
major hits were cut between 1954 and 1964 at the Chess
studios in Chicago and, more often than not, featured the
excellent Hubert Sumlin on lead guitar. Wolf's work has
made a significant impact on the rock world, prompting
dozens of cover versions of his hits, including 'Smokestack
Lightning' (Yardbirds, Manfred Mann), 'Spoonful' (Cream,
Ten Years After), 'Little Red Rooster' (Rolling Stones), 'I
Ain't Superstitious' (Rod Stewart/Jeff Beck, Savoy Brown),
'Back Door Man' (Doors), 'Killin' Floor' (Electric Flag) and
'How Many More Years' (Little Feat). In 1972, Wolf went
to London to record an album at the request of the Rolling

Stones. On the session were such rock luminaries as Eric Clapton, Ringo Starr, Stevie Winwood, plus several of the Rolling Stones.

H. P. Lovecraft, formed in 1966 in Chicago. The group comprised: George Edwards, guitar; Dave Michaels, keyboards; Tony Cavallari, lead guitar; Mike Tegza, drums and Gerry McGeorge, ex-Shadows of Knight, bass, replaced by Jeffrey Boylan – all shared vocals. They made their earliest recording in February, 1967 – the Troggs' 'Anyway That You Want Me' (on *Early Chicago*) which featured only Edwards and Michaels plus three of Chicago's Roving Kind. *H. P. Lovecraft* later that year established them on the West Coast. The highpoint of the album is 'The White Ship', from an early story by their namesake, lingering and haunting, beautifully sung and sympathetically arranged. *H. P. Lovecraft II*, which followed their move to L.A., was their acid album, hypnotic and powerful, the psychedelics usually superfluous. There are no further recordings, though Tegza later formed Lovecraft and produced the lame *Valleys Of The Moon*. Another Lovecraft is reported to have signed a recording deal.

Englebert Humperdinck, born Gerry Dorsey on May 2, 1936, in Madras, India, had by 1967 been making a living, but little else, for over ten years as a dance-band singer. Under the astute guidance of Gordon Mills, and via a name change to Englebert Humperdinck, he won apparent overnight success. Mills had just clinched Tom Jones's middle-of-the-road immortality with 'Green, Green Grass Of Home' and Englebert was a natural with the timely release of 'Release Me' early in 1967 while 'Grass' was only just on its way down. Mills gave Englebert a moody image with a touch of the matinée idol to totally secure, yet not compete with, the same vast audience appeal Jones had recently captured. It's hard to visualize Englebert's success on such a scale other than in the wake of Tom Jones or under Mills' management. He notched up further chart hits, notably 'The Last Waltz' (a No. 1) and 'Man Without Love' in Britain and throughout the world and though the flow of hits petered out in the Seventies, he continues to remain at the top of his side of the profession as a cabaret performer.

Janis Ian, born in 1951, spent some years in New Jersey, then moved to Manhattan. *Broadside* magazine published her first song, 'Hair Of Spun Gold' in 1964, and she produced understandable shock waves when she first performed at a *Broadside Hoot* at the Village Gate. At only 15, she signed to MGM and recorded 'Society's Child', a bitter, personal protest at the hypocrisy of the older generation. An album full of angry 'generation gap' songs followed in 1967 – and for a writer of her age they showed astonishing maturity. After a couple of years performing, she quit and moved to California to write songs for others. Signed to Columbia, she later returned to recording and performing – but her ever-personal songs were now more varied, less bitter. She had an American No. 1 with 'At 17' in 1975.

The Impressions, formed in Chicago in 1957, were originally an anonymous drone behind Jerry Butler's beautiful recording debut, 'For Your Precious Love' (Falcon, 1958). Three years later, it was another founder-member, Curtis Mayfield, who came to dominate the group with his distinctive songs, soft expressive voice, mellow, fluid guitar, and unique ideas in production. He made the Impressions the most readily identifiable group of the Sixties and eventually emerged as one of black music's superstars.

After Butler's departure, Mayfield led the revamped group (Richard and Arthur Brooks, Sam Gooden, and Fred Cash) and supplied most of the songs for the rest of their unsuccessful recordings on Abner. When the label was absorbed by the parent company, Vee Jay, the Impressions were dropped. While Gooden and Richard Brooks took the lead on singles for Bandera (Chicago) and Swirl (New York), Mayfield created his first hits, writing and accompanying several of Butler's early Vee Jay releases, before doing the same thing for the Impressions with their first ABC-Paramount release, 'Gypsy Woman' (1961), cut in New York. Five more singles were less successful, perhaps because Mayfield was busy giving his most interesting songs to Gene Chandler and his most commercial to Major Lance. Then, back in Chicago as a trio, Mayfield, Cash and Gooden recorded their biggest hit, 'It's All Right' (1963). Arranged by Johnny Pate, its gentle, infectious rhythm and lilting harmonies supported two more years of solid hits – bouncy love songs ('Talking About My Baby', 'You Must Believe Me', 'Woman's Got Soul') – the wistful ('I'm So Proud') – and the first stirrings of deeper thought ('Keep On Pushing', 'Amen', 'People Get Ready', 'Meeting Over Yonder').

With the group at their peak, and many other performers recording his songs, Mayfield made two premature attempts to launch his own record companies, Windy C (1966) and Mayfield (1967). While these ventures quietly collapsed, the Impressions' records started to sound like out takes from Motown sessions. 'You Been Cheatin'' (1965), 'Since I Lost The One I Love', 'Can't Satisfy' (1966), and 'You Always Hurt Me' (1967) were all hits that owed more to the sound of Detroit than Chicago, and it seemed that Mayfield had lost his touch. In their last year with ABC, they recovered with two prophetic titles ('We're A Winner' and 'We're Rolling On') which they promptly confirmed by transferring to Mayfield's third, successful, company – Curtom. From their first release, subtle changes in his guitar playing and the overall production showed that he acknowledged the new wave of young black musicians and the use of modern technology. With heavier songs like 'This Is My Country' (1968), 'Choice Of Colours', 'Mighty Mighty Spade and Whitey' (1969), 'Check Out Your Mind' (1970) he began attracting audiences who wouldn't have listened to his earlier work, and left the group for a solo career in 1970.

Replacing Mayfield with Leroy Hutson, the Impressions survived as a trio for two more years without a memorable hit. When Hutson also left to go solo, Cash and Gooden brought in Reggie Torian and Ralph Johnson, recorded the successful 'Three The Hard Way' film soundtrack, and by 1974 were back at the top with 'Finally Got Myself Together', written and produced by veteran Ed Townsend.

They had their first British hit in 1975 with 'First Impressions'.

The Incredible String Band began as a three-man jug band in 1965, playing in Glasgow at Clive's Incredible Folk Club. Only after Clive Palmer left did the other two, Robin Williamson (born on Nov. 24, 1943) and Mike Heron (Dec. 12, 1942), blossom out to invent a new, global folk form. Using instruments and influences from anywhere they could, and actually being able to play the gimbris, mandolins, whistles, or other assorted instruments they got hold of, they were popular in both the folk clubs and the emergent 'Underground'. The freshness and unspecific idealism in their early work summed up the best in the new, vague hippy culture, notably on *The 5,000 Spirits Or The Layers Of The Onion* (Elektra, 1967) and *Wee Tam And The Big Huge* (1968).

As they became more successful they moved to the rock circuit and expanded the band. For many years it included two girls, Rose and Licorice, and then a dancer turned musician, Malcolm Le Maistre. During the Seventies the String Band moved to Island where they gradually lost their magic, and moved to a conventional rock line-up. The band broke up in 1974, with Heron forming his own band, Mike Heron's Reputation.

Iron Butterfly began life in Los Angeles in 1967, soon settling to a line-up of Doug Ingle (born Sept. 9, 1945) organ, vocals; Ron Bushy (Sept. 23, 1941) drums; Lee Dorman (Sept. 15, 1942) bass; and Eric Braunn (Aug. 10, 1950) guitar. Danny Weiss also flirted with the band for a while before joining Rhinoceros and can be heard on their first album, *Heavy*. The album, released in 1968, established the group as unsubtle and instrumentally obvious, with a too solid rhythm section and an overweight sound only lightened by Ingle's ponderous organ work. Despite an inauspicious start, a strong following launched their second album, *In A Gadda Da Vidda*, to massive sales. It remains Atlantic's largest grossing rock album – and maybe their largest gross selling album. Braunn was replaced in 1971 by twin guitarists Mike

Pinera (Sept. 29, 1948) – later with Cactus – and Larry Rheinhardt (July 7, 1948) but their contribution failed to raise *Metamorphosis* to a higher critical standpoint. The group ground to a halt in 1972 but resurfaced in 1975 under the dual helm of Eric Braunn and Ron Bushy, assisted by Phil Kramer, bass, and Howard Reitzes, keyboards, to produce another tiresome and expendable album, *Scorching Beauty.*

It's A Beautiful Day, a second-generation San Franciscan group – David LaFlamme, electric violin (born April 5, 1941); Bill Gregory, guitar; Val Fuentes, drums (Nov. 25, 1947); Tom Fowler, bass; and Pattie Santos, vocals (Nov. 16, 1949) – had their first album, *It's A Beautiful Day* (Columbia) released in the summer of 1969. It featured a blend of rather ordinary rock and the impassioned violin-playing of their leader, the classically trained LaFlamme, seen at its best on the group's one memorable number, 'White Bird'. With each subsequent album, *Marrying Maiden*, *Choice Quality Stuff* and *Live At Carnegie Hall*, the group shed members and changed styles until, by 1973, they were unrecognizable as the group who originally performed 'White Bird'.

Chuck Jackson, born on July 22, 1937 in Winston Salem, North Carolina, moved to Pittsburgh to join the Del-Vikings shortly after the group's 'Whispering Bells' hit in 1957. His lead singing can be heard on recently released records on Bim Bam Boom. He made solo discs for Clock and Beltone before producer Luther Dixon signed him to Wand. The resulting rich-voiced soul ballads were constantly in the middle reaches of the charts between 1961 and 1964. Among them were 'I Don't Want To Cry', 'I Woke Up Crying', 'Any Day Now' (a fine Burt Bacharach song), 'I Keep Forgetting' (a Leiber/Stoller composition), 'Tell Him I'm Not Home', 'Beg Me' and 'Since I Don't Have You'. In 1965, Jackson's partnership with Maxine Brown produced a series of hits, including 'Something You Got'. Two years later, he joined Motown where 'Are You Lonely For Me Baby' was a small

191

R&B hit. Subsequent records for Dakar and ABC-Paramount were less successful although he returned to the charts with the Steve Barri production, 'I Only Get This Feeling', in 1973. Always a distinctive singer, Chuck Jackson is now firmly established in the cabaret soul market.

Eric Jacobsen, originally a member of the Plum Creek Boys, a bluegrass style group in the hootenanny era of the early Sixties, followed Al Grossman – another Chicagoan – to New York where Grossman took over management of the now renamed Knoblick Upper Ten Thousand. The trio – Jacobsen, Duane Storey and Peter Childs – toured heavily and cut two albums for Mercury before Jacobsen, like countless other folkies, had his head turned around by the Beatles' music. It decided him on a new role in nurturing new talent, producing, arranging, even managing them and publishing their music. Surprisingly he more than lived out his fantasy, initially with Tim Hardin, producing his first and arranging his second album. *Tim Hardin 2* was produced by Charlie Koppelman and Don Rubin who were originally scheduled to handle the electric folk group which Jacobsen helped build around Village musician and songwriter John Sebastian. The Lovin' Spoonful, as they became, were in their early stages indebted to Jacobsen who produced their first two albums, and *You're A Big Boy Now*. It was Jacobsen who put up the money for the single 'Do You Believe In Magic', but with their publishing signed to his Faithful Virtue Music he was well compensated. Later Jacobsen involved himself in a whole roster of fascinating projects: the Charlatans (their unreleased Kama Sutra album), the Sopwith Camel and in 1968, as if to prove he still had the touch, he discovered Norman Greenbaum in the Troubadour and produced the imaginative (and successful) 'Spirit In The Sky' single.

Dick James began his music career in 1936, at 15, singing in a North London dance band. After the war, he sang with many of the leading British bands, but quit touring in 1953 to join the publishing staff of Sydney Bron. Meanwhile, he sang the theme to the television series *Robin Hood*, a 1955 session produced by George Martin. In 1960, he set up his own publishing company which was given a spectacular boost in October, 1962, when George Martin put him in contact with Brian Epstein to publish songs for the Beatles and future NEMS artists. James then set up Page One Records, with Larry Page, in November, 1965, scoring immediately with the Troggs' 'Wild Thing'. Four years later, when James and Page parted company, he set up DJM. His luck and judgment continued – in James's studios cutting demos was Reg Dwight, whom James teamed with Bernie Taupin to launch another English rock phenomenon, Elton John.

Elmore James, an important blues figure of the Fifties and Sixties, was born on Jan. 18, 1918, at Richland, Mississippi. He started out playing at Saturday night dances, occasionally working with Sonny Boy Williamson (Rice Miller) and blues legend Robert Johnson. His first record was a cover of Johnson's 'Dust My Blues', recorded in Jackson in 1951 for the Trumpet label. The single made the R&B Top Ten, which inspired James to adapt the theme for several of his later songs. His best known sides were cut for the Chess, Chief and Fire labels between 1957 and 1962. This period produced such contemporary-sounding blues classics as 'It Hurts Me Too', 'The Sun Is Shining', 'Rollin' And Tumblin' ' and 'Shake Your Money Maker'. His regular band on these sessions included his cousin Homesick James (rhythm guitar), Little Johnny Jones (piano) and J. T. Brown (tenor sax). All the songs were characterized by James's intense, tortured vocal delivery and fierce, heavily amplified slide-guitar playing. His records influenced countless British blues groups during the mid-Sixties, in particular Fleetwood Mac and John Mayall's Bluesbreakers. But recognition came too late for Elmore, who died of a heart attack on May 23, 1963.

Tommy James and the Shondells emerged in 1964 as the Shondells, who released a cover version of the Raindrops' 'Hanky Panky' on the small Snap label in Michigan. Two years later, it was heard by a deejay in Pittsburgh, and released nationally by Roulette the record climbed to No. 1.

Tommy James – born April 29, 1947 – and his new Shondells (the original group had long since split) – Mike Vale, bass (born July 17, 1949); Ronnie Rosman, piano (Feb. 28, 1945); Peter Lucia, drums (Feb. 2, 1947); Eddie Gray, guitar (Feb. 27, 1948) and others – followed that with another Top Thirty record in the same vein, 'Say I Am', but eventually they changed their style to become a less raunchy, more candy-coated bubble-rock group. Their many hits during 1967–9 (mostly written by James and Bob King) included 'I Think We're Alone Now', 'Mirage' (both Top Five) and 'Gettin' Together' (1967), 'Mony Mony' (a No. 3), 'Do Something To Me' and their second No. 2, 'Crimson And Clover' (1968), 'Sweet Cherry Wine', 'Crystal Blue Persuasion' and 'Ball Of Fire'. Since 1970, James has had more than ten chart singles as a solo artist, particularly 'Draggin' The Line' (Roulette, 1971), a sizeable hit, also covered by Dave Clark. The rest of the Shondells recorded briefly as Hog Heaven.

Jan and Dean. Jan Berry, born in Los Angeles on April 3, 1941, and Dean Torrence, born in the same city on March 10, 1940, were entrenched in an era when pop was fun and by no means culture. Had their career not been abruptly terminated, it's difficult to imagine that their success would have continued much beyond 1966. Both attended Emerson Junior High School in L.A. and discovered their singing capabilities in the shower room after football practice. The season over, it was into the garage with two tape recorders and a few friends, among them Bruce Johnston, the future Beach Boy, to record 'Jenny Lee' as Jan and Arnie – Arnie Ginsberg – a song about a local burlesque stripper. A few months later in 1958, it was a Top Ten hit (on Arwin). Further hits followed as Jan and Dean, notably 'Baby Talk', a No. 10 in 1959 (on Dore), produced and arranged by Herb Alpert and Lou Adler, while they were still at college, Berry studying to be a doctor and Torrence studying design.

For 'Heart And Soul', a Top Thirty hit in 1961, they moved to Challenge, and then signed with Liberty in 1962 and started singing about one of their favourite pastimes – surfing. The group had been gigging with the Beach Boys, and when Brian Wilson played them a demo of 'Surf City', which they recorded and took to No. 1 in 1963, it opened up a vintage period for Jan and Dean who alongside the Beach Boys fought off the British Invasion with a string of hot rod, surfin' and high-school epics like 'Deag City', 'Little Old Lady From Pasadena' and 'Dead Man's Curve', all Top Ten hits 1963–4 on Liberty. They hosted the *TAMI Show*, disastrously took on folk-rock with a 1965 album, *Folk'n'Roll*, and frequently sang on Beach Boys sessions: for example, Jan actually sang lead on the *Beach Boys' Party* hit, 'Barbara Ann'. Brian Wilson had a hand in most of their classic hits between 1963 and 1965.

Then while filming *Easy Come – Easy Go* early in 1966, Jan crashed his car into a parked truck and all but sliced off the top of his head. He has been recovering gradually since, determined to return at some stage and recently cutting sides for A&M; though no permanent return of Jan and Dean is likely. Dean has been involved with the Legendary Masked Surfers and California Music but more importantly now runs a flourishing studio in Hollywood, Kittyhawk, designing posters and album sleeves. Their contribution to the less complicated Sixties pop is best remembered through their hits on either their *Legendary Masters* or *Gotta Take That One Last Ride* albums released in 1974.

Bert Jansch, born in Glasgow on Nov. 3, 1943, worked as a gardener in Edinburgh before moving to London to become one of the most successful guitarists on the folk scene. Originally influenced by bluesmen like Big Bill Broonzy and Lightning Hopkins, he followed Davy Graham as a leading exponent of the 'folk baroque' style. Jansch applied this guitar technique to his own songs, of which 'Needle of Death' (on *Bert Jansch*, Transatlantic, 1965) was the best known. He then concentrated on using this technique on traditional songs (as on the 1966 Transatlantic album *Jack Orion*). On all his solo recordings the voice is weak but effectively propped up by the intricate accompaniment.

In 1966, Jansch recorded an excellent album of jazz-tinged instrumentals with his friend, John Renbourn, and the following year he and Renbourn formed a band, Pentangle, along with Danny Thompson, Jaqui McShee and Terry Cox. Pentangle was an amplified acoustic band, and mixed folk with jazz, blues and contemporary songs. It was a success, internationally, but the muted, sophisticated approach often sounded monotonous. In 1974, after Pentangle had broken up, Jansch recorded an album for Charisma backed by American country musicians and produced by Mike Nesmith – a fusion that brought new life to his excellent guitar technique.

Jay and the Americans in 1962, the year of the twist and hootenanny epidemics, climbed their way to the American Top Five with 'She Cried' (United Artists). Jay Black (born Nov. 2, 1947) provided the plaintive lead voice while Kenny Vance (Dec. 9, 1943), Sandy Deane (Jan. 30, 1960), Marty Saunders (Feb. 28, 1941) – also their lead guitarist – and Howie Kane (June 6, 1942) added the neatly dovetailed chorus and harmonies. Sincere and emotional and anachronistic; simple arrangements in the age of Spector; cleancut, All-American image in the era of the British Invasion – despite or because of it all they had a steady flow of hits – 18 between 1962 and 1970, mostly produced by Wes Farrell, notably 'Come A Little Closer' and 'Cara Mia' (both Top Five) with Jay Black also enjoying some favour on solo ventures. They seemed oblivious to all that was changing around them, perhaps the key to their surprising longevity. Black and Vance both recorded solo albums for Atlantic in 1975.

Jefferson Airplane became synonymous with the 'San Francisco Sound' in 1967 when both 'Somebody To Love' and 'White Rabbit' were Top Ten hits on RCA. Although the critical consensus is that the Airplane reached their peak in 1970, they remain, with the Grateful Dead, the most longlasting and prolific of the groups to emerge from Haight-Ashbury in the late Sixties. Formed on the initiative of singer Marty Balin, who had recorded solo sides for Challenge in the early Sixties, the group was born out of a bunch of ex-folk musicians, who began playing folk-rock at the Matrix in the summer of 1965. One of the earliest San Francisco bands to establish themselves at the centre of the growing local culture, they were the first to secure a recording contract. The advance paid by RCA was said to be $25,000, and by the time the first album (*Jefferson Airplane Takes Off*) was recorded the following winter, the group was fully electric.

Although it was, in parts, derivative of the Beatles and the Lovin' Spoonful, the record showed how innovative the Jefferson Airplane were to be. From the beginning they saw their music as a means of breaking down established traditions and mores: hence the unabashed way they celebrated the drug culture, as early as 1965. Following the release of *Takes Off*, singer Signe Anderson left to be replaced by Grace Slick from the Great Society, another San Francisco group. Drummer Skip Spence also departed, to form Moby Grape. The remaining personnel remained together for the next four years. They were Jorma Kaukonen, lead guitar (born Dec. 23, 1940), Jack Casady, bass (April 4, 1944), Paul Kantner, guitar and vocals (March 3, 1941), Marty Balin, vocals (Jan. 30, 1943), Grace Slick, vocals (Oct. 10, 1939) and Spencer Dryden, drums (April 7, 1938). They were a co-operative, multi-media band, with posters, album-sleeves, dance promotion and Glenn McKay's Headlights light show all integral parts of their activity. The late Sixties also saw them at a creative zenith as a recording group with *Surrealistic Pillow* (1967), *After Bathing At Baxters* and *Crown Of Creation* (1968), the live *Bless Its Little Pointed Head* and the politically oriented *Volunteers* (1969). Grace Slick was an important addition to the band. She strengthened its visual and musical identity (through her harmonies with Balin). And she was the composer of the Airplane's two hit singles, 'White Rabbit' and 'Somebody To Love'. Equally important was the group's electronic experimentation, in the extended instrumental passages of songs like '3/5 Of A Mile In 10 Seconds' and 'The Ballad Of You, Me And Pooneil'. The pressures on the Airplane during these four years were immense and the cracks started to appear in 1970 when Casady and Kaukonen, who wanted to get back to playing blues again, formed Hot Tuna. Similarly Balin, whose contributions on each successive album were becoming less and less, left the band he had nurtured, a disillusioned figure, and although involved at the outset of Hot Tuna, left them, too, to form his own band, Grootna. Not even the arrival of violinist Papa John Creach prior to Balin's departure could cement the Hot Tuna/Balin/Slick/Kantner factions of the band together. It wasn't until 1971 after Slick's car crash and baby, the formation of their own record label, Grunt, the second Hot Tuna album and the bombastic *Blows Against The Empire* of the retitled Jefferson Starship that *Bark* appeared to prove that Airplane was still in existence.

Although members of the band contributed to splinter Grunt productions like *Sunfighter*, *Papa John Creach*, *Burghers* and *Black Kangaroo*, it was another year before the insipid *Long John Silver* appeared. Technically the last Airplane album, it showed that the totality of the band was no longer the primary interest of its members. Ex-Quicksilver bassist, David Freiburg, joined for the 1972 American tour and afterwards went into the studios with Slick and Kantner to produce the impressive *Baron Von Tollbooth And The Chrome Nun* (1973), followed by Slick's first 'solo' venture, *Manhole*.

The next 'group' venture, with Craig Chaquico on lead guitar and Pete Sears on bass and keyboards, was the Starship's *Dragonfly* (1974), an even more marked return to form that was indeed worthy of the Jefferson prefix. With Balin returning to the band (he sang one track on *Dragonfly*), the vocal depth of the band was strengthened and the content of songs became more diverse; it was when Balin's love songs were phased out in the Sixties, that iconoclasm had become the order of the day. Significantly, it was with his 'Miracles' from *Red Octopus* that the band returned to the singles (and album) charts in 1975.

The Airplane/Starship were and still are a very important band. Pioneers in many fields, they created sensuous music of the highest order, and if at times over-emphatic lyrically and self-indulgent, they were powerful spokesmen for a generation intensely critical of prevailing American values.

Bob Johnston was a staff producer for Columbia's country division throughout the Sixties, working on albums by Bob Dylan, Simon and Garfunkel, Johnny Cash and Leonard Cohen. He is the 'Bob' addressed by Dylan when he calls out 'Is it rolling, Bob?' on the *Nashville Skyline* album. A Texan, Johnston's first success was with middle-of-the-road singer Patti Page. He went on to produce six Bob Dylan albums, from *Highway 61 Revisited* to *Self Portrait*, and the Simon and Garfunkel hit, 'Homeward Bound'. In the late Sixties he succeeded Don Law as head of Columbia's Nashville operation, but was ostracized by the country music establishment and replaced by Billy Sherrill. As an independent producer in the Seventies, he worked with several artists on the British Charisma label, including Lindisfarne, whose *Fog On The Tyne* album was a Johnston production.

George Jones, influenced by Roy Acuff and Hank Williams, came out of Sarasota, East Texas, in 1954, at a time when rockabilly upstarts were threatening to make country music extinct. But even though he cut a couple of rockabilly sides under the name Thumper Jones, he was a purist, as his first hit ('Why, Baby, Why' for Starday in 1955) showed. Despite a long string of superb records, Jones didn't receive his due until 1962 and 1963, when disc jockeys voted him No. 1 male country singer.

His honky tonk music was matched by his debilitating lifestyle, and he did not maintain his position as 'King of Country Music'. Still, such mid-Sixties recordings as 'The Race Is On' were as 'traditional' as any in a field leaning increasingly towards middle-of-the-road music. Then he married country housewife queen, Tammy Wynette, and shared her label (Epic) and producer (Billy Sherrill), whose ornate, pop-oriented arrangements did much to blunt the classic Jones style. By the time the dream marriage dissolved in 1974, Jones had recorded some 100 albums (for Starday, Mercury, Musicor, United Artists, and Epic), embracing virtually every form of country music.

Paul Jones. Before joining the Manne-Hugg Blues Brothers

Manfred Mann's pixie-faced 'one-in-the-middle' had been a regular visitor to the Ealing Club throughout 1962, where as P. P. ('permanently pissed') Pond he would perform impromptu duets with Brian Jones behind huge sunglasses. A moderate singer, Jones – born on Feb. 24, 1942 – left Manfred Mann in 1966 to pursue a solo career. He recorded two British Top Ten singles on his own – 'High Time' (1966) and 'I've Been A Bad Bad Boy' (1962) – but had stronger ambitions as an actor. He appeared in dramatic roles on stage, television, and in films, starring in Peter Watkins' *Privilege* (1967).

Tom Jones, born in Treforest, Glamorgan, on June 7, 1940 as Thomas J. Woodward, first changed his name to Tommy Scott as a bar-room rock'n'roller in the late Fifties, singing for beer and change, brawling enough to bust his nose several times, and working by day as a labourer to support the wife and child he'd had since sixteen. Turned down in 1963 by Joe Meek, he was 'discovered 'in a Pontypridd club a year later by ex-novelty singer and harmonica player, Gordon Mills, who was there to watch Mandy Rice Davies' act.

Then a songwriter, Mills took him to London as a demo-singer, changed his name to Jones, and let him record a song he'd demoed, 'It's Not Unusual' (Decca), which made No. 1 in Britain in March, 1965. Over the next two years Jones had more flops than hits, but then found his true audience on TV and in cabaret and never looked back. The mawkish, manly 'Green, Green Grass Of Home' stayed seven weeks at No. 1 over Christmas, 1966, and Tom went on to win the housewives' hearts in America as a substitute Presley.

Janis Joplin, born in Port Arthur, Texas on Jan. 19, 1943, spent the first seventeen years of her life in the South, acquiring a love of the blues through listening to the recordings of Leadbelly and Bessie Smith. Then she joined the national odyssey to San Francisco, on her first visit singing alone in folk clubs and bars, on her second joining Big Brother and the Holding Company as lead singer. The band played a raucous amalgam of rock and blues behind Janis's dramatic vocals. Little subtlety was in evidence; above all the music expressed enthusiasm, in the making of music and in the community it was made for. The *Cheap Thrills* album (Columbia, 1968), for all its musical shoddiness, saw Janis at a peak. In particular the classic 'Ball And Chain' and 'Piece Of My Heart' displayed her power as singer and symbol. They were desperate cries for love and security, transforming themselves in the emotional energy of the performance into triumphs of a will to continue.

In late 1968 Janis left the band, convinced that they had exhausted their collective potential. But with the undoubtedly more competent musicians with whom she thenceforth worked, Squeeze and later Full Tilt Boogie, the old enthusiasm was never quite recaptured, although her singing perhaps showed a finer control. Both *Kosmic Blues* (1969) and the posthumously released *Pearl* (1971) are fine records but somehow lack the bite of *Cheap Thrills*' joyous intensity. Janis was now a superstar, confronting greater expectations with less human support. In addition, she faced the contradiction of the tomboy superstar, defying the feminine stereotypes, but also the traditional female blues persona of the eternal loser. A combination of these pressures eventually overwhelmed her. She died of a heroin overdose on Oct. 4, 1970, in Hollywood.

Kaleidoscope are a reminder of the danger of over-eclecticism in rock. Their first two remarkable albums *Sidetrips* (Epic, 1967) and *A Beacon From Mars* (1968) range through old-timey music, English ballads, Cajun fiddle music, Eastern modal music, R&B and brilliantly sustained feedback work by guitarist David Lindley who also played fiddle, harp guitar, and banjo. The rest of the crowd were Solomon Feldthouse, guitar, caz, oud and other stringed instruments; Chris Darrow, bass, mandolin; John Vidican, drums, and Fenrus Epp, keyboards, fiddle and harmonica.

On each of the four albums Epp masqueraded under a different name (Max Buda, Templeton Parceley and Connie Crill) while for their final albums more changes brought in Paul Lagos, drums, and Stuart Brotman, bass. Under that line-up they cut *Incredible* (1969), the brilliant but obscure single 'Just A Taste', and the weakish *Bernice*, the last before they split up in 1970. Their live performances deserve the legendary tag, showcasing their eclectic tendencies in spectacular fashion. Flamenco dancers would accompany Feldthouse's Spanish guitar piece and a belly dancer their Eastern jam, 'Taxim'. Kaleidoscope went unnoticed while less deserving L.A. bands monopolized the critical acclaim until it was too late. Chris Darrow later followed a solo career (with three albums to date) while Dave Lindley is best known for his work with Jackson Browne.

Kama Sutra Records, the focal point of 'good-time' music (the East Coast equivalent of California's folk-rock sound) in 1965–6, was launched in mid-1965 by Artie Ripp and his associates as an outgrowth of Kama Sutra Productions, a publishing/production company that in a year had scored many hits (including the Shangri-Las) working through young producers like Bo Gentry, Richie Cordell, Artie Butler, Jimmy Wisner, and the prolific Koppelman-Rubin team, who brought Kama Sutra a Top Ten smash with its second release, 'Do You Believe in Magic', by the Lovin' Spoonful. Originally distributed by MGM, the label became known for the melodic, happy-style rock epitomized by the Spoonful. Other hit acts included the Sopwith Camel ('Hello, Hello', 'Postcard From Jamaica'), the Vacels ('You're My Baby'), the Tradewinds ('Mind Excursion'), and the Innocence ('There's Got To Be A Word'). After the Lovin' Spoonful's demise, Kama Sutra began its decline, and in 1970 left MGM to become a subsidiary of Buddah.

Albert King, one of today's top blues guitarists and a major influence on the rock world, was born in Indianola, Mississippi, on April 25, 1923. Inspired by the guitar-playing of T-Bone Walker, King travelled to Chicago where he ended up playing drums behind Jimmy Reed and on a few of the early Vee Jay sessions, including those of the Spaniels. But he did manage to sing and play guitar on 'Bad Luck Blues', a one-off single for Parrot Records which he cut in 1953. He didn't record again until 1959, when he signed to the St

Louis-based Bobbin label. These sides were later leased to King Records. In 1965, he cut a few things for the Coun-Tree label of East St Louis, before signing with Stax in 1966, the turning point in his career. Together with the solid house-band at Stax, he recorded some of the most dynamic blues sides of the early Sixties, such as 'Laundromat Blues', 'Crosscut Saw' and 'Personal Manager' on the album *Born Under A Bad Sign* (1967).

An extremely imposing figure, King stands six feet four inches and weighs about 250 lb. He plays a left-handed Gibson Flying Arrow guitar in a distinctly recognizable style which more than complements his raw and husky vocals. His guitar breaks build to a climax, incorporating clusters of fast, single-note runs – usually on a minor scale – with hard, biting notes that almost scream. This technique has influenced dozens of rock guitarists, and his songs have been covered by the Free ('The Hunter'), Paul Butterfield ('Born Under A Bad Sign'), John Mayall/Mick Taylor ('Oh Pretty Woman') and Electric Flag ('You Threw Your Love On Me Too Strong').

B. B. King, perhaps the best known and influential blues-man of them all, was born Riley King on Sept. 16, 1925, in Itta Bena, Mississippi. After the war, King travelled to Memphis, where he renewed a friendship with his cousin, the legendary blues singer/guitarist, Bukka White. Encouraged by White, and influenced by the guitar-playing of T-Bone Walker, Django Reinhardt and Charlie Christian, King began working sessions on local radio shows, eventually landing a job as deejay on station WDIA. He became known as the Beale Street Blues Boy, which he later abbreviated to just B. B. In between radio shows he kept playing, often sitting in with whichever jazz and blues artists were in town.

In 1950, he signed with Modern Records, cutting his first million-seller, 'Three O'Clock Blues', which stayed at No. 1 in the R&B charts for eighteen weeks. The song featured King on vocals and guitar, Ike Turner (piano), Willie Mitchell (trumpet) and Hank Crawford (alto). It was the first of a string of hits for Modern/RPM, as King recorded literally hundreds of sides for the label over a ten-year period. They included 'Everyday I Have The Blues', a million-seller in 1955, 'Sweet Little Angel' (1956) and 'Sweet Sixteen' (1960). All were polished city blues, mostly featuring horns and occasionally strings.

Initially, B. B. played guitar to accompany himself, but by the time he cut his first records, he was playing single-string runs in a group context. Gradually he began to develop different ways of punctuating phrases. He sometimes played a barrage of notes to introduce a whole section of extended improvisation, and to this would add a vibrato sound while 'bending' notes. The idea did not originate with him, since a number of jazz guitarists had done the same thing before – but the frequent use of bent notes has since become a B. B. King trademark. He also possesses a potent vocal style, most distinctive, again, in the way he tends to punctuate phrases with his clear falsetto wail and gospel-blues voice.

In 1961 King signed with ABC, which led to hits like 'Don't Answer The Door' and his second million-seller in 1969, 'The Thrill Is Gone', the latter revealing a more contemporary approach to his material. During the early Seventies, King teamed up with Leon Russell and Carole King for *Indianola Mississippi Seeds*; with Joe Walsh and Taj Mahal for *LA Midnight*, and worked with Ringo Starr, Pete Wingfield, Steve Marriott and others on *B. B. King In London*. But his best album remains *Live At The Regal*, recorded in Chicago during the early Sixties.

Freddie King, a pioneer of modern blues guitar, was born on Sept. 30, 1934, in Longview, Texas. While in his teens he moved to Chicago, jiving and jamming with numerous bands including Muddy Waters'. He first recorded under his own name for El-Bee in 1956–7. In 1960, he signed with the Cincinnati-based Federal label, a subsidiary of Syd Nathan's King Records. The first session produced three hits: 'Have You Ever Loved A Woman', 'See See Baby' and his best known number, 'Hide Away', a superb instrumental dedicated to a Chicago blues lounge of that name. Over a six-year period, Federal released 77 titles by King via singles and albums and of these 30 were instrumentals. In 1968 he switched to Atlantic, cutting two King Curtis-produced albums. This eventually led to Leon Russell signing King to his newly formed Shelter Records. Three Shelter albums and numerous tours with Russell brought King superstar status. In 1974, however, Mike Vernon managed to lure him away to RSO Records, where in England he recorded 'Burglar', produced by Vernon and featuring Eric Clapton and Gonzales.

King's influence on today's generation of rock guitarists has been enormous. His many hits have been covered by Clapton/Derek And The Dominoes ('Have You Ever Loved A Woman', Clapton/John Mayall ('Hide Away'), Mick Taylor/John Mayall ('Driving Sideways'), Pete Green/John Mayall ('The Stumble', 'Someday After A While'), and Stan Webb/ Chicken Shack ('San-Ho-Zay').

The Kingston Trio was formed at Stanford, California, in 1957 by Dave Guard, Bob Shane and Nick Reynolds who all played guitar and banjo and sang. As purveyors of folk songs to a larger pop audience, they marked a transitional and very successful phase between the more committed (Old Left) Weavers and (New Left) Peter, Paul and Mary. Their accessible harmonies (which owed as much to the cabaret tradition of the Four Freshmen and others as to folk) took them to No. 1 in 1958 with 'Tom Dooley' on Capitol. This was followed by a stream of successful albums and singles, including 'Worried Man' and 'Greenback Dollar'. In 1961, Guard was replaced by John Stewart. The Trio disbanded in 1966, outmoded by the newer folk-rock artists.

The Kinks. At the centre of the mass of seeming contradictions that the Kinks represent is Ray Davies; his obsessions have charted the course the group have followed since the days when they were the Ravens, a smartly dressed – pink hunting jackets, frills and lace – if musically inept R&B group on London's deb circuit in 1962–3. The nucleus of the group was the Davies brothers, Raymond Douglas Davies (born in Muswell Hill, London on June 21, 1944) and Dave (born on Feb. 3, 1947), who while at Art School graduated from a passing interest in rock'n'roll and blues to fully fledged would-be R&Bers. They met up with ex-skiffler and drummer, Mick Avory (born Feb. 15, 1944), and bassist Peter Quaife (born Dec. 23, 1943), and got together originally to back singer Robert Wace who later became their manager.

Signed by Pye Records in the wake of the Merseybeat/ R&B boom, the Kinks', as the group was renamed, first record, a very Beatles-influenced version of Little Richard's 'Long Tall Sally', failed, as did their second, 'You Do Something To Me'. However, their next single, 'You Really Got Me', was a British No. 1 and American Top Ten record (on Reprise) in 1964. It marked the beginning of Ray Davies' songwriting career and the Kinks' prominence in the British (and world) charts for a couple of years. Produced by Shel Talmy, 'You Really Got Me' was both utterly primitive in conception and construction and completely devastating in performance. Over the next two years it was followed by seven British Top Ten, and sizeable American hits, all hewn from the same 'Chunka Chunka Chunk' mould – as Ray Davies laconically put it later, 'Those three chords are part of my life, G, F, B♭.' These included 'All Of The Day And All Of The Night' (1964), 'Tired Of Waiting For You' (a British No. 1), 'Set Me Free', 'See My Friends' and 'Till The End Of The Day' (1965), which when taken together as a group of songs gave a foretaste of the aura of disenchantment and melancholy that was to pervade most of Ray Davies' songwriting. 1966 saw the first indication of the group's change in direction. At a time when the rest of the world was glorifying the idea of 'Swinging London' and Britain was smugly celebrating her lead in fashion and pop music, the Kinks chose to question the whole giddy scene in songs like 'Well Respected Man' and 'Dedicated Follower Of Fashion' (1966). Amazing though they were at the time, these songs and others like 'House In The Country', 'Session Man' and 'Exclusive Residence For Sale', from *Face To Face*, their first thematically linked album, can in retrospect be seen as transitional. They showed that Ray Davies was quite sure of what he *didn't* like, but, as yet, this was only expressed in a superficial and wholly negative way. It wasn't until 'Sunny Afternoon' (a British chart-topper), 'Dead End Street' (1966), the glorious 'Waterloo Sunset' and 'Autumn Almanac' (1967) that Davies found the mellow melodic sound that was to characterize the Kinks' next musical phase and began to write compassionately rather than merely satirically.

For a while the change in direction seemed a smart move and the hits kept coming, though at a slower rate. But 'Days', a British Top Twenty hit in 1968, marked the group's end as consistent hitmakers, especially in America where, after a disastrous tour in 1965, they weren't to perform again until 1969, due to their banning by the American Federation Of Musicians for 'unprofessional conduct'. In part the reason was that Ray Davies was involved in other projects. He wrote the music for the film *The Virgin Soldiers*, as well as songs for a variety of acts – e.g. 'I Go To Sleep', recorded both by the Applejacks (which included Ray's sister Megan on bass) and Peggy Lee, and 'Dandy', a Kinks album track that was an American Top Five hit for Herman's Hermits in 1966 – and produced *Turtle Soup* for the Turtles.

Face To Face (1966), *Live At Kelvin Hall* and *Something Else* (1967) – Shel Talmy's last production for the group – found Davies still writing three-minute songs, but they were no longer aimed purely at specific audiences, the charts or at the underground, as was demonstrated most noticeably on the live album. It consisted not of lengthy solos by the group but of one long 30-minute scream of applause by the audience, over which the Kinks could hardly be heard. And it wasn't an accident, as the credit 'musical direction: Ray Davies' made clear.

As the group was no longer performing very frequently, Dave Davies decided to temporarily branch out on his own as well. His first single, 'Death Of A Clown' (1967), on which he was backed by the Kinks, was a British Top Five hit. He planned a solo album, but when follow-up singles flopped, as did the Kinks' records of this period, it was scrapped. Despite the group's absence from the charts for a year, the

Kinks had amassed a lot of material similar to that on *Something Else.* Currently only available in America – on *The Kink Kronikles* (Reprise, 1972) and *The Great Lost Kinks Album* (1973) – where the group had developed a fanatical cult following that saw them as the most English of all British groups, this material wasn't released in Britain at the time because Pye was only interested in hit singles and thought that if they couldn't sell singles, they certainly couldn't sell albums.

(The Kinks Are) The Village Green Preservation Society (1968), the group's first 'official' concept album, saw Ray Davies looking back at a make-believe Edwardian Britain when life seemed more ordered. Its follow-up, *Arthur (Or The Decline And Fall Of The British Empire)* (1969), which began life as a TV musical Ray Davies had written with Julian Mitchell, and saw John Dalton (born May 21, 1943) replacing Peter Quaife on bass, was again a look back. But this time the past was not seen as a haven but as a burden on the present and flight – whether from the town to the country as in 'Drivin' ', or from Britain to Australia in 'Australia' – seen as the only solution. Having summed up the pressures of the past, the Kinks next moved on to a description of their own situation in *Lola Versus Powerman And The Moneygoround* (1970), produced while the group were preparing to leave both Pye and their old managers. More importantly, in career terms the album and its hit single, Ray Davies' salute to the ambiguous charms of 'Lola' – 'I'm Glad I'm A Man And So Is Lola' – which reached both the British and American Top Tens in 1970, marked a new lease of life for the group.

In 1971, the group signed with RCA and recorded *Muswell Hillbillies*, by which time John Gosling had joined the group on piano and organ to fill out the group's sound. That and the next (double) album, *Everybody's In Showbiz – Everybody's A Star* (1972), which included another marvellous flop of a single, 'Celluloid Heroes', continued the themes of *Village Green* and *Lola* into the present day and, equally importantly, were relatively successful commercially. The tide seemed to be turning, and the group even began touring regularly again in America where they gained a new generation of fans with the increasingly theatrical approach to material which replaced the sloppy stage act of the Sixties. So successful were they with rock-theatre that all the following albums, *Preservation Act 1* (1973), which saw Alan Holmes, Laurie Browne and John Beecham joining as full-time Kinks, *Act 2* (1974), *Soap Opera* (1975) and *The Kinks Present Schoolboys In Disgrace* (1976), would be accompanied by a stage presentation of sorts. While *Preservation* was too unwieldy to work either on stage or record, *Soap Opera*, which had its origins in a TV musical commissioned from Ray Davies by Granada and tells the story of a 'star' (Ray Davies) surveying suburbia for material for a new album and slowly succumbing to its 'attractions' until in the end he isn't sure if he's Norman Normal or Ray Davies, was the group's most successful album of the Seventies and boded well for the future.

During their stay at RCA, the Kinks formed their own record label, Konk, which signed Claire Hammil among others, and Ray Davies returned to production with Café Society.

Don Kirshner made his mark in New York's music business as the manager of Bobby Darin and Connie Francis in the mid-Fifties. His initial experience was in songwriting, management, publishing and related activities, which led him (1958) to form Aldon Music (with Al Nevins, formerly with the Three Suns), publishing and supplying songs for the new teenage music industry. They were the first to set up such an organization on a professional basis, and they attracted the best young writers, including Neil Sedaka and Howard Greenfield, Carole King and Gerry Goffin, and Tony Orlando.

From there, Kirshner became involved with Screen Gems, a film concern whose record label, Colpix, was just being launched. With the assistance of Lou Adler and Stu Phillips, Kirshner built Colpix into a fairly successful teen label, with hits by Shelley Fabares, Paul Peterson, James Darren and others, utilizing his same stable of writers. Those same writers also composed and performed most of the hits on Dimension, a new label launched by Kirshner under the aegis of Screen Gems. Hits by Little Eva, Carole King and others followed.

Kirshner's greatest success, however, came in 1966 when he assembled a group of musicians known as the Monkees for another Screen Gems label, Colgems. With the double-barrelled concept of a recording group whose records could be promoted through a popular weekly TV series (the proto-type for *The Partridge Family* and other shows), the Mon-kees were, within months, the biggest selling record act in the world, using songs written mainly by Aldon writers Tommy Boyce and Bobby Hart, with a few by Goffin-King and other Kirshner regulars. Following a dispute over per-centages to be received by Kirshner for the Monkees, he left Screen Gems, but wasted no time in starting a label of his own, Kirshner, and outdoing the Monkees with a new idea – the Archies. The concept was similar: great records by studio musicians hyped to the kids on weekly TV; but, and this was the key difference, using cartoon characters instead of humans who might develop ego and personality prob-lems. Naturally, the Archies were a stupendous success, and during the years 1968–71 Kirshner's songwriting mills were bustling. He brought in new writers such as Ron Dante, and brought back old ones including Howard Greenfield, re-uniting him with Sedaka for a series of albums which led to the latter's 1974 comeback.

In 1972, Kirshner got involved with ABC-Television in creating a weekly late-night rock show to be called *In Con-cert*. He produced the first few shows, then turned it over to Dick Clark when the network began insisting on artistic con-trol. True to form, he showed up soon thereafter with *Don Kirshner's Rock Concert*, a syndicated live concert show that has since become a successful institution. *Rock Concert* accounts for most of Kirshner's activities as of 1975, al-though he still keeps up his publishing and songwriting in-terests, and makes sporadic attempts at launching new artists, such as his 1974 discovery, Kansas.

210

The Knickerbockers formed in 1964 as the Castle Kings. The group – Buddy Randell from the Royal Teens (he co-wrote 'Short Shorts'), vocals and saxophone; Jimmy Walker, drums and vocals; John Charles, bass; and his brother Beau, guitar – took their name from Knickerbocker Avenue in their hometown of Bergenfield, New Jersey. Discovered by Jerry Fuller, a moderately successful singer and very successful writer ('Travellin' Man', 'Young World', 'Over You' and 'Young Girl') and producer (Union Gap and Ricky Nelson), they were signed to Challenge in 1965. They soon showed their skills as mimics when their Beatles pastiche, 'Lies' shot into the Top Twenty in the winter of 1965. Fuller's production of the Randell-B. Charles composition was perfect, sounding more like the Beatles than the Beatles. A follow-up, 'One Track Mind', made the Top Fifty in 1966 but then failure set in and the group disbanded. Jimmy Walker briefly 'replaced' Bill Medley in the Righteous Brothers before attempting a solo career on Columbia and Buddy Randell tried the same on Uni and then Paramount.

Curtis Knight, of mixed black/Indian parentage, was born in Fort Scott, Kansas, in 1945. He moved to New York in 1961 where his own records on a number of labels (Gulf, Shell, R.S.V.P.) have since been overshadowed by an association with Jimi Hendrix. *Jimi,* Knight's 'intimate biography' of Hendrix was published in 1974, but was not well-received by critics or fans. Knight's best solo record was 'That's Why' on Gulf, which bubbled under the Hot Hundred in 1961. Jimi Hendrix played and sang on tracks by Curtis Knight and the Squires made in 1965 for R.S.V.P.

Al Kooper. Few musicians have had a more chequered or more fascinating career than Al Kooper born in New York in 1943. At 13 he was a member of the Royal Teens who had a Top Ten hit with the novelty 'Short Shorts' on ABC in 1958. At 19, with a reputation as a session guitarist, he quit college to work as an apprentice engineer in a recording studio before teaming up with songwriters Bob Brass and Irvine Levine. Despite a No. 1 with 'This Diamond Ring' for

Gary Lewis and the Playboys in 1965, Kooper didn't enjoy Tin Pan Alley life and spent his time between session work gigging round the folk clubs. Then Tom Wilson invited Kooper to a session by Bob Dylan. Kooper was determined to play on the session, but Mike Bloomfield was there to play guitar so Kooper muscled in to play organ. He didn't know the first thing about the instrument but felt his way through the take. Dylan was impressed by the amateurish squeezed organ sound and the take was used on the record, 'Like A Rolling Stone'. Kooper later joined Dylan at the famous 1965 Newport Folk Festival electric set before completing the *Highway 61* album. His association with both Dylan and Mike Bloomfield stood Kooper in good stead in the future.

In 1966, through Wilson, Kooper came to join the Blues Project. He played on three albums by the group, the two live ones and the studio *Projections*, until friction with guitarist Danny Kalb caused him to leave both the group and New York. In L.A., he gigged around, and unveiled future Blood, Sweat and Tears songs at the Big Sur Folk Festival in 1967. Back in New York Kooper put together a temporary band to play a week at the Café A Go Go in order to fund a trip to England. It was these musicians who became the nucleus for BS and T. However, after the remarkable *Child Is Father To The Man* album he found the band slipping away into an alien direction and left them to start work with Columbia as a producer. Filling in studio time, he started another trend (which, like jazz rock, was later to get out of hand) by recording an album with Mike Bloomfield and Steve Stills (fresh from Buffalo Springfield) which became *Supersession* (1968). Its spectacular success led to a series of live concerts with Mike Bloomfield again captured on the, for the most part excessive album, *The Live Adventures Of Al Kooper And Mike Bloomfield* (1969).

In the Seventies, Kooper released a series of usually weak solo albums of which only *Easy Does It* and *New York City You're A Woman* do him any real credit. The latter was mostly recorded in England with members of Elton John's Band. A man never afraid to speak his mind and never the

212

darling of the critics, Kooper's involvement with great projects and seminal schemes singles him out as someone special. Currently he is living in Atlanta, having set up the Sounds Of The South label.

Alexis Korner. In the early Fifties Korner (born in 1928) flirted with traditional jazz and skiffle before opening the London Blues and Barrelhouse Club with Cyril Davies in 1955. The pair first played together at the club's Thursday evening sessions, which attracted visiting American bluesmen as well as local enthusiasts. Inspired by Muddy Waters, Chris Barber introduced R&B into his jazz band's repertoire, and Korner (guitar) and Davies (harmonica) backed singer Ottilie Patterson. The popularity of the sets encouraged them to form their own R&B band, Blues Incorporated, in 1961 and, in March the following year, to open their own club in Ealing. The band's original personnel included Art Wood (vocals) and Charlie Watts (drums), and among those who passed through the constantly changing line-up during the next year were Long John Baldry, Jack Bruce, Ginger Baker, Graham Bond, Ronnie Jones, and Phil Seamen.

Despite his seminal influence on British R&B, the boom passed Korner by and he spent much of the mid-Sixties working in television with his current rhythm section, Danny Thompson (bass) and Terry Cox (drums). In 1967, he formed a trio, Free At Last, with an initial line-up of Cliff Barton (bass) and Hughie Flint (drums), but which changed so much he decided to work on his own. While touring Scandinavia the following year he met Peter Thorup; their subsequent collaboration provided the nucleus of New Church in 1969, the studio band CCS, and Snape, formed by chance on an American tour in 1972 with ex-members of King Crimson. Though Snape broke up within a year, Korner and Thorup continued to work together both as a duo and in CCS, whose hits included a cover of Led Zeppelin's 'Whole Lotta Love' in 1970.

Billy J. Kramer and the Dakotas. Originally lead singer with a Mersey group, the Coasters, the handsome but bland-voiced Billy J. (born William Ashton, Aug. 19, 1943) was teamed by Brian Epstein with a Manchester group, the Dakotas, and signed to Parlophone. Between 1963 and 1965 he had six records in the British Top Twenty, four of them Lennon-McCartney compositions: 'Do You Want To Know A Secret?', 'Bad To Me', 'I'll Keep You Satisfied' and 'From A Window'. The others were composed by Mort Shuman ('Little Children') and Burt Bacharach ('Trains And Boats And Planes'). In America, only 'Little Children' and 'Bad To Me' reached the Top Twenty, and as his recording career began to fade, Kramer followed many of his contemporaries into the lucrative North of England cabaret circuit. The Dakotas (Mike Maxfield lead guitar, Robin McDonald rhythm, Ray Jones bass, and Tony Mansfield drums) had an instrumental hit in 1963 with the Shadows-styled 'The Cruel Sea'.

The Jim Kweskin Jug Band – Jim Kweskin, vocals, guitar; Maria D'Amato (Muldaur) vocals, kazoo, tambourine; Geoff Muldaur, guitar, vocals, clarinet, washboard; Bill Keith, banjo, steel, guitar; Fritz Richmond, jug, washtub bass – was formed at Al Grossman's suggestion from a nucleus of Club 47 folkies in 1963. They literally sparked off the whole jug band revival through their spectacular live appearances. Rarely captured on album, *Best Of Jim Kweskin And His Jug Band* is the closest approximation of their craziness. They spanned six years and various personnel fluctuations. Fiddler Richard Greene joined towards the end and earlier Mel Lyman (then a harmonica player) had helped start the collapse. It was inevitable anyway, as jug band music became a pleasant anachronism. Kweskin became part of Lyman's authoritarian religious sect, 'The Family', Geoff and Maria recorded together in Woodstock, then separated, Maria to spectacular success, and Geoff tastefully in Better Days and now solo. Richmond and Keith are still in demand as musicians, Richmond additionally as an engineer.

Denny Laine, born Brian Arthur Haynes in Birmingham on Oct. 29, 1944, led his first group, Denny Laine and the Diplomats – which also included drummer Bev Bevan – from 1962 to May, 1964, when he was sacked. He immediately formed the Moody Blues and sang the plaintive lead vocal on the group's international hit, 'Go Now'. He left, frustrated by the failure of the group's follow-ups in 1966. In 1967 he fronted the short-lived Electric String Band which recorded his 'Say You Don't Mind', later a hit for Colin Blunstone in 1972. With ex-Move member Trevor Burton, he formed Balls, a putative supergroup financed by Tony Secunda, in 1969. The group, which also included at various times Steve Gibbons, Dave Morgan, Keith Smart, Richard Tandy and Alan White, made one single, 'Fight For My Country', and played ten dates before breaking up in 1971. During the same period, Laine played briefly with Ginger Baker's Airforce and appeared on sessions for an unreleased Rick Grech solo album. In late 1971 Laine, always a Beatles fan, joined Paul McCartney's Wings where he remains playing a variety of instruments and contributing occasional songs. He released a pleasant but undistinguished solo album *Ahh . . . Laine!* in 1973.

Major Lance, born on April 4, 1941, in Chicago, recorded unsuccessfully for Mercury before finding success on the Okeh label. There, the combination of Carl Davis' production, Johnny Pate's brassy arrangements and Curtis Mayfield's songs gave him a stream of hits on both the pop and R&B charts between 1963 and 1967. 'The Monkey Time', 'Hey Little Girl', 'Um Um Um Um Um Um' and 'The Matador' were all Top Twenty records, while 'It Ain't No Use', 'Rhythm' and 'Come See' were lesser hits. With Mayfield often providing vocal backing, Lance's records were often indistinguishable from those of the Impressions, Mayfield's group. In 1968, he went with Carl Davis to Dakar Records and had a small R&B hit with 'Follow The Leader'. Later records on Curtis Mayfield's Curtom label included 'Stay Away From Me' and 'Must Be Love Coming Down'. In 1972, Lance recorded for Volt, toured Britain where he had become a cult figure on the Northern soul scene and recorded for Contempo and Warner Bros.

The Leaves were part of the first wave of Los Angeles folk-rock groups that followed in the wake of the Byrds' success in 1965. Led by Jim Pons and Bill Rinehart, the group also included John Beck, Robert Reiner and Tom Ray – when Rinehart left a few months later he was replaced by Bobby Arlin. Signed to the local Mira label, they recorded a number of fine protest songs, the requisite number of Dylan tunes, and two versions of a song that later became a folk-rock standard (done by the Byrds, Love, Tim Rose, Jimi Hendrix and countless others) – 'Hey Joe'. The second version gave them their only national hit (when it reached No. 31) in May, 1966. Its powerful beat, fuzz guitar and screaming vocals made it an all-time classic. Despite the fact that none of their follow-ups made the charts, the Leaves were later signed by Capitol who issued a second album. Later in 1967, Pons joined the Turtles, and Arlin left to form the Hook, a trio who recorded two albums for Uni.

The Left Banke were formed by Michael Brown in New York in early 1966. Other members were Steve Martin, Jeff Winfield, Tom Finn, Rick Brand and George Cameron. Their first single, 'Walk Away Renee' proved an instant Top Five hit on Smash in 1966, with an appealingly offbeat arrangement laden with heavy strings and harpsichord, and featuring ethereal vocals and strong melodies. This sound was explored further on 'Pretty Ballerina' (a Top Twenty hit) and the excellent album that followed. But several subsequent singles, including the brilliant 'Desiree', failed to click, and Brown left the group before their second album was recorded, to work with a group, Montage, ultimately forming Stories, which he also left after their second album, in 1973.

The Lemon Pipers were Bill Albough (born in 1948), drums; Reg Nave (1945), keyboards; Bill Bartlett (1946), guitar; Steve Walmsley (1949), bass and Ivan Browne (1947), vocals and guitar. They surfaced in 1968 with the million-selling 'Green Tambourine' (Buddah), an early piece of psychedelic bubblegum music that topped the American charts and made the British Top Ten. Producer Paul Leka, who co-wrote the song with S. Pinz, judged the moment perfectly with his ostentatious use of phasing but the subsequent releases to 'Rice Is Nice' (Top Forty in 1968) and the giveaway title 'Jelly Jungle (Of Marmalade)' (Top Sixty in 1969) failed and the group split.

Barbara Lewis, born in a Detroit suburb on Feb. 9, 1944, began her career after submitting her own songs to Ollie McLaughlin in 1961. A contract with Atlantic led to regional hits, including 'My Heart Went Do Dat Da' and finally to the hauntingly sensual 'Hello Stranger', which reached the Top Three in 1963. With various producers – McLaughlin, Bert Berns, Jerry Wexler – and good songs from Goffin/ King and Van McCoy, Lewis was consistently successful in the soul field throughout the mid-Sixties. Her hits included 'Straighten Up Your Heart', 'Puppy Love', 'Baby I'm Yours' and 'Make Me Your Baby' (both of which reached No. 11 in 1965) and 'Make Me Belong To You'. Her distinctive voice, suggesting both coyness and sophistication, coped equally well with strong blues material and soft, romantic ballads.

Gary Lewis and the Playboys emerged in the mid-Sixties when the sons and daughters of entertainers from the Forties and Fifties began their own careers. Mickey Rooney, Jr., Nancy Sinatra, Dino Desi and Billy had no trouble securing recording contracts in Hollywood, and Gary Lewis (born in 1946, son of the comedian Jerry) was no exception. Yet surprisingly in the course of his ten albums for Liberty, he made quite a few good pop records, notably 'She's Just My Style'. In 1965-6, Lewis had seven consecutive Top Ten hits (including 'This Diamond Ring', 'Count Me In', 'Save Your Heart For Me', 'Everybody Loves A Clown' and 'Sure Gonna Miss Her'), all with bright arrangements by Leon

217

Russell and a solid, teenage sound. Later he made several albums as a more 'sensitive' artist, an image he failed to establish, and since re-forming the Playboys in 1973 he's been working regularly, playing his oldies.

Ramsey Lewis, born in Chicago on May 27, 1935, studied piano at the Chicago College of Music and De Paul University. He formed his own jazz trio in 1956, working local night clubs and appearing on records by Sonny Stitt, Clark Terry and Max Roach, with albums of his own on American Argo. These, plus occasional gigs in New York City, earned the Ramsey Lewis Trio – bassist Eldee Young, drummer Isaac Holt and Lewis – a modest following until their 1965 recording of 'The In Crowd' (Argo) reached No. 5 on the Hot Hundred. Other big hits included 'Hang On Sloopy' (1965) and 'Wade In The Water' (1966) before the Trio broke up. Since then Lewis has made a huge commercial success of transforming a variety of material with his strong keyboard touch, thick gospel chording and a rocking blues beat; he's toured extensively, including several dates in Britain. Lewis' most recent records were for Columbia.

Light Shows. Traditionally, lighting in rock was limited to white spotlights. In 1966, as 'acid rock' caught on in San Francisco, the 'light show' was invented, as a means to intensify the sense of 'total environment' supposedly being created. Introduced by Ken Kesey at his Trips Festival, these light shows employed opaque projectors, slide projectors, gels, movies and whatever other visual effects could be played over the walls and ceiling of a dark dance hall, augmented by strobe and ultraviolet lights above the floor. The basic, and most common, technique was to push coloured oils around on an opaque projector with an inverted clock face, creating pulsating bubbles in time with the music. Light-show art became quite advanced by 1968, at which point every hall and club in the land had some kind of light show, but after that its popularity fell off. Today they are extremely rare, and those used by groups like Hawkwind are very simple by 1968 standards. Among the earliest leading

San Francisco light-show artists were Bill Ham, Tony Martin, Ben Van Meter and Roger Hillyard. At their peak, there were many large light-show companies that often charged – and changed members – as much as the groups they were lighting.

Bob Lind, born in 1942 in Baltimore, had a transatlantic Top Ten hit in 1966 with 'Elusive Butterfly' (World Pacific, Fontana in Britain). The subsequent album, *Don't Be Concerned*, was a typical post-Dylan singer/songwriter production, with selfconsciously poetic lyrics set to soft music. The follow-up, 'Remember The Rain'/'Truly Julie's Blues' reached the lower end of the American charts, but Lind's later albums on Verve and Capitol (*Since There Were Circles*, 1971) made no impact.

Little Milton, one of today's leading contemporary blues singer/guitarists, was born Milton Campbell in Inverness, Mississippi, on Sept. 17, 1934. As a child he sang in his local church choir and became interested in the guitar at 10. His first public performance was at 14 and his inspirations included T-Bone Walker, B. B. King and Roy Brown. In 1950, a trio Milton was leading became popular around Memphis and he came to the attention of Sun records where he was recorded with Ike Turner's band. From Sun he switched to Meteor and, in 1958, to the St Louis-based Bobbin label where he cut several successful singles with bandleader/ arranger, Oliver Sain. In 1961, Chess/Checker took over his contract, and Milton was turning out such hits as 'Who's Cheating Who', 'Grits Ain't Groceries' and 'We're Gonna Make It', a No. 1 R&B hit in 1965. All feature Milton's throaty, gospel-inflected vocals, tastefully underscored by a full band – often with arrangements by Donny Hathaway and production by Gene Barge. This consistency led to his 1971 signing with Stax, where he re-established himself on the black music scene. An appearance in the film *Wattstax* plus recent, more commercially oriented, single hits, like 'Behind Closed Doors', has turned Milton into an international pop/soul name who still retains his blues roots.

219

Little Walter, born Marion Walter Jacobs on May 1, 1930 in Alexandria, Louisiana, revolutionized blues harmonica technique with a style steeped in jazz phrasing which remains, to this day unsurpassed. Influenced by Sonny Boy Williamson No. 1 and 'jump' saxophonist Louis Jordan, he arrived in Chicago in 1947, singing and playing for a living in the Maxwell Street market. But Walter's obvious talents resulted in his recording for several small Chicago labels, like Ora Nelle and Regal. In 1951, he was hired by Chess Records as accompanist on the Muddy Waters sessions, his powerful, heavily amplified harp embellishing such hits as 'Mannish Boy', 'Standing Around Crying' and 'I'm Ready'. He also backed Jimmy Rogers on most of his big-selling singles like 'That's All Right' and 'The World Is In A Tangle'. In 1952, Chess signed Walter to their subsidiary, Checker, and his first session produced 'Juke', his best-known instrumental and a huge R&B smash. Then came 'Mean Old World', 'Off The Wall', 'Blues With A Feeling' and 'Last Night', all self-penned R&B chart hits featuring accompaniment by top Chess sessionmen Louis and David Myers, guitars, and Fred Below, drums. 1954 and 1955 were Walter's most successful years. He stayed in the national R&B Top Ten throughout that period. More hits followed, including 'My Babe' and 'Confessin' The Blues' before Walter switched sidemen, cutting 'Everything's Gonna Be Alright' and several other sides with Freddy Robinson on lead guitar, who was later to succeed Mick Taylor in John Mayall's Bluesbreakers. Walter died on Feb. 15, 1968, from a fatal thrombosis brought on by injuries received in a fight.

Liverpool. Virtually every major British city in the early Sixties had its nucleus of rock musicians dedicated to playing rougher and more rewarding music than the current Top Twenty. What made Liverpool different was the size of its beat group population and the richness and variety of their American musical influences.

As a port, Liverpool had strong connections with America, and local seamen would return from New York with ciggies, comic books and the latest R&B and pop records.

Thus local groups were able to graft on to their rock'n'roll repertoire the music of early Motown, the Shirelles, the Isley Brothers and Ritchie Barrett (whose Ray Charles-styled 'Some Other Guy' became a Merseybeat standard). By 1960 local entrepreneurs like Alan Williams were booking Liverpool groups led by Kingsize Taylor and the Dominos into the clubs along Hamburg's notorious Reeperbahn and, on Merseyside, folk and trad jazz clubs were switching to beat music. By 1962 the Cavern, opened four years earlier as a jazz cellar, was given over to the pounding rhythms of the Big Three, the Beatles, Rory Storm and the Hurricanes, Faron's Flamingos and many more of the 350 groups which Liverpool's own music paper, *Mersey Beat*, estimated were operating in the area. The same thing happened at the Iron Door, the Jacaranda, the Beachcomber, the David Lewis and Litherland Town Hall.

All this activity made little impact outside Merseyside and Hamburg until local record-shop owner Brian Epstein got the Beatles their EMI recording contract. The success of 'She Loves You' in early 1963 sent recording managers scurrying from London to find their Liverpool group. Pye signed the Searchers, the Undertakers, black vocal group the Chants and Johnny Sandon and the Remo Four. Decca had the Big Three, the Clayton Squares, Lee Curtis and the All-Stars, Freddie Starr and the Midnighters and the Dennisons. Philips/Fontana grabbed the Merseybeats, Earl Preston and the TTs, Ian and the Zodiacs. EMI (Parlophone and Columbia) released the records of the Epstein stable.

Over 200 singles by Liverpool groups were released in Britain over the next few years. Most were sloppily produced and undistinguished and no groups outside the charmed circle of the Epstein stable and the Searchers and Swinging Blue Jeans established themselves on a national or international scale. When the first or second single failed, most Liverpool groups were dropped by the record companies as quickly as they had been snapped up.

Merseybeat was, in any case, essentially created in live performance. It was captured best on live recordings, notably those of the small Oriole label, which recorded a dozen or so groups in a short recording session at the Cavern under live conditions (some of the tracks are now available on a British United Artists album, *This Is Mersey Beat*). At its best it represented an exciting collision between the enormous enthusiasm of the musicians and their fairly rudimentary technique. Its essence was in the chugging rhythm section, with metallic guitar chords cutting across thumping bass lines and solid four-square drumming. Few of the groups could reproduce the atmosphere and energy of a packed night at the Cavern in a London recording studio with an unsympathetic producer, and hardly any wrote their own songs.

By 1965, the Liverpool music scene was almost dead. Drained of its best musicians by the record companies, yesterday's trend, its only consolation was that the graduates of Merseybeat had changed the face of pop music internationally. Today the city is full of ex-musicians and kids who know more about the local soccer team than the Beatles.

Alan Lomax was an important figure in the folk revivals of both Britain and America. With his father, John A. Lomax, he went on field recording trips in the 1930s, collecting songs for the Library of Congress archive for which he also recorded Woody Guthrie. On one of these they met Leadbelly, who was brought by the Lomaxes to perform in front of white, urban audiences. A later trip included the first recordings of a young singer, McKinley Morganfield, better known as Muddy Waters. In the post-World War II period, Lomax travelled to Britain to collaborate with Ewan MacColl in such ventures as the *Ballads And Blues* radio series. He returned to America in the Fifties to undertake the last major field recording journey in the South, the results of which were issued on Atlantic's *Southern Folk Heritage* series.

Shorty Long. Born Frederick Long in 1940, he first recorded for Harvey Fuqua's Tri-Phi label in 1961. The company was absorbed by Tamla-Motown in 1963, and Long's bluesy records appeared on the Soul subsidiary label. He co-wrote most of his discs, including 'Function At The Junction', 'Night Fo' Last' and his biggest hit, 'Here Comes The Judge', which reached the Top Ten in 1968 and was covered by Pigmeat Markham. Originally from Birmingham, Alabama, Long drowned when his boat capsized off Sandwich Island, Ontario, on June 29, 1969.

Trini Lopez emulated Peter, Paul and Mary and took 'If I Had A Hammer' into the American Top Fifty for the second time in a year, in 1962, with a totally different treatment. Born in Dallas, Texas, on May 15, 1937, Trini Lopez was discovered by Reprise's Don Costa who produced and arranged 'If I Had A Hammer' – which made the Top Three – and his subsequent recordings, giving them a party atmosphere of handclapping and enthusiastic yelping – from Hollywood's PJ's club – around rhythm guitar and Lopez's clear vocal. The formula was used over the years on a string of hits – 'Kansas City', 'America' (like 'Hammer', from the gold album *Trini Lopez At PJ's*), 'La Bamba' and 'Lemon Tree'. Throughout the mid-Sixties he enjoyed a large following in South America and Europe, particularly in France. He later turned up singing and acting in the film, *The Dirty Dozen*.

Los Angeles. The (white) music industry quickly followed the movies to Los Angeles. This connection gave a particular slant to the popular music made there, a devotion to topicality and craftsmanship in production. The result, in the early Sixties, was the surfing/hot rod music of the Beach Boys, Jan and Dean and a host of lesser groups. At the same time, a nucleus of session musicians was forming who would play on nearly all the L.A. hits of the decade. Mainly migrants to California, often from Arkansas or Oklahoma, they included Leon Russell, Glen Campbell, David Gates, Jim Gordon, Joe Osborne and Larry Knechtel.

In 1965, the new thing was Dylan and protest. The L.A. session crew played behind Roger McGuinn on the Byrds' 'Mr Tambourine Man', an immaculate and influential record. The key figure of this era in Los Angeles, however, was

Lou Adler, who brought together P. F. Sloan's punk lyrics and Barry McGuire's hairy 'protest' image to make 'Eve Of Destruction' a million-seller on his own Dunhill label. Other Los Angeles protest successes came with Sonny and Cher (records which owed a lot to arranger Harold Battiste), Glen Campbell and the Turtles. The latter group soon became recognized as part of the Los Angeles vocal group trend into which 'protest' evolved. Adler had the Mamas and the Papas, blending rich harmonies with hip or witty lyrics. There were Spanky and Our Gang, and two San Francisco-based groups who came south to record with Lenny Waronker when Warner Bros. bought out their label, Autumn: Harpers Bizarre and the Beau Brummels.

The local club scene blossomed in the mid-Sixties, through venues like Ciro's, the Moulin Rouge (later the Kaleidoscope), the Crescendo and the Cheetah and Shrine Explosion ballrooms. From them came a series of groups from the Byrds to the Doors. Los Angeles also had a youth culture centred on Sunset Strip, scene of anti-curfew riots which were the subject of 'For What It's Worth', Stephen Stills' song for Buffalo Springfield. They also inspired a series of teen-exploitation movies and soundtracks which often featured local punk-rock groups like the Standells and the Chocolate Watch Band. By 1968, Los Angeles was established as the major pop music recording centre outside New York, the home base of a number of major record companies and producers, as well as songwriters like Randy Newman, Van Dyke Parks and David Gates, all employed by the Metric Music publishing house. In the Seventies it would again be the home of a new major trend in rock, as acoustic singer-songwriters and country-rock groups came to record in the city.

Love was the brainchild of Arthur Lee. The group started off playing the Los Angeles club scene in 1965, with a music that synthesized black R&B and the new 'folk-rock' of the Byrds. The original line-up was Arthur Lee (born in Memphis, Tennessee, 1944), John Echols (guitar), Bryan Maclean (guitar, vocals), Ken Forssi (bass), Alban ('Snoopy') Pfisterer (drums), Tjay Cantrelli, and Michael Stuart (percussion). Their first two albums, *Love* (1966, Elektra) and *Da Capo* (1967), featured Lee's eerie voice intoning surreal lyrics over a smooth blues sound dominated by acoustic guitars. It was the third album, though, with which they are most associated. Tjay and 'Snoopy' had left, and Lee's musical schizophrenia was given its fullest expression. *Forever Changes* (1968) contains the same elements, but rather than peacefully coexisting, they now glare at each other, R&B being as absent from the music as traditional folk-rock themes are from the words.

L.A. groups have a reputation for performing badly outside the city. Love solved this by simply staying there, rarely leaving their horror-film mansion in Hollywood. The triumph of *Forever Changes* was followed by an album, apparently too awful to release, and the old Love was no more. From 1968, the name belonged to Arthur Lee and whatever musicians he chose to work with. Among these was Jimi Hendrix, an indication of Lee's progression into straighter, blacker R&B. Hendrix performed on one track of *False Start* and made a whole album with Lee which has never been released.

Darlene Love, born Darlene Wright in 1938, is the sister of Edna Wright who sang in the Honey Cone. In 1958, Darlene joined the Blossoms, a Los Angeles high-school girl group which recorded unsuccessfully for Capitol in 1958–60. Between 1960 and 1962, the Blossoms, now a trio, recorded for Challenge and Okeh but mostly did session work in L.A. for James Darren, Bobby Darin, Nino Tempo and April Stevens and many others. As a session singer, Darlene sang lead on several Phil Spector-produced singles on Philles, including 'He's A Rebel' and 'He's Sure The Boy I Love' (credited to the Crystals) and 'Zip-A-Dee-Doo-Dah' by the dubiously named Bob B. Soxx and the Bluejeans. She also recorded six singles for Philles in her own right, notably the classic 'Christmas (Baby Come Home)', 'Today I Met The Boy I'm Gonna Marry' and 'A Fine Fine Boy', and scored in 1963 with 'Wait Till My Bobby Gets Home' which reached No.

26 in America. Throughout the Sixties, the Blossoms continued to work sessions (they were regulars on the *Shindig* TV show) and went on the road with Elvis during an early Seventies tour.

The Lovin' Spoonful came together in Greenwich Village in 1964. John Sebastian (born March 17, 1944) was a local boy, the son of a classical harmonica player. He had played mouth-harp himself on sessions for Tim Hardin, the Even Dozen Jug Band and others before producer Eric Jacobsen encouraged Sebastian to put a group together to record his own songs. Zally Yanofsky (born Dec. 19, 1944, in Toronto) had been with Sebastian in the Mugwumps, which also contained Cass Elliott and Denny Doherty, later of the Mamas and Papas. Joe Butler (born Jan. 19, 1943, Glen Cove, Long Island) was one of the few drummers in the Village and Steve Boone (Sept. 23, 1943, North Carolina) was a rhythm guitarist in search of a band. All were extroverts with a wild sense of humour who combined traditional folk and blues elements with updated rock'n'roll to produce a streamlined jug-band sound that came to be known as good-time music.

The Spoonful signed to Kama Sutra and followed the success of their first record, 'Do You Believe In Magic', with six successive Top Ten singles in 1965–6. At a time when everyone else in America seemed to be imitating the Beatles, the Spoonful were among the few to create an American equivalent to the Merseybeat synthesis. They had a similar zany, casual image which, however, seemed to extend to their musical activity as well. They did not progress in the way the Beatles or Dylan did: each album was just a collection of songs, nearly always Sebastian originals or reworkings of traditional songs, from which hit single after hit single was taken – lazy, old-fashioned celebrations of love on a summer's day like 'Daydream'; eulogies to the power and appeal of pop music like 'Do You Believe In Magic' and 'Nashville Cats'; delicate descriptions of adolescent love like 'You Didn't Have To Be So Nice' and 'Younger Girl'. Sebastian was a supreme pop craftsman and an unashamed romantic, yet he was best at capturing a mood – the sweaty

226

tension of 'Summer In The City', their only American No. 1, or the utter resignation of 'Didn't Want To Have To Do It'.

The Lovin' Spoonful had an effect on nearly everybody, including the Beatles, whose 'Good Day Sunshine' had exactly the same carefree attitude as Spoonful tracks like 'Daydream' (their biggest British hit, reaching No. 2 on Pye). But by 1967, they had begun to dissipate their energies and were producing things like Sebastian's uneven score for Francis Ford Coppola's first film, *You're A Big Boy Now*. The break-up of the group was, however, precipitated by a non-musical event. A drug bust in San Francisco in 1967 resulted in Zal Yanofsky incriminating others involved in the city's drug scene, under threat of deportation – he was still technically a Canadian citizen. The band were ostracized by their peers on the rock scene, and Yanofsky left. He was replaced by Jerry Yester, former Association producer and folk singer, but the band was never quite the same again and after a couple of worthy albums they split up.

Sebastian made a comeback in 1970 when he took the stage at the Woodstock Festival during a storm and for a couple of years his records sold well and his live appearances drew the crowds, though mostly on the strength of his association with the Spoonful. His new material was nowhere near as good, but rather more like his new adopted stage manner, too cloying and too sentimental. Four years later he re-formed the Spoonful, apparently without consulting Joe Butler, and the band were preparing to make their own nostalgic comeback.

Lulu, born Marie Laurie on Nov. 3, 1948, in Glasgow, led the Glen Eagles in the Lindella and various other Glasgow clubs when she was 15. A year later, in 1964, renamed Lulu and the Luvvers – Ross Nelson, Jim Dewar, Alec Bell, Jimmy Smith, Tony Tierney and David Miller – they gave Scotland its first beat hit, 'Shout' (Decca). She had a potentially great blues-shouting voice, but parted with the Luvvers in February, 1966 to become a successful if unremarkable all-round entertainer. She appeared in the film *To Sir With Love*, singing the title song – a million-seller and a chart topper for five weeks in America. Today, she fronts a regular British television show, increasingly accepting the show business trappings.

Victor Lundberg featured in one of the more amusing by-products of the Protest/Generation Gap trend of 1965-7: a series of records debating, in broad generalities and loaded emotional terms, various aspects of the social revolution, from long hair to draft-card burning. 'An Open Letter To My Teenage Son' by Lundberg (Liberty, 1967); like Sgt. Barry Sadler's 'Ballad of the Green Berets' (RCA, 1966), was a right-wing refutation of the protest movement, and it inspired a raft of answer-records, including 'A Teenager's Answer' by Keith Gordon and 'Letter From A Teenage Son' by Brandon Wade. All featured stirring marching-band backgrounds and impassioned arguments for their cause, but Lundberg (who throughout it all was represented only as a concerned parent – he was born in 1923) – had the last word. His record, a Top Ten hit, was the only one which made the charts.

Barbara Lynn was born Barbara Lynn Ozen on Jan. 16, 1942 in Beaumont, Texas. She was discovered singing blues in Louisiana clubs by Huey P. Meaux, who has produced all her records.

Early sides were cut in Cosimo's New Orleans studio but leased to the Philadelphia-based Jamie label. The first of these, 'You'll Lose A Good Thing', was written as a poem when Lynn was 16. It topped the R&B chart and reached the national Top Ten in 1962, later becoming an R&B standard. Other Jamie singles (12 in all) made the middle reaches of the Hot Hundred, including 'Second Fiddle Girl' (1963), 'Oh Baby We Got A Good Thing Goin'' (1964 – it was revived by the Rolling Stones) and 'You're Gonna Need Me' (1965).

After a less eventful period on Meaux's Tribe label, she returned to the charts on Atlantic with 'This Is The Thanks I Get' (1968), 'Until Then I'll Suffer' (1971) and 'Daddy Hotstuff' (1972). Barbara Lynn's recordings consistently display a bluesy experience-laden voice, low-key, frequently throwaway vocal style, her own simple but gutsy left-handed guitar work, and Meaux's tasteful horn arrangements. The lack of strings and lazy, down-home flavour of her work is redolent of Jimmy Reed.

The MC5 – Rob Tyner, vocals, harmonica; Fred 'Sonic' Smith, guitar; Mike Davis, bass; Dennis Thompson, drums; Wayne Kramer, lead guitar – a 'killer' band from Detroit, were thrust to national prominence in 1969 by manager John Sinclair. Originally part of the Trans Love commune that housed Sinclair's White Panther Party, the raw revolutionary energy and 'punk' stance of the live *Kick Out The Jams* was rejected, along with Sinclair, as their attitudes and political ideas diverged. They replaced Sinclair's philosophy with rock'n'roll, and guided by rock critic Jon Landau, they recorded *Back In The USA* (Atlantic, 1970), one of the most interesting rock albums of the Sixties. Sandwiched between two rock'n'roll classics was a new expression of teenage consciousness Seventies-style, but in concise, three-minute epics ('Teenage Lust', 'American Ruse', 'Call Me Animal'). *High Time* had the same drive and energy and instrumental precision. They toured Europe in 1972, but were badly received. Davis stayed behind, and the others moved back to Detroit and called it a day.

The McCoys were formed in 1962 when Rick Zehringer (guitar) then 13, and his younger brother Randy (drums), 11, formed a high-school rock group with Randy Hobbs (bass) and Bobby Peterson (keyboards) in Union City, Indiana, and named it after a Ventures track, 'The McCoy'. They supported and backed leading acts in Dayton, Ohio, and three years later, after a few name-changes (Rick and the Raiders, Rick Z. Combo), reverted to the McCoys to record Bert Berns's 'Hang On Sloopy', a smash throughout America and Britain. Only one big hit followed – the Top Ten 'Fever'/ 'Sorrow'. They lived down the teenage image with *Infinite McCoys*, and through regular appearances at Steve Paul's Scene in New York. Paul took over management in 1969, and later they became back-up for Johnny Winter, recording

Johnny Winter And with Rick producing. Peterson had already left and Randy split after the album. Rick, now Derringer, teamed up with Edgar Winter and subsequently recorded, solo, *All American Boy* for Steve Paul's Blue Sky label.

Jimmy McGriff, brought up in a classical music environment, in Philadelphia, where he was born on April 3, 1936 – learned to play violin at music school, but an early interest in jazz was fostered at college. He joined the Philadelphia Police, and later went to Temple University where he met Bill Crosby, who helped set up some jazz gigs where McGriff met, and learned from, Jimmy Smith and Milt Buckner. In 1962, he signed with Sue Records, and his jazz/blues organ instrumental interpretation of 'I've Got A Woman' became a Top Twenty hit. Three subsequent Sue discs were small hits, and following years of jazz session work 'The Worm' was a 1968 hit on Solid State. Later recordings have appeared on Capitol and Groove Merchant.

Barry McGuire, born on Oct. 15, 1937 in Oklahoma, met Lou Adler and P. F. Sloan at Ciro's in Los Angeles at the Byrds' opening. He had been the gruff lead voice on the New Christy Minstrels hits like 'Green Green' (1963), but in autumn 1965 he recorded Sloan's 'Eve Of Destruction' for Adler's Dunhill label, the archetypal protest song. A rushed album of mainly Dylan and Sloan's imitatory Dylan material preceded *This Precious Time*, for which Adler brought the future Mamas and Papas to the sessions. The Mamas and Papas' 'California Dreamin'' is the same as McGuire's hit with Denny Doherty's voice substituted for McGuire's. His finest album was *Barry McGuire And The Doctor* (1969), after which he discovered salvation in Christianity – and the musical inspiration for albums like *Seeds* and *Lighten Up* for the religioso Myrrh label.

Lonnie Mack, born in Harrisburg, Indiana in 1941, had but one big hit, and that was a fluke. In the summer of 1963, at the end of someone else's session, he cut an instrumental version of Chuck Berry's 'Memphis'. His terse, rhythmic guitar style propelled it straight into the Top Ten, on the Fraternity label, resulting in some lesser-selling follow-ups, a fine album, and a few months of fame before he disappeared. The album was re-released on Elektra in 1970.

In 1969, he tried again, recording three albums for Elektra. His voice still carried the fullness and conviction of the gospel singer and his guitar work was still roadhouse tough – his music was a unique and fully realized blend of black music (gospel, blues and soul) with a country tinge, best exemplified by such tracks as 'Why', 'What Kind Of World Is This', and 'Where There's A Will There's A Way'. A shy, retiring man with none of the flash (or drive) essential for stardom, he dropped out of the music business, citing religious reasons. Though he returned to Indiana to drive a truck for a while, he cut singles for various labels in the Seventies including the Troy Seals-produced 'Highway 56' (Roulette, 1975).

Scott McKenzie, born on Oct. 1, 1944, in Arlington, Virginia, was a member of the Journeymen by 1964. The group also included John Phillips. When Phillips moved to California to start the Mamas and Papas, McKenzie stayed in New York and recorded a few ballads for Capitol. By early 1967, folk rock had become a booming industry in L.A., and Phillips persuaded McKenzie to come out and join in. The Phillips-produced 'No, No, No, No, No' (Epic, 1967) established McKenzie's ability within the genre and, soon thereafter he appeared on Lou Adler's newly formed Ode Records with Phillips' 'San Francisco (Be Sure to Wear Flowers in Your Hair)'. Perhaps the ultimate hippie anthem, it was a heart-tugging production with a genuine innocence and sense of wonder that inspired thousands of kids to make pilgrimages to San Francisco when it became an international hit in 1967. According to interviews, McKenzie was apparently very sincere in his flower philosophy, which may also explain why he stopped recording when the Summer of Love ended, save for a lack-lustre country-rock album (Ode, 1970) three years later.

Taj Mahal, one of the new breed of intellectual/cosmic bluesmen, was born in New York City of Caribbean descent on May 17, 1942. He grew up under the influence of Marcus Garvey and of Haile Selassie rather than Muddy Waters and Howlin' Wolf, eventually taking a degree at the University of Massachusetts. His debut album for Columbia in 1967, *Taj Mahal*, none the less highlighted a driving, electric blues-band that included such notables as Ry Cooder and Jesse Ed Davis who had been with him in the Rising Sons. His two best singles came from the same period: 'Statesboro' Blues' and 'Give Your Woman What She Wants'. He subsequently cut nine albums for Columbia, each one more ethnic in approach and many featuring acoustic African instruments.

The Mamas and Papas produced music that, for some, was the epitome of high-class folk rock, a perfect merging of California beat and Greenwich Village melody. But despite their beginnings in the New York folk club scene of the early Sixties and their close association with the Lovin' Spoonful, the Mamas and Papas' musical style owed little to the American folk and blues tradition and was more a contrived product of shrewd pop thinking on the part of producer-manager Lou Adler. His policy was to match their sweet vocal sound with a rock backing and to market them in terms of their hippy image, which, though fairly common among solo performers, was almost unheard-of in groups.

Most of the Mamas and Papas' material was written by leader John Phillips (born in Parris Island, South Carolina, on Aug. 30, 1941) and his wife Michelle (née Gilliam, born in California in 1944), who harmonized neatly with Cass Elliott (Alexandria, Virginia, Sept. 19, 1943) and Denny Doherty (Halifax, Nova Scotia, 1941). Their first hit was 'California Dreamin'' (Dunhill, 1966) which rivalled Scott McKenzie's 'San Francisco' as a popularizer of the flower-power philosophy. A dozen more hits followed in the next two years, including 'Monday Monday', 'I Saw Her Again', 'Creeque Alley' and a revival of 'Dedicated To The One I Love'. But the group did not progress and after a while their records began to sound pedestrian, too much like the Ray

Conniff cover versions of their songs. In 1968, they finally split. Cass Elliott and Denny Doherty went solo, with varying degrees of success. John made the intriguing solo album, *The Wolfking of LA*, then with Michelle joined the rock jet-set.

Manfred Mann was formed late in 1962 as the Manne-Hugg Blues Brothers after Manfred Mann (born on Oct. 21, 1940 in Johannesburg) and Mike Hugg (born on March 11, 1940 in Andover) had played in the same jazz quartet, on piano and vibes respectively, at a Butlin's holiday camp that summer. Mann took up organ, Hugg swapped to drums, and with Paul Jones (vocals, harmonica, born on Feb. 24, 1942), Mike Vickers (alto, clarinet, born on April 18, 1941), and Dave Richmond (bass), dropped jazz for R&B. An immediate success on the rapidly expanding R&B club circuit, they made their first single, 'Why Should We Not?' (HMV), in July, 1963. Their third release, '5-4-3-2-1', in January, 1964, coincided with Richmond's replacement by Tom McGuinness (born on Dec. 2, 1941 in London); its gimmicky pop qualities made it the theme tune of British television's *Ready Steady Go!* and a big hit. Thereafter Manfred Mann's A-Sides – e.g. 'Do Wah Diddy', 'Pretty Flamingo' (both British No. 1s) – stuck to a strong pop formula with a consistent success unaffected by the departure of Vickers – McGuinness switched to lead and was replaced by Jack Bruce on bass – at the end of 1965; the brief addition of a brass section (Lyn Dobson and Henry Lowther), and the substitution of Mike D'Abo from A Band Of Angels for Paul Jones and Klaus Voorman for Bruce, who left after six months for Cream. No material was exempt from the Manfred touch and the group's string of 15 British hits includes two Dylan numbers, 'Just Like A Woman' and 'The Mighty Quinn'. After the group split in 1969, Mann and Hugg stayed together for a while in Manfred Mann Chapter III, then Mann formed his own Earthband in 1971.

The Mar-Keys, originally known as the Royal Spades, had a Top Ten hit with their first disc, 'Last Night' (Satellite), written and arranged by Chips Moman, in 1961. Other, smaller, hits included 'Morning After', 'Popeye Stroll' and, in 1966, 'Philly Dog'. All were for the Stax Company.

The first of many Mar-Keys line-ups contained Packy Axton (tenor sax), Don Nix (baritone sax), Wayne Jackson (trumpet), Jerry Lee Smith (organ), Steve Cropper (guitar), Don 'Duck' Dunn (bass) and Terry Johnson (drums). All were white boys, two of whom (Cropper and Dunn) also played in the MGs with black musicians Booker T and Al Jackson, who in turn went on to play in both groups. As staff musicians at the Stax-Volt studios, the Mar-Keys were at the centre of the Memphis soul boom of the mid-Sixties, providing the accompaniment to hits by Otis Redding, Sam and Dave, Wilson Pickett *et al.* Axton subsequently formed the Packers ('Hole In The Wall' was a hit on Pure Soul in 1965), while Wayne Jackson, Andrew Love (tenor sax) and Floyd Newman (baritone sax) played in both the Mar-Keys and the famed sextet, the Memphis Horns.

Marmalade – Dean Ford, lead vocals (born Sept. 5, 1946); Junior Campbell, lead guitar (May 31, 1947); Pat Fairlie, rhythm guitar (April 14, 1946); Graham Knight, bass (Dec. 8, 1946) and Raymond Duffy, drums – first appeared as Dean Ford and the Gaylords. A leading Scottish group since 1963 – on a par with the Poets and the Beatstalkers – British impact eluded them despite entertaining and inventive singles such as 'The Name Game' and 'Little Egypt'. As Marmalade, 'Lovin' Things' (CBS) broke the spell in 1968, and a cover of the Beatles' 'Ob La Di Ob La Da' took them to No. 1 that year. Duffy was replaced by Alan Whitehead, the first in a series of changes. More serious was the departure of Junior Campbell, co-writer with Dean Ford of their finest hit, 'Reflections Of My Life' (Deram). He made highly commercial Tamlaesque singles by himself while his successor in Marmalade, Hughie Nicholson, soon formed the much-praised Blue, with other ex-Poets like himself. Reduced to a fourpiece, Ford and Knight, plus Duggie Henderson (drums) and Mike Japp (lead guitar) continued to make polished singles though with less good fortune, their brand of pleasant pop outmoded. Dean Ford released a solo album on EMI in 1975.

Martha and the Vandellas – Martha Reeves (born July 18, 1941), Rosalind Ashford (born Sept. 2, 1943) and Annette Sterling, the original Vandellas – were all natives of Detroit. Martha was employed as a secretary by Motown Records where one of her jobs was to sing song lyrics on to tape for artists to learn. When an artist fell ill, Martha was asked to sing on a session and the studio, impressed with the results, formed a group round her to do backing work. Their first disc as a session group was backing Marvin Gaye's 'Stubborn Kind Of Fellow' hit. The girls were then given a contract with Gordy Records – 'Vandellas' was derived from 'vandal'; they were jokingly accused of stealing the limelight from Marvin Gaye on disc.

The group's second record, 'Come And Get These Memories', a husky beat ballad, was a Top Thirty hit in 1963, and the follow-up, 'Heatwave', which saw a change of style to a rocking, brassy dance sound, set the charts alight, rising to No. 4. At this point, Annette quit the group to marry and was replaced by Betty Kelly, another Detroiter (born Sept. 16, 1944). The follow-ups 'Quicksand' and 'Livewire' were equally successful and in 1964 'Dancing In The Street', another storming dance record with crashing percussion, hit the No. 2 spot. Numerous other hits followed, and in 1967 the billing changed to Martha Reeves and the Vandellas. The following year Martha's sister Lois replaced Betty, but in 1969 Martha's illness interrupted activities. When they resumed in 1970, ex-Velvelette Sandra Tilley had replaced Rosalind, but success now dwindled, and the group split in 1973. Martha Reeves became established as a solo singer on MCA in 1974, singing with Arista in 1975.

George Martin, born in London on Jan. 3, 1926, trained at the Guildhall School of Music and joined EMI Records in 1950. Before signing the Beatles to the company's Parlophone label in 1962, Martin had principally produced comedy acts and ballad singers. He had been responsible for hits

235

by the Goons, Peter Sellers, Matt Monro and Shirley Bassey. He produced all the Beatles' recordings from 1962 to 1969, with his role as arranger becoming more crucial as the group's music grew in complexity. In addition to his string arrangements ('Eleanor Rigby') or harpsichord playing ('In My Life'), Martin's knowledge of studio techniques enabled Lennon and McCartney to translate their musical intuitions into sound collages on innovative tracks like 'Tomorrow Never Knows', 'A Day In The Life' and 'Strawberry Fields Forever'. In 1965, Martin left EMI to set up his own company, AIR London and after the Beatles' dissolution, turned to other projects, including the West Coast group Sea Train and the British band Stackridge, but most successfully, America.

The Marvelettes – Gladys Horton (lead singer), Katherine Anderson, Wanda Young, Georgeanna Tillman and Juanita Cowart (all born in 1944) – were formed at Inkster High School in Detroit. The girls won the school talent contest and a teacher introduced them to Berry Gordy, who signed the group to Tamla Records. Their debut disc 'Please Mr Postman', an intense, gospelly beat ballad featuring Gladys Horton's rasping lead vocal, was a No. 1 hit and million-seller in 1961. The next four years brought a succession of Top Fifty hits with such songs as 'Playboy', 'Beechwood 4-5789' and 'Too Many Fish In The Sea', but it was the Motown sound with a difference since the Marvelettes' vocal delivery had a bluesy edge not found in most of the Corporation's teen dance output. 1966 brought a return to the Top Ten with the mellower, gospel blues-flavoured 'Don't Mess With Bill', notable for its searing tenor sax solo. The group was reduced to a trio when Georgeanna and Juanita quit, but continued to make hit records. When lead singer Gladys left in 1968 – replaced by Anne Bogan – the distinctive sound went, too, and the group's final hit, a revival of 'That's How Heartaches Are Made', which crept into the Hot Hundred at 97 for just one week in 1969, reflected an altogether softer pop sound. The group disbanded soon afterwards.

Barbara Mason, born in Philadelphia on Aug. 9, 1947, first recorded in 1964 for Crusader. The following year her recording of her own song 'Yes I'm Ready', on Arctic, reached the American Top Ten. Jimmy Bishop (Mason's manager, producer and owner of the Arctic label) framed her mock-Motown soul ballads with a mixed chorus and strings while Mason's warm but girlish voice kept her from slipping into an easy-listening sophisticated style. Other hits on Arctic were 'Sad Sad Girl', 'I Need Love' (1965) and 'Oh How It Hurts' (1968). In 1970 Barbara Mason recorded for National-General, moving the next year to her current label, Buddah, where her answer disc to Shirley Brown's 'Woman To Woman' sold well in 1975.

John Mayall, a protégé of Alexis Korner, had been developing a multi-instrumental technique since the Fifties, playing harmonica, piano, organ and guitar. Born in Manchester on Nov. 29, 1933, he established his group, the Bluesbreakers, on the R&B club circuit with a line-up of Roger Dean (guitar), John McVie (bass) and Hughie Flint (drums), which remained unchanged until Eric Clapton replaced Dean in April, 1965. When Clapton left to form Cream just over a year later after making his own reputation – and Mayall's – with his unparalleled virtuosity, both live and later on record with *Blues Breakers* (Decca, 1966), his replacement, Peter Green, introduced a new and equally creative phase in the band's career. Mayall was the Midas of British rock: Green and McVie went on to form Fleetwood Mac; Green's successor, Mick Taylor, joined the Rolling Stones; his drummers included Aynsley Dunbar, Keef Hartley and Jon Hiseman; and both Jack Bruce and Andy Fraser played bass for a while. As each musician came and went Mayall's reputation grew. He has experimented frequently with the Bluesbreakers' line-up, adding horns, a violin, excluding drums, and attempting a fusion of jazz and blues with *Jazz-Blues Fusion* (Polydor, 1971) and *Moving On* (1972), recorded in America where he now lives. In 1974 he signed with ABC.

Huey Meaux, variously disc jockey, barber and independent record producer, was born on March 10, 1929 in Kaplan, Louisiana. He is of Cajun origin and a number of his own local record labels were devoted to this ethnic music, including Crazy Cajun, on which Meaux himself recorded. His first pop production, Jivin' Gene's 'Breaking Up Is Hard To Do', became a hit in 1959. Meaux's influence throughout Texas and Louisiana spread as his ability to pick hit records increased. 'My plan,' he told *Billboard*, 'is to pick up masters and place them with various companies. I want to set aside certain hours every day when I do nothing but listen to masters.' The degree of his responsibility was somewhat blurred, and he was often credited with producing records which he may simply have arranged for a major company to purchase or distribute. Meaux's name has cropped up in connection with Dale and Grace's 'I'm Leaving It All Up To You' (from Sam Montel) and Archie Bell's 'Tighten Up' (from Skipper Lee Frazier). But Meaux certainly produced many records himself, including Joe Barry's 'I'm A Fool To Care', 'She's About A Mover' by the Sir Douglas Quintet (released on his own Tribe label), Barbara Lynn's major hit 'You'll Lose A Good Thing', the profits from which he ploughed into his own studios, including Pasadena Sounds in Houston and Grits and Gravy Studios in Jackson, Mississippi.

Other records he 'placed' include the Hombres' 'Let It Out' (1967), Roy Head's 'Treat Her Right' (Backbeat in 1965), and B. J. Thomas's 'I'm So Lonesome I Could Cry' (Scepter in 1966). He also worked with T. K. Hulin, Jimmy Donley, Joey Long (three key but little-known figures in Texas rock), Chuck Jackson, Johnny Copeland, T-Bone Walker and Jerry Lee Lewis, whose fine *Southern Roots* album was a Meaux production. Freddy Fender's huge success in 1975 with three hit singles and two albums was in great part due to Meaux's 'old fashioned' approach to production: 'always highlight the song',

Terry Melcher, born on Feb. 8, 1942 in New York City, is a leading West Coast record producer. He made his singing debut in 1962, cutting several solo sides for Columbia under the name of Terry Day. They failed miserably, so he shifted into production work, turning out a string of moderate hits in the surf-sun *genre* by people like Pat Boone, Wayne Newton, the Rip Chords and his mother, Doris Day. In between sessions, he cut a few singles with future Beach Boy Bruce Johnston as Bruce and Terry. But it was as a producer that Melcher really excelled, and when his work with groups such as Paul Revere and the Raiders and the Byrds established him as a consistent hit-maker, his singing career faltered. During the years 1963–71 Melcher was responsible for the numerous hit albums by the Byrds: *Mr Tambourine Man*; *Turn, Turn, Turn*; *Easy Rider*; *Untitled* and *Byrdmaniax* as well as eight best-selling albums by Paul Revere and the Raiders, two by the Rip Chords, and one by Doris Day.

In 1973, Melcher signed to Reprise as a solo artist and cut the introverted *Terry Melcher*, which featured names like Clarence White, Roger McGuinn, Chris Hillman and Ry Cooder. However, it didn't sell, and Melcher redirected his energies into his own company, Equinox Records. Distributed by RCA, Equinox includes California Music (Bruce Johnston's group) and, of course, Melcher. As a production subsidiary, it has made albums by such diverse artists as Barry Mann and David Cassidy.

Memphis, having gained a reputation, through Sam Phillips and Sun Records, as one of the prime centres of Fifties musical development, retained its importance in the popular music field through the following decade. Former Sun sessionman Bill Black moved to Joe Cuoghi's Hi outfit in 1958 and had a series of hits during the early Sixties with his sax-led small combo. Paralleling this success with a similar sound was altoist Ace Cannon, while Willie Mitchell followed on from Black in the mid- and late Sixties.

Cuoghi died in 1968 and Mitchell largely took control of Hi's output, being responsible for the success of Ann Peebles and Al Green. In each case, Mitchell's band provides support with mellow, precise horn/rhythm arrangements, and his hornmen, Wayne Jackson and Andrew Love, provide a link with rival Memphis giant, Stax, formed in 1959 as Satellite by Jim Stewart and Estelle Axton, but changed to Stax to avoid confusion with a like-named West-Coast label. The Stax sound, developed throughout the mid-Sixties with artists like Rufus and Carla Thomas, Sam and Dave, Johnny Taylor and the Mar-Keys, is characterized by more punchy, riffing horn arrangements played by the Mar-Keys (including Jackson and Love), who backed most Stax artists on sessions. House arrangers included Isaac Hayes and David Porter, also prolific songwriters, who were both later to become successful solo artists with styles divergent from the 'Stax Sound'.

Short-lived competition emerged in 1964 with Quinton Claunch and Doc Russell's Goldwax label, successful with the Ovations and James Carr, with an intense, deep-soul style. In 1967, Chips Moman and Tommy Cogbill quit Fame Studios to set up their own American Group Productions in Memphis, and were successful with the Box Tops, B. J. Thomas, Dionne Warwick, Elvis Presley and Dusty Springfield among others. Among AGP's regular sessionmen was Reggie Young.

The Merseybeats – Tony Crane (lead guitar), Aaron Williams (rhythm guitar), Billy Kinsley (bass) and John Banks (drums) – were one of the few Liverpool groups to achieve a recorded sound worthy of their impact in live performance. Produced by Jack Baverstock on Fontana, they made a series of slow, atmospheric rock ballads (the Shirelles' 'It's Love That Really Counts', Jackie De Shannon's 'Wishin' And Hopin' '), though none was as successful as the jaunty Peter Lee Stirling number, 'I Think Of You', which got to No. 5 in 1964. Various personnel changes led, in 1966, to the dissolution of the group, but Kinsley and Crane re-emerged as the Merseys to score a massive hit with 'Sorrow', later to be enshrined as a Sixties classic by David Bowie on his *Pin-Ups* album.

Buddy Miles, an erratic rock drummer, was born in Omaha, Nebraska on Sept. 5, 1946. He backed the Ink Spots at 15.

While in the Wilson Pickett band he was approached by Mike Bloomfield to join Electric Flag. Miles' soul combined with Bloomfield's blues background, their personalities outweighing the other players, to create in the Flag both adventuresome ideas and consolidatory rock/soul music, as on *A Long Time Coming*. Following Bloomfield's departure, the Flag fell apart. Miles, in the driving seat for their second indifferent album *An American Music Band*, formed Buddy Miles Express out of its ruins. More brass-oriented, the Express folded when Miles joined Hendrix and Billy Cox in the Band Of Gypsies' tour through the winter of 1969-70. After Hendrix's death, Miles and Cox picked up the pieces in the Buddy Miles Band, and had a hit with 'Them Changes', a song continually recycled by Miles' bands ever since. He relinquished his James-Brown-meets-BST sets to tour with Carlos Santana, releasing a live album in 1972 on which their styles rarely met convincingly. Another band in between led to the re-formation of Electric Flag in spring 1974 and a typically uneven album.

Jody Miller, who was born on Nov. 29, 1941 in Phoenix, Arizona, contributed several up-beat ballads to the pop charts during the mid-Sixties. Her dramatic voice was produced with success by Steve Douglas at Capitol Records, with the aid of strong orchestral arrangements by Billy Strange. Hits ensued in 1965 with 'Queen Of The House' (Epic), the answer record to Roger Miller's 'King Of The Road' and 'Home Of The Brave'. Later, Jody moved to Epic and has consistently been around the country charts, singing in a more subdued style.

Roger Miller – born Jan. 2, 1936 in Fort Worth, Texas – worked in Nashville for a decade (as songwriter, backing musician and recording artist) before scoring his first hit in 1964, 'Dang Me', immediately after signing to Smash. Both it and his other 1964 million-seller, 'Chug-A-Lug' represented his best qualities; humorous lyrics sung tongue-incheek and set to infectious melodies. The following year he scored again with the much blander 'King Of The Road'.

Miller's style can go both ways, from typical up-tempo country novelties to coy tackiness ('England Swings') and into schmaltz ('Little Green Apples').

The Steve Miller Band. Miller was born on Nov. 5, 1943 in Milwaukee, Wisconsin and raised in Texas. He learned about the blues when he was still a child and T-Bone Walker would play at parties for Steve's father, a doctor. When he went to San Francisco and formed a band in 1966, Miller had already worked in a Fort Worth recording studio and played in the bars on the South Side of Chicago.

The Steve Miller Blues Band was a tighter, more professional unit than most in San Francisco; with fellow-Texan Boz Scaggs sharing guitar leads with Miller plus Tim Davis (drums), Lonnie Turner (bass) and Jim Peterman (keyboards), the quintet picked up a large ballroom following in no time. They signed with Capitol in 1967 for an unprecedented $75,000 and changed their name to simply the Steve Miller Band. *Children Of The Future*, their first album, showed why – they were stepping well past the blues. The first side of the LP was an extended suite that meshed electronic effects and meticulous harmonies with the basic band tracks. *Sailor*, their second, was in the same vein. Then Scaggs and Peterman left the group in 1969. After that, Miller usually stuck to a trio or quartet, and featured himself much more than in the original band. There was a constant turnover of sidemen, and the sound became more diffuse. By releasing albums and touring often, Miller managed none the less to keep a stable, good-sized audience without ever scoring a hit single. That finally came in 1974, when 'The Joker – and its accompanying album – went to the top of the charts.

Millie, born Millie Small in Jamaica where she recorded a few unmemorable sides for Coxsone Dodd and one classic, 'Oh Shirley' with Roy Panton, was brought to England at the peak of the bluebeat craze by the astute Chris Blackwell, who produced her international hit, 'My Boy Lollipop' (1964). Her follow-up, 'Sweet William', in similar vein,

242

failed to register and from then on it was the long road down – a high-pitched screech based on Shirley of Shirley and Lee being the sum of her musical vocabulary.

Garnet Mimms (and the Enchanters). After unsuccessful recordings with the Gainors on Cameo Mercury and Big Top, Mimms (born Nov. 26, 1937 in Ashland, West Virginia) struck lucky with the Enchanters (Sam Bell, Charles Boyer, Zola Pearnell) under the guidance of fellow-Philadelphian, Jerry Ragavoy. The group recorded twelve beautiful sides for United Artists, including million-selling 'Cry Baby', 'Baby Won't You Weep', and a revival of 'For Your Precious Love' (1963) before splitting into two acts for the price of one. Enchanters releases on Warners and Loma were ignored, but Mimms succeeded with further recordings for United Artists ('Tell Me Baby', 'One Woman Man' – 1964; 'It Was Easier To Hurt Her' – 1965; 'I'll Take Good Care Of You' – 1966) and its subsidiary Veep ('It's Been Such A Long Way Home' – 1966; 'My Baby' – 1967). By then, however, Ragavoy was getting more reaction with another ex-Gainor, Howard Tate, and his sporadic productions with Mimms on Verve (1968–70) were a poor second-best. Two more releases on GSF (1972) fared no better.

The Mindbenders, formed in Manchester in 1963 and led by Wayne Fontana, comprised Eric Stewart (guitar), Bob Land (bass) and Ric Rothwell (drums). As the Mindbenders, they stepped into the limelight after cutting their first solo single, 'Groovy Kind Of Love', in December, 1965 for Fontana. An attractive beat ballad, it reached No. 2 in January, 1966, and a month later the group officially split from Wayne. They recorded five more singles, but only one, 'Ashes To Ashes', reached the charts. Two albums were released – one in 1966 and one in 1967 – containing mostly cover versions of R&B hits like 'Just A Little Bit' and 'Cool Jerk'. The group made its final bow in the 1967 film *To Sir With Love.* In later years, Eric Stewart formed Hotlegs – of 'Neanderthal Man' fame – which eventually became 10cc.

Moby Grape was put together by Matthew Katz, one-time manager of Jefferson Airplane. Built around Skip Spence, the Airplane's original drummer, as rhythm guitarist and singer, Moby Grape boasted two other lead guitarists – Jerry Miller and Peter Lewis – plus Bob Mosley on bass and Don Stevenson on drums. All sang and their vocal diversity and harmonies set against the fluency of three guitars established their melodic style. After playing the Fillmore late in 1966, only weeks after formation, they were inundated with record offers. David Rubinson, of Columbia, won out and then was responsible for a wave of promotional overkill in launching their album, *Moby Grape*, in May, 1967, culminating in the simultaneous release of five singles drawn from it. The group's credibility was destroyed.

Ironically, *Moby Grape* was a rare attempt by an early 'Frisco group to actually create a structured album rather than simply capture a live sound. Each member contributed songs and the magic of interweaving guitars and rapturous singing ('8.05', for example, clearly foreshadows Crosby, Stills and Nash) resulted in an album that has matured well with time. Dogged by more hype techniques and, later, an ever-fluctuating line-up, the group floundered. *Wow* was a fascinating exercise in excess with only occasional glimmers of their potential. Skip Spence left soon after to make the extraordinary *Oar* and the four-piece cut *Moby Grape '69*, complete with a disclaimer about the earlier hype. However, it was a poor album and when Mosley quit before its release, the Grape folded. Clutching at straws, the remaining trio went to Nashville to record the unimpressive *Truly Fine Citizen*, with local bassman Bob Moore depping for Mosley. They fell apart again only to return *in toto* in 1971 for the largely forgettable *20 Granite Creek*.

There's little doubt that the Grape were something special, but a never-ending saga since 1974 of re-forming and splitting neither augurs well for the future nor helps redeem their tarnished past reputation. Despite it all, *Moby Grape* alone reveals what a tragedy it was that they were never able to develop freely.

George 'Zoot' Money, after a brief spell with Blues Incorporated in 1963, formed Zoot Money's Big Roll Band. Backing his keyboards and vocals were Paul Williams (bass, vocals), Andy Somers (guitar), Nick Newell (tenor), Clive Burrows (baritone), Colin Allen (drums). Although the band had no success on record, either with Decca or Columbia, Zoot rapidly became a favourite of the Flamingo audience for both his music and his clowning and took over Georgie Fame's residency. A victim of psychedelia and flower power – he appeared in robes and short-lived euphoria as Dantalion's Chariot – he re-emerged in 1971 with Steve Ellis in Ellis. After recording two albums for Epic, bad luck broke up the group. He subsequently performed in the rock revue, Grimms, and backed Kevin Coyne.

The Monkees were formed in the spring of 1966 to star in a new television comedy series about the life of a mythical pop group. The chosen four from among the hosts of unknowns auditioned for the parts were former British child star Davy Jones (born in Manchester on Dec. 30, 1945), former American child star Mickey (*Circus Boy*) Dolenz (March 8, 1946 in Los Angeles), Peter Tork (Feb. 13, 1945 in Washington D.C.) and Michael Nesmith (Dec. 30, 1942 in Houston, Texas). They had talent but, initially at least, were given no chance to develop it: they were told what to sing and how to sing it and were not allowed to play their respective instruments on recording sessions. For two years virtually every single made under the Monkees' name (on Colgems, and RCA in Britain) reached the Top Ten in both America and Britain and for a short time it really did appear, in terms of the hysteria they created and actual record sales, that here were the new Beatles.

The musical supervision of the series was by Don Kirshner, the head of Screen-Gems Music, who used material from the people he had worked with earlier in New York: Carole King and Gerry Goffin ('Pleasant Valley Sunday'), Neil Diamond ('I'm A Believer', 'A Little Bit Me, A Little Bit You'), Neil Sedaka and Barry Mann. A few of the hits were from newer writers, who would later make their mark elsewhere. Harry Nilsson wrote 'Daddys' for them while 'Day-dream Believer' was by John Stewart. Kirshner's approach, like that of the show's producers and publicity men, was unashamedly commercial. It secured ten gold records within eighteen months, but it also ensured that the group would rebel against the machine that had created them. When, led by Nesmith, they won greater control over their records – at the time of *Headquarters*, the third album – Kirshner was content to manufacture another television pop group who existed only in cartoon form, the Archies.

The Monkees themselves never quite made the leap from teen idols to 'serious' rock group, 1967 style, though *Head* (the soundtrack of their one feature film) was an above-average album. Each member of the group went his own way, although the impact of the Monkees operation itself is still being felt in pop. A new, sub-teenage audience had been identified – an age-group which previously had shown no interest at all in pop – and it was proved that the centralization of control over an artist's material, production and the means of exposing them to the public could hardly fail. The creators of the Partridge Family and the Osmonds were not far behind. In 1975, the Monkees re-formed with Dolenz and Jones joined by Tommy Boyce and Bobby Hart who had written many of the group's early songs (e.g. 'Valeri'), as well as having hits of their own ('I Wonder What She's Doing Tonite', 1967, and 'Alice Long', 1968). They toured successfully and recorded for Capitol.

Bob Montgomery, born in Lampasas, Texas in 1936, moved to Lubbock where he met Buddy Holly in 1949. Buddy and Bob, 'Singers Of Western And Bop', recorded a number of unimpressive bluegrass and country sides (later released by American Decca as the *Holly In The Hills* album) before Holly formed the Crickets.

Montgomery helped with the engineering in Norman Petty's Clovis studios and wrote a number of songs with and for Holly, including 'Heartbeat' and 'Love Made A Fool Of You'. In 1959, he moved to Nashville and his songs were soon recorded by Bob Luman, Sue Thompson ('Two Of A

Kind') and Mel Tillis. After several successful compositions including 'Misty Blue' (Wilma Burgess) and 'Wind Me Up' (Cliff Richard), he joined United Artists as a staff producer in 1966. There his work with Johnny Darrell, Buddy Knox, Earl Richards and Del Reeves resulted in a stream of country hits, while Montgomery's silky and imaginative productions of Bobby Goldsboro – 'Honey' and 'Summer The First Time' – helped to bring 'country pop' into being.

Derrick Morgan, born in Jamaica, began his recording career while still in his teens and achieved national fame almost immediately with 'Fat Man', a disc that, although different from the Fats Domino title, nevertheless betrayed the New Orleans artist's influence. He was a consistent seller with the Jamaican audience throughout the Sixties, recording, in the style and manner of early Ben E. King, sides like 'Look Before You Leap'. His recorded outings with sister Patsy on 'Housewives' Choice' and 'Troubles' were very popular, as was his feud with Prince Buster on 'Blazing Fire' and 'Let Them Talk'. An idiosyncratic vocal style was his forte.

During the rock-steady period 'Tougher Than Tough' and 'Court Dismiss' made him popular with British skinheads, a position he consolidated with a whole series of 'popatop' and 'moon hop' recordings. In the Seventies he was still going strong with 'Rasta Don't Fear' and others high in the charts.

George 'Shadow' Morton is somethinb of a cult-figure, his reputation as a record producer by far outweighing his actual achievements which amount to a few hits in the middle-to-late Sixties by the Shangri-Las, Janis Ian and Vanilla Fudge. Born in 1942 in Richmond, Virginia, he nicknamed himself 'Shadow' – possibly because of his tendency to excuse himself from business meetings, ostensibly to visit the toilet and not to be seen again for several days. Raised in Brooklyn, he sang with a local vocal group, the Gems, during the late Fifties, then held down numerous jobs including bouncer, ice-cream vendor and hairdresser before launching his record career in 1964 with a hit song he wrote in twelve

247

minutes – the exotic 'Remember (Walkin' In The Sand)' by the Shangri-Las. Although Morton wrote the song he did not produce the session, as has been commonly supposed. However, he did produce the group's subsequent output on the Red Bird label and established a reputation for his theatrical approach to production exemplified on Top Ten American hits such as 'Leader Of The Pack' (a No. 1 in 1964) and 'I Can Never Go Home Anymore' (1965) and on such minor hits as 'Past, Present And Future' (1966), 'Out In The Streets' and 'Give Us Your Blessing' (1965).

In 1968 Morton entered the heavy-rock field with his 'pop-art' production of 'You Keep Me Hanging On' by Vanilla Fudge and also scored with 'Society's Child' by singer-songwriter prodigy Janis Ian. He also supervised Richie Havens' debut album for Verve but achieved very little commercial success in subsequent years although he was hired to produce the New York Dolls' second album in 1974. An autocrat in the studio, Morton does his own arranging and most of his engineering.

Mickie Most, born Michael Hayes in 1938 in Aldershot, Hampshire, moved to Harrow, North London, with his family and befriended Terry Dene during the skiffle craze. They both appeared as extras in a crowd scene in the film *Joan of Arc*, made at Pinewood in 1956. The following year, Dene shot to stardom as an early British teen idol while Most worked the espresso machine at the famed 2 1's coffee bar in Soho. In 1958, Most and friend Alex Murray formed the Most Brothers, recorded unsuccessfully for Decca and toured with the young Cliff Richard. Following his marriage in 1959 to a South African girl, Most spent the next three years there where he formed Mickie Most and the Playboys and covered American hits for the South African Market, achieving eleven consecutive local No. 1s.

Returning to England in 1962, Most attempted to break into the burgeoning R&B/beat scene but turned instead to record production after failing as an artist. His first known production, 'Baby Let Me Take You Home' by the Animals, reached the Top Twenty but the follow-up, 'House

Of The Rising Sun', topped charts internationally. From then on, Most achieved an impressive success ratio with a stream of international pop hits by the Nashville Teens ('Tobacco Road'), Brenda Lee ('Is It True'), Herman's Hermits, the Animals, Donovan and Lulu. The latter pair were both 'cold', chartwise, when Most took over their recording careers and furnished them both with comeback hits – respectively, 'Sunshine Superman' and 'The Boat That I Row'. He also recorded the original Jeff Beck group and put Beck in the Top Ten with 'Hi-Ho Silver Lining', but was criticized for treating the guitarist like any other pop singer whose career depended on chart success. In 1969, Most formed his own label, RAK, which achieved an all-time high ratio of hits in 1973 with 14 from 18 releases. Most is uncompromising in his attitude towards producing straightforward commercial pop, adjusting to the dominant tastes of each era.

Motown. In the beginning, there was Berry Gordy Jr. He spent the mid-Fifties working part-time on Ford Motor Company's production lines in Detroit, but the rest of his time was spent rather more creatively – writing songs and producing record sessions. By early 1960 he had written or collaborated on 18 Hot Hundred entries, six of which made the Top Twenty and four selling over a million. There had also been innumerable misses and album fillers. Moreover, Gordy produced virtually all of those hits, and often ensured that the songs were published by his own firm, Jobete. His collaborators included his sister Gwen, Tyran Carlo, Janie Bradford and Smokey Robinson, and artists to record his songs included Jackie Wilson, Marv Johnson and Etta James. Berry's production work included the Miracles, and he leased their masters first to End, then to Chess where 'Bad Girl' made the Hot Hundred late in 1959. At this time, his sister Gwen had her own Detroit label, Anna (named after another sister), distributed by Chess, on which Paul Gayten made the Hot Hundred in November, 1959, and the following February Barrett Strong began a climb to the Top Thirty with 'Money'.

These successes prompted Berry into action, and in June, 1960, the Motown label (derived from Detroit's 'Motortown' tag) was launched with 'My Beloved'/'Sugar Daddy' by the Satintones, followed a month later by Tamla – he wanted to call it Tammy, after Debbie Reynolds' 1957 hit, but was prevented for copyright reasons – whose first release was a pickup of Barrett Strong's 'Money' hit from Anna. The eighth release on Tamla was 'Shop Around' by the Miracles, which by early 1961 had risen to No. 2 in the charts, selling a million copies on the way. At the same time, Motown's fourth release, Mary Wells' 'Bye Bye Baby', reached the Top Fifty, and by the end of that year the Marvelettes' 'Please Mr Postman' had provided Tamla's second gold disc and first chart-topper, while Eddie Holland's 'Jamie' was soon to put Motown in the Top Fifty again. Success followed success, and another string was added to the Motown Recording Corporation's bow with the debut of the Gordy label early in 1962. By autumn, the Contours' 'Do You Love Me' had given the new label a No. 3 hit and a gold disc. Meanwhile several small Detroit independent labels with Gordy family connections were experiencing financial difficulties, having scored hits but not received payment from distributors. By the end of 1962 such labels as Harvey, Tri-Phi, Miracle, Melody and Anna had been absorbed into the Motown Corporation, and with them came the contracts of Lamont Anthony (Dozier), Jimmy and David Ruffin, Johnny Bristol, Junior Walker, the Temptations and Spinners. Dozier forsook his performing career to employ his writing talents in partnership with Eddie and Brian Holland – a trio that was to provide Motown with a constant stream of hit records over half a decade – and Bristol also turned his attention to writing and producing, while the others were placed with the Corporation's now established labels.

The Temptations went to Gordy, where after a shaky start they reached the Top Twenty in 1964 with 'The Way You Do The Things You Do', and the next year went to No. 1 with 'My Girl', written by Miracles' leader and Motown vice-president, Bill 'Smokey' Robinson, arguably the most poetic popular songwriter of his time. The Temptations have proved to be the label's most consistent hitmakers over the years, despite numerous changes of personnel and style. Their closest rivals on Gordy were Martha and the Vandellas, whose 1963/64 hits 'Heatwave' and 'Dancing In The Street' were followed by consistent chart entries up to 1970. Other artists to enjoy chart success on Gordy include the Contours, Bobby Taylor and the Vancouvers and Edwin Starr, who joined the label following Motown's acquisition of the Ric Tic/Golden World combine in 1967. Tamla's success continued with the Miracles and Marvelettes, while in 1963 Marvin Gaye – married to Anna Gordy – began a string of Top Thirty hits with 'Hitch Hike', later augmenting his success in duets with Mary Wells, Kim Weston and Tammi Terrell, and the million-selling chart-topper 'Fingertips' set blind, harmonica-playing keyboard virtuoso Stevie Wonder on the road to fame and fortune; 1966–7 saw a brief spell of chart entries for the Isley Brothers.

Motown's initial momentum was maintained by Mary Wells with a succession of hits up to her departure in 1964, when the Supremes inherited the mantle of prime hitmakers, followed by the Four Tops – the Supremes recorded no less than 12 chart-toppers between 1964 and 1969 and the Tops were rarely out of the Top Fifty. In 1970, when these groups were waning somewhat, the Jackson 5, a male sub-teen group signed from the small independent Steeltown label, revitalized Motown's potency with four consecutive No. 1s, spending a total of ten weeks at the top of the charts that year. 1964 had also seen the opening of two further outlets, VIP and then Soul. VIP seems to have been intended for experimental product, with novelty items by Ray Oddis ('Happy Ghoul Time') and the Vows, material licensed from overseas (Richard Anthony), a tentative dabble with local white acts (R. Dean Taylor, Lewis Sisters, Chris Clark) and 'mainstream' soul. It is perhaps significant that only the latter brought chart success: the Velvelettes' 'Needle In A Haystack' reached the Top Fifty late in 1964, and there were subsequent hits by the Monitors, Elgins and Spinners. Meanwhile, Soul soon became established when the seventh release, Junior Walker's 'Shotgun', reached the Top Five early in 1965, the first in a succession of hits for his combo. Shorty Long (killed in a boating accident in 1969), Jimmy Ruffin, the Originals and Gladys Knight and the Pips subsequently kept the label well-represented in the charts.

In 1970, the Motown Corporation took a step into the rock market with the Rare Earth label, which achieved four Top Ten hits in its first year – three by Rare Earth, a group of white Detroiters restyling Sixties hits in 'heavy' fashion, and one by R. Dean Taylor. The following year, the Corporation moved its administrative quarters to Hollywood as Berry Gordy became involved in movies, grooming Diana Ross for stardom in the title role for a biographical film on Billie Holiday, *Lady Sings The Blues*. The move also brought a new label, aptly named Mowest, with a roster including Gloria Jones, Sisters Love, G. C. Cameron and Tom Clay, a disc jockey who took the second release into the Top Ten, 'What The World Needs Now Is Love – Abraham, Martin and John', a bizarre but striking collage of radio station tape clips pertaining to various political assassinations, with tasteful musical background. In 1973 Gordy took chairmanship of his conglomerate, relinquishing the presidency to Ewart Abner, whose pedigree included presidency of Vee Jay during the Sixties and Motown staff production duties, and by the mid-Seventies, having lost Gladys Knight, the Four Tops, Martha Reeves and the Spinners to other labels and the mists of time, the Corporation was 'hot' again with successful acts including the Jackson 5, Eddie Kendricks, Miracles (minus Smokey Robinson, now an established solo artist), Willie Hutch and the Commodores. Meanwhile the label's established stars – Diana Ross, the Temptations, Marvin Gaye and Stevie Wonder – sustained their success.

The Move, formed in late 1965 from the cream of the Birmingham beat groups comprised Roy Wood, guitarist and songwriter, born Nov. 8, 1946; Bev Bevan, drummer, born Nov. 25, 1945; Ace 'The Singing Skull' Kefford, bassist; Trevor Burton, guitarist, born 1949; and Carl Wayne, vocalist. Manager Tony Secunda booked them into London's Marquee Club in late 1966 where their violent and dramatic approach caused a sensation and rapidly won them a following among London's burgeoning underground. Their first record, 'Night Of Fear' (Deram), a pastiche of Tchaikovsky's '1812 Overture', which reached No. 2 in Britain in January 1967, was a Roy Wood composition, supposedly inspired by Secunda's prompting. Subsequent Top Twenty hits of note included: 'I Can Hear The Grass Grow', 'Flowers In The Rain', 'Fire Brigade', 'Blackberry Way', 'Curly', 'Brontosaurus', 'Tonight' and 'California Man' – all by Wood, who developed into a successful and consistent formula pop-writer of little originality but with a flair for mimicking and reworking styles.

The Move veered uneasily between psychedelia and a career as a hit singles band with only one minor hit album, their first *The Move*, at a time when singles and album charts were developing in different directions. A late flirtation with heavy metal on *Looking On*, which yielded 'Brontosaurus', was largely unsuccessful. Secunda's flamboyance backfired when Prime Minister Harold Wilson sued successfully over a postcard caricature designed to publicize the 1967 single, 'Flowers In The Rain' (Regal Zonophone). Internal dissent led to the departure of Ace Kefford, then Trevor Burton, and finally, after a disastrous excursion into cabaret, Carl Wayne. Birmingham musicians Rick Price, bass, born June 10, 1944, and Jeff Lynne, guitar and vocals, born Dec. 30, 1947, replaced them; the latter avowedly to launch a new project with Wood – the Electric Light Orchestra. The final line-up made one brief trip to America in 1971 before coming off the road for good. The last hit, 'California Man' (the B-side of which, 'Do Ya', was their only American chart entry), appeared in May, 1972, just three months before ELO's first hit '10538 Overture' signalled the end of the Move.

Muscle Shoals' repute as a recording centre is the result of the industry and perseverance of Rick Hall of Fame Studios. After years of touring locally with a small combo, doing session work for Hi in Memphis and writing songs with Billy Sherrill, Hall opened his studios in 1961 in Florence, Alabama, where he lived – the Muscle Shoals 'tag' stems from the airport which serves Florence. He quickly collected around him a group of white musicians with their heads and hearts steeped in Southern R&B to form the nucleus of the Muscle Shoals sound. Among them were Spooner Oldham and Barry Beckett, organ; Jimmy Johnson, guitar; David Hood, bass; and Roger Hawkins, drums. However, unlike Memphis or New Orleans, there is no readily identifiable 'Muscle Shoals Sound' as such, though on slow numbers arrangements tend to be 'churchy' with solemn, elegiac keyboard work, like the organ on Percy Sledge's 'When A Man Loves A Woman', and on fast songs Hall tends to feature a repeated guitar riff. During the early Sixties, artists like Tommy Roe and the Tams, from Bill Lowery's Atlanta-based stable, recorded at Fame. In 1964, Rick Hall launched his own Fame label, scoring immediately with Jimmy Hughes' 'Steal Away'. That year Joe Tex's 'Hold What You've Got' was a Muscle Shoals creation, and in 1965 Hall signed Fame to an Atlantic distribution deal, prompting Jerry Wexler to venture south with such artists as Aretha Franklin and Wilson Pickett. Arthur Conley's first hits were cut at Fame, while Chess used the facilities for Etta James, Irma Thomas, Maurice and Mac and Bobby Moore's Rhythm Aces, and in later years the diverse styles of Otis Rush and Ronnie Hawkins have benefited from the Rick Hall touch.

The Nashville Teens – Arthur Sharp, vocals; Ray Phillips, vocals, bass; John Allen and Pete Shannon, guitars; Barry Jenkins, drums; John Hawken, piano – were formed in 1962 in Weybridge, Surrey, and learnt their craft in Hamburg clubs through 1963–4. From this period, only a live album, their contribution mixed down, backing Jerry Lee Lewis at the Star Club, remains. In 1964, managed by Don Arden and produced by Mickie Most, they cut 'Tobacco Road' – strident piano, fierce beat and the two singers up front, it made the British and American Top Ten. Their label, Decca, didn't grasp how original an R&B outfit they were – as 'Parchman Farm' and 'I Need You Baby' from a 1964 EP bear witness – and their pop singles were a travesty of their excellence. The band continued working into the Seventies, though much changed; Jenkins joined the Animals and Hawken went to Keith Relf's Renaissance.

Fred Neil, a songwriter and singer, came to the fore in the Greenwich Village folk scene of the early Sixties. Although Neil made five albums between 1962 and 1970, his public performances were rare and other artists have been responsible for bringing his songs to large audiences. Born in St Petersburg, Florida in 1937, he appeared on the *Grand Ole Opry* before moving to New York. His first Elektra album, *Bleecker And MacDougal*, contained the definitive versions of 'Candy Man' and 'Other Side Of This Life', later recorded by Roy Orbison and the Lovin' Spoonful respectively. Neil later moved back to Florida, emerging only to cut occasional albums, the most recent of which was *Other Side Of This Life* (Capitol, 1970). Meanwhile, his songs were still being recorded by other artists, notably 'Everybody's Talkin'' (Nilsson on the soundtrack of *Midnight Cowboy*) and 'Dolphins' (Linda Ronstadt, Tim Buckley).

Aaron Neville, born in New Orleans in 1941, achieved national prominence in early 1967 when 'Tell It Like It Is' on Parlo reached No. 2. His delicate voice was well suited to this bluesy ballad, which was taken up as the anthem for the rising Black Power movement. Neville started out in the late Fifties with the Hawketts and in the early Sixties had some regional successes when he recorded for Minit. He is signed to Sansu Enterprises in New Orleans along with his elder brother, Art Neville of the Meters. He has also recorded for Instant, Safari and Bell.

The Newbeats were a three-man group, based in Nashville and purveying the sort of shrill, falsetto singing that was popular in the early Sixties (e.g. Lou Christie, Four Seasons, etc.). Originally a duo called Dean and Mark (who had a Top Fifty hit with a cover of Travis and Bob's country number 'Tell Him No' on Bullseye, 1959) they became the Newbeats when joined by Larry Henley – born June 30, 1941, in Arp, Texas – in 1964. Their first release, 'Bread And Butter' (Hickory),was a No. 2 hit in August of that year and was followed by two other Top Twenty hits ('Everything's Alright', 'Run Baby Run') and several other chart entries over the next two years. A good, firm dance beat and strong material kept them going through 1965, after which they remained on Hickory. Larry Henley now records for Capricorn, while Dean and Mark Mathis – born on March 17, 1939 and Feb. 9, 1942 respectively, in Hahira, Georgia – kept the Newbeats' name alive on Playboy Records.

New Orleans. By 1963, the New Orleans recording scene seemed quite derelict. Imperial/Minit Records had been sold by owner Lew Chudd to Liberty and the new management retreated to their West Coast home; AFO, likewise, had moved to California and Ace was having problems with its distributor, Vee Jay. Other major labels were not happy with the recording facilities available at Cosimo's tiny studio in Gov. Nicholls Street, nor were they pleased with the obstructing tactics of the local musicians' union. So, with the hits drying up and rock'n'roll and R&B in fast decline there seemed good reasons for long faces.

But there was light in the darkness and, as singer Earl King said, 'It seemed that New Orleans was at a standstill in production, but they had more recordings done during the Sixties, I imagine, than they did during the Fifties.' The departure of the outside independent labels had given the small local labels the chance to cash in on the homegrown talent. One of the first to come up with a local hit was Frisco, with Danny White, in late 1962 with 'Kiss Tomorrow Goodbye'; Rip did likewise with Deacon John, Reggie Hall and Eddie Bo and Watch had minor successes with Benny Spellman, Johnny Adams and Professor Longhair. The man responsible for these productions was Wardell Quezergue, who had learnt his trade with Dave Bartholomew's band and now ran the most popular aggregation in the city, the Royal Dukes of Rhythm. Along with fellow-producer Allen Toussaint, Wardell more or less kept the New Orleans scene alive in the

Sixties. Like Toussaint, he was very much aware of the trend away from the old rocking R&B music towards the funkier, slicker soul sounds and this was reflected in his modern productions.

In late 1964, Wardell formed Nola Records with Clinton Scott and had early good-sellers with Smokey Johnson, Warren Lee and Willie Tee. Early problems with pressing, distributing and promoting facilities were solved when studio owner Cosimo Matassa formed his Dover Records Corporation to cover these vital aspects. Nola soon had a No. 7 hit with Robert Parker's dance record, 'Barefootin'', in 1966 and another group label, Parlo, had a gold record with Aaron Neville's 'Tell It Like It Is' in early 1967. But Dover grew too big too quickly and collapsed in financial ruin in 1968 taking with it the 20 or so labels by then under its umbrella. Out of this debacle, only Instant and Sansu survived. Although Instant, who had early hits with Chris Kenner, was merely jogging along, Sansu – headed by Marshall Sehorn and Allen Toussaint – was enthusiastically clocking up international hits with Lee Dorsey on Amy. It was these two record-men who were willing and eventually able to inject new life into the long-standing New Orleans scene.

The Nice – Keith Emerson (born Nov. 2, 1944), keyboards; Brian Davison (born May 25, 1942), drums; Lee Jackson (born Jan. 8, 1943), bass, vocals; David O'List, guitar, vocals – had individually thorough groundings in the seminal British club scene of the mid-Sixties. They came together to back P. P. Arnold, often upstaging her with their impressive warm-up act. Managed by Andrew Oldham, the original quartet made only one album, *Thoughts Of Emerlist Davjack* (Immediate, 1968), featuring the climactic 'Rondo'. O'List left the group, as he did Roxy Music later, on the verge of their breakthrough, removing one of the dynamic cornerstones of the band. Without O'List, Emerson's keyboard pyrotechnics dominated as he developed his penchant for rocked-up classics on *Ars Nova Vita Brevis* and his showmanship – exemplified by setting fire to the Stars and

257

Stripes during 'America' – in live performances. Their three subsequent albums, including *Five Bridges* (Charisma, 1970), all reached the Top Ten. Following the break-up in 1970, Emerson nurtured these aspects with ELP, while Davison and Jackson, after abortive attempts with their own groups, formed Refugee with another keyboard virtuoso, Patrick Moraz. In 1975 O'List formed Jet with Andy Ellison and Clive Townson (from John's Children), and Peter Oxendale and Martin Gordon (from Sparks) while Refugee folded when Moraz replaced Rick Wakeman in Yes.

Nirvana originally consisted of Patrick Campbell-Lyons and Alex Spyropoulos, who came together in 1967 to produce two superb dreamlike singles, 'Tiny Goddess' and 'Pentecost Hotel'. They went on to produce *The Story Of Simon Simopath* (Island, 1967) an impressive 'concept' album before the idea had got out of hand. Their second album, *All Of Us* (1968), was in many ways more successful. However, the team began moving apart and Campbell-Lyons dominated the awkward-sounding *Dedicated To Markos III* (Pye, 1970). By the next album, Spyropoulos had vanished altogether and the three later Nirvana albums, solely under Campbell-Lyons's control, have only quiet flashes of their former excellence. Campbell-Lyons has also worked as producer of a series of mostly unsuccessful albums by 'progressive' bands like Clear Blue Sky, Sunburst and Jade Warrior.

Cliff Nobles & Co. A one-time group singer whose old rock'n'roll cuts are available on Moonshot, Nobles' brief moment of glory came in 1968 when 'The Horse' went to No. 2 on both the pop and R&B charts on the Phil L.A. Of Soul label. It had originally been the B-side of an unexceptional Nobles' vocal. The label kept his name on smaller hits – 'Horse Fever' and 'Switch It On' when, in fact, 'The Horse' had been made by Leon Huff and other Philadelphia sessionmen, most of whom turned up in the MFSB band in 1974. Nobles, born in Mobile, Alabama, in 1944, had previously recorded in 1966 for Atlantic. His regular group

(And Co.) included Benny Williams (bass), Bobby Tucker (guitar) and Tommy Soul (drums).

Phil Ochs, a singer-songwriter primarily identified with Sixties topical protest, was born on Dec. 19, 1940 in El Paso, Texas. Ochs went as a disenchanted Ohio State University journalism student into the Greenwich Village radical folk scene as a logical progression. First influenced by Bob Gibson, he fell in with Dylan, Paxton, Dave Cohen and the *Broadside* magazine movement. He sang out against the Vietnam War as early as 1962, recorded for Elektra beginning in 1963, then switched to A&M, which released the controversial *Gunfight At Carnegie Hall* (1970). His best known songs include 'There But For Fortune' (a hit for Joan Baez), 'Power And Glory', 'Changes', 'I Ain't Marchin' Anymore', 'Draft-Dodger Rag', 'Flower Lady', 'Love Me, I'm A Liberal' and 'Small Circle Of Friends'. Especially fluent in the sardonic talking-blues style, Ochs eschewed the 'poetic' lyric fashion to stress logic and clarity, with a fine sense of melodic shaping. His career line became jagged as causes he espoused were either won, lost or abandoned. Yet he made a lasting contribution to the topical songwriting outburst during the period of mass radicalization of the Sixties.

Andrew 'Loog' Oldham, a failed teenage pop star and former publicist, used his own persuasiveness – and Eric Easton's financial backing – to lure the Rolling Stones away from their verbal and unofficial understanding with Georgio Gomelsky one night in April, 1963, at Gomelsky's Crawdaddy Club in Richmond. Though generally credited with moulding the group's unruly image – he sacked pianist Ian Stewart because he didn't look right – he initially tried to smarten up the Stones, forcing them into dog-check stage suits for their first British television appearance to promote 'Come On' on *Thank Your Lucky Stars.* He also controlled their early recordings, ignoring material from their popular club repertoire and, for a while, succeeded in diluting their style.

He modelled his own image – and some of his early productions – on Phil Spector and in 1966 formed his own record company, Immediate, whose artists included Chris Farlowe, the Small Faces, P. P. Arnold and the Nice. He split with the Stones in 1967 and retired altogether when Immediate folded in 1970, but returned to the business as a producer in 1973.

Spooner Oldham came to prominence during the Sixties, initially as keyboards player at Rick Hall's Fame Studios, becoming part of the Muscle Shoals Sound, and later as a prolific songwriter with partner Dan Penn, the duo being responsible for such hits as 'Out Of Left Field' (Percy Sledge), 'She Ain't Gonna Do Right' (Clarence Carter), plus material for James Carr, James and Bobby Purify and many others. Oldham – full name Dewey Lyndon – was not, however, contracted to Rick Hall, and success spurred him to farm out his talents (with Penn) to other studios before setting up as an independent production team at the Lynn-Lou Studio.

Roy Orbison had a string of nine American Top Ten hits and even more in Britain between 1960 and 1966. In a period when most successful pop music was decidedly lightweight, his records were sensitive, sombre and overpoweringly emotional. Born in Vernon, Texas on April 23, 1936, Roy Kelton Orbison began as a rockabilly singer with the Wink Westerners and then the Teen Kings, who included Johnny 'Peanuts' Wilson on rhythm guitar. His first records were cut at Norman Petty's studio in Clovis, New Mexico, and released on Jewel. In 1956, Orbison recorded for Sun and 'Ooby Dooby' reached No. 59 in the national charts.

Further Sun Singles – hard rockers, unsuited to Orbison's voice – were unsuccessful. In 1958, Orbison's song 'Claudette' was recorded by the Everly Brothers and he moved to Nashville to concentrate on songwriting. One single for RCA followed, then Orbison signed with Fred Foster's Monument label. His second release on the label was 'Only The Lonely' which went to No. 2 in America and topped the British charts. It set the pattern for the string of big, mournful, almost operatic ballads which followed – 'Blue Angel', 'Runnin' Scared', 'Dream Baby', 'Crying' and 'Blue Bayou' were among them. 'In Dreams' (Top Ten in 1963 on both sides of the Atlantic) was the Orbison song *par excellence*, with its spoken introduction, ringing tear-jerking theme, soaring falsettos and storming crescendo. His romanticism was a legacy of his Southern upbringing. Many of his best songs reflect the emotional honesty of the best country music and tell of situations well loved by the Dixie audience: Orbison was the loner, the rejected lover, the born loser. He took his initial cue, no doubt, from country singer Don Gibson but there was something magical about the qualities of his songs which transcended even the best Gibson numbers. His voice, too, developed into something great – it contained within it something of Don Gibson's blue, lamenting quality, but it also exhibited much of the raw emotionalism of black music: it was the combination of these two qualities which created the mystique of the Big O's voice. It was tender, but the tenderness never seemed to slip into sentimentality – it was a tenderness permeated by toughness. The mystique of the Orbison voice was emphasized even more strongly at personal appearances, where his stunning lack of movement seemed oddly contradictory in the age of the Shadows and Freddy Cannon. Not only did he stand completely motionless, but he also managed to sing his hard-hitting material (exact re-creations of the records) without appearing to move his lips any more than the average ventriloquist.

In the middle Sixties, Orbison's popularity and the quality of his material declined, although 'Too Soon To Know' (on MGM, where he moved in 1965) reached the British Top Ten. He was also dogged by domestic tragedy when his wife, Claudette, died in a motorcycle accident in 1966 and his house was destroyed by fire in 1968. His was the most distinctive voice in the pop music of the early Sixties.

Buck Owens was born on Aug. 12, 1939, in Sherman, Texas as Alvin Owens. He moved to Bakersfield, California, in the early Fifties to play guitar in the bands of Bill Woods and then Tommy Collins. He also worked as an occasional sessionman for Capitol's Ken Nelson – he appears on some Gene Vincent recordings – before forming his own band, the Buckaroos, and signing with Capitol (after an abortive stay with the local Pep label) in 1957. Owens and his tight, spare 'Bakersfield Sound' have produced over 20 country chart-toppers since 1963 and, in the relatively small country market, have sold almost ten million records. His success meant the end of Nashville's dominance of the country charts and helped pave the way for Bakerfield's other country superstar, Merle Haggard, whose records are also firmly in the honky tonk tradition. Although he is still active as a performer, the Seventies have seen Owens, like Roy Acuff before him, increasingly turn his attention to business, building up his OMAC Artists Corporation into a base for a possible future in Republican politics as well as in music.

Jimmy Page, born in London, on April 9, 1944, rapidly became one of London's busiest session guitarists in the early Sixties. He turned down his first chance to join the Yardbirds when Eric Clapton left in March, 1965, preferring to experiment with production – he produced John Mayall's 'I'm Your Witchdoctor' (Immediate) later that year – continue his session work and make the occasional single, e.g. 'She Just Satisfies' (Fontana). However, he eventually joined the Yardbirds as bass guitarist in place of Paul Samwell-Smith in June, 1966, but soon swapped roles with Chris Dreja to share lead with Jeff Beck. He took over lead guitar work entirely when Beck quit at the end of the year. When the Yardbirds split up in the summer of 1968, Page formed the New Yardbirds, later Led Zeppelin.

Felix Pappalardi, born in the Bronx in 1940, had an active musical education at Michigan University. Thrown out, he gravitated to Greenwich Village, playing guitarron, singing and backing others like Tom Rush and Fred Neil. He did early sessions for Vanguard and Elektra, backing or arranging for an impressive roster – Mimi and Dick Fariña, Tim Hardin, Richie Havens, Buffy St Marie and Joan Baez, and producing New York's first folk rock, the Mugwumps. Later he worked with the Lovin' Spoonful and the Youngbloods, producing their first two albums, before making his name with Cream as producer/arranger/writer on all their studio albums after *Fresh Cream*, and Jack Bruce's *Songs For A Tailor*. In 1969, he produced and played bass on Leslie West's album (with whom he'd worked earlier in the Vagrants) which led to the formation of Mountain. Initially Cream-influenced, they made some of the most original heavy music on record on *Nantucket Sleighride*. They split up in 1972 but re-formed in 1974.

Junior Parker, born Herman 'Little Junior' Parker on Mar. 3, 1927 in West Memphis, Arkansas, was a well-respected and influential bluesman of the Fifties and Sixties. Originally a member of the legendary Beale Streeters – along with Bobby Bland, B. B. King, Johnny Ace and Rosco Gordon – he first recorded in 1952 for the Modern label, switching to Sun in 1953 where he scored a massive R&B hit with 'Feelin' Good'. His second Sun release, 'Mystery Train', was covered by Presley in 1955. Parker then signed with Duke, where he achieved his greatest success. His straightforward Sonny Boy Williamson-influenced harmonica-playing did not appear on record until 1956, but thereafter he played harp on many sessions. His best sides included 'Next Time You See Me', 'Mother-in-Law Blues' and 'Barefoot Rock', all featuring superb accompaniment by the Bill Harvey/Joe Scott band. (These tracks can be heard on *Blues Consolidated*, Duke.) Apart from 'Drivin' Wheel', 'Country Girl' and a few other titles, Parker's later records were pretty dismal, his velvet-tinged vocals fighting a losing battle with gimmicky arrangements and a huge, brass-dominated band. During the late Sixties, he recorded a number of contemporary-sounding soul and blues sides for Mercury, Capitol, Blue Rock, Minit and UA. Parker died in a Chicago hospital on Nov. 18, 1971, following surgery to correct an eye problem, which through complications turned into a brain operation.

Robert Parker, born in New Orleans on Oct. 14, 1930,
263

played alto saxophone on numerous R&B recording sessions, beginning with Professor Longhair's Atlantic sides in 1949. Between other sessions for Irma Thomas ('Don't You Mess With My Man'), Joe Tex ('You Little Baby-Faced Thing'), Eddie Bo and Ernie K-Doe ('Mother-In-Law'), he cut unsuccessful solo discs for Ron, Imperial and Booker. In 1966, Parker signed with Nola and reached No. 4 on the national charts with his own composition 'Barefootin'', a pounding dance number with spectacular accompaniment from New Orleans' finest sessionmen. 'Tip Toe' was a smaller hit on Nola. Parker also recorded for Silver Fox.

Gary Paxton was part of a circle of young producer/songwriter/singers who formed the second generation of Los Angeles studio manipulators. Others included Kim Fowley, Skip Battyn, Bruce Johnston, Lou Adler, and Terry Melcher. Paxton's first success was with the Hollywood Argyles, singing the lead on 'Alley Oop', a No. 1 record in 1960, and with Battinas and Skip and Flip. He and Fowley subsequently sent over a dozen 'Hollywood Argyle' groups out on the road, and recorded, produced and released hundreds of records by groups of kids they found on the street, on a wide array of one-shot labels. Paxton's Lute and Paxley labels were among the longer-lived of these, featuring many novelty releases along the lines of 'Alley Oop', notably Bobby 'Boris' Pickett's 'Monster Mash'. Around 1965, Paxton became involved with the growing country scene in Bakersfield, California, and went on to write and produce many country hits there and in Nashville, though never entirely leaving novelty records behind – 'The Clone Affair' (Private Stock, 1975) had enough of the old spirit to satisfy any Hollywood Argyles fan.

Tom Paxton was the only topical folk singer of the early Sixties who retained his influence until the end of the decade with minimal changes in style, as proved by his triumphant appearance at the 1971 Isle of Wight Festival. Born in Chicago, Illinois, on Oct. 31, 1937, he studied at the University of Oklahoma before travelling to New York, the centre of

264

the folk revival. Many of the songs Paxton wrote in those early years have become folk club standards. They include the love songs ('The Last Thing On My Mind', 'Leaving London'), highway songs ('Rambling Boy', 'Bound For The Mountains And The Sea') and, above all, the topical/protest lyrics. These range from the early 'Daily News' and 'Lyndon Johnson Told The Nation' through 'Talking Vietnam Pot Luck Blues' (1968) to 'The Hostage' (1973) and 'Forest Lawn'. In 1971, Paxton signed with Reprise after cutting seven albums with Elektra. In 1975, he moved to the British company MAM.

Peaches and Herb. Marlene 'Peaches' Mack (born in Virginia in 1945) left session group the Joytones in 1966 to join Herb Fame, an unsuccessful solo artist, and the duo signed with Columbia's newly formed Date label. Recording in the style of an updated Brook Benton/Dinah Washington, blending Herb's easy tenor with Peaches' wistful voice, their debut, 'Let's Fall In Love', produced by Van McCoy, was a Top Thirty hit. Their follow-up, 'Close Your Eyes', made the Top Ten, and seven subsequent discs were Hot Hundred hits over two years. When Date was discontinued, the duo reappeared briefly on Columbia in 1971, Francine Barker having taken over as 'Peaches', before moving to Mercury and then to BS Records.

Pearls Before Swine -- Tom Rapp, guitar vocals; Wayne Harley, autoharp, banjo, mandolin, oscillator; Lane Lederer, bass, guitar, various horns; Roger Crissinger, organ, harpsichord -- after two ESP albums became Tom Rapp plus whoever he gathered around him in the studio. Rapp's individual songs were always the heart of the group, shrouded in innovative, mysterious arrangements and presenting a philosophical aura (especially *Balaclava*, 1968) that suggest his influence on his New York peers the Velvet Underground, especially Lou Reed. After *Balaclava*, he abandoned the dominant abstract themes (shared by the earlier *One Nation Underground*) for a series of more conventional-sounding albums, erratic, but containing brilliant humanistic

265

('The Jeweller'), allegorical ('Rocket Man') and romantic ('Island Lady') songs. After six albums under the aegis of Pearls Before Swine, he now records under his own name. The first, *Familiar Songs* (Reprise, 1972), was a re-recorded collection of some of his best earlier songs.

Dan Penn first came to the fore as the 14-year-old writer of 'Is A Bluebird Blue?', a substantial hit for Conway Twitty in 1960. In the late Fifties, he formed a group, Dan Penn and the Pallbearers – adopting their name after buying a hearse as a bandwagon – with David Briggs (piano), Norbert Putnam (bass), Jerry Carrigan (drums). They made several unsuccessful records, playing local Alabama clubs and bars, before Rick Hall hired them as a session band for his new Fame studio, where Penn began a lengthy and fruitful partnership with another Fame sessioneer, Lyndon 'Spooner' Oldham. As a songwriting partnership, Penn and Oldham produced several hundred songs, some used by artists from Hall's own Fame label, some artists from other labels doing individual sessions at the studio, and some passed on to artists in other local studios since Penn and Oldham were not contracted to Fame as writers. Penn also wrote with other renowned sessioneers, most notably with Chips Moman, which team was responsible for 'Do Right Woman – Do Right Man', a million-seller for Aretha Franklin and the magnificent doomy, country-soul ballad 'Dark End Of The Street', recorded by James Carr, Roy Hamilton and numerous others. As a producer Penn worked with the Box Tops amongst others. He continued his partnership with Spooner Oldham, however, and they went on to form their own independent production company, working from Lynn-Lou Studios. He has recorded in his own right for MGM, Earth, Fame, Atlantic and Happy Tiger.

Peter and Gordon – Peter Asher and Gordon Waller (vocals/guitar) – always had a lot going for them. Peter (born June 22, 1944) looked like every mother's hoped-for son, quiet and well-educated. Gordon (June 4, 1945) had the sex appeal. Peter also had an actress sister, Jane, who was Paul McCartney's girlfriend. McCartney and Lennon contributed unrecorded songs to give them their early hits ('World Without Love', 'Nobody I Know' on EMI's Columbia label) and Paul also wrote 'Woman' for them under a pseudonym, but the secret leaked out. Their other hits were timely revivals and vaudevillian songs such as 'Lady Godiva'. Like Chad and Jeremy, their real success was in America, on Capitol, where their commerciality and 'Englishness' had great appeal, and where they toured frequently. They split up in 1968; Gordon went solo, unsuccessfully, and Peter Asher became a staff producer for Apple before going on to even greater success as the manager and producer of James Taylor as well as managing Linda Ronstadt.

Peter, Paul and Mary were the most successful American pop-folk group of the Sixties, bringing countless pop fans into contact with both the folk and protest movements. Peter Yarrow (born May 31, 1938 in New York), Paul Stookey (Nov. 30, 1937, Baltimore, Maryland) and Mary Allin Travers (Nov. 7, 1937, Louisville, Kentucky) were brought together in 1961 by manager, Albert Grossman, to provide a contemporary equivalent to the Kingston Trio and the Weavers. In addition to their topical and protest songs – they were the first to introduce Bob Dylan compositions to mass audiences – their repertoire included comic and children's songs, notably 'Puff The Magic Dragon', which was claimed to have drug connotations by conservative critics of the folk revival. Under musical director Milt Okun, the trio had nearly 20 chart entries on Warner Bros. between 1962 and 1969, when John Denver's 'Leaving On A Jet Plane' provided them with their first No. 1. Peter, Paul and Mary were the most popular attraction on campuses, but also sang at civil-rights, peace and liberal-Left meetings throughout the Sixties. Their light, ebullient harmonies and two-guitar backing were technically polished, appealing to audiences worldwide. They disbanded in 1971 to pursue solo careers.

Wilson Pickett, one of the first of the new breed to carry aggressive black emotion to a mass audience, eventually hammered spontaneous excitement into a stylized cliché, lost his sense of purpose, and is currently struggling to revive a lukewarm career. Born in Pratville, Alabama on March 18, 1941, but raised in Detroit, he was first noticed on record as the shrieking lead vocalist on the Falcons' apoplectic R&B smash 'I Found A Love' (Lupine) in July, 1962. Leaving the group (and after one dismal release on Correctone) he wrote and recorded two impressive wailers for Lloyd Price's Double L label – 'If You Need Me' and 'It's Too Late' (1963) – before joining Atlantic the following year. After two unsuccessful releases, Atlantic took him to the Stax studios in Memphis for sessions with Steve Cropper, Booker T and co., resulting in the hits – 'In The Midnight Hour' and 'Don't Fight It' (1965), and to Muscle Shoals for '634-5789', 'Ninety-Nine-And-A-Half (Won't Do)' (1966). These launched Pickett as a major soul star.

For the next three years, at Fame studios, Muscle Shoals, he recorded constant variations on the dance themes, scoring his biggest hits with coarse, pounding tunes – 'Land Of 1,000 Dances', 'Mustang Sally' (1966), 'Soul Dance No. 3', 'Funky Broadway' (1967), 'She's Looking Good', 'I'm A Midnight Mover' (1968) – although his best performances were slow, searing ballads – 'I'm In Love' and 'People Make The World' (1967) written and accompanied by Bobby Womack; the Beatles' 'Hey Jude' (1968); and 'Back In Your Arms' and 'Hey Joe' (1969). By the end of the Sixties that particular brand of sock-it-to-'em soul was pushed aside by far more complex productions, and after one session in Miami and a hit with tribute record 'Cole, Cooke, And Redding', he was teamed with the new black money-spinners, Gamble and Huff, at Sigma Sound in Philadelphia, who gave him 'Engine No. 9' (1970) and 'Don't Let The Green Grass Fool You' (1971) – reputedly his first million-seller. Back in Miami, he recorded a last big hit for Atlantic, 'Don't Knock My Love', before signing with RCA in 1972. Predictably, their attempts to transform 'The Wicked Pickett' into a black Tom Jones largely misfired, but he did succeed with 'Soft

Soul Boogie Woogie' in 1974 and seems to be slowly getting to grips with the demands of a new era.

The Pink Floyd first found fame as London's premier psychedelic band. But unlike most celebrities from the summer of 1967, they have not only survived but have continued to evolve as performers and composers. Founded in 1966, the initial line-up was Syd Barrett, vocals and guitar (born in Cambridge, Jan. 6, 1946); Roger Waters, bass (Great Bookham, Surrey, Sept. 6, 1944); Richard Wright, keyboards (London, July 28, 1945); and Nick Mason, drums (Birmingham, Jan. 27, 1945). Originally a rhythm'n'blues group, they moved towards 'psychedelic music', largely under the influence of Barrett. The Floyd acquired a hippy management (Blackhill Enterprises), a recording contract with EMI's Columbia label, and a hit single – the bizarre 'Arnold Layne' – in April 1967, just as flower power was being discovered by the national media.

The group played frequently at UFO, London's leading hippy club, and consolidated their underground pre-eminence with an excellent first album, *The Piper At The Gates Of Dawn* (1967). The album was dominated by Barrett's songs, their childlike imagery and unexpected structural twists skilfully combining the sinister and the naive. Also impressive were Wright's keyboard work, and the band's instrumental evocations of space travel. 'Astronomy Dominé' and 'Interstellar Overdrive' established their image as a psychedelic space-rock band. However, during the next year, Barrett's behaviour became increasingly erratic and the other members of the band decided to part company with him. Dave Gilmour, born in Cambridge on March 6, 1944, was brought in to replace him as lead guitarist.

Without Barrett, the Floyd felt unable to develop as a singles band, and concentrated on their instrumental abilities. The title track of their second album, *A Saucerful Of Secrets* (1968), was an extended instrumental which evolved skilfully through several shifts of mood to a beautiful, choral climax. 'Set The Controls For The Heart Of The Sun' continued their space identity, again through musical, rather than verbal, skills. Barrett appeared once, on one of his own compositions, 'Jugband Blues', singing his own epitaph: 'And I'm most obliged to you for making it clear/That I'm not really here'. The Floyd began using more sophisticated lighting effects in their live shows and introducing their innovatory 'Azimuth Co-ordinator', a PA system which moved the sound around the auditorium, emphasizing the spatial quality of their music. As testimony to their prowess as a live band, they released a double album, *Ummagumma* (Harvest, 1969). One record contained live recordings, showing that the band's energy and willingness to take chances enabled them to carry off their complex music live; the other contained a studio contribution from each member of the band, and was not so successful: the band appeared to possess more awareness of studio techniques than musical ideas on this record. After *Ummagumma*, the Floyd's career went through a quiet phase. They continued to develop the theatrical elements of their spectacular live shows, but their recordings were relatively unadventurous. They created soundtracks for a few films: *More* (1969), *The Body* (1970), *Obscured By Clouds* (1972), but only Antonioni's *Zabriskie Point* (MGM, 1970) began to match the power of their music, particularly in the closing sequence where 'Careful With That Axe, Eugene' was played over an apocalyptic sequence of explosions.

Their next major album, *Atom Heart Mother* (1970), seemed to find the Floyd short of inspiration, utilizing choirs, orchestras, and diverse sounds (doubtless the influence of Ron Geesin who helped to record the album) to curiously little effect. Mere musical spectacle proved inadequate, and the Floyd responded well to this problem by tightening their sound and focusing their effects to create *Meddle* (1971), which was chiefly remarkable for 'Echoes', an extended piece occupying one side of the album. It wove together hard-rock improvisation, powerfully melodic themes, and passages of abstract sound to create a richly integrated kaleidoscope of music. At the same time as developing a form of subtle, but emotionally charged, electronically flavoured mood music, the Floyd also began to create powerful songs.

Probably the most successful piece on *Atom Heart Mother* was 'If' by Roger Waters, a movingly understated account of fear of an approaching mental crack-up, and this theme subsequently expanded to form the basis of a cycle of songs, *The Dark Side Of The Moon* (1973), about the mental and emotional devastation wrought by the social pressures of fear of failure, growing old, poverty, loneliness, and, lurking behind them all, madness. The album was an extraordinary and quite unpredictable triumph for the Pink Floyd. The instrumental passages with which they fleshed out their songs were recognizable developments from their earlier musical experiments; but the theme of the lyrics (all written by Waters) and the overall mood of bleak pessimism were an explicit rejection of escapism, romanticism, rural retreats, and space travel – the major themes previously utilized by the Floyd – in favour of an acknowledgement of immediate, everyday pressures. *The Dark Side Of The Moon* was a massive commercial, as well as artistic, triumph. It was conspicuously successful in the British and American charts, and had sold four million copies within two years of release. Despite lukewarm critical reaction, *Wish You Were Here* (1975) looked like repeating that success.

Gene Pitney, one of the most popular American singers of the Sixties – born on Feb. 17, 1941, in Hartford, Connecticut – had no less than 23 chart-making singles, and at least that many albums. Although he occasionally wrote (his first hit, 'Love My Life Away', on Musicor, 1961) Pitney was best known as a pop singer who worked with other people's songs and arrangements. He had a strong, distinctive tenor that was at its best in big productions, which all of his hit records were. These included 'Town Without Pity' (1961), 'Liberty Valance', 'Only Love Can Break A Heart', 'Half Heaven – Half Heartache' (1962), 'Mecca' (1963), 'I'm Gonna Be Strong', 'It Hurts To Be In Love' (1964), 'She's A Heartbreaker' (1968) and '24 Hours From Tulsa', his best remembered British hit in 1963. From 1961 through 1966, Pitney averaged three hits per year. His hits continued through 1969, but dropped off after that. He's done little recording in recent years, remaining for ever on the verge of a chart comeback.

Brian Poole formed the Tremeloes in 1959 in Dagenham, Essex. A competent group, they turned professional after the first of many regular appearances on the leading British radio show, *Saturday Club*. Their speciality was other people's hits – they even recorded an album, *Big Hits Of '62*, for Ace of Clubs. However, their fortunes turned with the beat boom when, despite an anachronistic appearance and approach, they covered the popular Beatles' album track, 'Twist And Shout', in summer 1963. It was the first of six Top Twenty hits, including 'Do You Love Me', a No. 1. Poole's chart reign lasted only as long as the unqualified group fever, barely into 1965. In 1966, he left the Tremeloes (who continued successfully without him) for an abortive solo career and today follows his original chosen occupation, the family butcher's shop.

Sandy Posey (real name Martha Sharp) was born in 1945 in Jasper, Alabama, and in her late teens moved to West Memphis, Arkansas. She did session-work as a back-up singer in Memphis and Nashville, and sang on innumerable records including Percy Sledge's classic 'When A Man Loves A Woman'. She was also a songwriter, and in 1966 began to work with producer Chips Moman. Her first single, 'Born A Woman' (MGM), reached No. 12 in America; the follow-up, 'Single Girl', was equally successful and also reached No. 15 in Britain. Her most successful single came in the following year, 1967 ('I Take It Back'), preceded and followed by 'What A Woman In Love Won't Do' and 'Are You Never Coming Home' respectively. Sandy Posey has a distinctive country voice, although success in the pop charts has eluded her in recent years.

The Pretty Things, formed by the Rolling Stones' original bass guitarist, Dick Taylor, and Phil May (born on Sept. 11, 1944) at Sidcup Art College in the autumn of 1963, were doomed by their scruffy image and Bo Diddley-based rhythm and blues to the role of poor man's Stones. With Taylor switching to lead guitar, the rest of the line-up was May (vocals, harmonica), Brian Pendleton (rhythm guitar), John Stax (bass, harmonica), Viv Prince (drums). They were signed up almost at once as the R&B boom hit the music industry, but after early hits, the double-sided 'Big Boss Man'/ 'Rosalyn' (May, 1964), 'Don't Bring Me Down' (November, 1964) and 'Honey I Need' (March, 1965) on Fontana, they failed to make the Stones' shift to their own material until, in a reorganized line-up, May and Taylor composed the biographical *S. F. Sorrow* (Harvest, 1968), supposedly an encouragement – if not an influence – for Pete Townshend's *Tommy* project. Following the departure of Taylor and the failure of the highly regarded *Parachute* album in 1969, the band folded for a time, re-forming to record *Freeway Madness* (Warner Bros., 1972). In 1974, with May, Peter Tolson (guitar), John Povey (keyboards), and Skip Alan (drums) still together from the *Parachute* personnel, plus Jack Green (vocals) and Gordon Edwards (bass), they signed with Led Zeppelin's Swan Song label for *Silk Torpedo*.

Prince Buster, born in Kingston, Jamaica on May 28, 1939, achieved local fame as a boxer and deejay before escalating into national prominence with 'Wash Wash' and 'I Feel The Spirit' in 1962. A front-runner of the bluebeat craze, he pioneered ska on '30 Pieces Of Silver', 'The Lion Roars' and 'Sammy Dead' (adopted by Chelsea FC as their anthem in 1964). Always as popular with white British youth as with the Jamaican audience, he was first a hero of the mods in 1964 and later achieved similar status amongst their skinhead counterparts, during the brief rock-steady period, with rude boy litanies 'Judge Dread' and 'Ghost Dance'; unabashed sexism on 'Ten Commandments Of Man' and 'Big Five'; and straightforward cowboy/gangster deifications with 'Al Capone' (a British chart entry in April 1967) and 'Lawless Street'.

A prolific songwriter and recording artist – issuing over 200 singles – Buster invariably employed the best session musicians as his 'Blues Busters'/'All Stars', including the Georgie Fame Band on occasions. A long understanding

273

with Melodisc ensured that the majority of his sides were made available in Britain on Bluebeat, Fab and Prince Buster. By the Seventies he was no longer recording himself, but producing the likes of Dennis Alcapone, re-releasing his old hits, professing a distinct dislike of current reggae and appearing in a cameo role in *The Harder They Come*.

P. J. Proby, born James Marcus Smith in Houston, Texas, on Nov. 6, 1938, spent his early twenties in Hollywood, doing odd jobs, playing bit parts, cutting demos, and recording as Jet Powers. He was brought to England in 1964 by Jack Good – for a Beatles television special – who produced his first single as P. J. Proby, a raucous revival of a 1939 ballad, 'Hold Me'. Good sold the record to Decca and it became a big hit that summer. After a similar follow-up, he changed labels (to Liberty) and styles, with melodramatic versions of 'Maria' and 'Somewhere' from *West Side Story*. Established as a star, he toured Britain with Cilla Black in February, 1965, but provoked a furore, and eventually his expulsion from the tour, by frequently splitting his velvet breeches on stage. His lifestyle was tailored less tightly than his clothes and by 1968, long after the hits had ceased, he was bankrupt. He returned to America, but was tempted back to London at the end of 1971 to play Iago in Jack Good's long-projected rock *Othello, Catch My Soul*, and later revived his old stage act for Northern nightclub matrons.

Procul Harum's story begins in 1962 with a Southend R&B group, the Paramounts: Gary Brooker (born May 29, 1945) keyboards, vocals; Robin Trower (March 9, 1945) guitar; B. J. Wilson (March 18, 1947) drums; and Chris Copping (Aug. 29, 1945) bass. The Paramounts made a string of singles, 'Little Bitty Pretty One' becoming a minor hit, before frustration led to their break-up in 1966. Gary Brooker teamed up with lyricist Keith Reid (Oct. 10, 1946) and to record their songs they formed a group. Procul Harum in their original line-up – Gary Brooker, piano, vocals; Matthew Fisher (March 7, 1946) organ; Dave Knights (June 28, 1945) bass; Ray Royer (Oct. 8, 1945) guitar and Bobby Harrison (June

28, 1943) drums – made only one single: 'A Whiter Shade Of Pale' (Deram). The drum part was played by session musician Bill Eyden. Released in summer 1967 to spectacular British and American success, its mysterious words and haunting organ, based on a Bach cantata, seemed to epitomize the spirit of the day.

They began an album, but Royer and Harrison had to be replaced (they formed the short-lived Freedom) and Trower and Wilson were added. In this form they completed *Procul Harum* (Regal Zonophone, 1967) and made two stunning and highly praised albums, *Shine On Brightly* and *A Salty Dog*. Despite a second hit single, 'Homburg' in 1967, gigs had always been scarce in a Britain in the throes of a blues boom which, ironically, would have better suited the old Paramounts. America, where audiences were more appreciative, provided their salvation. Long periods between tours allowed them time to produce albums of continually high standard. *Broken Barricades* (Chrysalis, 1971), for which Chris Copping replaced Knights on bass, also marked Robin Trower's rising musical aspirations since it was the first album without organist Matthew Fisher. Trower himself left in July, 1971, finding Procul's panoramic sound too stifling for his Hendrix-inspired guitar trips. After forming the abortive Jude (with Frankie Miller) he has subsequently formed the very successful Robin Trower Band. Copping, meanwhile, switched to organ and Alan Cartwright (Oct. 10, 1945) came in on bass. They recorded *Live In Concert With The Edmonton Symphony Orchestra*, which with a hit (reissued) single 'Conquistador', opened things up in Britain once more. Finally they also achieved a settled line-up once Mick Grabbham took over on guitar from Trower's replacement Dave Ball (March 30, 1950) and in this form they have consolidated their packed house tours of Britain and America with neatly balanced albums like *Grand Hotel* (1973). They still concentrate on America although Britain is no longer a void. The continual influx of new musicians kept Procul fresh and inventive while the solid framework of Brooker's piano and Keith Reid's lyrics has ensured a necessary stability.

275

Gary Puckett and the Union Gap – Gary Puckett, vocals (born 1942); Dwight Bement, tenor sax (1944); Kerry Chater, bass (1944); Paul Wheatbread, drums (1945); Gary Withem, piano (1944) – were originally the Outcasts, a popular San Diego group noted for their ability to duplicate other people's songs. As Gary Puckett and the Union Gap since 1967, they proceeded to write a string of hits, each one remarkably like the one before. 'Woman Woman' broke the ice, but 'Young Girl' made No. 1 both sides of the Atlantic in 1968 (making a return visit in 1974). They made six albums (plus a hits volume) all produced by Jerry Fuller and built on their familiar formula with Puckett's voice as the core of their sound. They disbanded in 1971, Puckett working with brother David on an album and studying acting.

Punk Rock was a style that flourished during the years 1964–7, reflecting America's grassroots response to the British Invasion, setting the stage for American rock as it evolved in the late Sixties, and also accounting, in its time, for perhaps the most prolific outpouring of records and groups in the history of rock. Punk rock was the music of thousands of bands, mostly of high-school age, who formed in the aftermath of the Beatles and the British rock invasion. Sociologically, they were an outgrowth of the local bands who played surf and twist music in the early Sixties. Musically, most were derived to greater or lesser degree from either the Stones or the Beatles, with occasional exceptions who took their style from the Pretty Things or the Small Faces.

But where these groups had a modicum of style, innovation, and either an innate sense of cool or a genuine innocence, the punkers took a stance of spoiled suburban snottiness. Most classic punk records shared a number of common attributes, from fuzztone on their guitars to an arrogant snarl in the vocals, and lyrics usually concerned with uncooperative girls or bothersome parents and social restrictions. In every city of America there were a few punk bands, and the larger cities often boasted hundreds. And, it seems, nearly all of them issued records locally, leading to the development of active local scenes and recognizable regional sounds. Despite its pervasiveness, however, punk rock never caught on commercially. Most of the records were either too crude or too intense for mass radio standards, and on the whole there were less than 20 punk groups who had hit records, and few of those ever had more than one. Some exceptions were Paul Revere and the Raiders, the Standells, the Seeds, the Outsiders, and the Knickerbockers. The music's main exposure was through live performances at teen clubs, teen fairs, high-school dances and local TV dance shows.

The product of kids who had little exposure to the music business mainstream, the punk idiom (much like its antecedent in the Fifties, the short-lived rockabilly style that was unimportant commercially but proved crucial in defining the basic spirit of the decade in its purest form) gave birth to a great deal of experimentation, resulting in some of the most bizarre, extreme, and ingenuously eloquent recordings of all time – and also some of the most powerful. Punk rock had its musical equivalents in other countries such as England and Holland, but the spirit that motivated it was peculiarly a product of the American youth of the time. With the increased popularity of psychedelic drugs in 1966, it was a logical development from there to acid rock, although something indefinable was lost in the transition. Among the most noteworthy punk groups were the Kingsmen ('Louie, Louie'), the Seeds, the Standells, the Thirteenth Floor Elevators, the Music Machine ('Talk Talk'), the Shadows of Knight, the Knickerbockers, the Barbarians, Count Five, Question Mark and the Mysterians, the Trashmen ('Surfin' Bird'), the Chartbusters ('She's The One'), Mouse and the Traps, the Gants, Blues Magoos, the McCoys, and the Clefs of Lavender Hill. Most punk groups released only ephemeral local singles, but the cream of the crop can be heard on the superbly compiled anthology, *Nuggets* (Elektra, 1973).

Bernard 'Pretty' Purdie learned to play drums as a child. Born in Elkton, Maryland, on June 11, 1939, Purdie gained his first practical experience deputizing in a local club when the resident drummer became drunk and incapable. He played in a variety of bands in a variety of styles and, after graduating, went to New York in 1961 for a one-week gig and session with Mickey and Sylvia – and stayed. In the early days he mixed gigs with Lonnie Youngblood and Les Cooper with a laundry job, but he gradually became established as a first-rate session drummer: by 1966 he was doing up to 20 sessions a week in various styles (i.e. James Brown, Tom Jones and Nina Simone), but later could afford to be more selective. 1967 saw his debut as a 'name act' on Date, and 'Funky Donkey', a plodding, heavily percussive opus, reached the Hot Hundred. Purdie continued as a prolific sessioneer with various solo ventures, but is now resident with Aretha Franklin's backing combo as musical director.

James and Bobby Purify are cousins – James Purify, born in Pensacola, Florida, on May 12, 1944 and Robert Lee Dickey, born in Tallahassee, Florida, on Sept. 2, 1939 – who teamed up professionally in 1965. Bobby played guitar with the Dothan Sextet, accompanying Mighty Sam, and when Sam quit, Bobby brought in his cousin, James, as feature vocalist. Their duets became a highlight of the group's act; Don Schroeder heard them, signed them to Bell Records, and took them to Muscle Shoals studios in 1966 where they cut 'I'm Your Puppet', a gospelly beat ballad and an immediate Top Ten smash. Subsequent discs also sold well, though by 1969 their appeal had cooled. Following a period of in-activity, the duo returned in 1974 on Casablanca Records.

Question Mark and the Mysterians made one of the most timelessly moronic records of all time, and one of the biggest hits of 1966, with '96 Tears' (Cameo). Question Mark and the Mysterians were a Mexican/American group from Texas who moved to Flint, Michigan, where they issued the record on their own label before it was picked up by Neil Bogart for release on Cameo. It was a good song, with properly arrogant vocals, but its true appeal lay in the relentless two-note 'punk' organ part that ran through the record. Later releases, particularly 'I Need Somebody', were good, but seemed to

278

lack that magic quality, so despite his seemingly unbeatable gimmick of remaining anonymous, Question Mark – Rudy Martinez (born in 1945), the composer of '96 Tears' – soon faded from the scene, as did the Mysterians: Bobby Balderamma, lead guitar (born in 1950); Frank Lugo, bass (1947); Eddie Serrato, drums (1947) and Frank Rodriguez, organ (1951).

Quicksilver Messenger Service's first consistent line-up was as a five-piece with Gary Duncan (guitar, born Sept. 4, 1946), Greg Ellmore (drums, born Sept. 4, 1946), David Freiburg (bass, born Aug. 24, 1938), John Cippolina (guitar, born Aug. 24, 1943) and Jim Murray (harmonica) and it was with this format that they appeared in the film *Revolution*, but by the time that the soundtrack was recorded, Murray had left. Wary of the fate of some of their colleagues, Quicksilver were one of the last San Franciscan bands to get a recording contract. Moreover, they played enough gigs locally not to have to worry unduly about money. Finally they signed with Capitol in January, 1968. Their uneasiness in the studio was evident on the first album and so they decided to record their second, *Happy Trails* (1969), in a more familiar 'live' environment and immediately found themselves with songs, like the side-long 'Who Do You Love? Suite' and 'Mona', which remain two of the finest guitar 'statements' ever recorded. At this stage the chemistry of the band was irrevocably altered; Dino Valenti (born Oct. 7, 1943), an early member who had twice spent time in prison on drug charges, reappeared and persuaded Gary Duncan to join him in a band called the Outlaws. Nicky Hopkins (born Feb. 24, 1944) was called in and they cut *Shady Grove* (1970) which lacked the grandeur of its predecessor. Despite the return of Duncan and Valenti a year later, the band never recaptured their early spark. Hopkins left and was followed by Cippolina, who had been occupying more and more of a backseat, after *What About Me* (1971). The group continued with Valenti at the helm but had quite clearly lost its original musical identity. Eventually Freiburg quit and the various permutations of musicians that made up the name of the group – and which released two albums, *Quicksilver* and *Comin' Thru* (1972) – were less than pale imitations of the band that had once been.

Quintessence, a true British underground band were formed through ads in the *Melody Maker* and auditions held in All Saints Hall, Notting Hill Gate. Raja Ram (born Ron Rothfield in 1940 in Melbourne), flute, vocals, and Sambhu, bass, were the moving spirit, adding Jake, drums; Alan, lead guitar, vocals; Shiva, vocals and Maha Dev on rhythm guitar. Their music was a blend of jazz/rock and Eastern music, built around heavy dependence on jazzy flute and rock guitar, that attempted to achieve spirituality through the chanting of mantras until 'the audience becomes the musicians'. Their cult following was won through club performances rather than usually unsuccessful albums – *In Blissful Company* (Island), the first in 1969 which was recorded within weeks of their formation. The partly live Self (RCA) in 1972 captured them best. Shiva and Maha Dev left after the album in spring 1972 (Shiva forming a similar group in Kala) and their final album *Indweller* features a band drifting apart. In spite of a tendency towards the pretentious, the group's concerts were often awesomely and powerfully constructed, achieving a high degree of contact with the audience. They represented a sense of 'spiritual revolution' among some sectors of the underground which, once it dissolved, left Quintessence stranded in an alien world.

Jerry Ragavoy. Among the backroom white soul brothers of the Sixties, Jewish writer and producer Ragavoy rates just below Jerry Wexler and Bert Berns. From Philadelphia, his career began around 1954 with George Grant and the Castelles, for whom he wrote 'This Silver Ring' and produced several more misty doo-wop classics including 'My Girl Awaits Me' for Herb Slotkin's Grand label. In 1959 Ragavoy formed a partnership with entrepreneur Bill Fox. He produced several hits for Fox's group, the Majors, in New York and co-wrote them under the name of Norman Meade. 'A Wonderful Dream', 'Tra La La', 'A Little Bit Now' and

'She's A Troublemaker' were all teen-styled falsetto bouncers on Imperial. Next Ragavoy switched to deeper soul. He produced everything by Garnet Mimms on United Artists, Verve and Veep, starting with the climactic 'Cry Baby', which Ragavoy has said he co-wrote with Bert Berns, although the label credits one 'Sam Bell'.

In 1966, he produced many records on the Loma label, including those by the Enchanters, Roy Redmond and Lorraine Ellison's classic 'Stay With Me'. In the same year, Ragavoy wrote and produced a series of minor hits for Howard Tate on Verve, following up with Miriam Makeba's 'Pata Pata' and 'Malayisha' in 1967–8. At this time he was also involved with more middle-of-the-road artists like Gene Pitney ('Mecca'), Kai Winding and Ritchie Adams. Ragavoy also wrote and co-wrote (often with Berns with whom he shared the Webb IV/Ragmar company) for Erma Franklin ('A Piece Of My Heart'), Freddy Scott, Bobby Freeman, Irma Thomas ('Time Is On My Side'), Baby Washington, Jon Thomas and many others. Lou Courtney enjoyed moderate success on Ragavoy's own short-lived label, Rags, in 1973. More recently, he has produced Bonnie Raitt and Dionne Warwick, who sang back-up vocals on Garnet Mimms' 'Cry Baby'.

The (Young) Rascals didn't merely play soul – they understood its inner tensions. The Rascals – Felix Cavaliere, organ, vocals (born Nov. 29, 1944); Eddie Brigati, vocals (born Oct. 22, 1946); Gene Cornish, guitar (born May 14, 1945) (all three simultaneously leaving Joey Dee and the Starlighters) and Dino Danelli, drums (born July 23, 1945), began in February, 1965, at the Choo Choo Club in Garfield, New Jersey where, as the Young Rascals, they were known for their odd apparel – plus-fours and knickerbockers – and for their crowd-pulling brand of rock'n'roll and R&B. They dropped the 'Young' two years later, having reached their twenties.

The group's first single 'I Ain't Gonna Eat Out My Heart Anymore' fractured the outer layers of the Top Fifty but it was 'Good Lovin' ', a No. 1 in 1966, that really set them on their way. They were particularly influential on the East Coast, spawning a virtual 'New York Sound' among groups like the Pigeons (later Vanilla Fudge) and the Vagrants. Significantly, their appeal was right across the line to black and white audiences alike – they also had the distinction of being the first white rock group on Atlantic. In Europe, they were a musicians group until the dramatic (and phenomenally successful) change of style on 'Groovin'' exploded them worldwide. The classic 1967 song, depicting a long, ecstatic afternoon, established a pattern which became the basis of the group's finest album, *Groovin'*, but in the long run saw them absorbed in goodvibe jazzy rock with more than an air of pretension on albums like *Freedom Suite* (1969) and *Island Of Real* (Columbia, 1972). At the same time the group were actually doing something positive, announcing a new appearance policy of no more shows that didn't include at least one black act; as such they were cutting their own financial throats by effectively banning themselves throughout the South. They also played the Soul Together show for Martin Luther King and the UNICEF benefit in London where they upstaged John Lennon's massive Ono Band. Right up to their demise, they were a live band of the first order and only towards the end did they fail to communicate this on record. Cavaliere has since recorded two impressive solo albums on Bearsville, notably *Destiny* (1975).

RCA Records, during the Sixties, achieved greater sales than ever with Elvis Presley and continued to thrive in the rock, pop and country fields. As mainstream pop sounds softened in the early Sixties, RCA scored heavily with Neil Sedaka, and Chet Atkins added a stream of smooth Nashville country-pop product by Don Gibson ('Sea Of Heartbreak'), Skeeter Davis ('End Of The World'), Eddy Arnold ('Make The World Go Away') and Jim Reeves, around whose death RCA built a multi-million dollar legend. In the year of Reeves' death, 1964, country artist Bobby Bare had a pop hit with 'Detroit City', for by now RCA had developed a promotional organization that could maintain a country-music hit factory while also enabling a really successful country record to be crossed over into the pop market.

RCA were able to repeat this in the soul field with Sam Cooke and Nina Simone. In pop, they were supplied with a series of massive hits by Don Kirshner, whose records with the Monkees and the Archies they distributed, plus hits from Duane Eddy and Little Peggy March. The company also entered uncertainly into the progressive rock developments of the late Sixties, signing the Jefferson Airplane and the Youngbloods, although their grandiose 'Groupquake' marketing campaign, with groups like Autosalvage, was less successful. In Britain, their 'progressive' label Neon made little impact.

Red Bird Records. Jerry Leiber and Mike Stoller formed Red Bird and its subsidiary Blue Cat in 1964, in an attempt to rectify the failure of their previous attempts at running their own label, Daisy and Tiger. They jointly owned the companies with veteran New York record man, George Goldner, who took care of the promotion side. Apart from blues singer Alvin Robinson, Leiber and Stoller took little interest in the creative end of Red Bird, leaving the song-writing and production to a younger generation of pop operators: Jeff Barry and Ellie Greenwich, Gerry Goffin and Carole King, Barry Mann and Cynthia Weil, Steve Venet, George 'Shadow' Morton, Artie Ripp and Joe Jones.

Red Bird was a tremendous success, with 25 Hot Hundred hits in its two-year existence, beginning with 'Chapel Of Love' by the Dixie Cups and 'Remember (Walking In The Sand)' by the Shangri-Las. Both groups had further hits, as did two more all-girl teams, the Butterflies (in fact Ellie Greenwich double-tracking) and the Jelly Beans. In the summer of 1965, there were two dance hits, 'The Boy From New York City' by the soulful Adlibs (Mary Ann Thomas, Hughie Harris, Danny Austin and David Watt) and 'New York's A Lonely Town' by the Tradewinds, a harmony surfing record by Anders and Poncia. By 1966, Leiber and Stoller were increasingly unhappy with their involvement with music they felt no sympathy for – Greenwich and Barry

283

had brought Neil Diamond to them, but they saw no potential in him – and withdrew from the company. Goldner was not capable of holding it together and soon after, Red Bird ceased operations.

Otis Redding – born in Dawson, Georgia, on Sept. 9, 1941, the son of a Baptist minister – imbibed gospel influences in his earliest years, but grew up in the late Forties and early Fifties to the sound of R&B and jump-blues shouters. As a high-school student in Macon, Georgia, he was so impressed by the adulation showered upon local luminary Little Richard, whose style was also modelled around intense blues-shouters like Roy Brown, that he decided to become a full-time performer, having already established a reputation in local clubs as a talented musician.

The road to fame began when high-school friend Phil Walden, later to become his manager, booked the band with whom Redding was vocalist, for a college party. Through Walden he met another local band, Johnny Jenkins and the Pinetoppers, whom he joined as general assistant and sometime singer. This outfit gave Otis his recording debut when, as Otis and the Shooters, they recorded 'She's Alright', a mid-tempo Little Richard imitation featuring reedy organ, in 1959, for the local Finer Arts label. The following year they tried again, this time billed as Otis Redding, with an even more frantic Richard soundalike, 'Shout Bamalama', on Confederate, which made a little more noise and was picked up for national release by the King subsidiary, Bethlehem. Meanwhile Johnny Jenkins was signed to Atlantic, and during 1962 was booked for a session at the Stax studios in Memphis. Otis drove the band to the studio that day, and with a little time left at the end of the session Jim Stewart was persuaded to record Otis singing one of his own songs. The song was 'These Arms Of Mine', a tender blues ballad, which Stewart released on his new Volt label, and its sheer simplicity carried it into the lower reaches of the Hot Hundred in 1963. His third release, 'Pain In My Heart', another poignant ballad, was a Hot Hundred hit, and the following four years brought a succession of chart hits on Volt, all recorded in Memphis, including ballads like 'That's How Strong My Love Is', 'I've Been Loving You Too Long', 'My Lover's Prayer' and 'Try A Little Tenderness'; and brassy, raunchy, up-tempo items like 'Mr Pitiful', 'Respect', 'Satisfaction' and 'Fa Fa Fa Fa Fa'. The biggest hit of this period was 'I've Been Loving You Too Long', an intense deep-soul ballad written by Jerry Butler, which reached No. 21 in 1965, but it was generally the up-tempo items which were more successful, though none rose higher than No. 29 ('Fa Fa Fa' in early 1967).

It is significant that Redding's somewhat gruff baritone voice seems to have been more acceptable on up-tempo material, carried by raunchy horn arrangements, than on ballads where the emotional intensity of his delivery was striking, yet his voice lacked depth. This is evident in his version of the Temptations' 'My Girl', which took him into the British Top Twenty in 1966 – the poignant pitch of the original version is lost as he stretches for falsetto notes that aren't his to reach; instead he produces a sound of straining emotion but tending to verge on the histrionic.

His appearance at the Monterey Pop Festival in 1967 brought Redding massive acceptance by American rock fans, just as his European tour later that year enlarged his audience there – so much so that he was voted World No. 1 Male Singer by *Melody Maker* readers. His cult-like following was deeply shocked when on Dec. 10, 1967, his aircraft plunged to the bottom of the frozen Lake Monona, Wisconsin, killing Redding and members of his Bar-Kays band. 'Dock Of The Bay', a wistful, shuffling ballad, was a posthumous American chart-topper and million-seller a month later (his only Top Ten hit), reaching No. 3 in Britain. Later in 1968, Stax/Volt was sold to Gulf & Western, but the previous distributors, Atlantic, retained Redding's material and managed to gain chart hits with six further posthumous releases, but on songs like 'Hard To Handle', 'Day Tripper' and 'Love Man', his exaggerated delivery had become a self-parody, worlds away from the soulful simplicity of his first Volt hit.

Jerry Reed was born in Atlanta, Georgia, on March 20, 1939 and first gained attention for his guitar-playing, though in the Fifties he had recorded Rockabilly for Capitol and written songs for Gene Vincent. He was a protégé of Chet Atkins and soon became a sought-after Nashville session musician. But it was as a songwriter that Reed's impact spread beyond country music. Two of Reed's songs were hits for Elvis Presley in 1968 – 'Guitar Man' and 'US Male' – while Gene Vincent had previously recorded 'Crazy Legs' in 1956. Other much-recorded Reed songs include 'A Thing Called Love' and the boasting 'Tupelo Mississippi Flash'. That song and the tall tale of 'Amos Moses' represent the 'swamp-rock' side of Reed's somewhat erratic writing talent. His own albums for RCA have tended to include more than their fair share of dross as well as good songs.

Jimmy Reed, one of the greats in the field of R&B, was born in Mississippi on Sept. 6, 1925. He learnt guitar from bluesman Eddie Taylor, who was to contribute much to Reed's infectious boogie-blues sound of later years. By the late Forties, Reed had settled in Chicago, where he became well-known singing and playing electric guitar with a harmonica strapped to a harness. In 1953, he signed with Chicago-based Vee Jay Records, scoring his first R&B chart hit two years later with 'You Don't Have To Go'. Reed's biggest successes came during the rock'n'roll era, and included 'Ain't That Loving You Baby' and 'Honest I Do', which reached No. 32 on *Billboard*'s Hot Hundred.

Easily the most popular bluesman recording in Chicago, topping even Muddy Waters, Reed's earthy, down-home sound was immediately identifiable by his lazy, dragged-out vocals and fierce, high-register harp playing set against a heavy, almost absurdly uncomplicated back-beat. His accompanying musicians usually included Taylor on second guitar and drummer Earl Phillips. The hits kept coming, and in 1960 Reed was back in the Top Forty with 'Baby What You Want Me To Do'. A year later came 'Big Boss Man' and 'Bright Lights, Big City', while, in 1964, he even dented the British pop charts with 'Shame, Shame, Shame'. Over a twelve-year period, Reed notched up 22 chart entries, mostly for Vee Jay. His style influenced many blues artists in the Sixties, including Slim Harpo, Tommy Tucker and various British rock bands of the Sixties, especially the Rolling Stones, who featured his 'Honest I Do' on their first album. Other artists to cover Reed songs include Elvis Presley ('Big Boss Man'), Pretty Things ('Big Boss Man') and the Animals and Them ('Bright Lights, Big City').

Reparata and the Delrons, one of the many groups who produced one classic record during the 1962–5 'girl group era', had their moment of glory with 'Whenever A Teenager Cries' (World Artists, 1965). Despite a number of fine follow-ups, particularly 'I'm Nobody's Baby Now' (RCA, 1966), the group had no more hits in America, though in 1968, 'Captain Of Your Ship' (Bell) was a British Top Twenty hit. Reparata has, none the less, continued recording through the years and, interestingly, all her records – on labels including Mala, Kapp, Avco, Laurie, Big Tree and Surrey – have featured the same arranger, producer and engineer. The Delrons were Mary Aiese, Lorraine Mazzola (who joined to sing lead on 'Captain Of Your Ship') and Nanette Licars.

Reprise Records was formed by Frank Sinatra in 1960, after his contract with Capitol Records expired. Sinatra headed the company and appointed Mo Ostin, a former Verve Records accountant, as Executive Vice-President, to run it. The first Reprise single was 'Second Time Around' by Sinatra, released February, 1961; the first album was Sinatra's *Ring-A-Ding-Ding!* Into the Reprise fold, attracted by Sinatra, came many of the friends of the showbiz world: Sammy Davis was the first to join, followed by Dean Martin and Bing Crosby.

In June, 1963, negotiations between Sinatra and Warner Bros.' film division began – Sinatra was hot property in film terms, and Jack Warner wanted to sign him up for four films. Sinatra's terms were that Warners should buy Reprise. Capitol, Sinatra's former label, had reissued his albums at cut-price, affecting his Reprise product, and there was a law-

287

suit between Sinatra and Capitol, later settled out of court. It was a large headache. Reprise was $2 million in debt and Sinatra wanted out. He retained a one-third interest in Warner-Reprise; Warner Bros. bought two-thirds for $2 million and a four-picture deal. A month later, Reprise scored its first hit single – Lou Monte singing 'Pepino The Italian Mouse'. Then Trini Lopez's 'If I Had A Hammer' was a hit, and Reprise moved into the Warners Burbank office in February, 1964, and released albums by Allan Sherman and Freddy Cannon. In late 1964, Reprise, now merely a section of Warner Bros., signed a deal with Pye Records in Britain, thus acquiring Petula Clark, Sandie Shaw and the Kinks. Petula's 'Downtown' gave Reprise their first gold disc in March, 1965. Dean Martin followed with 'Everybody Loves Somebody'.

Even bigger hits followed in 1966 – Nancy Sinatra's 'These Boots Are Made For Walking' became the company's biggest ever single; Sinatra's own 'Strangers In The Night' was No. 1; Petula Clark continued unabated. Then, in 1967, Reprise signed Jimi Hendrix, whose every release was to become a gold record. That same year, the label signed Randy Newman, Arlo Guthrie and Joni Mitchell. A year later came Neil Young, Ry Cooder, Gordon Lightfoot, the Beach Boys and their Brother Records.

Paul Revere and the Raiders, originally the Downbeats from Portland, Oregon, built up a strong high-school and college following on the North-west circuit on the strength of 'Like Long Hair', their progressively titled first hit. Disc jockey Roger Hart gave them their next break, financing a tape that won them a Columbia Records contract. The result was a raunchy version of 'Louie Louie', but another local group, the Kingsmen, got in first with the hit. In 1965 'Steppin' Out' gave them their first national Top Fifty hit; then Dick Clark signed the group for the weekly rock show *Where The Action Is.* It turned them, overnight, into the most heavily exposed group in the country and their well-rehearsed, slick stage act, eighteenth-century costume of jackets and tights, and comedy routines won over a vast

288

audience. It also killed their underground appeal as they consistently put out Top Ten hits over the next two years – 'Kicks', 'Good Thing', 'Just Like Me', etc., many of which, usually recorded by Bruce Johnston or Terry Melcher in single studio visits and in only one or two takes, still hold up as instant pop classics. The original group were Mark Lindsay, lead vocals (born March 9, 1942); Paul Revere, piano, organ (born 1942); Drake Levine, guitar; Michael Smith, drums and Philip Volk, bass. Soon, however, they grew unhappy with the fantasy world of *Where The Action Is*. The resulting personnel shake-ups left Lindsay and Revere with the group's name, after the others formed the spin-off band, Brotherhood. Jim Valley, guitar (later replaced by Freddy Weller, born Sept. 9, 1947); Joe Correro Jr., drums (born Nov. 19, 1946) and Charlie Coe, bass (born Nov. 19, 1944) were brought into the group who, by 1968, were just the Raiders. Their later material had a more pop amorphous sound which gave them their only No. 1, John D. Loudermilk's 'Indian Reservation', in 1971. They were far less at home than in the punk metier of *Just Like Us* or *Greatest Hits*, which included their pastiche single, 'The Great Airplane Strike', from their best album, *Spirit Of '67*. In 1969 Lindsay launched himself on a parallel solo career with a string of hits beginning with the Top Ten 'Arizona' in 1971 on Columbia. He also produced the later records by the group.

The Righteous Brothers – Bill Medley (born Sept. 19, 1940, in Los Angeles), and Bobby Hatfield (born April 10, 1940 at Beaver Dam, Wisconsin) – were not related, but got their name from the patrons of the Black Derby, a small club in Santa Ana, California, where they played a six-month engagement in 1962 and whose patronage was about 25 per cent black. In 1963 they began recording for the small Moonglow label in Hollywood and had a small hit that year with 'Little Latin Lupe Lu' penned by Medley who had earlier recorded with a group called the Paramours.

Although they grew steadily popular in Southern California, they did not break nationally until Jack Good heard them at Hollywood's Purple Onion Club and signed them to appear on *Shindig*, one of several dance-oriented TV rock shows which dominated American pop between 1964 and 1966. Through *Shindig*, the duo quickly reached a national audience of white teenagers while retaining a significant following in the black market. At this point Phil Spector stepped in and offered to record them, providing that Moonglow would permit him to release their records on his label in certain territories, notably America and Britain. Spector produced 'You've Lost That Lovin' Feelin' ', which topped charts internationally and is considered by some to be his greatest production. There followed a samey sequel, 'Just Once In My Life' (No. 9 in America) and big-selling revivals of 'Ebb Tide' and 'Unchained Melody'. By late 1965, however, Medley and Hatfield had grown restless with Spector. In 1966, they broke their contract to record the Spectoresque '(You're My) Soul And Inspiration' for Verve which topped the American charts, but they could not sustain their impetus for more than two records. In 1968, they parted company; Medley recorded solo while Hatfield recorded solo and with new partner Jimmy Walker, but neither achieved any notable success. In 1974, Medley and Hatfield reunited and scored American Top Ten hits on Haven with the death-disc 'Rock'n'Roll Heaven' and its follow-up, 'Give It To The People'.

Jeannie C. Riley, a native of Anson, Texas, who moved to Nashville as a secretary-cum-hopeful singer, had the rare distinction for a country singer of becoming a worldwide pop star at the same time as she first made the country charts in 1968 with 'Harper Valley PTA', a story song with a 'message'. It launched Jeannie C., her writer Tom T. Hall, and also Shelby Singleton's Plantation label. The campaigning, liberated young mother in the song was an image the media propagated to such an extent that it could not be erased by other, different, hits for Plantation, Capitol and MGM. Despite fine country recordings like 'The Girl Most Likely', 'Back Side Of Dallas' and 'Houston Blues', her record sales declined in the Seventies. She had first recorded in 1966, unsuccessfully, for Little Darlin' records.

Alvin Robinson, born in New Orleans on Dec. 22, 1937, was originally a guitarist with the Joe Jones band. As a solo artist he recorded for Imperial in 1961 and Post the following year before the Chris Kenner song 'Something You Got' provided him with his first hit on Tiger in 1964. Arranged by Jones, it was a fine performance, slow and heavy, with a vocal reminiscent of Robinson's idol, Ray Charles. The B-side, a revival of the Coasters' 'Searchin' ', was stark, deep and fiercely black. Other Robinson sides – notably 'I'm Gonna Put Some Hurt On You' – captured the essence of New Orleans R&B, and though his chart success was slight, the quality and influence of his work was undeniable. The Leiber/Stoller composition 'Down Home Girl' (on Red Bird) was later recorded by the Coasters and the Rolling Stones, while on 'Let The Good Times Roll' (Bluecat), Robinson's thick, cracked and guttural voice was in fine form. He also recorded for Joe Jones (his arranger/manager's label) and Atco, before moving to the West Coast to work with Harold Battiste and Mac Rebennack and record for Pulsar.

Smokey Robinson (and the Miracles). 'America's greatest living poet' was what Bob Dylan called him some years ago, and America's most influential living poet wasn't joking. Robinson has, without question, written some of the finest words and melodies in pop's entire canon; he is also one of the most expressive of its singers, and a producer of brilliant resource.

Born in Detroit on Feb. 19, 1940, as William Robinson, he was just fifteen when – with a group of school friends – he made his first private tape recording, a version of a song called 'Adios, My Desert Love' which had been popularized by Nolan Strong and the Diabolos. The tape betrays Smokey's debt to Strong – even at that early age he'd developed a very personal falsetto voice, half-choked and pleading. Smokey and his friends quickly coalesced into a group called the Miracles, and in 1957 they were heard at an audition by a young composer called Berry Gordy Jr., who'd just written 'Reet Petite' for Jackie Wilson. Gordy saw the potential of the six 17-year-olds – Smokey, lead; Claudette Rogers, first tenor (born 1942); Bobby Rogers, second tenor (1940); Ronnie White, baritone (1939); Warren 'Pete' Moore, bass (1939) and Marvin Tarplin on guitar – and helped them acquire a record deal for one of Smokey's own songs, 'Got A Job' (an 'answer' record to the Silhouettes' smash hit 'Get A Job'). The record came out on End in 1958. The group's next record, 'Bad Girl', was released by Chess in 1959. An aching ballad, 'Bad Girl' provided an early definition of one aspect of Smokey's unique writing; the subsequent release, 'Way Over There' (Tamla, 1960), provided another. A straight dance record, it featured Smokey at his most frothy and bubbling. Where 'Bad Girl' previewed a whole series of heart-wrenching tragedies, 'Way Over There' was the forerunner of many matchless dance classics.

The group's first major hit was 'Shop Around', an up-tempo song which revealed Smokey's increasingly clever way with words which made No. 2 on the pop charts in 1960. On 'You've Really Got A Hold On Me' (Top Ten in 1962), 'I Gotta Dance (To Keep From Crying)', 'I Like It Like That', 'That's What Love Is Made Of', and 'Mickey's Monkey' (Top Ten in 1963) all part of the group's first golden age, Smokey's use of the 'Hitsville USA' session musicians quite paralleled that made by Motown's other top producers, Holland-Dozier-Holland and William Stevenson. In his writing for other Motown artists, Smokey was showing even greater talent: 'The Way You Do The Things You Do' for the Temptations, for instance, displayed a wholly idiosyncratic deployment of homespun similes, piling one atop another with an almost dizzying effect. Similarly, 'What's Easy For Two', 'The One Who Really Loves You', and 'My Guy' brought out all the romantic quality latent in Mary Wells' voice, and her version of Smokey's 'Two Lovers' is simply one of the finest R&B ballads of all time.

By 1964, Motown Records was established as one of the strongest single forces in popular music: it appeared to have less trouble than any of its competition in getting its records to 'cross over' from the R&B charts to the national pop lists. It was at this time that Smokey's period of highest achievement began. Exactly when is difficult to say, but it may have been with the Temptations' 'My Girl'. This initiated a sequence of luscious slow love songs which form a quite distinct body of work, including, amongst others, 'Since I Lost My Baby', 'Fading Away', 'It's Growing', and 'Don't Look Back' for the Temptations, and 'My Girl Has Gone', 'Swept For You Baby', 'You Must Be Love', and 'The Tracks Of My Tears' for the Miracles. This latter song, generally – and rightly – considered his greatest single piece, is a beautiful combination of thoughtfully contrived words, darkly introspective singing, and Marvin Tarplin's slowly unfolding melodies. Tarplin's contribution has been consistently underrated: besides his memorable guitar intros and mellow rhythm playing, he also wrote the music for some of their best songs. Smokey's up-tempo songs were at their best in this era, too: the Miracles scored with the Top Twenty 'Going To A'Go-Go' (1965), a discotheque anthem, while Marvin Gaye received a new impetus to his career from 'Ain't That Peculiar', 'One More Heartache', and 'Take This Heart Of Mine', all of which hummed along on the motorway of Smokey's crisp, driving production. Robinson's singing had by now achieved full maturity: on a neglected item like 'A Fork In The Road' he was producing some of the most audacious phrasing ever attempted by an R&B singer – the kind of inventiveness that his imitators, like the Stylistics' Russell Thompkins Jr. in recent years, could never begin to equal.

By 1967 his writing had lost some of its youthful freshness and had gained a new depth. With the loss of innocence came lyrics like those of 'I Second That Emotion' and 'The Love I Saw In You Was Just A Mirage': 'Just like the desert shows a thirsty man a deep oasis where there's only sand, you lured me into something I should've dodged . . . the love I saw in you was just a mirage'. There was, too, 'If You Can Wait', with the economy of this marvellous couplet: 'Just like "push" can turn to "shove", "like" can turn to "love".' Musically, though, some of the magic was disappearing, and the hits were now less frequent. Perhaps it was the rigours of touring, perhaps creative exhaustion, perhaps the demands on Smokey's time made by his other role as vice-president of the Motown Record Corporation. Whatever the reason, the most interesting songs were now usually buried in albums which consisted mostly of adequate versions of other people's songs. Understandably, the general audience never dug deep enough to find 'You Must Be Love' on *Make It Happen*, 'You Neglect Me' and 'I'll Take You Any Way That You Come' on *Time Out*, or 'A Legend In Its Own Time' on *Four In Blue*.

However, Smokey and the group never fell completely into the doldrums and in 1970 the British success of a 1967 track 'The Tears Of A Clown', prompted American Motown to issue the record, finally giving the group their first number one on the pop charts. Close listening to this magnificent record reveals the lines, 'Just like Pagliacci did, I try to keep my sadness hid', and the key to most of Smokey's lyrics. Preoccupied with people's masks, with the heartbreak behind the smile, with the 'lipstick traces from kisses you only pretended to feel', his most moving songs all concentrate on hidden pain.

In 1972, after a long series of farewell concerts, he left the Miracles, who continued with a new lead singer, and embarked on a solo career. *Smokey*, the first album, was uneven but promising; *Pure Smokey*, the second, was much more coherent and considered, showing him coming to terms with the preoccupations of men of his age. Instead of parties and discos, he sang about his wife and children, and the complexities of family relationships. 'It's Her Turn To Live', 'She's Only A Baby Herself', and 'The Love Between Me And My Kids' showed concern and understanding, as well as an awareness of changing fashions in music (he employed a tough, funky rhythm section well able to cope with the current clichés. *Quiet Storm*, the third solo album, appeared in 1975 and found him singing in a slightly lower register. Musically, it was sometimes more far-ranging than anything he'd done before: the title-track, for instance, included rhythmic figures which would not have been out of place on a Miles Davis Quintet album in 1965. Another track, the more straightforward 'Baby That's Backatcha', put him back at the top of the American R&B singles charts.

Like most of pop's great artists, Smokey Robinson peaked early in his life. His innate abilities, however, have never deserted him, and his professionalism alone will ensure that he makes interesting music for many years to come.

Rock Films. The new music of the Sixties produced parallel changes in the way rock was reflected on celluloid. The two Beatles films – *A Hard Day's Night* (1964) and *Help!* (1965) led the way. Although the first stuck to a showbiz theme, Dick Lester's direction and Alun Owen's script showed the influence both of zany British comedy (the Goons) and of the gritty realism which dominated British fiction and film-making at that time. *Help!* took the surreal comedy further, and in both the four Beatles were given parts which seemed to extend their natural wit. Other films featuring British beat groups were less enterprising (*Ferry Cross The Mersey* with Gerry and the Pacemakers, *Catch Us If You Can* with the Dave Clark Five) although *What A Crazy World* had Joe Brown as a cockney layabout in a film version of an excellent Joan Littlewood play.

In America, beach-party movies like Fabian's *Ride The Wild Surf* (1965) continued unabated and screen exploitation of the new rock was at first limited to television, though a series of low-budget movies began to appear about the 'youth question', including *Riot On Sunset Strip, Wild In The Streets* and *Revolution*. The soundtrack music for these was generally provided by punk bands such as the Standells and the Chocolate Watch Band, though *Revolution* included the Steve Miller Band, Quicksilver Messenger Service and Mother Earth. These films were the forerunners of more sustained examinations of rock and youth culture. In Britain, Peter Watkins' *Privilege* had ex-Manfred Mann singer Paul Jones as a pop star manipulated by the authorities to channel the energies of the kids in a conformist direction. And Peter Fonda's *Easy Rider*, the odyssey of two hippy bikers with a soundtrack featuring the Byrds and other luminaries, rivalled Mike Nicholls' *The Graduate* (music by Simon and Garfunkel) as the definitive late Sixties statement on American youth.

By this point, it was almost *de rigueur* for smart film-makers to use rock music almost as an earlier generation of directors felt it obligatory to set a scene in a sultry night-spot. Francis Ford Coppola had a John Sebastian soundtrack for his first feature film *You're A Big Boy Now* (1966), while Antonioni's relentlessly swinging *Blow Up* (1967) had a sequence in which the Yardbirds' Jimmy Page was shown smashing a guitar, Pete Townshend-style.

Perhaps the most important development in rock movies during the Sixties was the growing importance and sophistication of the documentary. Starting with D. A. Pennebaker's film of Bob Dylan's 1965 British tour, *Don't Look Back*, the genre accurately reflected the rock experience at key moments throughout the decade. Most notable were the festival movies – *Monterey Pop*, *Woodstock*, and *Gimme Shelter* (Altamont) which, using hand-held cameras, triple screens and improved sound recording, chronicled rock's development perfectly.

The Rockin' Berries, a Birmingham-based group, finally scored in 1964 after a number of misses with a cover of the Tokens' American hit, 'He's in Town' (Pye). Their close harmonies and dominant falsetto lead (Geoff Turton) also sounded like the Tokens, and sustained the resemblance for their next two hits. In 1965, they made their debut in pantomime and subsequently began embellishing their act with comedy routines and impersonations by Clive Lea. In 1967, Lea quit to become a solo impersonator and the remainder of the group geared their appeal towards mums and dads. Today, as the Berries, they are a popular cabaret act. Personnel changes have been frequent, but the original line-up was Roy Austin (born 1943), Terry Bond (1943), Chuck Botfield (1943), Lea (1942) and Turton (1944).

Kenny Rogers and the First Edition will be remembered as a band that found success through accurately gauging the anti-Vietnam War mood of 1968–9. The Reprise recording of country artist Mel Tillis's 'Ruby, Don't Take Your Love To Town' was promoted with the First Edition's mock-hippy image and it took off internationally, just as Barry McGuire's 'Eve Of Destruction' had been a similar one-off success five years before. Rogers (born in 1941) had operated in the folk-music field previous to the First Edition. He organized the First Edition in 1967 with guitarist Terry Williams (born June 6, 1947), Mike Settle, rhythm guitar (born March 20, 1941) and Thelma Camacho, all of whom, like Rogers, had been members of the New Christy Minstrels. Three lesser pop hits resulted besides 'Ruby', including Mickey Newbury's 'Just Dropped In (To See What Condition My Condition Was In)' in 1968.

The Rolling Stones played their first gig – depping for Blues Incorporated at the Marquee on July 21, 1962 – because Alexis Korner's group was appearing on BBC radio's *Jazz Club*. Mick Jagger was quoted in *Jazz News* as saying, 'I hope they don't think we're a rock'n'roll outfit'. The magazine also announced the line-up: Mick Jagger (vocals), born July 16, 1944 in Dartford, Kent; Keith Richard, born Dec. 18, 1943 in Dartford and Elmo Lewis (guitars); Ian Stewart (piano), Dick Taylor (bass), Mick Avory (drums). Whether the future Kinks drummer played that night is not clear, though he did rehearse with the group, as did one Tony Chapman, before Charlie Watts – June 2, 1941 – who had previously worked with Korner, joined. Elmo Lewis turned out to be Brian Jones's – Feb. 26, 1944 – notion of an appropriate name for a bluesman; Dick Taylor quit to stay in art school, whereupon Bill Wyman – Oct. 24, 1941 – took his place; and Ian Stewart was kicked out less than a year later by Andrew Oldham because his face didn't fit. The 'sixth Stone' became the group's roadie and occasional session pianist.

Following their debut at the Marquee, the Stones played a few support gigs there and then were dropped because, as Chris Barber put it, 'they weren't authentic enough'. However, if their repertoire of Chuck Berry, Bo Diddley and Jimmy Reed and their energetic, unsophisticated style were too close to rock'n'roll for the smug purists of the self-styled London Jazz Centre, they impressed Giorgio Gomelsky sufficiently to offer the group a residency at his Crawdaddy Club in Richmond. There the Stones' reputation spread so rapidly by word of mouth that within a matter of weeks Gomelsky was faced with long queues and the need to move to larger premises. Then, in the first week of May, his unwritten contract with the group ended when Andrew Oldham, with immense self-confidence and Eric Easton's financial support, signed a management deal with them.

Easton purchased the demo tapes the group had made at IBC studios, and under Oldham's supervision they recorded 'Come On' and 'I Wanna Be Loved', which were released as the group's first single in June on Decca. The choice of the A-side, a Chuck Berry song not featured in the Stones' club repertoire, and its vocal harmonies and double-tracking were early indications of Oldham's attempt to mould the group into a form that would be more readily acceptable to the pop public; another was their appearance on television's *Thank Your Lucky Stars*, to promote the record, in matching check stage suits, and photographic sessions in collar and tie. The success of this manipulation was limited, for the record failed to reach the Top Twenty. Nevertheless, 'Come On' did well enough to land the group a spot on a national package tour headed by the Everly Brothers, Little Richard, Bo Diddley and Gene Vincent, and their second single, 'I Wanna Be Your Man', Lennon and McCartney's concept of the Stones' sound and a further step away from the group's original style, eventually made No. 10 at the beginning of January, 1964.

Their third single, released in February, was a reworking of the Crickets' 'Not Fade Away' and the group's first significant interpretation, for their Diddleyesque adaptation made Buddy Holly's song their own; along with their treatment of the Valentinos' 'It's All Over Now', their fourth single and first British No. 1, it anticipated the approach of Jagger and Richard's songwriting partnership. Not unnaturally, however, their first efforts – 'Little By Little' and 'Tell Me', for example – were heavily derivative of the R&B they'd been playing. It wasn't until they had moved beyond R&B to the more openly emotive and declamatory style of soul that the writing of Jagger and Richard flourished. To do this, they had first to confront Oldham who, though he had quickly learnt how to manipulate the group's improvised image and was especially good at capitalizing on the group's frequent brushes with the authorities, was less astute in his proposals for their musical direction. Obsessed with Phil Spector, whose Philles label he hoped to emulate with his own Immediate Records, Oldham – as can be clearly seen on the out-takes of that period finally released in 1975 on *Metamorphosis* (London) – made inept attempts at his own 'Wall of Sound'. Fortunately, however, the Stones found their own way, as 'Satisfaction', their first American No. 1 in the summer of 1965, demonstrated. That record was the perfect synthesis of the musical styles that had influenced the group – particularly Solomon Burke, Chuck Berry and Muddy Waters – and, for the first time, generalized feelings entered the Stones' lyrics as Jagger screamed out his anger at the attempt at complete manipulation he saw around him. Aggression also marked the songs Jagger and Richard fashioned out of their election to the exclusive, but supposedly egalitarian, club of 'Swinging London' – 'Play With Fire', 'Out Of Time' and 'Stupid Girl' – songs in which class hatred, and sexual aggression and frustration are to be found in equal parts.

However, 'Satisfaction' marked not only the Stones' discovery of a musical way forward, it also confirmed the social stance the group had evolved in the two years since 'Come On'. For the Stones had not merely won pop polls, topped the charts and toured the world, they had also caused riots in Blackpool, Belfast and Paris, at London Airport and on *Ready Steady Go!*; been barred from hotels and restaurants; walked out on press receptions; been banned by the BBC, and convicted for driving offences and using insulting behaviour; and they'd incensed hairdressers, schoolteachers, television viewers and magistrates. Seen from this perspective, the phenomenal popularity of 'Satisfaction' said as much for the accuracy with which it reflected the feelings of a generation in the mid-Sixties as it did for the song's construction and the group's performance. None the less, because of a stylistic restlessness that verged on whimsy, only a few of the half-dozen hits of the next two years came near to matching 'Satisfaction', though success was assured for every single and album – 'Get Off Of My Cloud' (1965), 'Paint It Black' (1966) and 'Ruby Tuesday' all made No. 1 in America.

The albums of that period, *Out Of Our Heads* (1965), *Aftermath* (1966) – the first to consist entirely of Jagger–Richard originals – and *Between The Buttons* (1967), were equally eclectic, but the most significant development in the group's career between 1965 and 1967 was the inordinate growth of their image and the increasing seriousness with which it was treated by the establishment, culminating in the *News Of The World* witch-hunt, the drugs busts in February (Jagger and Richard) and May, 1967 (Jones), and the subsequent disproportionate jail sentences which prompted the famous *Times* editorial, 'Who Breaks A Butterfly On A Wheel?' and were quashed on appeal. Out of all this came a wilting flower-power single, 'We Love You' (August, 1967), featuring back-up vocals by Lennon and McCartney, who also introduced them to the Maharishi; a break with Andrew Oldham; virtual withdrawal from public performances; and the unsuccessful post-*Sergeant Pepper* psychedelic album, *Their Satanic Majesties Request* (December, 1967). Then in May, 1968, the group emerged from the months of retirement with 'Jumping Jack Flash', their finest single since 'Satisfaction', and played their first British concert in two years. And finally, after a five-month delay due to Decca's opposition to the sleeve artwork, *Beggar's Banquet* was released in December. Though its superficially radical themes drew the Stones greater attention than they perhaps deserved, it was the group's most complete album to date, seeing the cutting edge of their music restored (in part by Jimmy Miller's production) as Jagger–Richard returned to their musings on anger and frustration in songs like 'Street Fighting Man'.

In June, 1969, Brian Jones left the group, explaining his

decision in the unquestionable understatement, 'I no longer see eye-to-eye with the others over the discs we are cutting', and within a week Mick Taylor – born Jan. 17, 1941 – had left John Mayall to join as lead guitarist. Jones announced his intention to form his own band, but on July 3 was found dead in his swimming pool. Mick Jagger transformed the group's free concert in Hyde Park that weekend into a memorial service by quoting Shelley and releasing several thousand butterflies. Following the sensation of Jones's death, the group continued to provide newspaper copy : Jagger with his girlfriend, Marianne Faithfull, and the shooting of *Ned Kelly* in Australia, but more disturbingly at the year's end when, during their set at the notorious Altamont Festival, a black youth was stabbed to death by Hell's Angels in front of the stage as they played. The killing made prophetic sense of 'Gimme Shelter', the opening cut on their excellent *Let It Bleed* album (December, 1969) : 'Rape, murder – it's just a shot away', and in turning the Woodstock dream into a nightmare, it emphasized dramatically the group's complete remoteness from their audience.

After an initial burst of energy which brought about the foundation of their own record company – Rolling Stones Records, launched with *Sticky Fingers* in April, 1971, their last Decca recording being *Get Yer Ya Yas Out* (September, 1970), a live set to foil concert bootleggers – the Seventies saw complacency setting in. The group moved to France after a farewell gig at London's Roundhouse in March, 1971, and thereafter public attention drifted away from their music to focus on Jagger's much-publicized courtship of Bianca Perez Morena de Macias and their trendy San Tropez wedding in May. The couple at once joined the international jet set, attending society parties and winning fashion polls. The rest of the group declined to follow suit. They worked less, and not surprisingly the music suffered. Jagger's songs, especially, lost the force provided by his earlier stance outside conventional society. *Exile On Main Street* (1972) was a sprawling double album with no core; *Goat's Head Soup* (1973), old-fashioned : and although *It's Only Rock'n'Roll* (1974) revived confidence in their universally unquestioned status as 'the greatest rock'n'roll band in the world', it's as a live act that their reputation has been best preserved.

Keith Richard's collaboration with Ron Wood in 1974 – his first work outside the group – gave rise to speculation about the future of both the Stones and the Faces, and when Mick Taylor quit at the end of the year it was indeed Wood who took his place in the Stones' 1975 American tour.

The Ronettes, comprising sisters Veronica (born Aug. 10, 1943) and Estelle Bennett (July 22, 1944) and their cousin Nedra Talley (Jan. 27, 1946), began as a pubescent dance-act, the Dolly Sisters, before branching out into singing after taking harmony tuition at New York's Camilucci Studios. In 1961, at the height of the twist craze, they worked as resident dancers at the Peppermint Lounge and in 1961 they went out as a utility dance-act, touring with the Clay Cole Twist Package and appearing with Cole (a deejay) in the exploitation film, *Twist Around The Clock.* Signing with Colpix in 1961, they recorded five singles without success until 1963 when the Phil Spector-produced singles, 'Be My Baby' and 'Baby, I Love You', sold a million copies each on Spector's Philles label. Several smaller hits followed, including 'Walkin' In The Rain' and 'Breakin' Up', but the trio faded with the demise of Philles in 1966. They re-emerged, briefly, in 1969 on A&M and with a revised line-up, on Buddah, in 1973. The only original member, Veronica (Ronnie) Bennett, is married to Phil Spector although they separated in 1973.

Biff Rose, who owes much to hip comedians like Lenny Bruce, is an eccentric singer, composer and raconteur who still commands a cult following in both Britain and America. His idiosyncratic performing and writing style repels as many people as it attracts, although David Bowie (who recorded Rose's 'Fill Your Heart' on *Hunky Dory*) has acknowledged Rose as a substantial influence on his work. Rose's main fault has always been his tendency to undercut his often brilliant satirical sense by recording songs of horrible sentimentalism, possibly due to the fact that he never fully survived the flower-power era of 1966–7, when he appeared on American television propagating the virtues of the new lifestyle and unintentionally sentimentalizing it. His recent output has been low and of poor quality, compared to his 1971 Buddah record, 'The Thorn In Mrs Rose's Side'.

Tim Rose, born in 1940, gained attention in 1967 with his first Columbia album which included a song he had composed with Bonny Dobson, 'Morning Dew', and a slow arrangement of 'Hey Joe'. He had earlier been a member of the folk-rock group the Big Three, with Mama Cass. A second Columbia album followed in 1969, and in 1971 he signed to Playboy Records, for whom he made one album. This was finally released in Britain in 1974. Since then he has been resident in Britain, playing clubs with his own (English) band. Rose is a powerful singer, injecting drama and contrast into his performance.

Paul Rothchild, a staff producer for Elektra Records in the mid-Sixties, produced records by the label's main rock bands, including the Doors, the Paul Butterfield Blues Band and Love. He was involved in six records by the Doors, and once tried to record the group on LSD. Before joining Elektra, Rothschild had worked with Tom Rush for the Prestige label, and though he did not continue to produce Rush at Elektra, he was a prolific producer throughout the Sixties. Clear Light, Goodthunder and the heavy rock 'supergroup' Rhinoceros (which he had been instrumental in forming) were among his later, mainly unsuccessful, projects. Leaving Elektra he produced John Sebastian's first solo album and, in 1973, made an abortive attempt to set up his own label, Buffalo Records.

The Royal Guardsmen were a classic case of the 'one-hit wonder' phenomenon when the 1967 record of 'Snoopy Versus The Red Baron' made the American Top Ten on Laurie and the British Top Ten on Stateside. Worldwide, the record – a gimmicky tribute to Charles Schulz's famous cartoon character – sold over three million copies. The Royal

Guardsmen were all from Ocala, Florida, and included John Burdett (drums), Bill Balogh (bass), Barry Winslow (rhythm guitar, vocals), Tom Richards (lead guitar), Billy Taylor (organ) and Chris Nunley (percussion and vocals). A series of predictable but largely unsuccessful follow-ups included 'The Return Of The Red Baron', 'Snoopy For President' and even 'Snoopy's Christmas'.

Ruby and the Romantics – Edward Roberts (first tenor), Ronald Mosley (baritone), Leroy Fann (bass, from Ohio) and Alabama-born George Lee (second tenor) – changed their name from the Supremes to the Romantics when Ruby Walsh (also from Ohio) joined them as lead singer in 1962. Their recording of Bob Hilliard's Latin-flavoured song, 'Our Day Will Come' on Kapp, topped both pop and R&B charts the following year. They were managed by orchestra leader Leroy Kirkland and their other Top Fifty hits, all on Kapp, included 'My Summer Love', 'Hey There Lonely Boy' (later revived by Eddie Holman with a change of gender), 'Young Wings Can Fly' and 'When You're Young And In Love'. The group also recorded for ABC-Paramount.

David Ruffin, son of a Baptist preacher, began singing gospel with the Dixie Nightingales. Born in Meridian, Mississippi, on Jan. 18, 1941, Ruffin had a brief spell as a racehorse jockey in Arkansas, where he met Billy Davis and signed with Anna Records, which Davis was forming with the Gordy family. In Detroit he soon joined the Temptations, and it was his distinctive, gritty baritone voice that carried such hits as 'Ain't Too Proud To Beg'. He left the Temptations in 1968 to go solo, scoring a Top Ten hit with 'My Whole World Ended', and after a short period of duetting with his brother Jimmy in 1970, he reverted to his successful solo career with Motown.

Jimmy Ruffin, born in Collinsville, Mississippi on May 7, 1939, moved to Detroit with his family in 1960, where a factory workmate – a member of Motown's Contours group –

introduced him to Berry Gordy, who signed him to the Miracle label. On the same label were the Temptations, whom he later refused to join, preferring to remain solo. His perseverance was rewarded when 'What Becomes Of The Broken Hearted', a plaintive beat ballad, was a transatlantic Top Ten hit in 1966. Subsequent discs were smaller hits, including a 1970 duet with brother David, but in 1972 he quit Motown, moving to Britain to join Polydor: 'Tell Me What You Want', a shuffle-funk ballad, was a minor 1974 hit, issued in America on Chess.

Tom Rush, born in Portsmouth, New Hampshire, on Feb. 8, 1941, started his folk career while he was still at Harvard. He soon gravitated towards the Boston/Cambridge coterie of the Club 47. Influenced by Eric Von Schmidt, he developed his twelve-string and bottleneck style to a highly individual level on his first Elektra album, *Tom Rush* and the acoustic side of the 1966 *Take A Little Walk With Me*. These, and two earlier Prestige albums, reveal a stronger traditional and country blues emphasis than his Dylanesque contemporaries. He shunned the protest era and though he fell in with the electric trend on the 1966 album, it was by playing rock'n'roll classics by Chuck Berry, Bo Diddley and Buddy Holly, with Al Kooper on lead guitar. In 1968 he abandoned folk music with *The Circle Game*, a lavishly arranged album of heavily poetic material, including the restrained 'No Regrets', his finest song, and others by then unknown writers Joni Mitchell, Jackson Browne, and James Taylor. Three patchier albums followed with more good interpretations but weaker self-written songs and less thoughtful arrangements. *Ladies Love Outlaws* (Columbia, 1975) glimpses at a return to former glory.

Mitch Ryder and the Detroit Wheels came along with the wrong sound at the wrong time and made it work anyhow. 'Jenny Take A Ride' (on New Voice), a frenetic Little Richard remake that broke at the end of 1965, was much earthier than just about anything else on the charts at a time when rock was becoming increasingly sophisticated. Mitch (real name Billy LaVere) had spent his teenage years roaming the black clubs of Detroit, sometimes getting onstage to test his pipes against those of his Motown idols. He was a screamer with style, perhaps the best of the white rhythm and blues singers, with a stage act modelled after James Brown's.

By 1968, the group – John Badanjek, Jimmy McCartney, Earl Eliot and Joe Cubert – had rocked up ten more chart items, the biggest of which were 'Devil With A Blue Dress On'/'Good Golly Miss Molly' (1966) and 'Sock It To Me Baby' (1967). But manager-producer Bob Crewe felt Ryder was the sole attraction, and neglected the rest of the band. He tried to mould a Las Vegas-type show with full orchestra and elaborate choreography. Ryder went along with it only for a few months before returning to Detroit, bitter and deep in debt. In 1971, at the height of the Motor City's heavy-metal mania, he resurfaced as the lead singer in a band of equals, Detroit, that included such respected local players as drummer Johnny Badanjek and guitarist Steve Hunter. Their one album was a metallic blues-rock classic featuring Mitch's rendering of the Falcons' 'I Found A Love', a song he had by then been singing for 11 years. But this band was short-lived, a victim of little promotion and much in-fighting. Mitch retired not to the car wash, but to the car factories of his home-town, where, as Billy LaVere once more, he worked as a foreman and nursed a throat infection that all but guaranteed he would never sing again.

Buffy Sainte-Marie was born in Maine, of Cree Indian descent, on Feb. 20, 1941. Her strong, idiosyncratic voice and compositions like 'Universal Soldier' (a hit for Donovan and Glen Campbell) made her an important figure on the New York folk scene in the early Sixties. A number of her songs dealt with the past and present situation of the American Indian, notably 'Now That The Buffalo's Gone' and 'My Country 'Tis Of Thy People You're Dying'. Her first album was released by Vanguard in 1964, and since 1968 when she cut *I'm Gonna Be A Country Girl Again* in Nashville, she has experimented with other musical styles. *Illuminations*

(1970) was in a progressive rock mould, using electronics, while *Moonshot* (1972) was a mainstream rock album. In 1974 she moved to MCA.

Crispian St Peters (real name Peter Smith), was an undistinguished singer who covered the We Five's huge American hit, 'You Were On My Mind'. The original had failed to take off in Britain, and as a result Peters had a No. 2 hit early in 1966. His follow-up, 'Pied Piper' (Decca), provided him with a second Top Five hit, which proved to be his last.

Sam and Dave – Sam Moore, born in Miami, Florida, on Oct. 12, 1935 and Dave Prater, born Ocilla, Georgia, May 9, 1937 – were discovered by Morris Levy, of Roulette, in 1960. Sam's musical grounding was singing gospel with the Melonaires, but he soon realized that only secular music would yield sufficient financial reward to support his family and began doing solo gigs around the Miami area. He was playing the King of Hearts Club in Miami, in 1958, when Dave Prater joined him onstage, and the audience response persuaded them to form a partnership. The duo signed with Roulette in 1960 and spent four years making fine gospel-soul discs under the wing of Henry Glover, but without any commercial impact. They left Roulette, in 1965, to sign with Atlantic. There, Jerry Wexler arranged for them to record at Stax, whose owner, Jim Stewart, required that their records were released on his label. They were teamed with writers/producers Isaac Hayes and David Porter to record a series of gospel-tinged hits supported by the renowned Memphis horn section, both up-tempo and ballads, commencing with 'You Don't Know Like I Know' and 'Hold On I'm Coming' (1966) and culminating with 'Born Again' (1969), peaking with million-selling No. 2 hit 'Soul Of Man' (1967). When Stax was sold to Gulf & Western in 1968, the duo reverted to the Atlantic label, but later discs, recorded in Miami, were unsuccessful and they split in 1970, intent on furthering solo careers, Sam with Atlantic and Dave with Alston. But a year later they teamed up again, signing with UA Records.

Sam the Sham, christened Samudio Domingo, was a Texan-Mexican who, with his Pharaohs (David Martin, Roy Stinnet, Jerry Patterson and Butch Gibson), also of Tex-Mex origin and musical inspiration, launched a rocking good-time sound at the public in the mid-Sixties. The group recorded unsuccessfully in Memphis in the early Sixties, but a cover version of Gene Simmons' novelty rock hit, 'Haunted House', was followed by 'Woolly Bully', 'Ju Ju Hand' and other top hits. 'Woolly Bully' was a monster hit for MGM in 1965, to whom it had been leased from Stan Kesler's Pen Records in Memphis. The group transferred permanently to MGM thereafter and followed up with 'Red Hot', an old rockabilly tune, and 'Lil Red Riding Hood'. In 1973 Sam attempted a comeback with an uneven album under the name of Sam Samudio on Atlantic.

San Francisco had long provided a hospitable environment for both artistic and political radicalism even before the growth of the 'hippie' culture in the mid-Sixties, whose main expression was the music of dozens of locally based rock bands. In the space of a few months during 1967, this localized phenomenon had an international impact as San Francisco groups, led by the Charlatans, the Jefferson Airplane and Country Joe and the Fish, were signed to major record labels. Scott McKenzie sold vast numbers of his ersatz hippie anthem 'San Francisco (Wear Some Flowers In Your Hair)', and the city's counter-culture was the subject of countless magazine and television features. In addition, the so-called 'psychedelic music' of San Francisco groups inspired other musicians to experiment within a rock format throughout America and Western Europe.

Before 1965, there had been a small but flourishing rock scene in the city itself and a lively folk music scene in the university centre of Berkeley across the Bay. The local labels were Fantasy (Lenny Bruce, Vince Guaraldi, the Golliwogs, later Creedence Clearwater Revival) and Tom Donahue's Autumn Records. Donahue was a well-known local deejay and pioneer of 'underground radio', who employed Sylvester Stewart (later Sly Stone) as producer on hits by the Beau

308

Brummels, the Mojo Men and others. By 1965, the city was feeling the first ripples from the British Invasion and the new American rock of the Byrds and Lovin' Spoonful. Dances were organized at the Longshoreman's Hall by a community organization called the Family Dog, at which the Charlatans, the Great Society (featuring Grace Slick), the Jefferson Airplane, the Warlocks (later the Grateful Dead) and the pre-Janis Joplin Big Brother and the Holding Company played. The music consisted of various fusions of blues, folk and beat. Meanwhile, in Berkeley, the Instant Action Jug Band was becoming Country Joe and the Fish as acid became as important as protest in their lifestyle. LSD was not yet illegal in California and soon the influence of its apostles, notably Ken Kesey, was felt in the scene. The Grateful Dead developed their long, meandering numbers as a kind of musical equivalent of an acid trip, while the Airplane reached the American Top Ten with a thinly disguised drug song, 'White Rabbit'. Closely associated with the groups and dances was the development of poster art and of light shows, both of which were also intended to relate to the psychedelic experience.

In 1967, the first major free outdoor concert, the Human Be-In, inspired the Monterey Festival at which the leading San Francisco groups appeared outside their hometown for the first time. The Airplane had just been signed to RCA, and, sensing a trend, other big companies moved in. The Grateful Dead joined Warner Bros., Moby Grape and Janis Joplin went to Columbia, the Fish to Vanguard, the Sons Of Champlin and Mystery Trend to Verve. As those groups began to have hit albums, other musicians were among the thousands flocking to San Francisco's Haight-Ashbury to join the 'love generation': Sir Douglas Quintet, Mother Earth, Electric Flag, Linn County and Mad River were among them. But the hippie community was crumbling, music had become big business (Bill Graham, former Mime Troupe member, was now a big-time promoter) and the successful local bands were setting their sights on wider horizons. By 1969, there was no longer a specifically San

Francisco sound. It was underground music and of international significance.

Scaffold, a trio of Liverpudlian humorists with an appeal similar to that of London's Alberts, first attracted national attention in 1966 with their recordings of such schoolboyish ditties as 'Thank U Very Much' and 'Lily The Pink' a million-seller in 1968. None the less, Scaffold are still primarily stage and club performers, who also maintain disparate individual careers. Mike McGear (Michael McCartney, step-brother of Paul, born Jan. 7, 1944) released a solo album in 1975; Roger McGough (Nov. 9, 1937) is a poet particularly renowned for his P. C. Plod cycle; John Gorman (Jan. 4, 1937) is a comedy actor. In the early Seventies, all three men became associated with the larger unit, Grimms.

Scepter/Wand Records had their start in 1958, when Florence Greenberg launched the Scepter label in New York. Her only act at the time was a female vocal quartet – the Shirelles – which she had discovered at a school talent show and subsequently managed. Early Scepter product was channelled through Decca's distribution, but when the third release, the Shirelles' 'Dedicated To The One I Love', sold a million in 1959 the label went into its own full-scale production, promotion and distribution. Two further Shirelles discs went gold over the next year, giving Scepter a firm financial footing, and, in 1961, the Wand subsidiary was started. The first five releases remain obscure but the sixth, Chuck Jackson's powerful ballad 'I Don't Want To Cry', reached the Top Ten, and the same year saw Lenny Miles and Tommy Hunt with solo debut hits. The Shirelles' 'Will You Love Me Tomorrow' was Scepter's first chart-topper, and the girls had some 20 further chart entries before moving to Bell in 1967, while Chuck Jackson also enjoyed a stream of hits before he, too, left in 1967 for Motown. Further major hits came with the Isley Brothers ('Twist And Shout', 1962), novelties by the Rocky Fellers (1963), the Kingsmen ('Louie Louie', 1964)

310

and B. J. Thomas's chart-topping original of 'Raindrops Keep Falling On My Head' (1969), but the company's biggest success was with Dionne Warwick, who between 1962 and 1971 achieved some 38 Hot Hundred entries, eight of them Top Ten hits, largely material written by Burt Bacharach and Hal David including 'Walk On By', 'I Say A Little Prayer', and 'This Girl's In Love With You'. Both Scepter and Wand remain active, mainly in the R&B field.

Freddy Scott, originally a Screen Gems–Columbia contract writer – he wrote 'The Door Is Open' for Tommy Hunt – first registered as a 'deep soul' singer in 1963 with 'Hey Girl' on Colpix, having previously recorded for Arrow, Joy and Enrica.. When the Shout label was established in New York, in 1966, it was intended as an exclusively black subsidiary to Bang, and Freddy Scott – born on April 24, 1933, in Providence, Rhode Island – left Columbia to join a roster which embraced George Freeman, Jerry O, and the Exciters. That year, with producer Bert Berns, he cut 'Are You Lonely For Me', later covered by Motown's Chuck Jackson, and reworked Solomon Burke's 'Cry To Me'. Other sides included 'Am I Groovin' You', 'Just Like A Flower', and Ben E. King's 'Spanish Harlem'. More recently he has recorded for Probe, Vanguard, Pip and Elephant V.

Peggy Scott and Jo Jo Benson. Peggy Scott – born in Pensacola, Florida, in 1948 – sang in various gospel groups before adopting a secular style in 1966. She toured with Ben E. King, but after hospitalization following a car crash became resident with the Swinging Sextet in Pensacola, where she met Jo Jo Benson in 1968. Jo Jo – born in Columbus, Ohio, in 1940 – sang with the Bluenotes before joining the Chuck Willis Show, with which he toured until Chuck's death, later singing with the Upsetters and Enchanters. The duo first hit the charts in 1968 with 'Lover's Holiday' (SSS International), a brassy, gospelly belter, and three further hits followed in similar style. Both recorded solo items too, but soon faded from the scene.

The Searchers, named after the John Ford movie, were second only to the Beatles on Merseyside in terms of musicianship and local popularity. On their signing to Pye in 1963, the line-up was Mike Pender, lead guitar (born Mike Prendergast, March 3, 1942), John McNally, rhythm (Aug. 30, 1941), Tony Jackson, bass (July 16, 1940), and Chris Curtis, drums (Aug. 16, 1941). Their first single, the Drifters' 'Sweets For My Sweet' went to No. 1 and featured the high-pitched, light harmonies that became the group's trademark. Other covers of American hits followed and were equally successful: Jackie De Shannon's 'Needles And Pins' (written by Jack Nitzsche and Sonny Bono), the Orlons' 'Don't Throw Your Love Away' and 'When You Walk In The Room', another De Shannon hit. The Searchers were also regular visitors to the American Top Twenty on the Kapp label, and their combination of tight harmonies with jangling guitars anticipated the sound of the Byrds. By 1965, however, their lack of original songs for singles was becoming a liability. Two folk/protest numbers (Malvina Reynolds' 'What Have They Done To The Rain' and P. F. Sloan's 'Take Me For What I'm Worth') barely scraped into the Top Twenty and Jackson left to be replaced by Frank Allen from Cliff Bennett's band. In 1969, the Searchers lost Curtis who tried a solo career briefly and then went into production. By this time they were establishing themselves on the cabaret circuit, like many of their fellow-Mersey groups.

The Seeds were one of the more unusual groups spawned in Los Angeles during the folk-rock era. Formed by the charismatic Sky Saxon (real name Richard Marsh) in early 1965, the group included Jan Savage, Daryl Hooper and Rick Andridge. Their music was raw, simplistic, and featured one-note guitar runs, but it was Saxon's weird, idiosyncratic growls and free-association ramblings that made them special. After being out nearly a year, 'Pushin' Too Hard' (their second single) was picked up by a local radio station and spread to become a national Top Forty hit at the end of 1966. Although they had only three subsequent chart singles – 'Mr Farmer', 'Can't Seem To Make You Mine' and

'Thousand Shadows' – the Seeds remained immensely popular with L.A.'s discotheque audiences, and with fans around the country who saw them on tours and bought their albums, which were full of overt (if innocent) drug references and blatant sexual overtones. Everything they did was grossly overdone, notably their 'psychedelic' album, *Future*, and a ridiculous blues album with liner notes by Muddy Waters. But through it all Saxon's appeal remained. They dissolved around 1969, with no further recordings by any of the members – although Saxon still makes the rounds of record companies with tapes he describes as 'better than the Beatles'.

Pete Seeger, generally acknowledged as 'the father of the American folk revival' through 30 years of performing, collecting, songwriting and proselytizing, has always linked music and radical humanism. Born on May 3, 1919 in New York, he is the son of ethnomusicologist Charles, and half-brother of singers Peggy and Mike. After 'conversion' at a 1935 visit to a North Carolina folk festival, he dropped out of Harvard and established contact with the Lomaxes, Leadbelly and Woody Guthrie. During the War, he performed with The Almanac Singers before Army service. He helped found the Weavers in 1949 and made several hit records with them. Seeger went solo in the Fifties, and became a perennial on the college, camp and union benefit concert circuit. He helped reactivate the Newport Folk Festival in 1960, and has long been a leading columnist on *Sing Out!* and a patron of *Broadside*. Seeger's many recordings on Folkways, Vanguard and Columbia have shown an enormous range of style and material, with his light tenor voice and commanding instrumental work. He is a great believer in audience singalongs, and has been the greatest popularizer of the five-string banjo, though he also plays six- and 12-string guitar, chalil, and steel drums. His nicknames – 'the Johnny Appleseed of folk song' and 'America's tuning-fork' – indicate the missionary appeal. Among his most famous songs are 'If I Had A Hammer', 'Where Have All The Flowers Gone', 'Waist Deep In The Big Muddy', and 'Guantanamera'.

313

Shadows Of Knight. Punk-rock in Chicago was centred around the Dunwich label and Bill Traut's Dunwich Productions, and no group better typified this scene than the Shadows of Knight. Formed in 1965, the group (Jim Sohns, Warren Rogers, Jerry McGeorge, Tom Schiffour, Joe Kelley) paid the usual dues until their first single, 'Gloria', rose to the Top Ten nationally, nearly a year after Them's original version had flopped. Soon every garage band in the country was doing the song, although the Shadows of Knight were unable to follow this classic with anything of equal impact. 'Oh Yeah' and 'Bad Little Woman' (1966) presented the band's crude, Bo Diddley-inspired sound at its best, and though the Kasenetz-Katz-produced 'Shake' (Team) was big regionally in 1968, like nearly every punk group, one hit was all they got. A reformed Shadows of Knight, without Sohns, has been playing the local circuit since 1974.

The Shangri-Las were Mary Weiss, her sister Betty, and Mary Ann and Margie Ganser (who were twins) who began singing semi-professionally while still attending Andrew Jackson High School in Queens, New York. Between 1964 and 1966, they cut a series of remarkable records best described as theatrical in their intensity, masterminded by producer George 'Shadow' Morton. The girls were brought to him by disc-jockey Babalu (Bob Lewis). Their first record was the defiantly morbid 'Remember (Walkin' In The Sand)', released on Leiber and Stoller's Red Bird label. It got to No. 5, but the follow-up, 'Leader Of The Pack', topped the charts. Morton dubbed on motorcycle noises (after the seagulls of the earlier disc) and faced opposition from the more conservative members of the company over the record's adulation of black leather boys.

Minor hits of a more conventional nature followed until 'I Never Go Home Anymore', featuring lead singing from Mary Weiss expressing almost unbearable desolation, became the Shangri-Las' third Top Ten record in 1965. The even more ambitious 'Past, Present And Future' followed, but in 1966 both Red Bird and the group folded.

Ravi Shankar was born in Benares, India, in 1920. Raised in an orthodox Hindu Brahmin family, he began his musical career as a member of his elder brother Uday's travelling music and dance company. In 1939 he returned to India to study his native classical music and the sitar under Guru Baba Khan, eventually to become one of the greatest virtuosos in music – Eastern or Western. By the mid-Sixties, the Eastern influence found its way into the creatively expanding field of pop. George Harrison's use of the sitar on 'Norwegian Wood', for example, had unleashed a torrent of interest in – and misuse of – the instrument. Few followed Harrison's example in studying the sitar seriously. He journeyed to Bombay to study under Shankar and later used his tuition well to produce the brilliant 'Within You Without You' on *Sergeant Pepper*. Others used the sitar like a fashionable gimmick; its ubiquity on albums was virtually the Carbon 90 test for 1967. In May, 1967, Shankar inaugurated his Kinnera School of Music in Los Angeles and performed at the Monterey Pop Festival later the same year. He also played at Woodstock in 1969 and at the 1971 Madison Square Gardens Concert for Bangladesh.

Sandie Shaw, born Sandra Goodrich in Dagenham, Essex, on Feb. 26, 1947, reputedly became the barefoot pop singer after demonstrating her vocal talents in Adam Faith's dressing room. In 1964, her second record '(There's) Always Something There To Remind Me' (Pye), a cover of Dionne Warwick's minor American hit, went to No. 1, and subsequent releases also did well. She faded in 1966 but returned to the limelight the following year when she sang the winning entry in the Eurovision Song Contest, the influential 'Puppet On A String'. After marrying Jeff Banks, the fashion designer, in 1968, her public appearances became sporadic. In 1974 she began a new career as an actress.

Simon and Garfunkel, two ex-rock and rollers and ex-folksingers, made the most successful album of the early Seventies with *Bridge Over Troubled Water*, which has sold nearly two million copies in America alone and over eight million worldwide. Previously, Simon and Garfunkel had provided songs for Mike Nicholl's award-winning movie, *The Graduate*, a skilful comedy about the 'generation gap', which interpreted the 'youth revolt' of the Sixties for anxious parents. The unparalleled sales of the *Bridge* album suggested a similar impact. It bridged the division between the rock generation and those outside it through Simon's enigmatic songs and Garfunkel's soft, soaring tenor.

Paul Simon (born Oct. 13, 1942) and Art Garfunkel (born Nov. 5, 1942) grew up together in Queen's, New York. At 15, they were Tom and Jerry, an Everly Brothers type harmony team, with a small hit on Big called 'Hey Schoolgirl'. They made a few public appearances and appeared on *American Bandstand* before returning to their studies. Simon continued recording under various names, including Jerry Landis and Tico and The Triumphs (whose 'Motorcycle' made 99 in the Hot Hundred on Amy in 1962). He met Carole King and tried unsuccessfully to write songs with her, and then took his acoustic guitar down to Greenwich Village to become a folk-singer. His earliest songs were recorded with Garfunkel for Columbia but remained unnoticed until Bob Dylan unveiled his electric sound in 1965 and suddenly folk-rock was the thing. Paul Simon was in England playing the folk clubs, producing Jackson C. Frank and cutting his acoustic *Songbook* album and Garfunkel was in college when producer Tom Wilson added a rock backing to their New York recording of 'Sounds Of Silence'. By early 1966 it was a No. 1 hit. Simon rushed back to America, got together with Garfunkel and began touring. The pattern of their work together for the next five years was set.

From the start it was clear that Simon had his finger on the pulse of a college generation whose high-school adolescent angst was deepened as the Student Movement began. These songs were sometimes portentous ('Patterns', 'Sounds Of Silence', 'I Am A Rock') but they were balanced by Simon's unequalled melodic sense and by a few love songs of enduring power, notably 'Kathy's Song' and 'Wednesday Morning 3 a.m.'. The singing, too, was exceptional: the restless generation had its own Everly Brothers.

On record, it took some time for Simon and Garfunkel to achieve an instrumental mode to match their songs and singing. Both Wilson's overdubbing and the 1966 studio album produced by Bob Johnston (then Dylan's producer) were shotgun marriages of folk songs and rock sounds. Later that year another album, *Parsley, Sage, Rosemary And Thyme*, included more revamped versions of Simon's earlier acoustic songs. Meanwhile they had scored two more Top Ten hits, 'Homeward Bound' and 'I Am A Rock', and two further singles went Top Thirty. Simon and Garfunkel now took greater control of their career, resisting the pressure for more and more product. Throughout 1967 they concentrated on *The Graduate* and on the first self-produced album, *Book-ends*, both of which appeared early in 1968. The latter is perhaps the finest Simon and Garfunkel album, with its sympathetic accompaniments to Simon's first 'State of the Nation' song, 'America', and the mysterious 'Fakin' It'. Like *Bridge Over Troubled Water* and their later solo albums, it involved the collaboration of master engineer Roy Halee.

The stage was set for their greatest triumph and in 1970 both the single and album of *Bridge* headed the charts. The overwhelming success seemed to induce musical inertia in the duo and when Art Garfunkel turned his attention to film acting (*Catch 22*), the split was inevitable. Simon's later solo work showed greater experimentation and intensity, while Garfunkel contented himself with relatively lightweight but exquisitely made records. They briefly re-united in 1975 for 'My Little Town', an American hit which also appeared on their 1975 solo albums.

Joe Simon is an immensely popular, smooth soul singer born on Sept. 2, 1943 in Simmesport, Louisiana. After mediocre issues on Irral, Hush, where he sang with the Goldentones, and a minor hit on Vee Jay, in 1966 he joined the Nashville-based Monument subsidiary, Sound Stage 7. Produced by John Richbourg – noted for his work in the country-flavoured soul area – Simon scored 16 hits in four years, including 'Teenager's Prayer' (1966), 'Nine Pound Steel' (1967), a version of the much-recorded 'You Keep Me

317

Hanging On' (1968), and million-seller 'The Choking Kind' (1969). Recording for Spring since 1970, he has maintained his success in a modern market with hits produced by Gamble and Huff ('Drowning In The Sea Of Love', 'Pool Of Bad Luck'), Brad Shapiro ('Step By Step', 'Carry Me') and further recordings with Richbourg.

Nina Simone, born Eunice Waymon in Tryon, North Carolina, in 1933 – played organ at her Methodist minister mother's church, having begun playing piano at the age of four. She had formal training at New York's Julliard School of Music, and worked around Philadelphia's clubs until signing with Bethlehem Records in 1959, her debut album yielding a million-selling single – a tortuous, gospel-drenched version of Gershwin's 'I Loves You Porgy'. She moved to Colpix in 1960, recording numerous LPs and scoring two minor hit singles before joining Philips in 1965, when 'Don't Let Me Be Misunderstood' and 'I Put A Spell On You' were R&B hits. She signed with RCA in 1967 and soon returned to the charts with 'Ain't Got No– I Got Life', from *Hair*, and the race anthem 'Young, Gifted And Black'. Still with RCA, her rather intense vocal and small combo jazz style has dropped from commercial favour.

Nancy Sinatra, born on June 8, 1940 in New Jersey, struggled for years to establish her own identity. She made some impact as an actress but signed with her father Frank's Reprise label in 1961, her early recordings doing better in Europe and Japan than in America. This changed following Lee Hazelwood's inspirational idea of tossing aside the all-smiling image for the aggressive, growling singing of 'These Boots Were Made For Walking', a No. 1 in America and England in 1966. Other hits followed, including two Top Tens in 1966, 'How Does That Grab You Darlin'' and 'Sugar Town' and the plum role of the James Bond film title song 'You Only Live Twice'. She had another No. 1 in 1967, with her father, singing 'Something Stupid'. She then teamed up with Lee Hazelwood to make countryish duets like 'Jackson' (1967).

318

Shelby Singleton's career has been the most phenomenal among the white Southern record entrepreneurs who emerged during the Fifties and Sixties. He was working in Shreveport, Louisiana, in the early Fifties as promotion manager for radio KWKH's country artists when he met his wife Margie, a singer whom he placed with Starday and eventually with Mercury. Singleton moved to Mercury in the late Fifties and climaxed a successful selling career by taking over as country product manager. Immediately, he began to find a string of top sellers like the Big Bopper and Johnny Preston.

When Mercury formed Smash Records in Nashville in 1962, Singleton was put in charge. He had by then successfully recorded Clyde McPhatter and Brook Benton, but his forte was making pop hits of country material, and in 1962 he produced Bruce Channel from Louisiana, whose 'Hey Baby' went to No. 1. In the same year he became a vice-president of Mercury, and he went on to sign Jerry Lee Lewis and Charlie Rich. In 1967 Singleton pulled off a financial coup by buying out Sun Records, forming his own Plantation, SSS and Silver Fox labels and coming up with hits in all fields. Jeannie C. Riley, Peggy Scott and Jo Jo Benson, Johnny Adams and Harlow Wilcox all made the national charts, while the original Sun product of Johnny Cash and Jerry Lee Lewis made a fortune all over again.

The Sir Douglas Quintet comprised Doug Sahm (born Nov. 6, 1942 in San Antone, Texas), Francisco Morin (born on Aug. 13, 1946), Harvey Kagan (born on April 18, 1946), Augie Meyer (born on May 31, 1940) and John Perez (born on Nov. 8, 1942). Sahm was a country music child prodigy – he played the steel guitar at the age of six and was a featured player on The Louisiana Hayride by the age of nine – who turned to rock'n'roll in the Fifties, recording solo and with a group, the Knights, for several local Texas labels, before forming the Sir Douglas Quintet in San Antone in 1964. Huey P. Meaux's simple recording of 'She's About A Mover', featuring the insistent organ of Meyer – which was to become the group's trademark – was a Top Twenty hit in 1965 on Tribe. After one more hit, 'The Rains Came' (1966),

Sahm decamped to San Francisco – a journey that was to provide the theme of much of *Mendocino* (Smash, 1969), Sahm's best album to date – where an enlarged group (including George Rains and Martin Fierro) recorded the charmingly uneven *Honky Blues* (Smash, 1968). Sadly, the infectious 'Mendocino', a surprise million-seller in 1969, came too late to rescue the band's commercial potential. Henceforth, despite satisfying and pioneering albums – *Together After Five* (1970) and *1+1+1=4* (1971) – which mixed country music, Mexican rhythms, the blues and rock with Meyer's organ and Sahm's idiosyncratic songwriting – the group's audience was to be a minority one. In 1971, Sahm folded the band to embark on an erratic solo career.

Percy Sledge, born in Leighton, Alabama in 1941, shot to international fame with his first release, 'When A Man Loves A Woman' (Atlantic), in 1966. An intensely performed love ballad, it was the archetype for many southern soul productions of the period and set the pattern for most of his own subsequent releases. Although several were better than the original hit, audiences gradually rejected his simple but compelling style in favour of the complex sounds of the Seventies. Among his greatest performances were 'It Tears Me Up' (1966), 'Out Of Left Field', two album tracks, 'Dark End Of The Street' and 'I Had A Talk With My Woman' (1967), 'Take Time To Know Her', 'Sudden Stop' (1968), 'Any Day Now' (1969), and 'Stop The World Tonight' (1971). In 1974, he made a welcome, if surprising, return to grace with 'I'll Be Your Everything' (Capricorn) which was in the style of his earlier records.

P. F. Sloan had his fling in 1965, the year of the harmonica holder and Dylan caps, as folk singers crammed image-laden syllables into all their rhymes. In Britain this trend was epitomized by Donovan, in America by David Blue and Sloan. Earlier, in partnership with Steve Barri, Sloan had been a writer of surfing songs in Los Angeles. There he had known Lou Adler, who brought him together with Barry

McGuire. Sloan wrote 'Eve Of Destruction', a classic hate-ridden supply of lines for McGuire to angrily spit out. A performer himself, he recorded an album for Adler, *Songs Of Our Times*, of original songs, some written in collaboration with Steve Barri who also produced the album which is *the* imitatory Dylan period piece. *David Blue* was *Highway 61 Revisited*; *Songs Of Our Times* was a mixture of *Bringing It All Back Home* and *Another Side*. Sloan's 'This Morning' borrowed the melody of 'Love Minus Zero – No Limit' and 'What's Exactly The Matter With Me' was Sloan's variation on 'All I Really Wanna Do'. Somehow though, Phil Sloan did it with great personal style though he was heavily slighted by 'hip' people. Jimmy Webb, on *Words And Music*, wrote a song, 'P. F. Sloan', in sympathy with Sloan's plight in the mid-Sixties. Later albums, like *Measure For Pleasure* (Atco), and *Raised On Records* (1972), didn't measure up to earlier expectations. Sloan failed to find a particular niche of his own.

The Small Faces, unlike the Who whose mod image was their manager's creation to exploit the growing cult, *really* were mods. Formed in 1965 by Steve Marriott, born Jan. 30, 1947 (vocals, guitar); Ronnie 'Plonk' Lane, April 1, 1946 (bass); Jimmy Winston (organ) and Kenny Jones, Sept. 16, 1948 (drums), the group grew out of their mutual liking for the mods' favourite music – R&B and soul – and their first single, 'Whatcha Gonna Do About It?' (Decca), a hit in September, 1965 took the riff from Solomon Burke's 'Everybody Needs Somebody To Love'. The Marriott–Lane follow-up, 'I've Got Mine', released when Ian McLagan – born May 12, 1945 – replaced Winston, flopped, but within six months they were chart regulars as 'Hey Girl', 'All Or Nothing' – their only No. 1 and probably their best record – and 'My Mind's Eye' followed each other into the Top Ten. The success of these singles – all Marriott–Lane compositions – linked the group for ever with the Top Ten, and despite a label change and less obviously 'pop' material, they couldn't stop the hits or change their image. Songs like the jokey 'Itchycoo Park' (Immediate, 1967) – their only American Top Twenty record – and 'Lazy Sunday' (Immediate, 1968), recorded for albums and released as singles against the group's wishes, only heightened the problem. After making the brilliant *Ogdens Nut Gone Flake* in 1968, Marriott quit and joined Peter Frampton in Humble Pie. Lane, McLagan and Jones stuck together, turned down offers to back solo performers and eventually teamed up with Rod Stewart and Ron Wood as the Faces.

Jimmy Smith, the award-winning jazz organist, was born on Dec. 8, 1925. His innovatory technique on many small-combo recordings for Blue Note in the late Fifties had already been highly acclaimed, was discovered by a mass audience when he was teamed with an Oliver Nelson-arranged big band in 1962 for his exciting adaptation of Elmer Bernstein's 'Walk On The Wild Side' theme (Verve). It hit the pop charts and catapulted him to stardom. His hit Verve albums – *Hobo Flats, Any Number Can Win, Who's Afraid Of Virginia Woolf*, etc. – followed the earlier less commercial Blue Note releases (*Home Cookin', Back At The Chicken Shack, Prayer Meeting*) which had set the style and pace for all the jazz organists to follow. In 1966, he tried his hand at singing, scoring minor hits with gruff interpretations of the Muddy Waters blues 'Got My Mojo Working' and 'Hoochie Coochie Man'.

O. C. Smith, born in Mansfield, Louisiana, on June 21, 1936, moved to Los Angeles with his family when he was three years old. Upon graduation, he was conscripted into the USAF, and on discharge signed with Cadence Records in New York. Smith's debut disc, 'Lighthouse', was a slow rock'n'roll ballad with dubbed-on seagull cries. He subsequently recorded for Citation, and in 1961 became vocalist with Count Basie's Band after recording under Leiber and Stoller on Big Top and Broadway. Further fame came in 1968 when 'Son Of Hickory Holler's Tramp', a country rockaballad on Columbia, was a transatlantic Top Fifty hit. Ensuing years have brought several further hits, largely sentimental ballads like 'Little Green Apples' and 'Honey'.

322

Soft Machine evolved through various jazz-oriented personnel. The group took their name from William Burroughs' novel after Australian guitarist, Daevid Allen, brought the influence of Terry Riley and tape-loops to the basic Kentish line-up of Kevin Ayers (bass, vocals), Mike Ratledge (keyboards, born 1943) and Robert Wyatt (drums, vocals). They appeared regularly opposite the Pink Floyd in London, participated in a couple of abortive recording sessions in 1967, and presented their music (free improvisation over a rock base, plus vocals) in France with great success. Allen was refused re-entry to Britain because of visa and passport difficulties, and it was as a trio that the band undertook a gruelling American tour with Jimi Hendrix in 1968; they broke up after cutting their first LP for Probe in New York.

When the album proved successful, they re-formed with Hugh Hopper (born 1945, a sympathetic sideman from the days when they called themselves the Wilde Flowers) replacing Ayers on bass. More albums (on CBS/Columbia) followed, featuring Wyatt's songs and Ratledge's angular experiments with time-signatures. Four jazz hornmen were added for a French tour, and saxophonist Elton Dean stayed with them; their now strongly jazz-influenced sound, with fewer Wyatt vocals, represented rock at the London classical music Proms in 1970, and Wyatt left to form Matching Mole in September, 1971, shortly after an appearance at the Newport Jazz Festival. The jazz flavour remained, with Phil Howard then John Marshall on drums, Roy Babbington replacing Hopper, and Karl Jenkins (keyboards, oboe and baritone saxophone) replacing Dean; on the *Six* album, jazz riff structures and Rileyesque pieces rub shoulders. More recently, jazz guitarist and violinist Alan Holdsworth has injected a slightly more urgent feeling into their brilliantly played, carefully structured improvised rock, as on their 1975 Harvest album.

Sonny and Cher. Born Salvatore Bono on Feb. 16, 1935, in Detroit, Sonny Bono worked for a while with his father on the Douglas Aircraft assembly lines in Los Angeles. A songwriter and would-be singer, he touted himself around local record companies in the late Fifties. In 1957, his 'High School Dance' was recorded as the flip of Larry Williams' million-seller, 'Short Fat Fannie' (Specialty). It actually sold well in its own right, reaching No. 46 in America. On the strength of this he became a staff producer at Specialty, also recording as Don Christy (after his first wife, Donna, and his daughter Christy) for that and other labels. After the demise of Specialty in 1959, Bono continued writing and formed his own Dak and Thrush labels, but without success. In 1963, the year he wrote 'Needles And Pins' – a huge hit for the Searchers later – with Jack Nitzsche, he began working for Phil Spector. In 1964, he married his girlfriend, Cher.

Born Cherilyn Sarkasian LaPier on May 20, 1946, of Armenian and Cherokee extraction, Cher took up session singing to earn extra money to pay for acting lessons. At a Ronettes recording session for Phil Spector in 1963 – she can be heard on 'Be My Baby' – Cher and Bono met and under his direction the couple began recording, as Sonny and Cher for the small Vault label and as Caesar and Cleo for Reprise. In 1965, they signed with Atco and recorded the million-seller, 'I Got You Babe'. Written, arranged and produced by Bono, the song owed a lot to Spector and Harold Battiste – who conducted the orchestra on it and subsequent Atco recordings – both of whom Bono had worked under. However, it was Sonny and Cher's image – both sported long hair and 'outrageous' clothes – as much as their sound and the generalized protest content of their lyrics that sustained their careers through 'Baby Don't Go' (a Reprise recording), 'Just You' (1965) and 'The Beat Goes On' (1967) until, in 1967, it became apparent that they were more inclined towards Las Vegas than Haight-Ashbury. 1965 also saw the release of solo records – Sonny had a Top Ten with the ersatz protest song, 'Laugh At Me' (Atco), while Cher began what was to become a stream of hits with a cover of Dylan's 'All I Really Want To Do' (Imperial). After four years of chart failure, the duo resurfaced on Kapp with 'All I Ever Need Is You' (No. 7, 1971) and 'A Cowboy's Work Is Never Done' (No. 8, 1972), both of which were produced by Snuff Garrett. Finally, their Las Vegas lounge-rock image was confirmed when in 1972 they began their own TV show. Early in 1974, the couple separated.

Soul Survivors – Kenneth Jeremiah, Richard Ingui, Charles Ingui (vocals), Paul Venturini (organ), Edward Leonetti (guitar) and Joey Forgione (drums) – was formed in New York in 1966. The vocal trio had previously performed as the Dedications, but changed their name with the arrival of the instrumentalists and gained a contract with Crimson Records. Their first disc, 'Expressway To Your Heart', was a Top Five pop and R&B hit in 1966, but R&B radio airplay ceased when the group was seen to be white, and subsequent Crimson releases were considerably lesser hits. 1974 saw their return to recording, on Philadelphia's TSOP label.

Spanky and Our Gang, fronted by singer Elaine 'Spanky' McFarlane, were Nigel Pickering (guitar, bass), Malcolm Hale (guitar, trombone, vocals), John Seiter (drums), Kenny Hodges (replaced by Geoffrey Myers, bass, vocals) and Lefty Baker (lead guitar, vocals). A pop-folk group in the style of the Mamas and Papas and the British group, the Seekers, they reached the Top Ten with 'Sunday Will Never Be The Same' on Mercury in 1967. It was the first of a string of hits ('Lazy Day', 'Like To Get To Know You') that celebrated the California pop myth of golden sands, beautiful sunshine, lazy days and walks in the park on Sunday mornings. When flower power withered away, they took up the Bonnie and Clyde craze and performed in Thirties gear, but they couldn't keep pace with the acid revolution and finally split in 1969. Like their contemporaries the Turtles, Spanky and Our Gang were basically a fun group.

Phil Spector was born on Dec. 26, 1940, in the Bronx, New York. His father died in 1949, and in 1953, his mother moved the family to California. The Spectors settled in Hollywood, and that year Phil enrolled at Fairfax Junior High School where he met Marshall Leib. In 1957, Spector – who was dabbling in songwriting – and Leib – who played piano – began working together on musical projects. Early in 1958 they roped in another Fairfax pupil, Annette Kleinbard, and formed a high school trio, the Teddy Bears. After graduation in June, they approached Dore Records, one of the many tiny labels scattered across L.A.'s huge sprawl, and were signed to a recording contract. Soon after, Spector wrote a soft teen ballad titled 'To Know Him Is To Love Him' (the title came from the inscription on his father's grave) and recorded it with the Teddy Bears. The record unexpectedly topped both the British and American charts and the Teddy Bears found themselves catapulted into national prominence. Like so many of their contemporaries, however, they were unable to consolidate their initial success and they disbanded in 1959. Spector worked as a part-time stenographer while also studying at UCLA. Late that year, he decided to re-enter the record business.

Still only 18, Spector approached the independent producers, Lester Sill and Lee Hazelwood, who agreed to take him under their wing. They were the immensely successful producers of Duane Eddy whom they recorded in an obscure studio in Phoenix, Arizona, and it was here that Spector was taken to observe and master the mechanics of record production. In 1960, Spector persuaded Sill to send him to New York where he studied under Leiber and Stoller as a studio factotum. Spector was then introduced to Stan Shulman, manager of Ray Peterson who had recorded the classic death-disc, 'Tell Laura I Love Her'. Peterson and Shulman had just formed their own label, Dunes Records, and they hired Spector to produce Peterson's follow-up for the new label. The result was a very professionally made revival of the old folk song 'Corrina, Corrina', which made the American Top Ten in December, 1960 – giving Spector his first hit as a producer.

On the West Coast, Sill allowed Spector an enormous amount of studio time to produce and during 1961, Spector spent close on $100,000 conducting what amounted to his own producer's course in the studio. But Sill's faith in his protégé was justified in December, 1961, when 'I Love How You Love Me', Spector's second production with a trio called the Paris Sisters, made the US Top Five on Sill's

Gregmark label. He also had a Top Ten hit with Curtis Lee's 'Pretty Little Angel Eyes' on Dunes and a Top Fifty hit with Gene Pitney's 'Every Breath I Take', though one of his most interesting early efforts, Johnny Nash's 'Some Of Your Loving', flopped. Late in 1961, Spector and Sill formed the Philles (Phil-Les) label with a distributor in Philadelphia. Spector began recording a girl group, the Crystals, in New York and had two straight hits with 'There's No Other' and 'Uptown'. However, despite these successes Spector grew increasingly dissatisfied with the existing Philles set-up and, late in 1962, he bought out his partners. At 21, Spector had become the youngest ever label chief and now had total control, with only the public to answer to.

He began recording on the West Coast, recruiting a team of session musicians and technicians. They included Leon Russell, Larry Knechtel, Glen Campbell, Hal Blaine, Earl Palmer, Barney Kessel, arranger Jack Nitzsche and engineer Larry Levine. Within two years, this set-up had produced fifteen consecutive hits for Spector and Philles, including the Ronettes' 'Be My Baby', the Crystals' 'Then He Kissed Me' and the Righteous Brothers' 'You've Lost That Lovin' Feeling'. This was the era of the famous 'Wall Of Sound', whose most formally perfect expression was perhaps the unusual *Christmas Gift For You* album (1963) on which all the Philles artists performed traditional seasonal songs. With the Wall Of Sound, Spector brought the art of record production to a new level of sophistication and complexity. Where others would employ a conventional four or five-piece rhythm section, Spector (through overdubbing) used instruments in multiples, skilfully interlocking them to create massive polyphonic sound structures. His was, as he said, 'a Wagnerian approach to rock and roll: little symphonies for the kids'.

As a personality, Spector tended to be sensitive and egocentric and he made enemies as a matter of course. In 1966, a mixture of circumstances led to the boycotting, in America, of a record he considered to be the highpoint of his career, 'River Deep – Mountain High' by Ike and Tina Turner. Its American failure (it was a smash hit in Britain) caused an embittered Spector to withdraw from production and go into seclusion for two years. In 1969, after a shaky resurrection at A&M records, Spector re-emerged as producer of the newly liberated Beatles, John Lennon and George Harrison. He knew better than to swamp them with the excesses of a bygone sound and million-selling albums like *Imagine* and *All Things Must Pass* proved that he was capable of making records which allowed the artist an identity within the overall framework of Spector's idiosyncratic production methods.

Leaving Apple in 1973, he formed Warner-Spector records with Warner Bros. in Los Angeles, while continuing to work with Lennon. Little of note came of the new arrangement and during 1974 rumours were rife of Spector's eccentric behaviour. He suffered a mysterious accident at this time, but returned in 1975 with a new company, Spector International, whose first signings included Dion and Cher. At that point it remained open as to whether Phil Spector would once again make his mark on rock music, or whether in retrospect his finest years would be seen as the Philles period of 1963–6.

The (Detroit) Spinners, formed in 1955, a five-man team (Pervis Jackson, Bobbie Smith, Henry Farnborough, Billy Henderson, George W. Dixon, later replaced by G. C. Cameron) from Detroit signed by ex-Moonglows leader, Harvey Fuqua, to his Tri Phi label, scored with their first release, 'That's What Girls Are Made For' in 1961. Absorbed by the expanding Tamla Corporation, the Detroit Spinners next appeared on Motown – 'I'll Always Love You', 'Truly Yours' (1965–6) – and its subsidiary VIP – 'Message From A Black Man', 'It's A Shame' (1970) – but transferred to Atlantic in 1972. Teamed with Thom Bell, a succession of classy soul ballads ('I'll Be Around', 'Could It Be I'm Falling In Love', 'I'm Coming Home', and 'Then Came You' with Dionne Warwick) have established them as one of the top black groups of the Seventies. In Britain the group have been known as both the Motown Spinners (on Tamla) and the Detroit Spinners (on Atlantic) to avoid confusion with a cabaret folk group.

Dusty Springfield, born Mary O'Brien in Hampstead, London, in April, 1939 had early successes with the folksy Springfields before she went solo in 1963 and appeared regularly in the British Top Twenty over the next four years, reaching No. 1 with the spectacular 'You Don't Have To Say You Love Me', on Philips, in 1966. Despite a later concentration on cabaret work, she still released the occasional gem – notably 'Son Of A Preacher Man' in 1968, now regarded as a soul classic, and 'Who Gets Your Love' (1972). Although her best singles were superbly assured performances of pop melodrama, Dusty's music has been heavily influenced by her love of soul. The brilliant *Dusty In Memphis* (1969, on Atlantic in America), produced by Jerry Wexler, showed her to be among the most funky and mellow of white soul singers, while the later *From Dusty With Love*, a Gamble/Huff/Thom Bell collaboration, is a lovely example of early Seventies soft soul.

Terry Stafford's 1964 ballad hit, 'Suspicion', a cover of an Elvis album cut, was a first-time success for a new label, Crusader. It was followed by 'I'll Touch A Star', but Stafford's career then went into limbo. He re-emerged in 1972 as part of Atlantic Records' country roster, gaining the country hit version of 'Has Anybody Seen Gypsy Rose' and he proved himself a fine country songwriter with 'Amarillo By Morning' and 'Road House Country Singer'.

The Standells' 'Dirty Water' (Tower, 1966) was one of the few truly classic punk-rock records. It contained all the essential elements: Stones riffs, taunting vocals, nasty lyrics, and burning fuzztone guitar. In their two follow-up hits, 'Why Pick On Me' and 'Sometimes Good Guys Don't Wear White', the Standells spoke for young men everywhere who felt like protesting, not for any political cause, but merely against the way they were treated by parents, girls and society. That was the stance the Standells took, and it carried them through four albums and an appearance in the legendary film, *Riot On Sunset Strip*. The Standells (Larry Tamblyn, Tony Valentino, Gary Lane, Dick Dodd – the latter of Mousketeer fame) formed in 1963 and were popular as a swim/twist discotheque group, recording for MGM, Liberty and Vee Jay, before joining the punk-rock movement on Tower Records. Since 1968 they have been without a label, but still perform (minus Dodd and Tamblyn) at local clubs.

Edwin Starr, born Charles Hatcher in Nashville, on Jan. 21, 1942, was educated in Cleveland. Upon graduation, he enlisted in the forces and was posted to Europe where he sang in clubs when off-duty. Discharged, he joined Bill Doggett's combo before forming his own group and joining Detroit's Ric Tic Records, where his solo debut, 'Agent Double O Soul', a storming dance song with a fashionable spy lyric was a Top Thirty hit in 1965. Further hits followed, including 'S.O.S.' and 'Headline News', before Ric Tic was swallowed by Motown. After some lean years, '25 Miles' and 'War' were Top Ten hits in 1969–70. With Motown's move to Hollywood, Starr began writing movie soundtracks. He joined Granite in 1975.

Stax Records. During the rock'n'roll heydays of 1957 a Memphis bank-teller and country fiddler, Jim Stewart, tried producing pop and country records in a garage after being turned down by Sam Phillips at Sun. Stewart's partner in this enterprise was local deejay Fred Bylar, but the crude results were unsuccessful, and Bylar soon pulled out. In 1958, Stewart formed another record company with his sister, Estelle Axton. Estelle mortgaged her house to finance Jim's purchase of an Ampex recording machine, which he installed in a garage with disastrous results – there was far too little space. Jim's barber offered him the use of a large store-room some 25 miles out of Memphis, and it was there that Satellite Records was launched in 1959.

The first release, Satellite 100, was 'Someday' by R&B vocal group, the Veltones. Success was not immediate, and country discs by Charles Heinz also failed to impress. In

1960, Jim found a vacant old theatre in McLemore Street, Memphis, and yet more property was mortgaged to finance the move back to the city. The theatre had a candy store out front, which Stewart turned into a record store, Estelle running it while Jim continued to work in the bank. Then Rufus Thomas, a deejay on local radio station WDIA, walked in with his daughter, Carla, to record ' 'Cause I Love You'. The disc was a regional hit, and was picked up by Atco for national release with a $1,000 advance, which was used to finance a solo disc by Carla, 'Gee Whiz'. This simple teen-ballad was a massive local hit, and again Atlantic took over national release and it became a No. 10 hit in the spring of 1961. The musicians on those sessions would work in the studios in their leisure time, and eventually they came up with an instrumental featuring a repetitive melody figure and horn riff, 'Last Night', which was issued in 1961 and hit the No. 3 spot that summer for the Mar-Keys. At this point, a name-change was necessary to avoid confusion with another company, so Jim and Estelle pooled their surnames and came up with Stax.

Further Mar-Keys releases sold reasonably well in 1961, plus local hits by Barbara Stevens and William Bell. Then, in 1962, Stax had the idea of recording the Mar-Keys without their horn section, letting young black organist, Booker T. Jones, carry the melody. The result was the moody, bubbling 'Green Onions', which took Booker T and the MGs to No. 3 in the charts in August, 1962. Early 1963 saw the arrival of the Volt subsidiary, and the Stax combine committed to Atlantic for national distribution. Volt was soon in the charts with Otis Redding's 'These Arms Of Mine', and both Stax and Volt continued to enjoy a prolific number of chart entries with artists like Rufus Thomas, Sam and Dave, the Astors, Johnnie Taylor, Eddie Floyd and the Staple Singers (the latter providing the label's first chart-topper, in 1972), the Mad Lads, Dramatics and Emotions (Volt). The late Sixties saw the inception of various smaller subsidiaries and distributed labels, including We Produce, KoKo, Respect, Hip, Weiss, Gospel Truth (now Truth) and Enterprise, which was introduced as a jazz outlet, but broke 'pop' when the elaborately arranged monologue/instrumentals of Isaac Hayes who with David Porter had been a prolific writer/ producer for the company, began to sell in vast quantities. His *Shaft* movie theme topped the charts in 1971.

The Atlantic distribution deal expired in 1968, and Stax opted to sell out for a production deal with the Gulf & Western conglomerate. The move was a financial and artistic disaster, and Stax bought themselves out of the contract, courtesy of a loan from Polydor, in return for international licensing rights. In 1972, they entered a distribution deal with Columbia, but despite a host of big-selling records on their various labels, they have encountered financial problems which, in 1975, led to almost all their major artists joining other companies.

Steppenwolf, formed in 1967 from the remnants of the Canadian blues group Sparrow, were John Kay (born April 12, 1944), vocals; Goldy McJohn (May 2, 1945), keyboards; Jerry Edmonton (Oct. 24, 1946), drums; George Biondo (Sept. 3, 1945) bass and Kent Henry, guitar. They were a hard rock band with a fashionable name and singles to match – 'Born To Be Wild', 'Magic Carpet Ride' (1968) and 'Rock Me' (1969) all of which made the American Top Ten. Their first albums, *Steppenwolf* and *Steppenwolf The Second* (Dunhill) saw them straining to mix heavy rock and the blues, while later albums, like *Monster*, saw them content to live out a leather/bike-boy fantasy. Never successful in Britain and decreasingly so in America, the group disbanded in 1972. Kay made two solo albums before re-forming the band in 1974.

Billy Stewart – born in Washington, D.C. on March 24, 1937 – gained his early musical experience in a family gospel group, the Stewart Gospel Singers, moving into the secular field at high school with the Rainbows, following which Billy joined Bo Diddley's band as pianist. His solo debut came in 1956 with the instrumental, 'Billy's Blues' (Chess), followed by 'Billy's Heartaches' (Okeh) in 1957. He resurfaced in 1962 to hit with vocal beat ballad 'Reap What You

Sow' (Chess) introducing his trademark 'word-doubling'. The following seven years brought a string of hits, largely with his own melodic beat ballads, such as 'I Do Love You' and 'Sitting In The Park', peaking in 1966 when his startling, original treatment of Gershwin's 'Summertime', laden with word-doubling, yodelling, scat-singing and a dynamic, jazzy tenor sax solo reached the Top Ten. Subsequent sales dwindled but Billy toured constantly. He was killed on Jan. 17, 1970 with three of his band when their car crashed off a bridge into the River Neuse, North Carolina, travelling between gigs.

Strawberry Alarm Clock, formed in 1967 in Santa Barbara, California, were Mark Weitz, organ; Lee Freeman, vocals; Ed King, lead guitar; Gary Lovetro, bass; George Bunnell, guitar and Randy Seol, drums. Merely another local punk band until they got involved with producer Frank Slay, who was actively searching for groups to record, they did 'Incense and Peppermints' on a local label. Released nationally (Uni, 1967) it shot to No. 1. A blatantly trendy record, it proved more acceptable to the masses than the more genuinely 'underground' records of the time, and the group's followups ('Tomorrow', 'Sit With The Guru') continued in the same vein. They were more significant as a product of their era than for their music.

The Supremes – Diana Ross, born March 26, 1944; Mary Wilson, born March 6, 1944; Florence Ballard, born June 30, 1944; and Barbara Martin, all natives of Detroit except Mississippi-born Mary – grew up together in Detroit's Brewster Housing Project. As the Primettes, they played local clubs as sister group to the Primes (later the Temptations) and recorded for Lupine. In their last year at school, they won a talent contest which brought them to the attention of Berry Gordy at Motown, who insisted they complete their education before signing a contract, which they did in 1960. Their first release, 'Your Heart Belongs To Me', entered the Hot Hundred in August, 1962, soon after which Barbara left the group. Four other discs, including the risqué 'Buttered

Popcorn', were small hits over the next two years, until the summer of 1964 when their seventh release, the husky, swinging 'Where Did Our Love Go', shot to the top of the charts, as did their next four releases, each selling a million on the way, including 'Baby Love' and 'Stop! In The Name Of Love'. Then came failure – 'Nothing But Heartaches' only reached No. 11! They were soon back on top with 'I Hear A Symphony', and 1966 and 1967 brought a further four consecutive chart-toppers, ending with 'The Happening'. 'You Can't Hurry Love' and 'You Keep Me Hangin' On' (1966), both Holland, Dozier and Holland compositions, were probably their finest recordings.

At this point Florence quit, replaced by Cindy Birdsong – born Dec. 15, 1939 – and the next No. 1, 'Love Child', in late 1968, saw the group listed as Diana Ross and the Supremes. A year later, in December, 1969, Diana Ross finally departed for a solo and movie career, and with her went the Supremes' last No. 1 – 'Someday We'll Be Together'. Jean Terrell replaced her as lead singer, but the magic touch was gone – 'Stoned Love' and 'Nathan Jones' were Top Twenty hits, but later discs were comparative flops. In June, 1972, Cindy Birdsong left to concentrate on married life, and was replaced by Lynda Laurence; later Jean Terrell left and was replaced by Shari Payne – born Nov. 14, 1944 – leaving Mary Wilson as the only original Supreme.

Surf Music, a broad trend that dominated grassroots teenage music in America during the years 1962–5, actually breaks down into four distinct phases. It started as early as 1961, with such transitional records as 'Mr Moto' by the Belairs (Felsted), 'Stick Shift' by the Duals (Sue), 'Moondawg' by the Gamblers (World-Pacific), and 'Church Key' by the Revels (Impact), which had what later would be called a surf sound, but no overt connection with surfing. This was instrumental music, a direct outgrowth of the hard rock, sax-and-guitar instrumentals that were 1959's biggest trend (Duane Eddy, Johnny and the Hurricanes, Viscounts, Ventures, Rockateens, Royaltones, etc.), a style taken over by local dance bands everywhere. The catalyst that turned these thousands of instrumental bands into surf bands was Dick Dale, whose Eastern-influenced, staccato guitar sound was designed to simulate the feel of being on a surfboard. Dale's popularity at Southern California dances became immense in 1961 and 1962, and he was soon imitated by a whole wave of surf bands including the Chantays, Rumblers, Tornadoes, Pyramids, Marketts, Surfaris, and Dave Myers and the Surftones.

This music established the audience for surf-related music, in California at least, but it took Brian Wilson and the Beach Boys to give it a commercial cast to which the rest of the world could relate. They pioneered surf lyrics in songs that were about going to the beach, surfing, partying, etc. In short, they had built surfing into a universal metaphor for being young and having fun. Their inspiration, however, had come from Jan and Dean, whose truly pioneering 1959 records such as 'Baby Talk' (Dore) had introduced the California style of falsetto and doo-wop-derived nonsense phrases used heavily in the early Beach Boys records. The vocal surf bands who followed made up the golden age of surf music – though, in reality, there were few real surf music bands besides the Beach Boys and the Surfaris who did vocal music. Most of the 'groups', including the Rip Chords, the Superstocks, the Four Speeds, the Rogues, the Fantastic Baggys, and many others, were the studio-created product of a small circle of writers/producers that included Bruce Johnston, Terry Melcher, Gary Usher, Roger Christian, P. F. Sloan, Steve Barri, and Brian Wilson and Jan Berry. These people, in various permutations, were so prolific they accounted for literally hundreds of surf (and later hot rod) recordings, including most of the acknowledged classics. Other notable acts of the period included the Astronauts and the Trashmen (the leading Midwest surfing bands), the Sunrays ('I Live For The Sun', Tower), and Nashville's Ronny and the Daytonas; plus, of course, Jan and Dean, whose records always reinforced the basic non-seriousness of it all, and in fact were usually parodies of the broadest sort – which didn't hinder their being huge hits.

Late in 1963, the record industry decided that surfing was

out, and hot rod music would be in. Cars and beaches were really part of the same culture and the same metaphor, so there was no problem adapting, as the Beach Boys, Jan and Dean, Dick Dale, the Surfaris, the Hondells, and others all contributed fine car tunes in the same basic instrumental and vocal style. This trend lasted a year or so, by which time the Beach Boys had evolved the music a stage further. Now it wasn't surf music or car music, but simply California music, or summer music. 'Summer Means Fun' by Bruce and Terry (Columbia, 1964) said it all. Summer means fun, California means summer, summer means beaches, beaches mean girls, girls mean cars, cars mean fun, etc., etc. Now 'fun' was the key word, and the world was given an image of California as a promised land where fun and summer were a year-round lifestyle. The Beach Boys' records of 1965–6, such as 'Dance, Dance, Dance', 'Help Me, Rhonda', 'California Girls' and 'Wouldn't It Be Nice' represented California music at its most sublime. The next step took it a little too far, however, as many California musicians began getting mystical and experimenting with drugs. From then on, nothing as literal as surf music, or anything reminiscent of it could be tolerated, although the effects of Scott McKenzie's 'San Francisco (Wear Some Flowers in Your Hair') showed the extent to which the rest of America still believed in California as the promised land.

Though surf music as a commercial trend died in 1966, 1974 saw a brief revival as a reissue of *Surfin' USA* by the Beach Boys became a large hit and several other surfing records made the charts. Surf concerts and surf revival bands have been popular in Southern California since the early Seventies, and surf music seems destined to survive indefinitely as a classic form, at least in its home territory.

Screamin' Lord Sutch, a somewhat legendary figure of the British rock netherworld, was born David Sutch in Harrow, Middlesex in 1942, and formed his group, the Savages, in 1958. His 'wild man' act owed as much to Fifties horror movies as it did to Screamin' Jay Hawkins, and Sutch caused much offence by running amok as Jack the Ripper or being carried onstage in a coffin. Rarely on television and never in the charts (although not for the want of trying) Sutch garnered much of his later publicity by standing for the British Parliament in the 1966 election, and opening a pirate radio station (Radio Sutch). Neither venture was financially rewarding, and he returned to the provincial club circuit from whence he came. His 1970 album, *Lord Sutch And Heavy Friends* (Atlantic), brought together ex-Savages like Nicky Hopkins, with superstars like John Bonham, Jeff Beck and Jimmy Page, but to no avail.

The Swinging Blue Jeans followed the classic Merseybeat route to success, from Liverpool skiffle groups to the Cavern and Hamburg and, finally, an HMV record contract in 1963. Previously known as the Bluegenes, they were made up of Ray Ennis (lead guitar, born May 26, 1942), Ralph Ellis (rhythm, March 8, 1942), Les Braid (bass, Sept. 15, 1941) and Norman Kuhlke (drums, June 17, 1942). Like many of their compatriots, the Blue Jeans were seldom able to reproduce the excitement of their live act on record, and they also suffered from a lack of strong original material. Their only three Top Twenty records were all covers of American songs – Chan Romero's 'Hippy Hippy Shake', Little Richard's 'Good Golly Miss Molly' and Betty Everett's 'You're No Good'. The first two in particular conveyed a certain enthusiasm and excitement which took them into the American charts on Imperial.

Shel Talmy, a onetime classmate of Phil Spector's, arrived in Britain in 1963 with a letter of recommendation from Nik Venet. Impressed, Decca gave him the Bachelors whom he transformed from a harmonica trio into a very successful pop group with songs like 'Charmaine', a Top Ten record in 1963. By 1964, Talmy had set up an independent production deal with Pye which led to his involvement with the Kinks – whose records he produced up to *Something Else* in 1967 – and then the Who, whom he first recorded as a Kinks soundalike.

In 1965, he set up Planet as a wholly independent label. It

337

failed to secure any hits – the closest being Creation with 'Making Time' – and ceased operation in 1967. More recently Talmy has produced less and less. Since 1970, Pentangle and String Driven Thing are the only major groups he has worked with. Instead he moved into film production and, more successfully, into book publishing with Talmy-Franklin.

The Tams originally consisted of Charles Pope (born Aug. 7, 1936), Joseph Pope (Nov. 6, 1933), Robert Lee Smith (March 18, 1936), Floyd Ashton (Aug. 15, 1933), and Horace Kay (April 13, 1934). They spent three years singing around the clubs in their hometown of Atlanta, Georgia, before their first hit, 'Untie Me', in 1962. It was recorded at Rick Hall's Fame Studios in Muscle Shoals for Harry Finfer's Arlen label. Under Bill Lowery's management and with Albert Cottle (born in 1941 in Washington D.C.) replacing Ashton, the Tams became one of the most popular soul acts in the South. Their long run of single hits on ABC-Paramount included 'What Kind Of Fool' (Top Ten in 1963), 'You Lied To Your Daddy', 'It's All Right', 'Hey Girl Don't Bother Me' (which topped the British charts in 1971), 'Silly Little Girl' and 'Be Young, Be Foolish, Be Happy'. The deliciously hoarse lead vocals, the rough gospel harmonies and a series of good songs by white soul brother Ray Whitley made the Tams an admirable foil to the slicker Motown soul of the North. In 1968 the group also recorded for Lowery's 1-2-3 label and for Capitol before rejoining ABC-Paramount in 1971.

Howard Tate, born in Macon, Georgia in 1943, moved to Philadelphia in the Sixties and spent two years singing with Bill Doggett's band. Between 1966 and 1968 he had a number of successes in both pop and R&B charts with gospel-tinged, climactic soul songs including 'Ain't Nobody Home', 'Look At Granny Run Run' and 'Stop'. All were written and produced for Verve by Jerry Ragavoy. Smaller R&B hits – 'These Are The Things That Make Me Know You're Gone' and 'My Soul's Got A Hole In It', followed on Lloyd Price's

Turntable in 1969–70. *Burglar*, the Ragavoy-produced album for Atlantic, was a classic of deep soul and, in 1974, Tate recorded for Epic.

Johnnie Taylor, the son of a church minister, born in Crawfordsville, Arkansas on May 5, 1938, sang in the choir at the age of six, and later enjoyed listening to Sonny Boy Williamson and Junior Parker on the radio. Leaving home at 15, he worked in a Cleveland chemical plant, singing with a gospel group in his spare time, then moved to Chicago and sang with the Five Echoes on Vee Jay. He joined the Soul Stirrers on Sam Cooke's recommendation (replacing him) and in 1961 reverted to secular music with Cooke's Sar label – 'Baby We've Got Love' was a 1963 hit on the Derby subsidiary, sounding very similar to Sam. In 1965, Johnnie signed with Stax, soon to find himself in the R&B charts with 'I Had A Dream', an intense blues ballad. Success grew and 1968 brought a million-seller when 'Who's Making Love', a brash, funky warning of infidelity was a Top Ten hit. Since then he has continued to take his rasping, blues-tinged presentations of Memphis soul into the charts for Stax with songs like 'Jody's Got Your Girl And Gone' (an R&B chart-topper in 1971) and 'Hijackin' Love'. He maintained his consistency with his 1975 album, *Taylored In Silk.*

Little Johnny Taylor, christened Johnny Young and born in Memphis, in 1940, adopted the 'Taylor' tag in the early Sixties, manufacturing a fraternal identity with soul singer Ted Taylor. He began singing gospel with the Mighty Clouds of Joy with whom he recorded for RCA, but later moved to Los Angeles to perform solo blues where he was spotted by producer Cliff Goldsmith and signed to Galaxy Records. Having scored an R&B hit with his debut disc, the follow-up 'Part Time Love', an intense, emotional blues ballad, was a 1963 Top Twenty smash. He recorded steadily for Galaxy throughout the Sixties in a soul-blues idiom before joining Ronn Records, where 'Everybody Knows About My Good Thing', in similar style, was a pop and R&B hit in 1971. He remains active on that label today.

Ted Taylor, brought up amid gospel music in Okmulgee, Oklahoma, and singing in spiritual groups, had his first taste of success in the R&B field as a member of the dual-identity West Coast group, the Cadets/Jacks, scoring as the former with the novelty 'Stranded In The Jungle' (Modern, 1956) and the latter with the ballad 'Why Don't You Write Me' (RPM, 1955). His distinctive, gospel-tinged tenor voice only once graced the pop charts solo, with a bluesy 'Stay Away From My Baby' (Okeh) in 1965. He moved to Atco in 1967, and on to Ronn in 1968, where he has recorded prolifically since scoring occasional R&B hits with storyline blues ballads. Over the years he has recorded for Ebb (1957), Top Rank, Duke, Warwick, Song-Craft, Apt and Dude.

The Temptations, a group subjected to a long and complex list of personnel changes and style variations, initially consisted of Eddie Kendricks (tenor) – born on Dec. 7, 1939 in Birmingham, Alabama; Otis Miles (baritone), subsequently known as Otis Williams – born Oct, 30, 1941 in Texarkana, Texas; Paul Williams – born July 2, 1939 in Birmingham, Alabama; Melvin Franklin, christened David English, by which name he was later known (bass) – born Oct. 12, 1942 in Montgomery, Alabama; and Eldridge Bryant. During the late Fifties they congregated in Detroit and were singing with local groups; Kendricks and Paul Williams with the Primes, Franklin and Miles with the Distants – along with Richard Street, destined to become a Temptation later on. Both groups had the same management, and when the Primes disbanded, Kendricks was drafted into the Distants as lead voice, Williams also joining. By 1959, the Distants had recorded for Northern and scored a local Detroit hit, gaining the interest of Berry Gordy, who signed them in 1960 and renamed them Temptations.

The group's first releases were on Gordy's Miracle label in 1961, basically straight doo-wop vocal style featuring baritone lead with burbling bass back-up. But with the introduction of the Gordy label in 1962 the Temptations were immediately switched to the new label, their first release, 'Dream Come True', becoming a substantial R&B hit that year. Follow-ups were less successful, however, and it was nearly two years later when their fifth Gordy release, 'The Way You Do The Things You Do', an imaginative Smokey Robinson beat ballad juxtaposing Kendricks' tender tenor lead with a tenor sax solo, soared to No. 11 in the national charts. By this time Eldridge Bryant had quit, replaced by baritone David Ruffin, born Jan. 8, 1941 in Meridian, Mississippi. Thus began the group's first 'golden age', lasting some four years with 17 Top Thirty chart hits, six of them Top Ten, including the 1965 chart-topper 'My Girl', another piece of poetry written by Smokey Robinson, and 'Ain't Too Proud To Beg', a pounding anthem led by Ruffin's searing baritone.

Ruffin left the group in 1968 to go solo and was replaced by Dennis Edwards, from Birmingham, Alabama, previously with the Contours. The Temptations, now teamed with writer/producer Norman Whitfield, entered a musically 'heavier' phase, featuring rock-angled performances with complex arrangements. 'Cloud 9' was an immediate 1968 Top Ten hit, and the next two years brought five more hits – four Top Ten, including their 1969 No. 1, 'I Can't Get Next To You'.

The year of great changes was 1971: 'Just My Imagination', a return to the tender ballad style, became their third No. 1 hit and then Kendricks left to go solo. His replacement, Ricky Owens from the Vibrations, proved unsatisfactory, and was himself replaced by Damon Harris after a mere six months. Meanwhile, Paul Williams had to quit on medical grounds (he was later found murdered in his car in Detroit), and ex-Monitor, Richard Street, joined. Success continued, however – 'Papa Was A Rolling Stone' was a 1972 chart-topper, and subsequent discs have sold well, the group having left Whitfield's influence and turned to a mixture of harmony ballads and thumping, discotheque-aimed funk.

Tammi Terrell, christened Tammy Montgomery and the daughter of an actress, was born in Philadelphia in 1946, and attended the University of Pennsylvania to study medicine, majoring in psychology. She appeared in many music talent shows and signed with Scepter Records in 1961, subsequently recording on Wand, Try Me and Checker before joining Motown in 1966. Briefly married to boxer Ernie Terrell, Tammi retained her married name and achieved two solo hits before being teamed with Marvin Gaye in 1967. Nine Top Fifty hits followed over three years, including 'Ain't No Mountain High Enough' and the transatlantic smash 'The Onion Song', before she died on March 16, 1970, following a series of operations on a brain tumour.

Joe Tex, born in Baytown, Texas, on Aug. 8, 1933, became one of the top soul names of the Sixties after ten years of unsuccessful hustling. His early records on King (1955–7) and Ace (1958–60) were an erratic assortment of R&B, derivative rock, and pop novelties. But, influenced by James Brown, by the time he recorded for Anna (1960) he was attracting attention with an athletic stage routine. His first memorable records were two sermonizing responses to other people's hits, 'All I Could Do Was Cry' (Etta James) and 'I'll Never Break Your Heart' (Jerry Butler), and his own 'Baby You're Right' which Brown took into the charts. The following year he cut one single with Brown's band, 'Wicked Woman' (Jalynne), and was then signed by Nashville song publisher, Buddy Killen, who founded Dial records specifically to market Tex and his growing folio of material.

National success eluded them until Atlantic assumed distribution of the label four years later, when 'Hold What You Got' introduced a string of preaching hits ('A Woman Can Change A Man', 'I Want To Do Everything With You', 'A Sweet Woman Like You', 'The Love You Save'), each record a tongue-in-the-cheek slice of homespun philosophy. Acclaimed by Atlantic as the New Boss of the Blues, he began calling himself Soul Brother No. 1 until an onstage duel with James Brown put him firmly in his place. On record, he was alternatively a country singer, soul man, preacher, pop star, or a peculiar mixture of each, so that it was never clear whether Tex took himself or his songs seriously. However, his ingenious and prolific writing talent kept up the run of hits ('The Letter Song', 'Skinny Legs And All', 'Men Are Getting Scarce', 'Buying A Book', 'You're Right Ray Charles') and after a brief 'retirement' to the church at the end of the Sixties he bounced back with 'I Gotcha' (1972), still on Dial, now distributed by Mercury.

Them were an Irish R&B group, formed in 1963 by Van Morrison (vocals), Jackie McAuley (keyboards), Billy Harrison (guitar), Alan Henderson (bass) and Ronnie Milling (drums). After a frenzied residency at Belfast's Maritime Hotel, Them crossed to London and enjoyed two British hits with Morrison's 'Gloria' and the soul-inflected 'Here Comes The Night' (Decca) produced by Bert Berns. The next year – 1966 – 'Gloria', 'Here Comes The Night' and 'Mystic Eyes' all entered the American charts on Parrot, and a tour followed. The group failed to consolidate their success, however, and Morrison returned to Ireland. A series of personnel changes ensued, with singer Ken McDowell and organist Peter Bardens among those passing through. 'Gloria' quickly became a punk-rock standard, while Them's own records remain of interest because of Morrison's adventurous vocals, combining the harshness of black R&B with a budding romanticism, which had its full flowering in his solo career.

Carla Thomas, born in Memphis in 1942, the daughter of Rufus Thomas, deejay/singer turned dancing-fool, gave the Stax studios their first hit with her own teen-dream ballad 'Gee Whiz (Look At His Eyes)', issued nationally on Atlantic in 1961. Noticeably more mature on her response to Sam Cooke, 'I'll Bring It On Home To You' (1962) and other successful releases on Atlantic, she reverted to Stax for duets with her father and solo hits, 'Let Me Be Good To You' and Isaac Hayes' composition 'B-A-B-Y' (1966). Dubbed the 'Memphis Queen', in 1967 she was teamed with 'King' Otis Redding for an album and hit singles 'Tramp' and 'Knock On Wood'. Later recordings with Johnnie Taylor and William Bell were not so popular, and her own hits are getting fewer and farther between, but she is still with the company that she helped to put on the map.

Irma Thomas is an outstanding singer – born in Panchatla, Louisiana, in 1941 – with a glowing reputation but little success to show for it. After local hits on New Orleans labels Bandy, Ron ('Don't Mess With My Man' – 1960), and Minit ('It's Raining' – 1962, 'Ruler Of My Heart' – 1963, the model for Otis Redding's 'Pain In My Heart'), she recorded her most famous performances for Imperial: 'Wish Someone Would Care', 'Anyone Who Knows What Love Is'/'Time Is On My Side' (1964), 'He's My Guy' (1965) and 'Take A Look' (1966). Although she had one more hit, 'Good To Me' (Chess) in 1968, equally fine records on Canyon, Roker, Cotillion, and Fungus have been ignored.

Rufus Thomas began his entertainment career as a comic with the Rabbit Foot Minstrels in 1935. Born in Collierville, Tennessee on March 28, 1917, he spent the war years in a Memphis textile factory by day and entertaining in the evenings, becoming a deejay on radio station WDIA. He began recording in 1949 with jump blues on Star Talent, appearing on Chess in 1951 and scoring an R&B hit on Sun in 1953 with 'Bear Cat'. Still with WDIA, he recorded a duet with daughter Carla, in 1959, for Satellite (soon to be Stax) and has since recorded a substantial quantity of solo hits on Stax with novelty dance songs like 'Walking The Dog' (1963), 'Funky Chicken' (1970), and 'Do The Funky Penguin' (1971).

Thunderclap Newman. Multi-instrumentalist Andy Newman, guitarist Jimmy McCullough and composer/drummer Speedy Keen, had an international hit in the summer of 1969 under the direction of Pete Townshend with 'Something In The Air' (Track). The connections with the Who began when Newman and Townshend met at art school and later Keen wrote 'Armenia City In The Sky' for *The Who Sell Out* album. Thunderclap Newman's album, *Hollywood Dream*, very effectively combined the surreal psychedelia of Keen's lyrics and the precision of McCullough's guitar with Newman's distinctive piano solos. However, recreating the sound live was a problem that not even the introduction of two more musicians – Jim Pitman-Avory and Jack Mc-Cullough – solved. A couple of singles followed, notably the fine 'Accidents', but were unsuccessful and the band split up. Both Andy Newman and Speedy Keen released solo albums – respectively *Rainbow* and *Previous Convictions* – while Jimmy McCullough moved on to Stone The Crows and, later, Wings.

Tiny Tim, prior to being 'discovered', was Herbert Khaury, born in New York in 1925, and for many years a well-known Greenwich Village eccentric. 'Tiny Tim' was one of several pseudonyms he used. In 1968, an appearance in the film *You Are What You Eat* led to his being booked for TV's *Laugh-In.* Accompanying himself on the ukelele, he sang falsetto renditions of some of his favourite Twenties tunes. American viewers were fascinated and snapped up copies of his Reprise single 'Tiptoe Through The Tulips' and album, *God Bless Tiny Tim.* His popularity lasted a good deal longer than the six months predicted by cynics and, at the end of 1969, he temporarily shot back into the public eye when he was married on a TV chat show.

Tomorrow. Keith West and John Wood were once half of the In Crowd – who had a minor British hit in 1965 with 'That's How Strong My Love Is' – and by 1967 were half of Tomorrow with Steve Howe and Twink. They built their reputation in early underground clubs, endorsed by 'My White Bicycle', a song about Dutch provos, produced by Pete Townshend. Halfway through their album, producer Mark Wirtz involved West in 'An Excerpt From A Teenage Opera'; originally to be a Keith Tomorrow release, it came out as by Keith West. Ironically, it marked the beginning of the end for the group. A second single, 'Revolution', and the album followed, though never the rest of the opera except a follow-up, 'Sam'. Tomorrow folded in 1968, Twink joining the Pretty Things and the Fairies and Steve Howe, whose guitar pyrotechnics shone in Tomorrow, eventually found fame with Yes in February, 1970. Keith West re-emerged in 1975 with 'Moonrider'.

The Toys were Barbara Harris, born in Elizabeth City, North Carolina on August 18, 1945; Barbara Parritt, born Wilmington, North Carolina, on Oct. 1, 1944; and June Monteiro, born New York, July 1, 1946. They began singing together at high school in Jamaica, New York, and contacted Vince Marc at Genius Inc. Records. He had a Bach melody arranged for their first session, and 'Lovers Concerto' became a 1965 million-seller on DynoVoice. Their novel style soon palled, however, and follow-ups were less successful. A 1968 Musicor disc was a small R&B hit, but the group soon disbanded.

Traffic, formed in 1967 after the break-up of the original Spencer Davis Group, comprised Stevie Winwood, vocals, guitars and keyboards (born on May 12, 1948); Dave Mason, vocals and guitars (May 10, 1945); Jim Capaldi, vocals and drums (Feb. 8, 1944) – all of whom had played together in the Birmingham-based group, Deep Feeling – and Chris Wood, flute and sax (June 24, 1944) from Locomotive. To 'get things together', the group took off to the famous Berkshire cottage in Aston Tirrold and only emerged some months later for the release of the wistful 'Paper Sun', their first single, highlighted by Mason's sitar runs, and which climbed into the Top Five in the summer of 1967. 'Hole In My Shoe', based on a dream of Mason's, reached No. 2 in the charts later that year, but resulted in cracks appearing in the band's set-up; Mason's more commercial tunes lent themselves to releases as singles – something which seemed to upset the others – and when the first album, *Mr Fantasy* (Island, 1967) was released it was clear that the songs fell into two distinct categories – Mason's and the others.

After 'Here We Go Round The Mulberry Bush' – their last Top Ten single – Mason split, but returned six months later. In his next brief stay, they got their second album together, *Traffic* (1968), which saw them expanding skilfully on their R&B roots. However, Mason's decision to leave again in October, 1968, resulted in the whole band disintegrating six months later. *Last Exit* (1969), a part live, part studio album released the following summer, was quite clearly a rushed job and didn't reflect the band's true potential.

After a brief spell with Blind Faith, Winwood started work on a solo album in January, 1970, tentatively titled *Mad Shadows*, but it wasn't long before Capaldi and Wood had rejoined him to bring Traffic back into existence once more. The album became *John Barleycorn Must Die* and proved the strength of the Winwood/Capaldi/Wood triumvirate – fusing R&B, rock, jazz and traditional folk into a style that was uniquely theirs. Playing live as a trio was limiting for Winwood and later that year ex-Family/Blind Faith bassist, Rick Grech, was called in, followed six months later by drummer Jim Gordon, conga-player Reebop Kwaku-Baah and the return of Dave Mason. They only played six gigs with this line-up but the live *Welcome To The Canteen* (1971) is a remarkable testimony of just how good they were.

Their next studio album, *The Low Spark Of High Heeled Boys*, released while they were touring America in December, 1971, featured both Grech and Gordon – yet when they returned to England both had, somewhat mysteriously, left. With Winwood ill with peritonitis for the first part of 1972, the band rested. Capaldi went to Muscle Shoals to make a solo album, *Oh How We Danced*, and established connections with David Hood and Roger Hawkins who were to become the rhythm section of the new Traffic. They played on the critically received *Shoot Out At The Fantasy Factory* (recorded in Jamaica in 1972) and on the following year's tour Traffic was augmented by another Shoalsman, Barry Beckett, on keyboards. This was probably the most impressive version of Traffic on stage and the magnificent *On The Road*, recorded in Germany in 1973, restored everybody's faith in the band; though the Muscle Shoals section left after the tour and returned to the States.

The remaining four went into their annual period of hibernation for the rest of 1973 to emerge again the following year for an English tour. They had a new member in Rosko Gee from Gonzales – a fluid bassist who featured prominently on *When The Eagle Flies* (1974), an album that saw Winwood almost abandon his guitar totally for piano, organ and synthesizer. With the departure of Reebop during the tour, the band returned to its original state as a four-piece. Traffic's long – and traumatic – history produced some of Britain's finest rock music, displaying an honesty and integrity which certainly equals that of their much vaunted West Coast contemporaries. In 1975 the band finally dissolved as Capaldi's solo career was launched.

The Tremeloes were Brian Poole's backing group, but when he left to go solo after a series of hits in 1963 and 1964, including the No. 1 'Do You Love Me?' (Decca), the rather homely Rick Westwood (lead, born in 1943), Alan Blakely (rhythm, born in 1942) and Dave Munden (drums, born in 1943) brought in young, handsome Len 'Chip' Hawkes (born in 1946) as bass guitarist and front man. As Poole's career spiralled from singing to butchery, the 'Trems' notched up seven Top Ten hits between 1967 and 1970, typified by the bright harmonies and optimism of 'Silence Is Golden' (a British No. 1) and 'Even The Bad Times Are Good' on CBS in 1967. Their popularity waned in the Seventies and Westwood spent two years out of the group, rejoining when a car accident forced Hawkes to quit at the end of 1974. Blakely left in January, 1975, leaving Aaron Woolley and Bob Benham alongside the two originals.

The Troggs came from Andover, in Hampshire. Originally the line-up was Reg Presley, vocals (born June 12, 1943); Chris Britton, guitar (June 21, 1945); Pete Staples, bass (May 3, 1944) and Ronnie Bond, drums (May 4, 1943); Presley and Bond are still in the group. Signed by manager/label owner Larry Page in 1966, they had a worldwide hit with Chip Taylor's 'Wild Thing'. Subsequent hits, which continued until 1968, were written by Presley, with the exception of Taylor's 'I Can't Let Go'. The Troggs' musical limitations were bolstered by good songwriting and production, and a streak of amusing suggestiveness runs through most of their material: 'I Can't Control Myself', 'Give It To Me' and 'Love Is All Around'. Leaving Page's management and the hit parade behind, the group survived 'the progressive revolution' playing cabaret dates. In the early Seventies, they began to get college bookings and critical notice again; a 'Trogg revival' was rumoured. In 1974 the band (who were joined by present bass-player Tony Murray in 1969, but who have had several lead guitarists) were reunited with Larry Page, but they've yet to reappear in the charts, even with their highly original version of 'Good Vibrations'.

Doris Troy, born Doris Payne in New York in 1937, the daughter of a Baptist preacher, sang in the church choir and subsequently with various gospel groups, later turning to jazz with a trio, the Halos. An established songwriter – she wrote Dee Clark's 'How About That' hit – Doris was spotted by James Brown while working as an usherette at the Apollo Theatre, and after recording in a Jay and Dee duo, signed with Atlantic in 1963 when the staccato, shuffling 'Just One Look' was a Top Ten hit. Subsequent discs for Atlantic, Capitol and Calla were less successful, and in 1969 Doris settled in England, becoming a prolific session singer and recording for Apple, People and Polydor.

Tommy Tucker, born Robert Higgenbotham in Springfield, Ohio, on March 5, 1939, began his career in the jazz field, soon forming his own band the Dusters, who recorded for Arc and Hudson in 1956. This was short-lived and he later played piano with jazz multi-instrumentalist Roland Kirk. After meeting Titus Turner, Tommy entered the R&B field on Atco in 1961 as Tee Tucker, and in 1963 recorded 'High Heel Sneakers' in simple, down-home style at Herb Abramson's A-1 Studio. It was leased to Checker and became a 1964 Top Twenty hit. Several subsequent discs in similar style failed to click, and after reviving 'That's Life' on Festival in 1966, Tommy returned to being simply a club pianist, though he visited Europe in 1975 as part of a 'Blues Legends' tour. 'High Heel Sneakers' is now an R&B standard that has been covered by everyone from the Rolling Stones to Tom Jones.

Ike and Tina Turner evolved one of the most dramatically successful rock stage acts of the Seventies after a career embracing most forms of blues and soul. Ike Turner was born in Clarksdale, Mississippi, deep in the Delta cotton belt, on Nov. 5, 1931. A disc-jockeying job at station WROX led to the formation of the Kings Of Rhythm, a band of local musicians led by Turner. Their first record was 'Rocket 88' (Chess, 1951), sung by Jackie Brenston, a disc which is often cited as the first rock'n'roll recording.

Next, he became a talent scout in the southern states for Modern Records, fixing sessions by Bobby Bland, B. B. King, Howlin' Wolf and others. With the arrival of rock'n' roll in 1956, Turner moved north to St Louis, recording and playing in clubs with the Kings Of Rhythm. With them he evolved a revue format featuring various singers, while playing piano and guitar himself.

He found the focal point for the act in Annie Mae Bullock, who was born on Nov. 26, 1938 in Brownsville, Tennessee, and moved to Knoxville, where she sang in the choir of her father's church. She was known at first as Little Ann, but her first record, 'A Fool In Love', was credited to Ike and Tina Turner. Released on Sue in 1960, it reached No. 2 in the R&B charts, No. 27 in the pop charts and eventually sold a million. That success led to the formation of the Ikettes (of which P. P. Arnold, Merry Clayton and Bonnie Bramlett have been members at one time) to back Tina, and the construction of the stage act which has persisted until the present day, in its essential features.

Like many black artists, Ike Turner has proved himself able to adapt to changing moods in both black and white audiences while still producing worthwhile music on many of the thirty-odd albums he and Tina have recorded for Sue, Warner Bros., Philles, Blue Thumb and United Artists amongst others. Perhaps surprisingly, they have had few major hits. 'It's Gonna Work Out Fine' (Sue, 1961), a fiery blues classic, was the most successful until their Top Ten version of 'Proud Mary' (Liberty, 1971), the funky, futuristic 'Nutbush City Limits' (United Artists, 1973) and 'Sweet Rhode Island Red' (1974). In 1966, Ike Turner relinquished production control to Phil Spector for the remarkable 'River Deep – Mountain High'. It reached only No. 88 in America but was a Top Three record in Britain.

By the Seventies, Ike had his own studios, Bolic, and recorded a highly personal solo album, *Blues Roots* (United Artists, 1971), which suggested that the increasingly spectacular and regimented stage act, centred on Tina's flaunting sexuality, might be less than satisfying for him.

The Turtles' records consistently echoed the old California surf sound while taking in contemporary influences – big-band arrangements, vast well-organized productions in the post-Spector style – and in America between 1966 and 1968 they had hit after hit ('Happy Together' and 'She'd Rather Be With Me' among them). They were labelled folk-rock artists because of their pop treatment of the Dylan song, 'It Ain't Me Babe' (on White Whale), but what eventually came to distinguish the Turtles was their character as performers: they looked odd, like a spruced-up Lovin' Spoonful, keeping the grins and funny hairdos but wearing suits. Although the emphasis in their act was on comedy, they became heavily involved in the flower power scene and never quite survived it. Leaving the group in 1969, arch-lunatics Howard Kaylan (born June 22, 1945) and Mark Volman (born April 19, 1944) joined Frank Zappa's Mothers of Invention but soon left to form their own act, Phlorescent Leech (Flo) and Eddie. Lead guitarist Al Nichol (born March 31, 1945) and drummer John Barbata started doing session work.

The Tymes – George Hilliard, Donald Banks (from Franklin, Virginia), George Williams, Albert Berry and Norman Burnett (from Philadelphia) – was formed in 1959. 'So Much In Love', their No. 1 hit on Parkway in 1963, heralded the sweet soul boom of the Seventies. They followed it with other hits in the same style, including 'Wonderful Wonderful', 'Somewhere' (both Top Twenty) and 'To Each His Own'. After less successful records for Winchester (a label they owned with Leon Huff) and MGM, the Tymes returned to the charts on Columbia with 'People' in 1968. Billy Jackson's productions of 'You Little Trustmaker' and 'Ms Grace' (a

British No. 1) kept the same personnel (minus Hilliard) in the charts on RCA-Victor during the mid-Seventies.

The United States of America were Joseph Byrd, electronic music, keyboards; Dorothy Moskovitz, vocals; Gordon Marron, electric violin, ring modulator; Rand Forbes, bass; Craig Woodson, electric drums, percussion – a collection of experimental California musicians. They cut their only album, *United States Of America*, for Columbia in 1968, a pioneering effort rarely surpassed in harmonizing electronics and rock. It was also an intelligent satire on contemporary rock, with an air of decadence. 'The American Metaphysical Circus' parodied *Sergeant Pepper* and 'Garden Of Earthly Delights', with Dorothy Moskovitz sounding like Grace Slick, suggested the Airplane's 'White Rabbit'. Byrd later indulged in self-parody, with the Field Hippies, on a 1969 album *The American Metaphysical Circus* (Columbia). Dorothy Moskovitz later played with Country Joe's All Star Band.

Gary Usher made his first mark as a songwriter in partnership with deejay Roger Christian from Los Angeles Radio KFWB. They churned out a string of surfing and hot rod hits, 'Hot Rod High', 'You're Gonna Ride With Me' and most of the Hondells' hits on Mercury. Mike Curb produced them and Usher did the arrangements before cutting his producing teeth with the Surfaris. Usher also wrote songs with Brian Wilson, such as 'In My Room' and others recorded by the Hondells and the Surfaris. Later he became a house producer with Columbia and his credits include Chad and Jeremy's *Of Cabbages And Kings* and *The Ark*, *Gene Clark*, the Millennium, the Peanut Butter Conspiracy and the Byrds on their classic albums *Younger Than Yesterday* and *Notorious Byrd Brothers* in which his sympathetic role was crucial. He also produced the Byrds' *Sweetheart Of The Rodeo*. With help in the arrangements and vocals from Curt Boetcher, and support from Terry Melcher and Bruce Johnston, he was the brains behind Sagittarius, a highly polished harmony and studio group, noted for their orchestrations. Columbia released *Present Tense* by Sagittarius, and from it took the 1967 hit 'My World Fell Down'. Their second album *Blue Marble* was released on Usher's own Together Records, which he established in March, 1969, with Curt Boetcher and Keith Olsen as an 'artist-oriented label'. Certainly it released an impressive array of material in its brief history, including the Byrds' *Preflyte, The Hillmen, Early L.A.* and other archive material.

Dino Valenti (born Oct. 7, 1943), a one-time carnival artist, became a leading light in Greenwich Village at the turn of the Sixties. Disillusioned, he split to Los Angeles – almost enticing Roger McGuinn away from the pre-flight Byrds – and then to the Bay area. About to unite with the foundling Quicksilver in 1964, he was arrested on an amphetamine charge. He sold some songs to Frank Werber to raise money, among them the 1967 anthem 'Get Together', though not 'Hey Joe', wrongly attributed to Valenti (whose pseudonym was Chester Powers) instead of folkie Billy Roberts. Usually over-pedantic about releasing material, he cut a strange, romantic album for Epic in 1968, and after an abortive group with Gary Duncan (the Outlaws) he stayed with Duncan on his return to Quicksilver in February, 1970. A powerful performer, he contributed many ideas to the later Quicksilver (*Just For Love*), though diehard Quicksilver fans resented his influence.

Vanilla Fudge were contemporaries of the Rascals and Vagrants in Long Island and New Jersey in the mid-Sixties (then as the Pigeons) with their brand of organ-based white funk. By 1967, they became Vanilla Fudge – Mark Stein, piano, organ (born 1947); Vince Martell, guitar (born Nov. 11, 1945); Tim Bogert, bass (born 1944); Carmine Appice, drums (born Dec. 15, 1946). They added semi-gospel harmonies and a familiar pop/soul repertoire which they immediately disguised. 'You Keep Me Hanging On' was a minor hit in Britain in 1967, and a year later, in America. The essence of their music, 'heaviness', caught on but with guitars replacing the Fudge's organ domination. They wallowed in pretentiousness through tedious, overambitious albums

353

before disbanding in 1970. Bogert and Appice formed Cactus, later joining Jeff Beck, while Stein formed the little-known and short-lived Boomerang.

The Velvet Underground consisted originally of Lou Reed, vocals (born March 2, 1944, New York); John Cale, viola, bass, keyboards (born Dec. 5, 1940); Sterling Morrison, guitar, and Maureen Tucker, bass. Reed came from Long Island, had dropped out of college to write songs and hustle music deals. Cale came from Wales, studied contemporary music in London, and reached America on a Leonard Bernstein fellowship. Reed and Cale met in New York in 1964 and began playing in various clubs. They impressed Andy Warhol and his clan, who decided that this was the right group to feature in the Exploding Plastic Inevitable mixed media show which Warhol staged in New York in 1966, and which then toured the States and Canada. Nico (Christa Päffgen from Cologne, West Germany), another Warhol protégée who had appeared in several of his films, was introduced to the Velvets as a *chanteuse*.

Warhol's newsworthiness helped the group to a contract with MGM, where their first album utilized a garish Warhol screenprint of a banana on the cover, and incorporated his name into the title: *The Velvet Underground And Nico Produced By Andy Warhol* (1967). However, Warhol did not exercise a record producer's usual control over their sound. This first album was dominated by Reed's fascination with elements of city life normally excluded from pop songs – an up-tempo account of the problems of heroin scoring ('I'm Waiting For The Man'), a haunting anthem of paranoia ('Sunday Morning') and a powerful amoral vignette of sado-masochistic obsessions ('Venus In Furs'). But Reed's interests were tempered by a true pop sensibility, and a sharp eye for authentic *demi-monde* detail. The sound of that first album drew additional power from Nico's deadpan, world-weary enunciation, and Cale's innovatory contributions on viola and bass, adding to rock the repetitive layers of sound that he had created with avant-garde composer LaMonte Young. The album was a powerful, original statement, and, of course, its subject matter rendered it unplayable on almost every American radio station.

In 1967, Nico left the group to pursue her own career, and the Velvet Underground parted company with Warhol's Factory and its financial support. Cale and Reed no longer totally agreed about musical policy, and out of the tensions surrounding the group in late 1967, they created their second album, *White Light/White Heat*. It lacked the pop elements of their first, its sound was aggressively harsh. This was not simply a result of Cale's avant-garde preoccupations swamping Reed's songs, for it was Reed who played the radical, screaming feedback guitar solos. Two tracks on the album stood out. 'The Gift' consisted of Cale's dry, Welsh voice reading aloud an elegantly macabre short story by Reed. And next to Cale's voice is set the murky, muddled instrumental sound of the band warming up. It remains a truly bizarre creation. 'Sister Ray' is a 17-minute rambling, deranged narrative about some sailors visiting a drag queen and being interrupted by the police, in which the words are frequently swamped by the maelstrom of music, and Cale plays some frighteningly unorthodox organ solos. Reed later commented he was trying to create the rock'n'roll equivalent of Ornette Coleman. In 1968, Cale quit to pursue his own career; he was replaced by Doug Yule on bass, guitar, and keyboards. Reed had written all the lyrics of the first two albums, and from this point the group became an undisputed vehicle for his vision.

Their third album, *The Velvet Underground* (1969), was again in contrast to its predecessor. Although there was a coherent plot with subtle implications, the sound remained delightfully light and tuneful: pure pop with heavy contents. The theme was a girl's search for significance through nihilism ('Candy Says'), religion ('Jesus'), adultery ('Pale Blue Eyes'), to some sort of moral liberation ('I'm Set Free'), followed by a relapse into schizoid incoherence ('The Murder Mystery') and ending with a desperately cheerful song of loneliness ('Afterhours') beautifully sung by Mo Tucker, the group's drummer. The final song seemed to point straight back to the opener, making the album a song cycle. But though the album was pop in sound, it was too subtle to grab popular attention, and for Velvets fans who thought the group were committed to depravity, songs about Jesus and liberation sounded like a sell-out. It was only with their final album, *Loaded* (Atlantic, 1970), that the group approached making a popular impact. This was a work of melodic rock, celebrating city kids with warmth and affection, qualities for which the Velvet Underground had not previously been famous. Particularly striking were 'Rock & Roll', an anthem to AM radio, 'Sweet Nuthin' ', an account of city kids able to live on nothing at all, which was both a survival guide and a set of existential values, and 'Sweet Jane', the archetypal, resilient city girl. But before *Loaded* was released, Reed abruptly quit in the summer of 1970, just when they appeared to be on the verge of achieving popular recognition. For a time, Doug Yule kept the group going and released another album, *Squeeze* (Polydor, 1970), but without Reed they had really ceased to exist. A poorly recorded live album from Max's Kansas City in the Velvet Underground's heyday was released by Atlantic in 1972.

They were probably the most influential New York group of the late Sixties, spawning a series of performers bent on outrageous statement and appearance. But popular recognition of a kind only came to Lou Reed and John Cale in the mid-Seventies, as solo artists.

Nik Venet, an ubiquitous figure on the Los Angeles recording scene, has worked with literally hundreds of artists since his arrival in the late Fifties. As a would-be teen idol, he released several singles but soon moved on to songwriting and production, often in collaboration with his brother Steve, whose own productions probably number in the hundreds. Venet's first big success was with the Beach Boys, whose early records he produced for Capitol – though according to the Beach Boys his involvement was minimal. His real talent was for making deals, getting musicians together for sessions, spotting potential talent, and getting the products out on wax. Through a production deal with Capitol, he brought many acts to that label in the mid-Sixties including the Stone Poneys, Fred Neil, Lothar and the Hand People, the Knack, Hedge and Donna, and many others less memorable. He favoured singles deals, and has been credited by a great many musicians as providing their first exposure to the recording business. In the late Sixties he operated an independent production company, supplying masters to a variety of labels. In 1972, Venet joined United Artists Records as head of A&R, remaining for a year, during which time he concentrated on producing Dory Previn, which has continued to be his major activity since then, although he has also been working with a number of acoustic singer/songwriters, notably John Stewart.

Mike Vernon, born in Harrow on Nov. 20, 1944, began collecting rock'n'roll records at school, which led to an interest in R&B, blues and jazz. In February, 1964, he teamed-up with fellow R&B fanatic, Neil Slaven, to edit and publish the authoritative *R&B Monthly* and later became a production assistant at Decca, working on records by such artists as Kenneth McKellar, Mantovani and Benny Hill. At the same time he launched the privately distributed Purdah record label – later Blue Horizon – issuing the first recordings by John Mayall and Eric Clapton, and Savoy Brown. Vernon soon had the London R&B scene tied-up, producing *John Mayall's Bluesbreakers With Eric Clapton* and *A Hard Road*, featuring Peter Green. He also worked on three Chicken Shack albums, plus singles and albums by Ten Years After, David Bowie, Duster Bennett, T. S. McPhee and Champion Jack Dupree. Then came Fleetwood Mac's 'Albatross', a million-seller on Blue Horizon in 1968. Vernon left Decca, in 1969, to concentrate fully on his fledgeling label, now distributed by CBS. Two years later he switched outlets to Polydor, for whom as an independent producer he scored heavily with both Focus' album *Moving Waves* and single, 'Hocus Pocus'. At the same time Blue Horizon fostered British talent including Jellybread (featuring Pete Wingfield) and co-ordinated a series of prestigious blues items by B. B. King, Lightnin' Slim, Otis Rush and others until the label folded. He came back in 1973, with the black

357

soul outfit, Bloodstone, with whom he cut four albums and a million-selling single, 'Natural High'. Vernon now works exclusively with black acts like Freddie King, Jimmy Witherspoon, and his new discovery, the Jades. He also runs his own recording studio at Chipping Norton.

The Vibrations were formed in 1959 by Don Bradley (born in St Louis on Aug. 7, 1936), Dave Govan (Los Angeles, Aug. 2, 1940), Carl Fisher (Quardon, Texas, Dec. 27, 1939), Ricky Owens (St Louis, April 24, 1939) and James Johnson (Brooklyn, New York, Sept. 13, 1939). In 1956, Johnson, Fisher, Govan and Carver Bunkum had hit the Top Thirty as the Jayhawks with the original version of 'Stranded In The Jungle'. Owens, who replaced Bunkum, came from the Sixteens. In 1961, the group had two hits: 'The Watusi' on Checker under their own name and 'Peanut Butter' on Arvee as the Marathons. H. B. Barnum had persuaded them to cut the latter record, but the Chess brothers sued successfully and 'Peanut Butter' was also released on their Argo label. The Vibrations' later successes included the original version of 'My Girl Sloopy' on Atlantic (Top Thirty in 1964) and several hits on Okeh between 1965 and 1968, including 'Misty' and 'Love In Them There Hills'. They have also recorded for Bet, Epic, Amy, Neptune and A&M.

Bobby Vinton, born in Canonsburg, Pennsylvania on April 16, 1935, helped form his high-school big band, which built a substantial following around Pittsburgh with Vinton playing clarinet and doubling on various instruments. Leaving the Army in 1961, he went back on the road as a band leader, releasing two albums for Epic, *Dancing At The Hop* and *Bobby Vinton Plays For His Li'l Darlin's*. His next recordings in February, 1962, were as a singer, among them 'Roses Are Red' which launched a new career. It was a No. 1 in America, and his only British hit. He notched up further usually schlock ballads (e.g. 'Blue Velvet', 'Mr Lonely').

The Walker Brothers – Scott Engel, vocals, bass (born 1944); John Maus, vocals, guitar (born 1943); Gary Leeds, vocals, drums (born 1944) – at their peak rivalled even the Beatles in Britain as the subjects of mass idolization. Jack Good suggested they try the British market after they had made little impact in their home country, America. Scott and John had recorded individually and together – John usually preferring the surname Stewart – before joining ex-Jet Powers (P. J. Proby) drummer Gary Leeds in 1964. The following year they struck the formula that propelled them to success, 'Love Her', with Scott and John pitting their voices in dramatic style against Spectoresque arrangements. Only a minor hit, it set them up for future international hits in 1965–6 ('Make It Easy On Yourself', 'The Sun Ain't Gonna Shine Any More'). Their first album *Take It Easy* (Philips) featured fine varied material, especially a version of 'Love Minus Zero'. They never totally cracked the American market, and after 'Sun' found their emotional and sexual impact wearing thin. Scott Walker began to take his moody image too seriously, and Gary Leeds' frustration reared forth in a terrible version of 'You Don't Love Me'. They split after the third album *Images*, Scott predictably doing well as a solo act. In 1975 they re-formed and recorded a fine version of Tom Rush's classic 'No Regrets'.

Junior Walker and the All-Stars. Walker was born Autrey deWalt in Blythesville, Arkansas in 1942, and picked up his stage name from his stepfather. Early influences were Illinois Jacquet and Earl Bostic, and his punchy, driving alto-sax style reflects the latter's approach. He formed a band around 1961, which was heard by Johnny Bristol, recommended to Harvey Fuqua in Detroit, and signed by him to his Harvey label, soon to be incorporated in the Motown organization. The shifting line-up of Junior and the All-Stars included Willie Woods, guitar; Vic Thomas, organ; James Graves, guitar and Junior on sax/vocal duties. They had three discs on Harvey, in 1962, and one on Soul, in 1964, before 'Shotgun' – a pounding dance tune, largely instrumental with shouted lyrics – became a No. 2 hit in 1965. Some 20 subsequent discs have climbed the American Hot Hundred, mainly crisp, rousing dance tunes, though latterly mellower ballads like 'These Eyes' and 'Way Back Home', augmented with strings, have pervaded the group's repertoire.

Warner Bros. Records, founded in 1958, represented the second venture into records by the famous film empire. In 1930, the three Warner brothers had bought Brunswick Records, a venture that ended in disaster a year later. Warner Bros. Records was run by former vice-president of Capitol, Jim Conklin. His first signings were middle-of-the-road performers like Henry Mancini and Buddy Cole. The new label's chart success began with a spin-off from a television series produced by the parent company: 'Kookie, Kookie Lend Me Your Comb', by Edd Byrnes, star of *77 Sunset Strip*. By 1960, comedian Bob Newhart and the Everly Brothers gave the company its first major album and singles hits. Two years later Warners moved into the growing folk field by signing Peter, Paul and Mary.

They were also extending their empire to other labels. Frank Sinatra's Reprise company was brought under the Warners umbrella in 1964, and in the next year two small West Coast labels, Valiant and Autumn, were acquired. The deal brought Warners Harpers Bizarre and the Beau Brummels, together with their producer, Lenny Waronker. He became a house producer, as did Ted Templeman, drummer and singer with Harpers Bizarre. In 1966, Warners signed their San Francisco group, the Grateful Dead, and had novelty hits with the Marketts and Napoleon XIV. In the following year, Warner/Reprise was itself taken over by Seven Arts, which then acquired the Atlantic group of labels. The Warners roster grew with artists like Van Dyke Parks, Van Morrison, Mason Williams and Alice Cooper, from Frank Zappa's Straight label. The take-over process continued in 1969 when the giant Kinney corporation, with interests in virtually every industrial area, purchased the Warner Bros.-Seven Arts group, including the WB film company and Atlantic.

Dionne Warwick was a session singer who became, in the mid-Sixties, the outstanding exponent of the ballads of Burt

Bacharach and Hal David. Born in East Orange, New Jersey on Dec. 12, 1941, she studied at Hart College of Music in Hartford, Connecticut, before joining Cissie Houston as backing vocalists on records by Garnet Mimms, the Drifters and others.

Her first solo disc was Bacharach's haunting 'Don't Make Me Over', which reached No. 21 on Scepter in 1962. Warwick's perfect phrasing was well suited to the almost operatic quality of later Bacharach classics, including 'Anyone Who Had A Heart' (No. 8 in 1963) and 'Walk On By' (No. 6 in 1964). Her ability was emphasized by the far cruder reading given to the former in Britain by Cilla Black.

Virtually every Dionne Warwick record of the Sixties entered the charts, though only a few were Top Ten hits. Like her mentors' songwriting, her work veered away from soul-tinged pop towards a less exciting cabaret style, on numbers like 'I Say A Little Prayer' (No. 4 in 1967) and 'I'll Never Fall In Love Again' (No. 6 in 1969). Nevertheless, the breathy, faultless vocals were highly influential, particularly in Britain where Dusty Springfield's outstanding style was indebted to Warwick's singing.

Moving from Scepter to Warner Bros. in 1971, she re-emphasized the soulful component of her approach on *Just Being Myself* (1973), with compositions by Brian Holland and Lamont Dozier. Later tracks were produced by Jerry Ragavoy while *Track Of The Cat* (1975) was produced by Thom Bell.

Muddy Waters, the king of Chicago blues, was born McKinley Morganfield on April 4, 1915, in Rolling Fork, Mississippi. He moved to Clarksdale at an early age where he grew up working on a plantation. In the summer of 1941, he was recorded for the American Library of Congress by folk-music researcher Alan Lomax, the two tracks being 'I Be's Troubled' and 'Country Blues'. Muddy moved to Chicago in 1943, where he met and played with Big Bill Broonzy, gaining invaluable experience.

In 1945, his uncle bought him an electric guitar, and a year later he was recorded, first for Aristocrat, and then

Columbia. The Columbia sides were never issued, and he signed an exclusive Aristocrat contract, which was later taken over by the newly formed Chess label. In 1948, Muddy cut his first solo single, 'I Can't Be Satisfied', accompanied by Big Crawford on string bass. It was a minor hit. He followed-up with 'Screamin' And Cryin'', and then 'Rollin' And Tumblin'', released in March 1950. Muddy's debut release under the Chess banner was 'Rollin' Stone', and was his first national R&B success. Soon after, he formed his now legendary group, which featured Little Walter on harmonica, Otis Spann on piano and Jimmy Rogers on second guitar. This was the classic Muddy Waters band, the pioneer city blues group that was to influence countless other blues musicians not to mention the entire white R&B movement of the mid-Sixties. Each member went on to record as a solo artist, and eventually Walter outsold Muddy, becoming the biggest-selling Chicago blues artist of the Fifties. But as a unit they recorded dozens of sides, the most famous being 'I've Got My Mojo Working', 'Hoochie Coochie Man', 'I'm Ready', 'Long Distance Call', 'I'm A Man', 'Honey Bee', 'Tiger In Your Tank', 'You Shook Me' and 'She's 19 Years Old'.

The Waters band at its best was tough and uncompromising. Muddy shouted and played bottleneck guitar over a pounding rhythm and amplified harmonica. This expressive technique reflected the spirit of the period – and was put across with almost terrifying effect. Between 1950 and 1958, Muddy notched up 12 *Billboard* national R&B chart hits. Still active today, he recently cut an album with The Band in support.

The Weavers stand beside the earlier Carter Family as one of the most influential early commercial American folk-song groups. The Weavers formed in 1949, disbanded three years later because of anti-Leftist blacklisting, reactivated in late 1955, and finally dissolved after a Chicago concert on December 29, 1963. The original group was Pete Seeger, Lee Hays, Ronnie Gilbert and Fred Hellerman. Their hits of the early Fifties included Leadbelly's 'Good Night, Irene', 'Kisses Sweeter Than Wine' and the traditional 'When The

Saints Go Marching In'. When Seeger decided on a solo career, he was succeeded as tenor by Erik Darling in 1958, then Frank Hamilton, and finally, in 1963, by Bernie Krause. The Weavers' name was chosen to suggest both rhythm and work. They cited Leadbelly as their earliest strong influence. The recordings of the Fifties with the Gordon Jenkins orchestra were extremely pop-oriented, but their later work was considered to be both pop and authentically true to tradition. Imitators by the score emerged after 1958. The group's various Carnegie Hall reunions were gala, sentimental occasions.

The We Five had their beginnings in 1962 when Mike Stewart formed the Ridge Runners in the mould of the Kingston Trio, of which his brother John was a member. The Trio's manager, Frank Werber, suggested they drop folk in favour of straight pop. Three years later, the result was the We Five – Mike Stewart, Beverly Bivens, Jerry Burgan and Pete Fullerton – and an archetypal pop-folk record, 'You Were On My Mind' (A&M) which made the Top Three in 1965. The follow-up, 'Let's Get Together', made the Top Forty, but subsequent records failed and the group disbanded.

Lenny Welch, born in New York City on May 31, 1940, began his solo recording career, on Decca, in 1958 with undistinguished rock'n'roll material. He was spotted by Archie Bleyer and signed to Cadence in 1959 and a change in style. Lenny hit the charts in 1960 as a most pleasant tenor balladeer with 'You Don't Know Me', but numerous follow-ups flopped until a revival of 'Since I Fell For You' reached the Top Five in 1963. Cadence folded the next year and he went to Kapp, recording easy-listening material with lush arrangements and scoring three small hits. Lenny has since recorded (with minimal success) for Mercury, Commonwealth United, Roulette, Atco and Mainstream.

Junior Wells, a contemporary of blues harmonica king Little Walter, was born Amos Wells Jr. in West Memphis, Arkansas, on Dec. 9, 1932. Inspired by the playing of Sonny Boy Williamson (John Lee), his big break came during the early Fifties, replacing Walter in the Muddy Waters band. Wells's first solo sides were cut in 1953 for the Chicago-based United/States label. Included in those sessions was the magnificent 'Hoodoo Man', with the Waters band in support. His later hits included 'Messin' With The Kid' (now a showstopper for Rory Gallagher) on Chief. In 1972, Wells teamed up with blues guitarist Buddy Guy, cutting one album for Atlantic, part-produced by Eric Clapton. The duo still work live dates together and have toured America and Europe supporting the Rolling Stones. He has also recorded for Shad, Profile, U.S.A., Delmark, Vanguard, Bright Star, Hit Sound and Blue Rock.

Mary Wells, born in Detroit, Michigan, on May 13, 1943, began singing at the age of 10, and in her teens played local clubs and talent shows. She was discovered during Motown's regular audition sessions, having walked in off the street in the hope of selling a song. The song, 'Bye Bye Baby', a gritty slow-rock ballad, became her debut disc and a Top Fifty hit in 1961. Mary's popularity soared and a string of hits followed, including Top Tenners 'You Beat Me To The Punch' and 'Two Lovers', peaking in 1964 with the chart-topping million-seller 'My Guy', a husky, loping minor-key ballad from the pen of Smokey Robinson. She then quit Motown for a lucrative 20th Century Fox contract, but the move was the beginning of the end – a handful of 20th Century releases climbed the charts, but fell way short of the Motown hits, and further moves to Atco and Jubilee failed to remedy the situation, though recent material on Reprise proved an artistic, if not commercial, improvement. She is married to songwriter Cecil Womack.

Kim Weston, born Agatha Natalie Weston in Detroit, Michigan, in 1943, originally planned to be a swimmer, and took to singing to improve her breathing control. Her minister father persuaded her to join a gospel group, whence she moved into R&B. After various auditions, Kim finally found

Berry Gordy receptive to her talents, and her 1963 debut on Tamla, 'Love Me All The Way', reached the pop and R&B charts. A switch to Gordy in 1965 brought a Top Fifty hit with the insistent, swinging 'Take Me In Your Arms', and 1967 saw a Top Twenty hit duet with Marvin Gaye, 'It Takes Two'. Kim married Motown executive Mickey Stevenson in 1966, moving with him to MGM, People, Banyan Tree and Pride. Kim latterly joined Enterprise and featured in the 1973 Wattstax show and film.

Ian Whitcomb, born in Surrey in 1941, was almost the only mid-Sixties British artist to have a major hit in America, but not in his home country, when the novelty falsetto record 'You Turn Me On' reached the Top Ten on Life in 1965. He had visited America while on vacation from Trinity College, Dublin, where his R&B group, Bluesville, had included the nucleus of Bees Make Honey, an important London pub rock band of the Seventies. Seattle record man Jerry Dennon recorded Whitcomb's version of the traditional blues 'Sporting Life', which was a minor hit and then flew to Ireland to record Bluesville. Follow-ups to 'You Turn Me On' failed and Whitcomb returned to his first love, the popular music of the early twentieth century. He wrote two books, produced a rock album by Mae West and recorded albums of music-hall songs and ragtime piano tunes which he performs to club audiences in Los Angeles.

The Who – Roger Daltrey, vocals (born Jan. 3, 1944), Pete Townshend, guitar (May 19, 1945), and John Entwistle, bass (Sept. 10, 1944) – had been through instrumentals, the Beatles songbook and R&B (as the Detours), acquiring Keith Moon on drums (Aug. 23, 1946) on the way, when publicist Peter Meaden changed their name to the High Numbers, dressed them in mod clothes, and transformed Slim Harpo's 'Got Love If You Want It' into the hip 'I'm The Face' (Fontana, 1964). The mod cult was spreading rapidly at that time in London areas like the group's base of Shepherds Bush, and Meaden's plan to associate the group with the mods was shrewdly timed. However, despite the superficial appropriateness of the words, the song was weak and flopped.

The group's following amongst the mod audiences of the London clubs continued to grow, and it was the crowd as much as the music that impressed Kit Lambert and Chris Stamp and prompted them to take over their management. The new managers not only restored the previous gimmicky name – the Who (who?) – but encouraged the development of the mod image, spending a great deal of money and time to create the correct appearance, and moulding to this identity a musical violence which matched the physical aggression of the mods. The Who, nevertheless, failed to impress EMI, and it was only through the influence of Shel Talmy, who had produced the demo of Townshend's song 'I Can't Explain', that they were offered a contract with American Decca. Released in January, 1965, on the Brunswick label, the record didn't take off until the group took their fanatical Marquee club audience with them to the mod-oriented TV show *Ready, Steady, Go*! In many ways closer to the Kinks' style than the Who's – Talmy produced both groups – it eventually made the Top Ten as did the more characteristic and innovatory follow-up, 'Anyway, Anyhow, Anywhere', which Lambert and Stamp energetically promoted as 'pop art'.

Despite the transitory, exploitative nature of the group's identification with the mods, the lifestyle held deep fascination for Townshend and provided the inspiration for his first compositions, culminating in the phenomenally successful 'My Generation', which conveyed the mods' inarticulate, pill-head rebelliousness as much by its style as its content. Townshend's subsequent songs introduced a cast of characters whose frequently eccentric personalities allowed him to explore such conventional themes as enforced transvestism ('I'm A Boy', Reaction, 1966), marital infidelity ('A Quick One While He's Away' on *A Quick One*, Track, 1966) and sexual fantasy ('Pictures Of Lily', Track, 1967). 'A Quick One While He's Away', a nine-minute song cycle which closed the group's second album – the first, *My Generation* (Brunswick, 1965), was a hurried, though powerful, collection of R&B readymades and early Townshend songs – was Townshend's first attempt at rock opera and, along with the incomplete 'Rael 1 and 2' on *The Who Sell Out* (Track, 1967), the precursor of *Tommy* (Track, 1968). The enormous critical attention and extravagant praise which *Tommy* attracted stemmed partly from its scale and ambitions, but it was an undoubted, if flawed, masterpiece. It brought wealth, international fame, and artistic respectability to the Who, and it was performed in opera houses throughout the world, later being given an orchestral treatment and all-star cast by Lou Reizner (Ode, 1972) and adapted into a typically excessive film by Ken Russell (1975), although in the group's live performances it was eventually condensed as a medley of old hits.

The release of 'Pinball Wizard' from *Tommy* virtually signalled the end of the Who as a singles group, and over the next five years only two singles – 'Won't Get Fooled Again' (1971) and 'Join Together' (1972) – made either the British or American Top Ten. *Live At Leeds* (1970), a set that only lacked the visual excitement of their stage performance, followed *Tommy*, while *Who's Next* (1971) contained material from the abortive *Lifehouse* project. Then, after a compilation of hits, *Meaty, Beaty, Big And Bouncy* (1971), came *Quadrophenia* (1974), an elaborate homage to the mods whose image the group had originally exploited and whose lifestyle had inspired Townshend's first songs. Though quadrophonic sound was abandoned, the theme of a four-sided personality as a reflection of the four members of the group remained, and the work's lack of unity underlined their divergent paths through the Seventies, a period which saw more emphasis on individual projects by the group's members. *The Who By Numbers* (1975) confirmed this process by virtue of its bittiness.

Sonny Boy Williamson. There were, in fact, two Sonny Boys; both were influential and innovative forces in the blues world. John Lee Williamson (Sonny Boy No. 1) was born in Jackson, Tennessee, on March 30, 1914. While in his teens he played harmonica behind Sleepy John Estes and Homesick James, coming to Chicago in 1937 where he cut his first sides for RCA's Bluebird label. They included the now classic 'Good Morning, Little Schoolgirl' and 'Sugar Mama'. During the early Forties, Williamson began to record, using a small group occasionally featuring Big Bill Broonzy on guitar. He was one of the first Chicago-based bluesmen to use accompanying musicians on record, thus anticipating by a decade the heavy, back-beat rhythm that characterized Chicago blues records of the Fifties. His style of harmonica playing, too, paved the way for artists like Little Walter and Junior Wells. Williamson died in Chicago on June 1, 1948, the victim of a brutal attack and robbery.

Rice Miller (Sonny Boy No. 2) was the better known of the two bluesmen, especially in Europe where he toured frequently during the early Sixties. Born in Glendora, Mississippi, in 1897, he first came to prominence in 1941, singing and playing harmonica on a highly successful daily radio show, *King Biscuit Time*, which was broadcast over KFFA in Helena, Arkansas. In order to gain even greater popularity, Miller claimed to be *the* Sonny Boy Williamson (who was safely based in Chicago, though scoring national hits) – a decision he must have certainly regretted in later years. He first recorded in 1951 for the Jackson-based Trumpet label, switching to Chess/Checker in 1955. Often accompanied by the Muddy Waters band, Sonny Boy's many hits included 'Don't Start Me Talking' and 'Fattening Frogs For Snakes'. He first came to Britain in 1963, where he caused a sensation dressed in a bizarre, two-tone suit with bowler hat. During subsequent visits he appeared on *Ready, Steady, Go!* and cut live albums with the Yardbirds and Animals. His records have been covered by such artists as Van Morrison ('Help Me') and the Moody Blues ('Bye Bye Bird'). Led Zeppelin's 'Bring It On Home' on *Led Zeppelin II* was remarkably similar to Sonny Boy's original. He died in Helena, Arkansas, on May 25, 1965.

Al Wilson – born in Meridian, Mississippi, on June 19, 1939 – joined the US Navy as a teenager and on demob settled in San Bernardino, where he joined a vocal group, the Jewels, in 1958. They changed names to the Rollers in 1961 and hit with 'Continental Walk' (Liberty), a typical dance disc of the time. Al started working solo, met Johnny Rivers at Liberty and signed with his Soul City label in 1965. 'Do What You Gotta Do' was an R&B hit while John Fogerty's 'The Snake', a moral saga, reached the Top Thirty in 1968; but Soul City folded and his 1974 million-seller, 'Show And Tell', was released on Rocky Road.

Brenton Wood, born Alfred Jesse Smith in Shreveport, Louisiana, on July 26, 1941, moved to Los Angeles with his family in 1943. His musical career began in the mid-Fifties with the Dootones vocal group, then he formed the Quotations in 1962 but they soon split, Alfred adopting the name of his home district, 'Brenton Wood', and going solo. Initial discs flopped, but in 1967 Hal Winn formed Double Shot Records, signed Brenton, and they hit when 'Oogum Boogum Song', a novelty ballad, reached the Top Fifty. The follow-up, 'Gimme Little Sign', in similar style, made the Top Ten, but the novelty then lost favour; a duet with Shirley Goodman as Shirley and Alfred flopped, and he slipped into obscurity, to return in 1975 on Warner Bros. Records.

O. V. Wright, born Overton Vertis Wright on Oct. 9, 1939 in Memphis, was ignored when his original recording of 'That's How Strong My Love Is' (Goldwax, 1964) was trumped by Otis Redding, and he has continued to be over-looked by a mass audience despite ten years of excellent soul releases on the Duke/Peacock subsidiary Back Beat. He first recorded with the Sunset Travellers on Peacock. Among his greatest performances were 'You're Gonna Make Me Cry' (1965), 'Gone For Good' (1966), '8 Men, 4 Women' (1967), 'Ace Of Spades' (1970), 'A Nickel And A Nail' (1971), and 'I'd Rather Be Blind, Crippled, And Crazy' (1974) – suggest that he's destined to be belatedly highly acclaimed. His later Backbeat sides (for example *Memphis Underground*, 1973) were produced by Willie Mitchell and featured the fine guitar work of Mabon Hodges.

The Yardbirds, inspired by the Rolling Stones' performances at the Station Hotel, Richmond, early in 1963, grew
out of a Kingston art school band, the Metropolitan Blues
Quartet. After a debut at Eel Pie Island, Keith Relf, vocals,
harmonica (born March 22, 1943); Anthony 'Top' Topham,
lead guitar; Chris Dreja, rhythm guitar (Nov. 11, 1946); Paul
Samwell-Smith, bass (May 8, 1943) and Jim McCarty,
drums (July 25, 1943) – took over the Stones' Crawdaddy
residency with Eric Clapton replacing Topham. However,
despite a strong following on the R&B club circuit and *Five
Live Yardbirds* (the quintessential British R&B album), the
Yardbirds had no chart success until 1965, when they recorded three Graham Gouldman compositions – 'For Your
Love', 'Heart Full Of Soul' and 'Evil Hearted You' – all of
which made the Top Three on EMI's Columbia label. The
overt commerciality of these caused Clapton to quit. He was
replaced by Jeff Beck, whose penchant for electronic effects
earned the group an American reputation as psychedelic
pioneers. In June, 1966, the endless touring forced Samwell-
Smith to retire and Jimmy Page, who had turned down the
chance to join when Clapton left, took his place. Dreja
moved to bass and Page joined Beck on lead: their unison
riffs and interchanged solos were exciting, if inconsistent, but
within six months Beck split. Their appearance in Italian
film director Michelangelo Antonioni's film of the 'Swinging
London' of the Sixties, *Blow-up*, had a lot to do with Page's
later impact with Led Zeppelin in the US. Although they
continued as a four-piece until July, 1968, the last eighteen
months produced little of merit and on stage they turned increasingly into self-confessed puppets. Following the break-
up, Relf and McCarty worked as a duo, Together, before
forming Renaissance; Dreja took up photography; and Page
put together the New Yardbirds – Led Zeppelin, managed
by former Yardbirds road-manager, Peter Grant.

The Youngbloods began performing in New York in 1966
as the houseband at the Café A Go Go. Jesse Colin Young
(born Nov. 11, 1944) had been a well-known New York folk
singer with two albums (*Soul Of A City Boy* and *Young*

Blood) behind him. He met up with Jerry Corbitt, a Cambridge folk singer, and as a duo they recorded 'Hey Babe' for Mercury who later released the earliest Youngbloods' sessions on *Two Trips With Jesse Colin Young*. The duo had added Banana Lowell Levinger, a onetime bluegrass musician (born 1946) and more recently member of Boston's Trolls, who played banjo, mandolin, guitar, bass and piano and ex-jazz drummer Joe Bauer (born Sept. 26, 1941). Young wound up playing bass. Their style was essentially East Coast : good-time, jug band, jazz and Beatles influences – highlighted by Young's delightful singing. He shared lead vocals with Jerry Corbitt, who wrote and sang their 'Grizzly Bear' (RCA), a minor hit when pulled from their album *The Youngbloods* in 1966. Their recording of Dino Valenti's summer 1967 anthem, 'Get Together' – a Top Ten record when it was re-released in 1969 – launched them in their future home on the West Coast. After *Earth Music* Corbitt departed (to record two disappointing solo albums), and the Youngbloods went on to complete *Elephant Mountain* as a trio. Their most acclaimed album saw Banana taking a more dominant role, his lilting piano and refreshing guitar underpinning a freer, jazzier album. *Elephant Mountain* and the comparable *Rock Festival* marked their peak, the self-indulgent *Ride The Wind* their zenith. They added Michael Kane, on bass in 1971, to record two rock'n'roll-oriented albums full of old rock classics (*Good 'N' Dusty* and *High On A Ridge Top*). After 1969 their albums, solo and spin-off projects (notably Jesse Colin Young's work with the remarkable Michael Hurley) were recorded for their own Racoon Records. By 1973 though, it seemed that comfortable living in Marin County and too much freedom under their own direction had stultified the Youngbloods and they folded. Only Jesse Colin Young has remained active, reverting to the style of *Elephant Mountain* in a series of tasteful and satisfying solo albums for Warner Bros.

Young-Holt Unlimited. As two-thirds of the Ramsey Lewis Trio, bassist Eldee Young (born Jan. 7, 1936) and drummer Isaac 'Redd' Holt (born May 16, 1932) were involved in undemanding discotheque hits like 'Wade In The Water', 'Hang On Sloopy' and 'The In Crowd'. They left Lewis in search of a more adventurous sound, but the addition of Canadian-born pianist Ken Cragen produced a number of similarly light but tight soul instrumentals on Brunswick including 'Wack Wack' (Top Forty in 1966) and 'Soulful Strut' (No. 3 in 1968). Both men were graduates of Chicago's Conservatory of Music and brought immaculate musicianship to their records. Young's acoustic bass was an unusual instrument to find in a soul context and he had also introduced the cello to a few Ramsey Lewis cuts. More recent Young-Holt Unlimited records have been issued on the Paula label.

Frank Zappa, born Francis Vincent Zappa Jr. in Baltimore, Maryland, on Dec. 21, 1940, was one of the great innovators in rock's development in the Sixties, though it was not until the Seventies that his records began to sell in large quantities. At the age of 10, Zappa moved with his family to California where he later emerged as a West Coast musician. A self-taught multi-instrumentalist, he passed through his school band and various other local groups before becoming a serious student of many musics: he studied harmony in college and was profoundly influenced by the recorded work of Stravinsky and Edgar Varese as well as by the likes of Howlin' Wolf. As interested in arranging as in playing, Zappa's first recording, in 1960, was his own sound-track for a film called *The World's Greatest Sinner*. Characteristically, Zappa's score involved 52 musicians. In 1963 another film soundtrack, for *Run Home Slow*, gave its writer enough money to buy a five-track recording studio in Cucamonga, California. Zappa was then 22.

He involved himself in a number of locally issued singles under various names and, in late 1964, pruned down the band with which he was working into a deliberately 'freak'-oriented group first called The Muthers and then The Mothers. The original line-up was Zappa, Elliott Inger (later of the Fraternity Of Man and then in Captain Beefheart's band), Roy Estrada (subsequently with Beefheart and Little Feat), Jimmy Carl Black (later in Geronimo Black) and Ray Collins. This band was signed to Verve/MGM by producer Tom Wilson in 1966 and a double album, *Freak Out!*, was issued. The album and its promotion emphasized the 'freak' element in Zappa's work, gave the leader a great deal of vivid publicity and implanted the Mothers Of Invention (their name by now) on the rock public's consciousness as a synonym for outrageousness. However, that first album, and those immediately following, were also innovative in their resourceful combinations of different kinds of music, lethally accurate parodies of other rock/pop genres. Zappa's writing contributed forcefully to the popularization of the revolt against Fifties suburban lifestyles which was taking place in America, through unforgettable songs such as 'America Drinks And Goes Home' on *Absolutely Free*. It was also apparent from even the earliest Mothers Of Invention albums that Frank Zappa was ahead of any other rock artist of the time as a tape editor. Under Zappa's auspices, the editing of his music became an essential creative ingredient of it. The second and third albums – *Absolutely Free* (1966) and *We're Only In It For The Money* (1967) – were predominantly satirical in their impact. The latter was presented as a parody of the Beatles' *Sergeant Pepper*, although its targets included the American Way Of Life as well as its ineffectual opponents, the flower children. Later records moved towards a greater emphasis on instrumental work or, with *Ruben and the Jets* (1967), the re-creation of the sound of Fifties vocal groups, inspired equally by affection and parody. In 1969, the Frank Zappa solo album, *Hot Rats*, established his claim as a significant jazz-rock guitarist: his strong and imaginative playing took many people by surprise.

Working with a consistent set of overall themes and methods, Zappa has, over a decade of work, continued to build up more pieces and new dimensions within what appears as the vast interlocking jigsaw of his output. This system also means that one album can act as a rehearsal for another, one track as an echo of one that went before; one marriage of time-signature and melody can counterbalance a different matching due to be made in the future. Zappa masters time in the additional sense that he manipulates the past through montages of nostalgia. This now seems unremarkable because the recording industry latched on to the commercial possibilities of the process. Zappa, however, kept it all under control and gave us, long before the 'Rock Revival', an inspired montage of the American Fifties, spliced into parallel evocations of Sixties hippie lifestyles and a personal musical vision.

This musical resourcefulness has been matched by the precision Zappa has always demanded of his many different line-ups (10 up to early 1975). On stage, the various different Mothers bands have usually radiated an image of freakish dishevelment, but their musical performances have always been outstandingly disciplined. Zappa has also been a considerable sponsor of other people's talent. His attempts to augment his original line-up in 1965 resulted in several names passing through his band – Dr John, Henry Vestine of Canned Heat, Jim Guercio, Van Dyke Parks, Jim Fielder, Alice Stuart and Kim Fowley. Subsequent Mothers have included Billy Mundi, Ed Marimba (Arthur Tripp III), Lowell George and Aynsley Dunbar. Zappa has also brought a number of jazz musicians before a wider audience, including Ian Underwood, George Duke, Jean-Luc Ponty, Don 'Sugarcane' Harris and Bruce Fowler.

In 1968, Zappa formed Bizarre Records with his manager, Herb Cohen, to ensure total artistic control over his work and to provide an outlet for his protégés, who included Alice Cooper, Wild Man Fischer and the GTOs (Girls Together Outrageously, the first groupie group). Artists on the sister label, DiscReet (founded in 1973) included Tim Buckley, also managed by Cohen. Thus despite his many failings – the disastrous film *200 Motels*, the dating of most of his Sixties social commentary, and in particular the tendency of his more recent work towards a cheap vulgarity (the kind of vulgarity he used to attack in others) – Frank Zappa has none the less proved himself a major figure in contemporary rock, and one who has largely carved out his own individual imprint. His music is jazz and rock without being conventional or clichéd jazz-rock; it is classical and pop without recourse to stereotyped combinations of four-piece bands and symphony orchestras. It is a deeply eclectic and strongly individual fusion of many different musics by a highly gifted composer, arranger, musician and producer.

The Zombies started off at the wrong end of the scale. Five school kids, they had a million-selling hit, 'She's Not There', the week they turned professional. Rod Argent, piano (born June 14, 1945); Colin Blunstone, vocals (June 24, 1945); Paul Atkinson, guitar (March 19, 1946); Hugh Grundy, drums (March 6, 1945), and Paul Arnold, bass, replaced within weeks of formation by Chris White (March 7, 1943) formed the group in St Albans in 1963. They won a beat group competition held by the *London Evening News* and were signed by Decca, who were impressed by their tapes of 'Summertime'. That was the group's choice for a single but Decca's was 'She's Not There', which surprisingly proved to be their only British hit. However, in America the follow-up 'Tell Her No' – a flop in Britain in 1965 – gave them their second Top Ten hit on Parrot. Instant success decided the group to leave school. Their image stressed their grammar-school status (with 50 'O' levels between them) at a time when other groups disdained to have any educational achievements. More important, their sound was quite devastating for 1964, dominated by Argent's jazz-tinged electric piano and Blunstone's breathy vocals. They anticipated a number of facets of future styles in a series of underrated singles and on their mixed, though at times adventurous, album *Begin Here* (1965). Far better appreciated in America, by 1967 they were at a low ebb, but before splitting up took three months to write and record an album. The result was *Odyssey And Oracle* (CBS, 1968), a breathtaking album by a virtually forgotten group in Britain. One of the singles taken from it, 'Time Of The Season', became a huge hit in America on Date, but the group had gone its separate ways and several bogus groups sprang up there, until they took legal action against them. The separate directions included a solo career for Blunstone, a namesake group for Rod Argent, working closely with Chris White, who took a non-playing but writing and producing role, being also part of Nexus.

INDEX

378

Dickey, Robert Lee, *see* Purify, James and Bobby
Dickson, Jim, 81
Dillards, The, 75, 128
Dillon, Jay, 158
Dino, Desi and Billy, 174, 217
Dion, 328
Diplomats, Denny Laine and the, 215
Distants, The, 340
Dixie Cups, The, 31, **114**, 283
Dixie Nightingales, 304
Dixon, George, 328
Dixon, Luther, 137, 191
Dixon, Willie, 169
Dobson, Lyn, 233
Dodd, Coxsone, 55, 242
Dodd, Dick, 330
Doggett, Bill, 338
Doherty, Denny, 226, 230, 232
Dolenz, Mickey, 245, 246
Dolls, The, 248
Dolphins, The, 181
Dolphy, Eric, 58
Domino, Fats, 247
Donaher, Thomas, 21, 22
Donahue, Jerry, 134
Donahue, Tom, 44, **114–15**, 308
Donays, The, 129
Donegan, Tony 'Lonnie', 62
Donley, Jimmy, 238
Donovan, **115–16**, 249, 306, 320
Doobie Brothers, 173
Doors, The, **116–18**, 128, 183, 186, 224, 303
Dootones, The, 369
Dorman, Lee, 190
Dorsey, Lee, **118**, 257
Dothan Sextet, 278
Douglas, Alan, 178
Douglas, Steve, 241
Dovells, The, 32
Dowd, Tom, **118–19**
Downbeats, The, 129, 288
Downliners Sect, The, 63
Dozier, Lamont, 148, 180–1, 250, 292, 361
Drake, Bill, 15
Drake, John, 14
Dramatics, The, 331
Dreamers, Freddie and the, **153–4**
Dreja, Chris, 262, 370
Drifters, The, 22, 47, 48, 49, 118, 130, 132, 312, 361
Driscoll, Julie, 21, **119**, 160
Dr John, 54, 172, 374
Dryden, Spencer, 197
Duals, The, 334
Duffy, Raymond, 234
Duke, George, 374
Dunbar, Aynsley, 237, 374
Duncan, Gary, 279, 353
Dunn, Donald 'Duck', 60, 61, 234
Dupree, Champion Jack, 357
Dusters, The, 349
Dwight, Reg, *see* John, Elton
Dwyer, Bernie, 154
Dyble, Judy, 133
Dylan, Bob, 8, 18, 19, 25, 28, 29, 30, 43, 53, 54, 57, 78, 79, 80, 81, 82, 83, 93, 98, 99, 104, 115, **119–25**, 128, 129, 136, 139, 144, 147, 158, 161, 167, 168, 171, 199, 212, 219, 226, 230, 233, 259, 267, 291, 296, 316, 317, 320, 321, 324, 351
Dymond, John, 112

Earthband, 233
Earth Opera, 128
Easton, Eric, 259, 298
Easybeats, The, **125–6**
Eaton, Wally, 96
Ebonies, The, 55
Echols, John, 224
Eckstine, Billy, 148
Eddy, Duane, 174, 283, 326, 334
Edmonton, Jerry, 332
Edwards, Dennis, 100, 341
Edwards, George, 187
Edwards, Gordon, 273
Edwards, Jackie, 103, 111
Edwards, Saundra, 129
Edwin Hawkins Singers, The, 74
Elbert, Donnie, **126**
Electras, The, 48
Electric Flag, The, 54, 79, 109, **126–7**, 158, 186, 203, 241, 309
Electric Light Orchestra, 253
Electric Prunes, The, **127**
Electric String Band, 215
Elektra Records, **127–9**
Elgins, The, **129**, 251
Eliot, Earl, 306
Ellington, Duke, 13
Elliott, Cass, 226, 232, 233, 303
Elliott, Jack, **129**, 143
Elliott, Mike, 146
Elliott, Ron, 44, 45
Ellis, Alfred, 70
Ellis, Ralph, 337
Ellis, Shirley, **129–30**
Ellis, Steve, 245
Ellison, Andy, 258
Ellison, Lorraine, 49, **130**, 281
Ellmore, Greg, 279
Emeralds, The, 129
Emerson, Keith, 257, 258
Emerson Lake and Palmer, 149
Emotions, The, 331
Enchanters, The, 130, 243, 281, 311
Engel, Scott, 358, 359
English, David, *see* Franklin, Melvin
Ennis, Ray, 337
Entner, Warren, 162
Entwistle, John, 365
Epp, Fenrus, 201
Epstein, Brian, 18, 40, 41, 43, 50, 51, 110, **130–1**, 146, 157, 193, 214, 221
Equals, The, 131–2
Esposito, Mike, 56
Estes, Sleepy John, 367
Estrada, Roy, 373
Eubanks, Jack, 145
Evans, John, 61
Eve, Mick, 135
Even Dozen Jug Band, 57, 226
Everett, Bernie, **132**, 337
Everly Brothers, 84, 119, 260, 298, 316, 360
Every Mother's Son, 137
Exciters, The, 31, 48, **132**, 311
Eyden, Bill, **275**

382

Fabares, Shelly, 11, 209
Fabian, 295
Faces, The, 322
Fahey, John, 132–3
Faier, Billy, 143
Fairies, The, 345
Fairlie, Pat, 234
Fairport Convention, 133–4
Fairweather Low, Andy, 14, 15
Faith, Adam, 18, 315
Faithfull, Marianne, 134–5, 301
Fakir, Abdul, 148
Falcons, The, 142, 268
Fame, Georgie, 13, 63, 103, 135–6
Fame, Herb, see Peaches and Herb
Family, 52
Family Dog, 309
Famous Flames, The, 69
Fann, Leroy, 304
Fantastic Baggys, The, 30, 335
Fariña, Richard and Mimi, 25, 128, 136, 262
Farlowe, Chris, 63, 135–6, 260
Farmer, Steve, 14
Farnborough, Henry, 328
Faron's Flamingos, 221
Farrell, Wes, 49, 137–8, 196
Farren, Mick, 113
Fason, Buddy, 84
Fast Bucks, The, 115
Fataar, Ricky, 38
Feldthouse, Solomon, 201, 202
Feliciano, José, 138, 173
Fender, Freddy, 238
Festivals, 138–9
Field Hippies, The, 352
Fielder, Jim, 53, 374
Fierro, Martin, 320
Fifth Dimension, The, 23, 140
Films, Rock, 295–6
Finfer, Harry, 338
Finn, Tom, 216
First Edition, Kenny Rogers and the, 296–7
Fischer, Wild Man, 140–2, 374
Fish, The, 104–5, 308, 309
Fisher, Bobby, 157
Fisher, Carl, 358
Fisher, Matthew, 274, 275
Five Echoes, The, 339
Five Stairsteps, The, 74
Flames, The, 176
Flanders, Tommy, 57
Flatt, Lester, 144
Fleet, Gordon, 125
Fleetwood Mac, 94, 141–2, 165, 166, 193, 237, 357
Fleming, Robert, 129
Flint, Hughie, 213, 237
Flood, Dick, 145
Flowerpot Men, The, 89
Floyd, Eddie, 108, 142, 331
Flying Burrito Brothers, 83
Fogerty, John, 368
Folk Revival (America), 142–4
Folks Brothers, 55
Fontana, Wayne, 144–5, 243
Forbes, Rand, 352
Ford, Dean, 234, 235
Ford, Perry, 89
Fordyce, Keith, 66

Forgione, Joey, 325
Forssi, Ken, 224
Fortunes, The, 145
Foster, Fred, 145–6, 260
Foster, Stephen, 92
Foundations, The, 146
Four Aims, The, 148
Four Freshmen, The, 34, 173, 205
Four Jays, The, 146
Fourmost, The, 146
Four Seasons, The, 89, 146–7, 255
Four Speeds, The, 335
Four Tops, The, 100, 148, 181, 251, 252
Four Vagabonds, The, 9
Fowler, Bruce, 374
Fowler, Pete and Annie, 8
Fowler, Tom, 191
Fowley, Kim, 148–9, 264, 374
Fox, Bill, 280
Foxx, Inez and Charlie, 149–50
Frampton, Peter, 178, 322
Francis, Connie, 209
Frank, Jackson C., 316
Franklin, Aretha, 105, 119, 150–2, 169, 171, 254, 266, 278
Franklin, Erma, 49, 281
Franklin, Melvin (David English), 340
Fraser, Andy, 237
Fraternity of Man, The, 372
Frazier, Dallas, 152–3
Frazier, Skipper Lee, 238
Freddie and the Dreamers, 153–4
Free at Last, 213
Free, The, 203
Freeman, Bobby, 114, 281
Freeman, George, 49, 311
Freeman, Lee, 333
Freiburg, David, 198, 279
French, John Drumbo, 86
Fried, Marty, 110
Friedman, Kinky, 85
Friesen, Gordon, 168
Fuentes, Val, 191
Fugs, The, 154, 158
Full Tilt Boogie, 201
Fuller, Bobby, 154
Fuller, Jerry, 211
Fuller, Jesse, 129
Fuller, Randy, 154
Fullerton, Pete, 363
Fulson, Lowell, 91
Funkadelic, 70
Fuqua, Harvey, 155, 222, 328, 359
Furay, Richie, 75
Fury, Billy, 135

Gabbidon, Basil, 55
Gaines, Bill, 84
Gainors, The, 243
Gallagher, Rory, 364
Gamble and Huff, 268
Gamblers, The, 334
Ganser, Mary Ann and Margie, 314
Gants, The, 277
Garcia, Jerry, 162, 163, 164, 165
Garfunkel, Art, see Simon and Garfunkel
Garrett, Amos, 79
Garrett, Bobby, see Relf, Bobby

387

388

McGeorge, Gerry, 187, 314
McGhee, Brownie, 62, 143
McGough, Roger, 310
McGowan, Cathy, 66
McGriff, Jimmy, **230**
McGuinn, Jim (Roger), 80, 81, **82**, 83, 84, 223, 239, 353
McGuinness, Tom, 233
McGuire, Barry, 11, 125, 224, **230**, 297, 320–1
McIntire, John, 165
McJohn, Goldy, 332
McKay, Glenn, 197
McKellar, Kenneth, 357
McKenzie, Scott, 11, **231**, 232, 308, 336
McKernan, Rod, *see* Pigpen
McLagan, Ian, 321, 322
McLaughlin, John, 21, 58, 135
McLaughlin, Ollie, 217
Maclean, Bryan, 224
McLemor, Lamont, 140
McNally, John, 312
McPhatter, Clyde, 319
McPhee, Skip, 132
McPhee, T. S., 357
McShee, Jaqui, 196
McVie, John, 94, 141, 237
Mack, Lonnie, 128, **230–1**
Mack, Marlene 'Peaches', *see* Peaches and Herb
Mad Dogs and Englishmen, 97
Mad Lads, The, 331
Mad River, 309
Maestro, Johnny, 74
Mae West, 365
Magic Band, *see* Captain Beefheart
Magicians, The, 59
Magick, 59
Maguire, Les, 157
Maha Dev, 280
Majors, The, 280
Makeba, Miriam, 281
Makins, Tex, 135
Mallard, 87
Mamas and the Papas, The, 11, 85, 138, 224, 226, 230, 231, **232–3**, 325
Manchester, Fanny, and Melissa, 18
Mancini, Henry, 360
Mandel, Harvey, 86, 158
Mann, Barry, 239, 245, 283
Mann, Manfred, 62, 90, 106, 132, 186, 200, **233**, 295
Mann-Hugg Blues Brothers, 199–200, 233
Mansfield, Tony, 214
Manuel, Richard, 27, 123
Manzarek, Ray, 116, 117
Marathons, The, 357
Marc, Vince, 346
March, Little Peggy, 283
Marcus-Hook Roll Band, 126
Mardin, Arif, 45
Marimba, Ed, 374
Marketts, The, 335, 360
Mar-Keys, The, 60, 108, **233–4**, 240, 331
Markham, Pigmeat, 223
Mark Leeman Five, 103
Marks, David, 34, 35
Marmalade, **234–5**

Marriott, Steve, 20, 204, 321, 322
Marron, Gordon, 352
Marsden, Beryl, 165
Marsden, Freddie, 157
Marsden, Gerry, 131, 146, **157**, 295
Marshall, John, 135, 323
Martell, Vince, 353
Martha and the Vandellas, 181, **235**, 251, 252
Martin, Barbara, 333
Martin, Dave, 132, 308
Martin, Dean, 287, 288
Martin, Dewey, 75
Martin, George, 40, 43, **131**, **157**, 193, **235–6**
Martin, Steve, 216
Martin, Tony, 219
Martinez, Rudy, 279
Marvelettes, The, 180, **236**, 251
Mascara Snake, The, 87
Mason, Barbara, 74, **237**
Mason, Bonnie Jo, 17
Mason, Dave, 149, 346, 347
Mason, Nick, 269
Massi, Nick, 146
Masters of the Airwaves, 149
Matassa, Cosimo, 257
Mathis, Dean and Mark, 256
Mattacks, Dave, 133, 134
Matthews, Bob, 162
Matthews, Ian, 133
Maurice and Mac, 254
Maus, John, 358, 359
Maxfield, Mike, 214
Maxim Trio, 91
May, Phil, 272, 273
Mayall, John, 63, 79, 86, 106, 165, 193, 203, 205, 220, **237**, 262, 301, 357
Mayfield, Curtis, 91, 188–9, 215
Mayorga, Lincoln, 183
Maytals, 55
Mazzola, Lorraine, 287
MC5, The, 128, 229
Meade, Norman, *see* Ragavoy, Jerry
Meaden, Peter, 365
Meagher, Ron, 44
Meaux, Huey, 175, 228, 229, **237–8**, 319
Medley, Bill, 93, 211, 289, 290
Medley, Phil, 48
Meek, Joe, 200
Melanie, 74
Melcher, Terry, 35, **238–9**, 264, 289, 335, 352
Mellow Larks, The, 55
Melonaires, The, 307
Melouney, Vince, 45
Melton, Barry, 104
Memphis Horns, The, 234
Memphis Jug Band, 85
Merseybeats, The, 51, 221, **240**
Messina, Jim, 75
Meters, The, 255
Metropolitan Blues Quartet, 370
Meyer, Augie, 319, 320
MGs, The, **60–1**, 108, 331
Micelli, Joe, 153
Michaels, Dave, 187
Mickey and Sylvia, 278

Reid, Keith, 274, 275
Reiner, Robert, 216
Reinhardt, Django, 203
Reitzes, Howard, 191
Reizner, Lou, 367
Relf, Bobby, 58
Relf, Keith, 255, 370
Remo Four, The, 221
Renaissance, Keith Relf's, **255**
Renbourn, John, 195, 196
Rendell, Don, 58
REO Speedwagon, 149
Reparata and the Delrons, **287**
Reputation, Mike Heron's, 190
Resnick, Artie, 72
Revere, Paul, 17, 99, 149, 239, 277, **288–9**
Reynolds, Malvina, 312
Reynolds, Nick, 205
Rheinhardt, Larry, 191
Rhinoceros, 128, 190, 303
Rich, Charlie, 153, 319
Richard, Cliff, 41, 170, 247, 248
Richard, Keith, 14, 53, 64, 134, 136, 297–302
Richards, Earl, 247
Richards, Tom, 304
Richbourg, John, 317, 318
Richmond, Dave, 233
Richmond, Fritz, 214
Rick and the Raiders, 229
Rick Z. Combo, 229
Rickfors, Michael, 183
Rieley, Jack, 37, 38
Righteous Brothers, The, 59, 93, 211, **289–90**
Riley, Jeannie C., **290**, 319
Riley, Terry, 323
Rinehart, Bill, 216
Rip Chords, The, 35, 239, 335
Ripp, Artie, 202, 283
Rising Sons, The, 232
Ritchie, Jean, 183
Ritter, Preston, 127
Rivers, Johnny, 11, 30, 140, 369
Rivingtons, The, 149
Roach, Max, 218
Robbins, Marty, 22
Robert Anderson Singers, 88
Roberts, Billy, 353
Roberts, Edward, 304
Robertson, Robbie, 27, 28, 30, 121, 172
Robin Trower Band, 275
Robinson, Alvin, 283, **291**
Robinson, Bobby, 118
Robinson, Freddy, 220
Robnson, R. B., 100
Robinson, Smokey, 103, 249, 250, 252, **291–5**, 341, 364
Rockateens, The, 334
Rockin' Berries, The, 145, 149, **296**
Rocky Fellers, The, 48, 310
Rodgers, Jimmie, 129
Rodriguez, Frank, 279
Roe, Tommy, 96, 254
Rogers, Bobby, 292
Rogers, Claudette, 292
Rogers, Jimmy, 220, 362
Rogers, Kenny, and the First Edition, **296–7**

Rogers, Warren, 314
Rogers, Will, 129
Rogues, The, 335
Rolling Stones, The, 8, 12, 62–3, 114, 121, 125, 140, 159–60, 237, 259, 260, 272, 276, 287, **297–302**, 349, 364, 370
Rollo, Zoot Horn, 87
Romantics, Ruby and the, **304**
Rondells, The, *see* Cyrkle, The
Ronettes, The, 17, 31, 114, **302**, 327
Ronk, Dave Van, 128, 143
Ronnie and the Daytonas, 35, 335
Ronstadt, Linda, 255, 267
Rooftop Singers, 143
Rooney, Herb, 132
Rooney, Mickey, Jr., 217
Rory Storm and the Hurricanes, 40, 221
Rose and Licorice, 190
Rose, Biff, 74, **302–3**
Rose, Slim, 9
Rose, Tim, 216, **303**
Rosman, Ronnie, 194
Ross, Diana, 252, 333, 334
Rothchild, Paul, 73, **303**
Rothwell, Ric, 243
Roving Kind, The, 187
Rowan, Peter, 128
Rowberry, Dave, 20
Rowland, Bruce, 97, 134
Roy C., 49, **84–5**
Royal, Billy Joe, 96
Royal Dukes of Rhythm, 256
Royal Guardsmen, The, 73, **303–4**
Royal Spades, The, 233
Royal Teens, The, 211
Royaltones, The, 334
Royer, Ray, 274, 275
Rubin, Don, 59, 192, 202
Rubinson, David, 244
Ruby and the Romantics, **304**
Rudolph, Paul, 114
Ruffin, David, 250, **304**, 341
Ruffin, Jimmy, 250, 252, **304–5**
Rumblers, The, 335
Rundgren, Todd, 79
Rupe, Art, 101
Rush, Otis, 158, 254, 357
Rush, Tom, 54, 128, 262, 303, **305**
Russell, Bert, *see* Berns, Bert
Russell, Doc, 240
Russell, Leon, 81, 97, 104, 173, 204, 205, 217–18, 223, 327
Ryan, Jim, 107
Ryder, Mitch, and the Detroit Wheels, **305–6**

Sadler, Sgt. Barry, 228
Sagittarius, 352
Sahm, Doug, 319, 320
Sain, Oliver, 32, 219
Sainte-Marie, Buffy, 85, 262, **306–7**
St Peters, Crispian, **307**
Salt, 27
Sam and Dave, 234, 240, **307**, 331
Sam the Sham, **308**
Sambhu, 280
Samudio, Sam, *see* Sam the Sham
Samwell-Smith, Paul, 262, 370
Sanders, Ed, 154

393

394

395

396